Making Policy Public

This book challenges the conventional wisdom that government bureaucrats inevitably seek secrecy and demonstrates how and when participatory bureaucracy manages the enduring tension between bureaucratic administration and democratic accountability. Looking closely at federal-level public participation in pharmaceutical regulation and educational assessments within the context of the vast system of American federal advisory committees, this book demonstrates that participatory bureaucracy supports bureaucratic administration in ways consistent with democratic accountability when it focuses on interdependent tasks and engages diverse expertise. In these conditions, public participation can help produce better policy outcomes, such as safer prescription drugs. Instead of being bureaucracy's opposite or alternative, public participation can work as its complement.

Susan L. Moffitt is the Mary Tefft and John Hazen White Sr. Assistant Professor of Political Science and Public Policy at Brown University. Before joining the faculty at Brown in the fall of 2009, she was a Fellow at the Center for American Political Studies and a Robert Wood Johnson Scholar of Health Policy Research at Harvard University. Her research program focuses on the development and use of knowledge in government agencies, with particular emphasis on the fields of K–12 education policy and pharmaceutical regulation. Moffitt's scholarship connects the study of institutional development with salient and enduring policy problems. Her first book, *The Ordeal of Equality* (coauthored with David K. Cohen), was published in 2009. Her work has appeared in the *American Journal of Political Science*, the *Journal of Politics*, the *Journal of Law, Economics and Organization*, the *American Journal of Education*, and numerous edited volumes. She holds a PhD and an MPP from the University of Michigan and a BA from the University of Rochester.

Making Policy Public

Participatory Bureaucracy in American Democracy

SUSAN L. MOFFITT

Brown University

CAMBRIDGE
UNIVERSITY PRESS

University Printing House, Cambridge CB2 8BS, United Kingdom

One Liberty Plaza, 20th Floor, New York, NY 10006, USA

477 Williamstown Road, Port Melbourne, VIC 3207, Australia

314-321, 3rd Floor, Plot 3, Splendor Forum, Jasola District Centre, New Delhi - 110025, India

79 Anson Road, #06-04/06, Singapore 079906

Cambridge University Press is part of the University of Cambridge.

It furthers the University's mission by disseminating knowledge in the pursuit of education, learning and research at the highest international levels of excellence.

www.cambridge.org
Information on this title: www.cambridge.org/9781107665972

© Susan L. Moffitt 2014

First published 2014

A catalogue record for this publication is available from the British Library

Library of Congress Cataloging in Publication data
Moffitt, Susan L.
Making policy public : participatory bureaucracy in American democracy / Susan L. Moffitt.
  pages cm
Includes bibliographical references and index.
ISBN 978-1-107-06522-2 (hardback) – ISBN 978-1-107-66597-2 (paperback)
1. Political planning – United States.   2. Bureaucracy – United States.   3. Administrative
agencies – United States.   4. Citizens' advisory committees – United States.   5. Government
accountability – United States.   6. Transparency in government – United States.   7. Education
and state – United States.   8. Pharmaceutical policy – United States.   I. Title.
JK468.P64M64   2014
320.60973–dc23   2014014934

ISBN 978-1-107-06522-2 Hardback
ISBN 978-1-107-66597-2 Paperback

To Michael Clark, for everything

Contents

Figures

Tables

Preface

"The Board helped me get my job done," former Indiana Director of Medicaid Managed Care, Sharon Steadman, recalled, referring to the Drug Utilization Review (DUR) Board that advised her on prescription drug formularies for Indiana's Medicaid Managed Care Organizations.[1] Director Steadman perceived the public board, which consisted primarily of physicians and pharmacists, as a valuable way to give ideas "legs" and buffer formulary decisions from industry pressure arising from both managed care organizations and pharmaceutical firms. Conventional portraits of public bureaucracy emphasize private information, closure, control, and cozy relationships with industry; but Director Steadman's account portrayed the board as offering independent information on formulary decisions. The disconnect between these two views of public bureaucracy caught my attention and launched my study of public committees well over a decade ago. I wanted to know when public bureaucrats would seek openness over secrecy and collaborative decision making over exclusive control, and why. I set out to understand public participation from the perspective of bureaucratic administration: when does participation through boards and committees help bureaucrats "get the job done," and when does it not?

Since both secrecy and technical expertise represent hallmarks of bureaucratic administration, assessments of public participation through public committees typically focus on their potential to promote or inhibit democratic accountability through *participatory oversight*: to induce an otherwise closed bureaucracy to attend to nonbureaucratic voices in the policy-making process and to enable individuals to monitor agency decisions. When, however, can public participation support public bureaucracy, and when is participation not imposed on but initiated by bureaucrats? As I answer these questions, I develop the concept of *participatory bureaucracy*: a systematic process of

[1] Personal communication with author.

public engagement that brings diverse expertise to bear on interdependent task implementations that exceed the scope of conventional bureaucratic hierarchy. When participation is bureaucratic, it advances competent policy implementation consistent with the core elements of bureaucratic reputation: unique agency expertise and diverse support. When bureaucracy is participatory, the scope of participation and policy decisions are fluid, not perfunctory means of rubber-stamping an agency decision or manipulating the masses.

The vast network of public committees in operation across the federal government provides prime venues for me to examine and assess participatory bureaucracy: when it manifests, how it works, how it impacts policy outcomes, and when it might contribute to democratic accountability. Federal public committees have been perennial features of the executive branch since the early twentieth century, and they remain prevalent. In 2010, U.S. federal agencies consulted 1,044 advisory committees composed of 66,389 public members.[2] More individuals, these estimates suggest, served on advisory committees across the federal government in 2010 than worked as civil servants in the Department of Energy, the Department of Labor, the Department of Housing and Urban Development, and the Department of Education *combined*. Federal public committees have also contributed to major federal policies, including the mapping of the human genome.[3] Though committee participation can yield forms of participatory oversight that monitor and constrain public bureaucracy, the origins and development of federal public committees reveal that bureaucrats have also actively initiated, cultivated, and structured public participation.

I focus my analysis on federal-level public participation for pharmaceutical regulation and for educational assessments, and I argue that participatory bureaucracy is more likely to manifest when participation engages diverse expertise focused on task implementation. Participation that abets domination by privileged interests does not support participatory bureaucracy, and neither does diffuse, unfocused participation. Participatory bureaucracy is also more likely to manifest for interdependent policy tasks rather than for tasks that occur fully within an agency's jurisdiction. The chief reason is that interdependent tasks entail evolving implementations that exceed the scope of the agency's hierarchical reach and thus require expertise that agencies do not command. Educational assessments sponsored by the federal government, for instance, can only succeed through interdependent action: implementation depends on the validity of the assessment instrument, on students showing up to take the test, on administrators letting special needs students take the test, on the people scoring handwritten essays, and on other implementers working in the vast space between the Department of Education and Classroom

#102. Federal officials cannot command educational assessment implementation the way they can command maintenance schedules for military aircraft. Interdependent tasks create incentives for bureaucrats to attend to not only their own learning and knowledge-gathering but also to getting information out the door to other parts of the implementation chain, creating new knowledge when none exists either inside or outside the agency, and legitimating the knowledge that is used.

When participation benefits bureaucracy, is there non-zero-sum potential for it to support democratic accountability as well? Participatory bureaucracy contributes to bureaucratic administration, the analysis suggests, when it fosters multidirectional flows of knowledge instead of just one-way or two-way closed information exchanges. This flow of knowledge can abet some degree of indeterminacy: the outcome of participation is not foreordained, nor is the value of the information flow restricted to a single point in time or to a single user. In other words, participatory bureaucracy is more than a way for bureaucrats to learn from the public; it also is a way to support learning in public. Learning in public both offers bureaucrats opportunities to distribute information to key implementers outside the agency's hierarchy on whom the agency may depend, and it provides opportunities to liquefy knowledge, to use John Dewey's metaphor. Open meetings can put knowledge into the public space that can, in turn, take on a life of its own: the information flow does not necessarily end when the votes are cast and the meeting comes to an end. The potential democratic contributions of participatory bureaucracy exceed the scope of a singular decision or information exchange and are ongoing. In these conditions of task interdependence, diverse expertise, and knowledge flow, my analysis suggests that public participation has the potential to support both bureaucratic administration and democratic governance in two respects: implementation quality and legitimacy. Instead of bureaucracy's opposite or alternative, public participation can complement bureaucracy.

Some theories of community organizing and participatory democracy discount information sharing as token or ancillary to true decision-making power. However, from a *bureaucratic* perspective, knowledge is power. As Weber claimed, "bureaucratic administration means fundamentally the exercise of control on the basis of knowledge."[4] While information sharing may seem insignificant or insufficient from a grassroots perspective, it can be monumental from a bureaucratic perspective.

The task interdependence that is a cornerstone of participatory bureaucracy, however, does not describe all tasks. Participatory bureaucracy is less amenable to supporting bureaucratic administration for tasks that occur fully inside the bureaucratic hierarchy, such as delivering the mail, or for tasks where private information is an end goal, such as spying. As the recent scandal over

---

[4] Max Weber, *The Theory of Social and Economic Organizations* (London: Free Press of Glencoe, Collier-Macmillan Ltd., 1947), p.339.

the National Security Agency's practice of gathering communication data from U.S. citizens and from allies attests, ample appetites for secrecy persist. Yet, some estimates suggest that governance is becoming more interdependent and less amenable to structural secrecy. The more policy problems and policy tasks embody interdependent implementations, the more participatory bureaucracy holds promise of both enabling opportunities for democratic accountability and helping bureaucrats "get the job done."

* * *

I am deeply indebted to many colleagues, scholars, family, and friends who patiently reviewed, challenged, and refined this project. I owe a special thanks to Daniel Carpenter, David K. Cohen, George Krause, Dave Lewis, and Patricia Strach for carefully reading the book manuscript at various stages of the project and providing extraordinarily constructive feedback. Daniel Carpenter also generously shared data on pharmaceutical safety outcomes used in Chapter 8. This work has also benefited greatly from thoughtful advice, challenging questions, and support from Scott Allard, Steve Balla, Jason Barabas, Nancy Burns, Chris Carrigan, Jacqueline Chattopadhyay, Ross Cheit, Cary Coglianese, Alan Cohen, Amy Connor, Nathan Dietz, Laura Evans, Martha Feldman, Archon Fung, Cynthia Grimm, Rick Hall, Hahrie Han, Cindy Kam, Anne Khademian, Miriam Laugesen, David Lazer, Ann Lin, Paul Manna, Moshe Maor, Lorraine McDonnell, Ken Meier, Clayton Nall, Yunju Nam, Anna Maria Ortiz, Genevieve Pham-Kanter, Christine Poulos, Janna Razaee, Elizabeth Rigby, Patrick Roberts, Wendy Schiller, Sharon Steadman, Ellen Adelman Stein, Kathy Swartz, Steven Teles, Michael Tesler, Rebecca Weitz-Shapiro, Susan Webb Yackee, and various anonymous reviewers. I am also grateful to Lew Bateman of Cambridge University Press for generously supporting this project. Scholars and participants in the Robert Wood Johnson Foundation Scholars in Health Policy Research Program provided tremendously helpful suggestions at various stages of this project, and the vibrant intellectual community provided by my colleagues at Brown University has been invaluable. A special thanks goes to Suzanne Brough, Isabel Costa, Patti Gardner, Sharon Krause, Jim Morone, Melissa Nicholaus, and Marion Orr for the many ways they have supported my work at Brown. Staff members at the National Center for Education Statistics and National Assessment Governing Board generously shared their time helping me access materials for this project. I am grateful for the careful research assistance I have received from Mark Bouchard, Kelly Branham, Jennifer Cassidy, Chris Chenoweth, Heather Creek, Lauren Finnessey, Kyle Giddon, Rob Kantner, Nick Lundholm, Domingo Morel, Carmen Sboczak, Chara Svaan, and Steve Vozar. All errors and shortcomings are my responsibility.

This research would not have been possible without generous financial support from the Robert Wood Johnson Foundation, the National Science Foundation (Grant No. 0241406), the Spencer Foundation, Brown University's Soloman Grant, and the University of Michigan's Rackham Graduate School,

Department of Political Science, and the Nonprofit and Public Management Center. Any opinions, findings, and conclusions or recommendations expressed in this book are mine and do not necessarily reflect the views of these institutions.

I am grateful to the Moffitts (Jim, Judy, and Michael) and to the Clarks (Michael, Ed, Linda, Julia, Madeleine, and Eleanor) for their enduring support, patience, and good humor while this manuscript consumed far more time, energy, and family holidays than we ever anticipated. I am especially grateful to Judy Moffitt for patiently reviewing multiple drafts of this book over the course of a decade and for the countless ways she has supported me every step of the way. This work is dedicated to Michael Clark, whose career in public service has inspired me and the work I do. I like to joke that I study bureaucracy to make sense of our marriage. Jokes aside, Michael embodies public service at its best, with his dedication to serving all the rest of us, with his unwavering commitment to making his corner of government work well and work justly, and with his unfailing courage to speak truth to power.

Abbreviations

AASA	American Association of School Administrators
ACES	Advisory Council on Education Statistics
AFT	American Federation of Teachers
APA	Administrative Procedure Act
APC	Assessment Policy Committee
BOB	Bureau of the Budget
CAB	Civil Aeronautics Board
CAPE	Committee for the Assessment of Progress in Education
CCSSO	Council of Chief State School Officers
CDER	Center for Drug Evaluation and Research
DOD	Department of Defense
DOJ	Department of Justice
DOL	Department of Labor
ECAPE	Exploratory Committee for the Assessment of Progress in Education
ECS	Education Commission of the States
ED	Department of Education
EPA	Environmental Protection Agency
ETS	Educational Testing Service
FDA	Food and Drug Administration
FOIA	Freedom of Information Act
GAO	Government Accountability Office/General Accounting Office
HEW	Health Education and Welfare
IES	Institute of Education Sciences
IND	Investigational New Drug
IOM	Institute of Medicine
NAEP	National Assessment of Educational Progress
NAGB	National Assessment Governing Board

NAS	National Academy of Sciences
NCES	National Center for Education Statistics
NCEST	National Council on Education Standards and Testing
NCLB	No Child Left Behind
NDA	New Drug Application
NEA	National Education Association
NELS	National Education Longitudinal Study
NME	New Molecular Entity
NRC	National Research Council
OE	Office of Education
OERI	Office of Educational Research and Improvement
OMB	Office of Management and Budget
SREB	Southern Regional Education Board
VEDS	Vocational Education Data System

Portals of Democracy in American Bureaucracy

"[K]nowledge is no longer an immobile solid; it has been liquefied; it is actively moving in all the currents of society itself."

John Dewey[1]

"Advisory committees can be of great value. They contribute to the "openness" of Governmental decision-making, and provide advice and information not otherwise available to the Government. Their functions range from providing policy advice on major national issues, to providing technical recommendations on particular problems."

Federal Advisory Committees: Sixth Annual Report
of the President, 1978

"Imagine planning your day around your life, instead of your osteoarthritis pain," enticed Merck's advertising campaign for Vioxx, its blockbuster arthritis drug. The drug Merck promoted "for everyday victories" soon became a symbol of regulatory failure as evidence emerged linking Vioxx with serious cardiovascular side effects and deaths. At the beginning of Senate hearings convened in 2004 to investigate Vioxx's withdrawal from the market, Senator Charles Grassley (R-IA) alleged that the FDA had "allowed itself to be manipulated by Merck" and, more broadly, that "the FDA has a relationship with drug companies that is far too cozy."[2] The remedy for coziness with industry and for regulatory failure, Senator Grassley continued, would include "changes inside the FDA that [would] result in greater transparency and greater openness." In its 2007 review of American drug safety, the Institute

---

[1] John Dewey, *The School and Society and The Child and the Curriculum* (Chicago: University of Chicago Press, 1956), p. 25.
[2] Statement of Senator Charles E. Grassley (R-IA), U.S. Congress, Senate, Committee on Finance, *FDA, Merck, and Vioxx: Putting Patient Safety First?* 108th Congress, 2nd Session, November 18, 2004 (Washington, DC: Government Printing Office, 2004), p. 3.

of Medicine (IOM) similarly claimed, "the FDA's reputation has been hurt by a perceived lack of transparency and accountability to the public."[3] As part of its package of proposals to improve the agency's impaired reputation, the Institute of Medicine called on the FDA to make greater use of its public advisory committees – groups of nongovernmental medical practitioners, researchers, and stakeholder representatives that the FDA consults on matters such as drug approval and labeling – to supplement agency expertise and to enhance transparency in the drug approval process. These proposals suggested public engagement could render FDA decisions both more accountable and less prone to regulatory failure.

The FDA, however, *had* publicly reviewed and discussed Vioxx long before the drug's withdrawal, before Senator Grassley's rebuke, and before the Institute of Medicine's charge: the agency consulted with its Arthritis Drugs Advisory Committee about Vioxx's safety and efficacy both in 1999 and in 2001. Neither FDA staffers nor the firm sponsoring the drug served on the agency's drug advisory committees as voting members. Instead, the firm sponsoring the drug summarized evidence from drug trials and offered justifications for the drug's approval and labeling claims. Agency staffers presented their findings and concerns about drug applications in testimony before the committee as well. Both Vioxx meetings invited nonbinding advice from the committee in front of public audiences, and a portion of the 2001 deliberation included debate over whether Vioxx caused heart attacks and strokes.[4]

Public meetings like the ones convened by the FDA suggest potential portals for public participation in agency policymaking that can challenge key aspects of traditional bureaucratic administration. They can provide a public forum for agency critics, reveal details of agency decision making that an agency may prefer to keep private, produce information an agency may not want to consider, and compromise agency jurisdiction over the ultimate policy decision.[5] As part of public meetings convened in 2005 to discuss Vioxx's withdrawal from the market, a representative of the consumer advocacy group, Public Citizen, publicly charged that the FDA knew about cardiovascular risks associated with Cox-2 inhibitors such as Vioxx and failed to reveal that information

---

[3] Institute of Medicine, *The Future of Drug Safety: Promoting and Protecting the Health of the Public* (Washington, DC: National Academy Press, 2007), p. 17.

[4] Food and Drug Administration, "Arthritis Advisory Committee Meeting Transcript: Vioxx, April 20, 1999"; Food and Drug Administration, "Arthritis Advisory Committee Meeting Transcript: Vioxx, February 8, 2001."

[5] Kenneth I. Kaitin, Ann Melville and Betsy Morris, "FDA Advisory Committees and the New Drug Approval Process," *Journal of Clinical Pharmacology* 29 (1989): 886–890; Steven J. Balla and John R. Wright, "Can Advisory Committees Facilitate Congressional Oversight of the Bureaucracy?" *Congress at Work, Congress on Display* (Ann Arbor: University of Michigan Press, 2000), pp. 167–187; Steven J. Balla and John R. Wright, "Interest Groups, Advisory Committees, and Congressional Control of the Bureaucracy," *American Journal of Political Science* 45 (2001): 799–812.

promptly.[6] Long before Vioxx, AIDS activists and groups representing other disease sufferers started using FDA advisory committees to chastise the FDA publicly and viscerally. "The FDA is incapable of doing its job expeditiously," a member of the AIDS organization ACT-UP New York charged at the June 12, 1991 Antiviral Drugs Advisory Committee meeting reviewing the drug Foscavir. He continued in his address to the committee:

> Tell [FDA Commissioner] David Kessler, [Center for Drug Evaluation and Research Director] Carl Peck ... that denying [Foscavir] to people who have nothing to lose because of their slow bureaucratic procedures is a moral outrage that this committee and the American public will not tolerate. Remind the FDA – and it is sick that they need to be reminded of this – but remind them that they work for us, the American taxpayers, and that we are dying because of their inefficiency.[7]

The conventional portrait of government bureaucrats depicts insatiable appetites for secrecy and exclusivity. This notorious closure fuels a fundamental and enduring tension facing American government: reconciling bureaucratic policymaking with democratic accountability. Yet, bureaucrats in American agencies across the federal government frequently make their information public, open their policymaking processes to public advice, and, in doing so, expose themselves to public rebuke as in the case of Foscavir. If public participation poses a fundamental threat to bureaucratic power, why do bureaucrats open their doors to participation and *choose* to convene thousands of public meetings each year? Does public participation in agency policymaking, of the kind that emerged for the Vioxx review, improve policy outcomes and provide a portal for democratic governance, or does it merely yield an additional platform for industry influence and privilege in executive branch policymaking? More broadly, what effects does public participation have on bureaucratic administration, on policy outcomes, and on democratic accountability?

***

"This is an idiotic policy," a member of the National Assessment Governing Board bluntly charged at the Board's May 2002 public meeting, referring to the portion of the No Child Left Behind Act (NCLB) that made the test questions on the National Assessment of Educational Progress more readily available to public inspection.[8]

---

[6] See comments from Sidney Wolfe, "Food and Drug Administration, Joint Meeting of the Arthritis Advisory Committee and the Drug Safety and Risk Management Advisory Committee Transcript, Volume II, February 17, 2005," pp. 240–241.

[7] David Kessler was the FDA commissioner at the time. Carl Peck was the director of the Center for Drug Evaluation and Research, in charge of the drug review process. Statement of Derek Link, in Food and Drug Administration, "Antiviral Drugs Advisory Committee Transcript: Foscavir for treatment of cytomegalovirus retinitis in patients with AIDS, June 12, 1991," p. 6.

[8] Author's field notes, May 17, 2002; See also National Assessment Governing Board, "Official Summary of Board Actions, Meeting of May 17–18, 2002," in August 2002 Briefing Book,

Since 1969, the National Assessment of Educational Progress (NAEP) has been routinely testing and reporting nationally on student achievement in reading, math, science, and other subjects.[9] It has earned the reputation as the "gold standard" for measuring student achievement across the United States, a reputation that depends on producing valid measures of student achievement. Such validity stems from the assessment's design, which has historically precluded teachers from teaching to the test.

From the view of agency leadership at the National Center for Education Statistics (the government agency responsible for helping administer the assessment) along with some members of the National Assessment Governing Board (the public board that sets policy for the assessment), provisions of NCLB designed to make National Assessment test questions more broadly accessible and transparent to the public threatened to jeopardize the assessment's integrity. Addressing the National Assessment Governing Board at its March 2002 meeting, the Acting Commissioner of the National Center for Education Statistics warned:

> [L]et's say, for example ... someone got all the [NAEP] booklets and put them on a web site. Well, that would basically as far as I'm concerned shut down our ability to conduct that assessment.[10]

Similarly, the public Board's Executive Director warned at the May 2002 meeting that these new requirements could "bring NAEP to its knees" and possibly damage the statistical integrity of the test.[11] The Board Chairman echoed these worries, stating that it might be the responsibility of board members to speak about these concerns. He remarked that if it appeared this part of the law would jeopardize NAEP's integrity, it could be the Board's job to say "Stop."[12]

For the past fifty years, public participation through public committees has figured prominently in the National Assessment's governance, design, and operation. Public committees helped design the original NAEP in the early 1960s. Public committees have helped design and review the questions that NAEP poses on assessments. Public committees have governed the assessment's

---

pp. 9–10; Lynn Olson "Board Acts to Bring NAEP in Line with ESEA," *Education Week* 21 (2002): 22–24.

9   Assessments in Science, Writing, and Citizenship marked the first round of NAEP assessments, conducted in 1969–1970. Assessments in Reading and Literature began in 1970–1971, followed by assessments in Music and Social Studies in 1971–1972. The first assessment in Math was conducted in 1972–1973. See National Center for Education Statistics, *Directory of NAEP Publications* (Washington, DC: U.S. Department of Education, 1999).

10 See National Assessment Governing Board, "Board Meeting Transcript, March 1, 2002." Page numbers are not reported on pages of the transcript.

11 Author's field notes, May 18, 2002. Participants at the meeting discussed the "good faith effort" the Board and agency had undertaken to implement the law.

12 Author's field notes, May 18, 2002. For further discussion, see National Assessment Governing Board, "Official Summary of Board Actions, Meeting of May 17–18, 2002," in August 2002 Briefing Book, p. 10.

policy decisions ever since the assessment began. Unlike the advisory committees the FDA consults, public boards for the National Assessment enjoy binding policymaking authority over some policy tasks.[13] And the relationship between the Governing Board and the education statistics agency has, at times, been fraught.[14] Yet, the Board found itself at odds with a portion of the president's signature education policy initiative and in agreement with bureaucratic leadership in the National Center for Education Statistics, the government agency: to protect the statistical integrity of the National Assessment by shielding it from unfettered public access to assessment questions. The conventional portrait of public committees suggests that public participation can interfere with agencies' abilities to deploy their technical knowledge in policy implementation, and that a trade-off exists between democratic control and agency expertise. In the case of the National Assessment of Educational Progress, public participation has instead appeared to help protect and promote the statistical integrity of the assessment, combining public participation and aspects of closure. When does public participation enhance expertise and when does it compromise the technical integrity of agency policymaking? When do bureaucratic administration and democratic governance appear fundamentally at odds, and when can they be reconciled through participation that offers both?

THE TENSION BETWEEN BUREAUCRATIC ADMINISTRATION AND AMERICAN DEMOCRACY

The opening narratives invite us to rethink and refine ideas about whether and when expert knowledge creates tension between bureaucratic administration and democratic accountability. Both secrecy and expertise represent traditional hallmarks of bureaucratic administration[15] and provide the crux of the Vioxx puzzle. Given the power that exclusive expert knowledge and closure can confer, why would the FDA open its policymaking process to outside advisers and to an audience of spectators? One conventional response looks for elected officials' fingerprints on agency structures and processes that yield greater openness. The idea that government agencies possess and capitalize on exclusive

---

[13] P.L. 103–382 stipulates that "Only sections 10, 11, and 12 of the Federal Advisory Committee Act shall apply with respect to the Board." Those sections bear on procedures for calling meetings, holding open meetings, transcript availability, and financial reporting.

[14] A historical review concludes NAGB and NCES "usually have worked closely and harmoniously together" despite "certain tensions and disputes." See Maris Vinovskis, *Overseeing the Nation's Report Card: The Creation and Evolution of the National Assessment Governing Board* (Washington, DC: National Assessment Governing Board, 1998), p. 31.

[15] Max Weber, *From Max Weber: Essays in Sociology* (New York: Oxford University Press, 1946), p. 233; Max Weber, *The Theory of Social and Economic Organizations* (London: Free Press of Glencoe, Collier-MacMillian Ltd., 1947), p. 339. This book defines secrecy as concealing information and defines transparency as revealing information, consistent with Sissela Bok, *Secrets: On the Ethics of Concealment and Revelation* (New York: Random House, 1983).

expert information is foundational to theories of oversight and delegation that strive to explain when elected officials cede policymaking to bureaucrats and what structures and procedures elected officials construct to prevent bureaucrats' policies from straying far from elected officials' wishes.[16] Given bureaucrats' presumed appetites for secrecy, the power such secrecy can confer and the potential threat it poses to democratic governance, American elected officials and government reformers have repeatedly sought ways to induce bureaucrats to reveal otherwise private information and provide organized groups opportunities to monitor bureaucratic policymaking. This includes requirements to share government records, to conduct open government meetings, and to require public participation in rulemaking.[17] The ensuing political influence over agency work, however, can threaten agency expertise and impair the quality of policy outcomes. Aspects of political control, for instance, appear to come at the expense of drug safety.[18] Some versions of democratic accountability can compromise bureaucratic administration, and vice versa, thus yielding an apparent trade-off between the two.[19]

These concerns about the tension between bureaucratic policymaking, in which unelected civil servants make significant policy decisions, and democratic oversight that vests governing authority in the public have long been stitched into the fabric of American governance. This tension has taken on heightened significance, however, with the dramatic expansion and development of American bureaucracy since the nation's founding.[20] The American bureaucracy wields significant power, and some estimates suggest that agency

---

[16] See Matthew McCubbins and Thomas Schwartz, "Congressional Oversight Overlooked: Police Patrols vs. Fire Alarms," *American Journal of Political Science* 28 (1984): 165–179; Mathew McCubbins, Roger Noll, and Barry Weingast, "Structure and Process, Policy and Politics: Administrative Arrangements and the Political Control of Agencies," *Virginia Law Review* 75 (1989): 431–482; David Epstein and Sharyn O'Halloran, *Delegating Powers: A Transaction Cost Politics Approach to Policy Making under Separate Powers* (New York: Cambridge University Press, 1999); John Huber and Charles R. Shipan, *Deliberate Discretion: The Institutional Foundations of Bureaucratic Autonomy* (New York: Cambridge University Press, 2002).

[17] On regulatory notice and comment procedures and its limitations, see Cornelius Kerwin, *Rulemaking* (Washington, DC: CQ Press, 2003), pp. 62–66; Jason Webb Yackee and Susan Webb Yackee, "Bias Toward Business?" *Journal of Politics* 68 (2006): 128–139; Steven J. Balla, "Administrative Procedures and Political Control of the Bureaucracy," *American Political Science Review* 92 (1998): 663–673. On the Freedom of Information Act provisions, see Alasdair Roberts, *Blacked Out* (New York: Cambridge University Press, 2006), pp. 13–18.

[18] Politics can never be fully separate from administration. However, imposing deadlines on the FDA to review drugs quickly – one manifestation of political influence over agency policymaking – can compromise the quality of the agency's regulatory process by putting drugs on the market that are more likely to pose safety problems associated with adverse events and deaths. Daniel Carpenter, Jacqueline Chattopadhyay, Susan Moffitt, and Clayton Nall, "The Complications of Controlling Agency Time Discretion: FDA Review Deadlines and Postmarket Safety," *American Journal of Political Science* 56 (2012): 98–114.

[19] Kathleen Bawn, "Political Control Versus Expertise: Congressional Choices About Administrative Procedures," *American Political Science Review* 89 (1995): 62–73.

[20] Stephen Skowronek, *Building a New American State: The Expansion of National Administrative Capacities, 1877–1920* (Cambridge: Cambridge University Press, 1982); William T. Gormley, Jr.

administrators – not Congress or the president – create the majority of American laws through the rulemaking process.[21] With the growth of the American administrative state has come responsibility for policies, services, and decisions on which Americans' health, safety, and financial livelihood depend. Failures in bureaucratic expertise can produce devastating consequences.

The chapters that follow depart from the conventional account that explains bureaucratic openness solely in terms of elected officials' handiwork and develops the concept of participatory bureaucracy: a form of public engagement in agency policymaking, which reframes the bureaucracy-democracy relationship as in tension but not necessarily as a zero-sum trade-off. When participation is bureaucratic, it supports competent policy implementation consistent with the core elements of bureaucratic reputation: unique agency expertise and diverse support.[22] When bureaucracy is participatory, the scope of participation and policy decisions are fluid, not perfunctory means of rubber-stamping an agency decision or manipulating the masses. Meeting the conditions of participatory bureaucracy can be difficult to attain. Yet, when they manifest, they have the potential to support both bureaucratic administration and democratic accountability.

PARTICIPATORY BUREAUCRACY: SOME GUIDING PRINCIPLES

When are federal-level bureaucrats more or less likely to seek public participation in agency policymaking? When is public participation more or less likely to support key features of bureaucratic administration: expertise and diverse support? My approach to these questions begins by considering bureaucrats as implementers broadly defined, who make policy in the course of implementation.[23] While putting policy into practice is a dynamic process,[24] knowledge and

and Steven J. Balla, *Bureaucracy and Democracy: Accountability and Performance* (Washington, DC: CQ Press, 2007).

[21] Kenneth F. Warren, *Administrative Law in the Political System*, 4th ed. (Boulder, CO: Westview Press, 2004), p. 282, cited in Susan Webb Yackee, "Lifecycle of Medical Product Rules Issued by the Food and Drug Administration," *Journal of Health Politics, Policy and Law* (Forthcoming). For comprehensive scholarship on bureaucratic power, see Daniel P. Carpenter, *Reputation and Power: Organizational Image and Pharmaceutical Regulation at the FDA* (Princeton, NJ: Princeton University Press, 2010).

[22] Carpenter specifies unique capacities and political legitimacy embedded in "multiple networks" as foundational elements of bureaucratic reputation and autonomy. Daniel P. Carpenter, *The Forging of Bureaucratic Autonomy: Reputations, Networks, and Policy Innovation in Executive Agencies, 1862–1928* (Princeton, NJ: Princeton University Press, 2001), p. 14.

[23] Though this view of implementation as creating policy is typically attributed to grassroots implementation, it applies to federal-level implementers as well. On grassroots implementation, see Michael Lipsky, *Street-Level Bureaucracy: Dilemmas of the Individual in Public Services* (New York: Russell Sage Foundation, 1980).

[24] On the factors affecting implementation, see David K. Cohen and Susan L. Moffitt, *The Ordeal of Equality: Did Federal Regulation Fix the Schools?* (Cambridge, MA: Harvard University Press, 2009), pp. 17–44.

turf provide the backbones of bureaucratic task implementation. Considered in the context of U.S. federal-level policy, neither knowledge nor jurisdiction for task implementation is a general or fixed property of an agency. Instead, knowledge and turf vary by task. Conditions conducive to participatory bureaucracy thus depend on characteristics of a policy task, the fundamental unit of bureaucratic work.[25]

For instance, federal-level bureaucrats may have knowledge superior to family physicians on Vioxx's cardiovascular risks, but Merck might have better information than the bureaucrats, and researchers at the Cleveland Clinic might have better information yet. Instead of assuming monopoly information – on anyone's part – bureaucratic implementers confront a range of informational contexts, including when bureaucrats have more information, when outsiders have more information, when nobody has information, or when everyone is informed.[26] Government agencies also face a continuum of implementation contexts, ranging from fully in-house, such as a budget examination housed in the Office of Management and Budget, to well outside the agency's hierarchical reach. The federal government, for instance, enjoys relatively little formal authority over local public schools. The extent to which federal bureaucrats can implement policy in local school contexts typically depends on thousands of loosely connected implementers populating the vast governance space between the federal Department of Education and Valley View Elementary.

Consider the schema in Figure 1.1 that depicts variation on two crucial dimensions of implementation: information and turf. The horizontal axis represents the agency's information relative to task demands: the right side reflects full agency information, and the left side pegs at agency ignorance. The vertical axis represents a continuum from task independence to task interdependence. The top reflects full independence: the task is performed entirely within the agency's hierarchy. The bottom reflects fully interdependent implementations. Considerable scholarship on bureaucratic politics focuses on quadrants A and B, and with good reason. Quadrant A represents an ideal bureaucracy with perfect information and full authority over implementation, rather like Internal Revenue Service tax audits. This is where Weberian expertise and secrets may reside in harmony. In Quadrant B, bureaucrats enjoy authority over implementation, but their information is less complete relative to task demands. Here is where the tenets of Weberian

---

[25] On the importance of tasks within an organizational context, see James Q. Wilson, *Bureaucracy: What Government Agencies Do and Why They Do It* (New York: Basic Books, 1989), pp. 25–26. The discussion that follows does not aim to provide an optimal strategy for bureaucrats or for elected officials. Instead, it focuses on the conditions when participation is more or less likely to be consistent with key features of bureaucratic reputation.

[26] For important work on the development of bureaucratic information and expertise, see Sean Gailmard and John W. Patty, *Learning While Governing: Expertise and Accountability in the Executive Branch* (Chicago: University of Chicago Press, 2012).

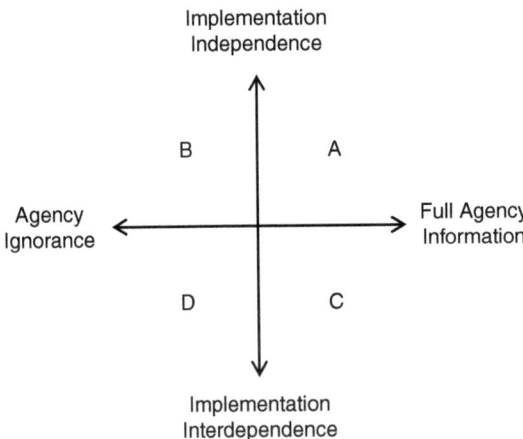

B: Private Agency Learning   A: Agency Closure

D: Creating Knowledge   C: Distributing Knowledge
    Legitimating Knowledge   Allocating Responsibility

FIGURE 1.1. Participation in American Bureaucracy by Task-Specific Information and Implementation Conditions.

power – technical knowledge and secrecy – may be at odds. The Atomic Energy Commission in the 1950s, for instance, enjoyed authority over the development of American nuclear power. When faced with insufficient information, the Commission engaged in private learning: talking behind closed doors with outsiders who had better information and more technical expertise than insiders.[27] Yet, Quadrant B is also where bureaucratic independence can allow bureaucrats to hide their ignorance: where secrecy enabled the Commission to avoid revealing their uncertainty over reactor safety, for instance. In his call for greater oversight of the Central Intelligence Agency in 1956, Senator Michael Mansfield (D-MT) lamented, "If we accept the idea of secrecy for secrecy's sake we will have no way of knowing whether we have a very fine intelligence service or a very poor one."[28] Secrecy can impair both expertise and democratic oversight.[29]

[27] On the Atomic Energy Commission, see Brian Balogh, *Chain Reaction: Expert Debate and Public Participation in American Commercial Nuclear Power, 1945–1975* (New York: Cambridge University Press, 1991).

[28] Comments of Senator Michael Mansfield, (D-MT), *Congressional Record* Senate, April 9, 1956, p. 5930.

[29] Francis E. Rourke, *Secrecy and Publicity: Dilemmas of Democracy* (Baltimore, MD: Johns Hopkins Press, 1961) pp. 5, 10–11, 138; Michel Crozier, *The Bureaucratic Phenomenon* (Chicago: University of Chicago Press, 1964), p.153; Daniel Patrick Moynihan, *Secrecy: The American Experience* (New Haven, CT: Yale University Press, 1998); Kenneth J. Meier and

Task implementations that appear in Quadrants C and D foster greater incentives for bureaucrats not only to learn *from* the public but also to learn *in* public than in A and B. These are conditions of greater task interdependence, when bureaucrats depend fundamentally on implementers who reside outside the agency's hierarchical jurisdiction. To implement its task of ensuring drug safety and efficacy, for instance, the FDA depends on firms to gather and reveal appropriate information both to the FDA *and* to doctors and patients. The agency depends on physicians and patients to use therapies judiciously. It depends on firms and physicians to report adverse events to the agency. The FDA cannot command safe drug use: safety and efficacy are ultimately matters of practice that transcend the agency's organizational boundaries. While drug reviews present general conditions of interdependence, each drug review produces a different information and implementation context. The case of the drug Lotronex presented in Chapters 6 and 8 offers an illustration of Quadrant D before the drug was approved: nobody knew if the drug caused the serious side effect ischemic colitis. Lotronex offers an illustration of Quadrant C after the drug was approved: the FDA had information on Lotronex risks it wanted to convey to the public, and it did so through public meetings.

Thus, one condition of participatory bureaucracy – public engagement in agency policymaking that supports both bureaucratic administration and democratic oversight – is *interdependent task implementation* that appears in Quadrants C and D. Interdependence renders the expertise or knowledge required for implementation contingent and emergent,[30] which creates incentives for public learning and learning *in* public, more so than for tasks with independent implementations. From a bureaucratic perspective, we would expect public participation to manifest in the same agency for some tasks but not for others. Participatory bureaucracy is less about whether or not the FDA reflects openness or closure overall, and more about whether and why openness appears for some tasks, such as drug reviews for novel indications, but not for others, such as drug reviews for supplemental indications. Participatory bureaucracy invites us to look beyond explanations that stop at the level of institutions and procedures and focus more closely on task-specific conditions.

John Bohte, *Politics and the Bureaucracy: Policymaking in the Fourth Branch of Government* (Belmont, CA: Thomson Wadsworth, 2007), p. 66; Harold Wilensky, *Organizational Intelligence* (New York: Basic Books, 1969), p. 144; Jeffrey Pfeffer and Gerald R. Salancik, *The External Control of Organizations* (New York: Harper and Row, 2003), p. 104.

[30] For careful distinction between the concepts of complexity, difficulty, and uncertainty, see Scott E. Page, "Uncertainty, Difficulty and Complexity," *Journal of Theoretical Politics* 20 (2008): 115–149. Task interdependence is consistent with public administration's concept of co-production and viewing the public as a partner. John Clayton Thomas, *Citizen, Customer, Partner: Engaging the Public in Public Management* (New York: M.E. Sharpe, 2012), pp. 10–12, 85–101; Jeffrey Brudney and Robert England, "Toward a definition of the co-production concept," *Public Administration Review* 43 (1983): 59–65; Sean P. Osborne, "Delivering Public Services: Time for a New Theory?" *Public Management Review* 12 (2010): 1–10.

Public participation can certainly occur for tasks that appear in Quadrants A and B, but participation in these contexts is more likely to yield participatory oversight than participatory bureaucracy. Public participation for tasks in Quadrants A and B are more likely to come at the expense of bureaucratic expertise and jurisdiction. The more that tasks are implemented in a traditional Weberian hierarchy – the more the tasks reside in Quadrants A and B – the less we would expect participatory bureaucracy to reconcile the democracy-bureaucracy tension, and the more we would expect the conventional trade-off, with more of one and less of another.[31] By some accounts, however, American government agency interdependence is both prevalent and expanding.[32] One estimate suggests that only 5 percent of "federal government activity" entails goods and services that government bureaucrats provide directly.[33] American government's reliance on third-party actors and public co-production renders public participation through public committees an increasingly feasible means of managing the bureaucracy-democracy tension.

However, complex tasks like those we would see in Quadrants C and D – such as regulator dependence on its regulatory target – can make agencies vulnerable to industry influence or capture,[34] which supports neither bureaucratic administration nor democratic oversight. Thus, a second condition for participatory bureaucracy is a public engagement process that yields *diverse expertise focused on implementation*. In the context of participatory bureaucracy, expert means possessing specialized knowledge that provides a baseline of knowledge or ability, but it does not inhere in fixed descriptive characteristics, such as being a woman or having a PhD. Instead, it can manifest from multiple sources, including the grassroots; and it depends on timing, location, and the nature of the policy task. Common critiques of participatory processes typically dichotomize "experts" and "public," defining expertise in terms of credentials or exclusive knowledge, and the public in terms of the mass that lacks formal credentials but has a potential interest in the issue. Participatory bureaucracy blurs the distinction between these categories. In participatory bureaucracy, disease sufferers may be expert in their ability to express how they are affected by disease, how they experienced pharmaceutical therapies, and their willingness to accept risk.[35] Expertise for participatory bureaucracy is

---

[31] For related discussion on this point, see Thomas, *Citizen, Customer, Partner*, pp. 129–130.

[32] Kenneth J. Meier and Laurence J. O'Toole, *Bureaucracy in a Democratic State: A Governance Perspective* (Baltimore, MD: Johns Hopkins University Press, 2006).

[33] Lester M. Salamon, *The Tools of Government: A Guide to the New Governance* (New York: Oxford University Press, 2002), p. 4.

[34] Nolan McCarty, "Complexity, Capacity and Capture," in *Preventing Regulatory Capture: Special Interest Influence and How to Limit It*, edited by Daniel Carpenter and David Moss (Cambridge: Cambridge University Press, 2013), pp. 99–123.

[35] Usable knowledge arises from many sources. Charles Lindblom and David K. Cohen, *Usable Knowledge: Social Science and Social Problem Solving* (New Haven, CT: Yale University Press, 1979). For related discussion, see p. 18 of Archon Fung and Erik Olin Wright, "Deepening

not restricted to a particular profession or perspective, but evolves along with the implementation context: who is "expert" depends on the task.[36] Rather than dichotomies between the public and experts, participatory bureaucracy can embody significant overlap between the two.

Within the context of broadly defined expertise, diversity brings different *perspectives* and heuristics. This cognitive approach differs from traditional models of participation in bureaucratic policymaking that frame participation strictly as opportunities for communicating and advocating for particular *interests*.[37] Building on a broadly defined baseline of expertise, diverse perspectives and diverse cognitive heuristics render suboptimal policy decisions less likely. Suboptimal from the perspective of bureaucratic administration means policy outcomes that are costly to reverse and/or damaging to agency reputation.[38] Participatory bureaucracy is better equipped to manage the bureaucracy-democracy tension when it marshals diverse expertise keyed to the policy task. These conditions – diverse expertise focused on interdependent task implementation – render public participation amenable to supporting core elements of bureaucratic reputation: expertise and diverse support.[39]

Given the conditions it imposes on public participation, participatory bureaucracy clearly differs from participatory democracy's inclusiveness and empowerment.[40] Yet, participatory bureaucracy is amenable to democratic accountability when it "liquefies knowledge," to use Dewey's metaphor. Participatory bureaucracy that manages the bureaucracy-democracy tension is *indeterminate*: both the participatory process and its outcomes are fluid and

---

Democracy: Innovations in Empowered Participatory Governance," *Politics and Society* 29 (2001): 5–41.

[36] For more discussion on the relativity of capability for policy implementation, see Cohen and Moffitt, *Ordeal of Equality*, pp. 17–44.

[37] For a summary, see Meier and Bohte, *Politics and the Bureaucracy*, pp. 198–205. On the distinction between representing interests and including diverse professional and social perspectives on public committees, see Mark B. Brown, "Fairly Balanced: The Politics of Representation on Government Advisory Committees," *Political Research Quarterly* 61 (2008): 547–560.

[38] For a review on group decision making, see Daan van Knippenberg and Michaéla C. Schippers, "Work Group Diversity," *Annual Review of Psychology* 58 (2007): 515–541. On the ability of diverse perspectives to render suboptimal policy less likely, see Scott E. Page, *The Difference: How the Power of Diversity Creates Better Groups, Firms, Schools and Societies* (Princeton, NJ: Princeton University Press, 2007). On the impact of diverse perspectives on the quality of deliberation, see James Bohman, *Public Deliberation: Pluralism, Complexity and Democracy* (Cambridge, MA: MIT Press, 1996). On costly reversals and agency reputation, see Daniel P. Carpenter, "Groups, the Media, Agency Waiting Costs and FDA Drug Approval," *American Journal of Political Science* 46 (2002): 490–505.

[39] Bureaucrats benefit from diverse support for their programs and policies, instead of support limited to a single dominant group. Carpenter, *The Forging of Bureaucratic Autonomy*, pp. 14, 32; Francis E. Rourke, *Bureaucracy, Politics and Public Policy*, 2nd ed. (Boston: Little, Brown & Co, 1976), p. 55.

[40] Carol Pateman, *Participation and Democratic Theory* (Cambridge: Cambridge University Press, 1970).

evolving rather than fixed or foreordained. Participatory bureaucracy creates openness and access to policymaking that can expand beyond the scope of the particular task. Scholarship typically assesses the impact of participation on the individuals who participated in the policymaking process. Examples include Chicago's Alternative Policing Strategy that brought community members and police together to develop and implement priorities for the police, or environmental regulatory negotiations conducted through stakeholder participation.[41] The potential democratic contributions of participatory bureaucracy, however, exceed the scope of a singular decision or information exchange. Consistent with open-systems theories of organizations, participatory bureaucracy can transcend fixed jurisdictions and offer access to policymaking through visibility and through opportunities for engagement from governmental and nongovernmental sources.[42] The potential for accountability is ongoing: it does not end when the votes are cast and the meeting comes to an end. Open meetings can put knowledge into the public space that can, in turn, take on a life of its own. The promise of participatory bureaucracy resides in part in the ongoing portal it may create.

Skepticism toward participatory processes abounds. Imbalanced power can limit the extent and scope of participation and stifle discourse.[43] Insufficient connections between knowledge and subsequent action can limit the usefulness of public information for individual behavior or policy outcomes. Knowledge may drip rather than flow, and do so in ways that exacerbate political, social, and economic inequality. Yet, consider the counterfactuals of Quadrants A and B, where accountability may be even more remote *and* come at the expense of expert or competent implementation.

Participatory bureaucracy is not the sole solution for the bureaucracy-democracy tension, and can complement other governing approaches including representative bureaucracy and performance management. But it is distinct in notable ways. For one, bureaucrats may initiate, design, and administer participatory bureaucracy. Participatory bureaucracy is not necessarily imposed

---

[41] Archon Fung, *Empowered Participation: Reinventing Urban Democracy* (Princeton, NJ: Princeton University Press, 2004), p. 3. On debate over the durability of policy made through negotiated rulemaking, see Cary Coglianese, "Assessing Consensus: The Promise and Performance of Negotiated Rulemaking," *Duke Law Journal* 46 (1997): 1255–1349; Laura Langbein, "Responsive Bureaus, Equity and Regulatory Negotiation," *Journal of Public Policy Analysis and Management* 21 (2002): 446–465. For a review of reg-neg, see Peter H. Schuck, and Steven Kochevar, "Reg Neg Redux: The Career of a Procedural Reform," *Theoretical Inquiries in Law* (Forthcoming 2014).

[42] Richard M. Cyert and James G. March, *A Behavioral Theory of the Firm* (Englewood Cliffs, NJ: Prentice-Hall, 1963); Pfeffer and Salancik, *The External Control of Organizations*; Karl Weick, "Educational Organizations as Loosely Coupled Systems," *Administrative Science Quarterly* 21 (1976): 1–19.

[43] For a classic illustration of power represented through "blue ribbon" advisory committees at the local level, see Robert Dahl, *Who Governs? Democracy and Power in an American City* (New Haven, CT: Yale University Press, 1961), p. 124.

on the bureaucracy by elected officials. Rather than curtail agency autonomy, public participation creates room for government agencies to frame policy issues, shape alternatives for the public agenda, and cultivate favorable agency images. In this sense, participatory bureaucracy departs from congressional dominance views, which leave little room for bureaucratic autonomy and credit elected officials with institution building. While participatory bureaucracy offers room for representing interests, akin to pluralism or representative bureaucracy,[44] it also allows direct public access to information and policy-making, not just access mediated through representatives or groups.[45] Unlike pluralism and representative bureaucracy where the direction of influence and information flow is from the representatives to the policy decision, moreover, participatory bureaucracy can enable information to flow in multiple directions: from the agency to the various publics as well as from the public to the agency.[46] In contrast to some aspects of New Public Management,[47] participatory bureaucracy does not assume that the local level or the consumer has "better" information essential to policy implementation, just as it does not assume federal-level bureaucrats enjoy superior information. Information for implementation depends on the policy task.

Public participation's ability to manage the bureaucracy-democracy tension depends on the design of the policy task, on the design of participation, and on the broader context in which the policy is implemented and participation occurs. Managing the tension offers a potentially non-zero-sum approach to government administration. Instead of dichotomies between democratic governance and bureaucratic administration, between legislative and executive branch control, between public and private, or between public and expert, participatory bureaucracy offers potential complements. Rather than zero-sum, both elected officials and bureaucrats can reap rewards from permeable

---

[44] Representative bureaucracy focuses on having individuals who serve in government reflect the broader population in terms of gender, race, ethnicity, sexual orientation, and other descriptive characteristics. When bureaucracy embodies the interests and preferences of the populace, it can offer a defensible substitute for more direct democratic accountability and can impact subsequent policy decisions. Meier and O'Toole, *Bureaucracy in a Democratic State*, pp. 67–92; Kenneth J. Meier, Eric Gonzalez Juenke, Robert D. Wrinkle, and J. L. Polinard, "Structural Choices and Representational Biases: The Post-Election Color of Representation," *American Journal of Political Science* 49 (2005): 758–768; Lael R. Keiser, Vicky M. Wilkins, Kenneth J. Meier, and Catherine A. Holland, "Lipstick and Logarithms: Gender, Institutional Context and Representative Bureaucracy," *American Political Science Review* 96 (2002): 553–564.

[45] As Thomas argues, representative bureaucracy offers a top-down, hierarchical approach to bringing broader community voice into agency policymaking, in contrast to co-production forms of engagement. Thomas, *Citizen, Customer, Partner*, pp. 20–29.

[46] On this point, see Thomas, *Citizen, Customer, Partner*, p. 177.

[47] For a consumer-oriented view, see David Osborne and Ted Gaebler, *Reinventing Government: How the Entrepreneurial Spirit is Transforming the Public Sector* (Reading, MA: Addison-Wesley, 1992).

bureaucratic policymaking.[48] Both elected officials and bureaucrats can benefit from competent task implementation.[49] One way bureaucracy can abet competence is through public participation that assembles diverse expertise for interdependent task implementations.

Participatory bureaucracy shares several key features with the development of administrative expertise modeled in Gailmard and Patty's *Learning While Governing*. Both challenge the conventional assumption that bureaucrats enjoy superior or sufficient information relative to other policy actors. Both recognize the importance of information and authority for structuring bureaucratic incentives. Both recognize that bureaucratic expertise and democratic accountability are not necessarily at odds. Gailmard and Patty offer an important model for understanding organizational designs that induce bureaucrats to "acquire, share and elicit information," to use their terms.[50] Participatory bureaucracy focuses instead on task-specific variation in bureaucratic knowledge and jurisdiction that yield different incentives for learning *from* the public and learning *in* public across organizational and institutional arrangements. The analysis that follows suggests that systematic variation in task conditions goes far to explain some policy outcomes, whereas some prominent organizational and institutional differences do not.

The potential democratic mechanism in participatory bureaucracy also differs from principal-agent models. When learning in public liquefies knowledge, to use Dewey's metaphor, the potential for democratic accountability exceeds the scope of any singular policy decision. The transparency that can manifest from learning in public may assist democratic accountability not merely by holding the agency accountable but also by creating opportunities to hold other implementers outside the agency accountable upon whom task implementation depends. Accountability in participatory bureaucracy may manifest not only by holding the FDA solely responsible, for instance, but also by shining the spotlight on firms and inducing firms to behave in ways consistent with policy implementation.[51]

---

[48] For related argument on the non-zero-sum potential of group engagement, see Jane J. Mansbridge, "A Deliberative Theory of Interest Representation," in *The Politics of Interests: Interest Groups Transformed*, edited by Mark P. Petracca (Boulder, CO: Westview Press, 1992), pp. 32–57. In her discussion of public boards from the perspective of democratic accountability, Mansbridge distinguishes between unitary and adversary issues (conflicting or common interests) as key to understanding different participatory arrangements. Jane J. Mansbridge, *Beyond Adversary Democracy* (Chicago: University of Chicago Press, 1983), pp. ix–x of the revised preface.

[49] Competently performing policy tasks can offer one expression of accountability. For an important theoretical approach that combines administrative balance and rationality to yield accountability, see Anthony Bertelli and Laurence E. Lynn Jr., *Madison's Managers: Public Administration and the Constitution* (Baltimore, MD: Johns Hopkins University Press, 2006).

[50] Gailmard and Patty, *Learning While Governing*, p. 11.

[51] Recall that the extent to which participatory bureaucracy yields competent task implementation can also support democratic accountability.

The policy conditions that make participatory bureaucracy promising, however, also render it fragile. Policies' interdependence can give way to imbalanced dependence, privilege, or even corruption. Emerging technologies and evolving expertise can expose nascent policies to unfounded attacks and equally unfounded sponsorship. The expansive, non-zero-sum potential of public knowledge generated through public participation can collide with zero-sum American politics. Appetites for secrecy persist. Public participation did not, for instance, prevent the arthritis drug Vioxx's post-marketing safety problems. Participatory bureaucracy is hard to pull off.

Given this mixed portrait of public participation in agency policymaking, this book explores the following questions:

- When do different forms of public participation emerge: participatory oversight, private learning, and participatory bureaucracy?
- What are the implications of participatory bureaucracy for policy outcomes and bureaucratic reputations?
- What are the implications of participatory bureaucracy for democratic accountability?

Managing the challenge of expert bureaucratic administration amid democratic accountability confronts policymakers and implementers across policy domains, from pharmaceutical regulation, to education testing, to defense contracting, to financial services reform. The vast U.S. federal advisory committee system offers an enduring venue for examining public participation in agency policymaking, for assessing its potential to yield participatory bureaucracy, and for addressing this book's guiding questions.

PARTICIPATORY BUREAUCRACY THROUGH PUBLIC ADVICE

Federal public committees are uniquely positioned among forms of federal level public engagement, such as notice-and-comment procedures and freedom-of-information requests, to address the three guiding questions introduced in the previous section. Committees like the ones that contribute to policymaking for pharmaceutical regulation are part of a vast American system of public committees and represent a defining feature of the American administrative state.[52] Federal public boards and committees offer durable and prevalent venues for policy development and deliberation, with roughly 1,000 committees currently in operation across federal agencies, such as the FDA's Arthritis Drugs Advisory Committee from the opening narrative. Committees typically consist of individuals who are employed outside of government but who advise government agencies on topics ranging from aviation security to electronic

---

[52] Rourke, *Bureaucracy, Politics and Public Policy*, p. 123. On committees that advise French pharmaceutical regulation, see Philippe Urfalino, *Le Grand Méchant Loup Pharmaceutique* (Paris: Les éditions Textuel, 2005).

medical records. Through the Federal Advisory Committee Act of 1972 and its amendments, common procedures govern advisory committee operations, including requirements for announcing meetings, setting committee agendas, transcribing meeting deliberations, and ensuring "balanced" committee membership. Although public meetings vary considerably, one common meeting format entails the agency presenting information on a policy, some nongovernmental individuals presenting information on that policy, some period of open public comment, and committee deliberation from members who are formally appointed to the public board and others in the room. Within the contours of Federal Advisory Committee Act provisions, committees vary considerably in terms of their meeting format, committee membership, meeting frequency, and their policy contributions.[53]

Federal public committees have the potential to make policy public in several ways. Committees are public in the sense that public officials – legislators, presidents, presidential appointees, bureaucrats – create them as portals for discussion and participation. Despite bureaucrats' legendary appetites for secrecy, government agencies have created nearly half of the approximately 1,000 federal advisory committees operating in 2010 and have played prominent roles in structuring many others, as Figure 1.2 illustrates.[54]

Committees are also public in the sense that they include members of the general public – individuals who work outside of government – in government policymaking.[55] This can provide individuals and interests a seat at government

---

[53] In *Organizational Intelligence*, Harold Wilensky offers a useful summary of the range of ways the government may use advisory committees, including representing constituencies, testing ideas, channeling public attention, mobilizing policy support, and broadening participation in the policymaking process. Harold Wilensky *Organizational Intelligence* (New York: Basic Books, 1969), pp. 169–172. On the development and use of public committees in various policy domains, see Sheila Jasanoff, *The Fifth Branch: Science Advisors as Policy Makers* (Cambridge, MA: Harvard University Press, 1990); Stephen Hilgartner, *Science on Stage: Expert Advice as Public Drama* (Stanford, CA: Stanford University Press, 2000); Rourke, *Bureaucracy, Politics and Public Policy*, pp. 121–124; David Truman, *The Governmental Process* (New York: Knopf, 1951), p. 458; Martha Derthick, *Policymaking for Social Security* (Washington, DC: Brookings Institution Press, 1979), pp. 100–101; Herbert Kaufman, *The Administrative Behavior of Federal Bureau Chiefs* (Washington, DC: The Brookings Institution, 1981), pp. 39–40; William T. Gormley Jr., *The Politics of Public Utility Regulation* (Pittsburgh, PA: University of Pittsburgh Press, 1983); Thomas A. Wolanin, *Presidential Advisory Committees: Truman to Nixon* (Madison: University of Wisconsin Press, 1975); Don K. Price, *Government and Science: Their Dynamic Relation in American Democracy* (New York: Oxford University Press, 1962) p. 130; Anthony Downs, *Inside Bureaucracy* (Boston: Little, Brown Downs, 1967), pp. 207–208; Bruce L. R. Smith *The Advisers: Scientists in the Policy Process* (Washington, DC: Brookings Institution Press, 1992), p. 8; Steven P. Croley and William F. Funk, "The Federal Advisory Committee Act and Good Government," *Yale Journal on Regulation* 14 (1997): 451–557.

[54] Jasanoff, *The Fifth Branch*, pp. 84–88; Derthick, *Policymaking for Social Security*, pp. 100–109. For a discussion of the ways in which committees are "public," see Wolanin, *Presidential Advisory Commissions*, pp. 8–9.

[55] For discussion on the state-society divide, see Jeffrey M. Sellers, "State-Society Relations," *The Sage Handbook of Governance*, edited by Mark Bevir (London: Sage, 2011), pp. 124–141.

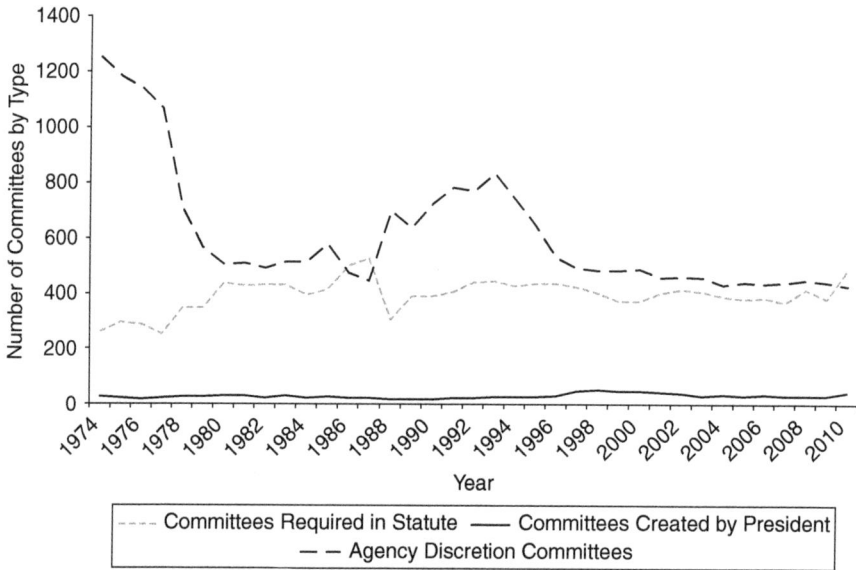

FIGURE I.2. Count of Active Public Committees by Institutional Authority, 1974–2010.

agencies' policymaking tables they would not otherwise enjoy.[56] Tens of thousands of people have served on public committees every year dating back to the 1950s. Some members serve as designated representatives of various interests. Other members serve as "special government employees" and are subject to government ethics provisions prohibiting conflicts of interest.

Committees are also public in the sense of promoting visibility: they can monitor and shine light on government agency policy processes. The Federal Advisory Committee Act contains provisions designed to promote committee transparency, such as requirements that advisory committees convene in public and make their meeting minutes publicly accessibly, affording room for visibility and for knowledge to spread. Through their visibility, public committees can expand participation beyond the boundaries of the officially convened discussion: information and arguments from open public participation can disseminate to other sites of governance outside the agency.

Despite public committees' longevity and ubiquity in the landscape of American governance, they have faced steady criticism for failing to be sufficiently public or sufficiently participatory. Proponents argue public participation, in general, may legitimate policy, promote a capable citizenry, advance policy implementation, and generate new knowledge. Public committees, as

---

[56] On the representation of interests on advisory committees, see Stéphane Lavertu, Daniel E. Walters, David L. Weimer, "Scientific Expertise and the Balance of Political Interests: MEDCAC and Medicare Coverage Decisions," *Journal of Public Administration Research and Theory* 22 (2012): 55–81.

one form of participation, may promote bureaucratic accountability to elected officials by allowing outsiders access to agency policymaking,[57] and can legitimize and encourage stable policy processes and outcomes.[58] Public participation in practice, however, habitually falls short of either a democratic or a bureaucratic ideal and has been described as "the most vilified approach to public involvement" in agency policymaking.[59] Participation can be constrained, opinions may become reinforced rather than evolve, and technical uncertainty can persist. Public advisory committees face enduring allegations of privileging particular interests, compromising agency expertise, promoting *secrecy* rather than transparency, or bringing validation, not participation, to agency work.[60] Public councils ranging from the Department of Justice Antitrust Division's advisory committees in the 1950s to the National Energy Policy Development Group convened by Vice-President Cheney in 2001 chose to close their meetings to public inspection and to public audiences. Critics of the NASA Advisory Council have argued that the council operates as "spokesmen on the agency's behalf" rather than as a venue for meaningful participation.[61] The EPA's Science Advisory Board faced allegations of insufficiently rigorous measures for preventing conflicts of interest among board members.[62] Some estimates suggest that thousands of committee meetings are closed to general public audiences each year.[63]

The analysis that follows offers an overarching portrait of the federal public committee system that extends throughout the executive branch, but it focuses primarily on public participation in the federal drug approval process and in the collection of educational statistics and assessments over the span of fifty years, from 1960 to 2010.

---

[57] Balla and Wright, "Can Advisory Committees Facilitate Congressional Oversight of the Bureaucracy?" pp. 167–187.

[58] Jasanoff, *The Fifth Branch*, p. 17; Hilgartner, *Science on Stage*; Heimann, *Acceptable Risks*, p. 154. Jasanoff discusses public committees' failures to achieve either democratic or technocratic ideals.

[59] Thomas, *Citizen, Customer, Partner*, p. 173. Thomas notes that this critique "unfairly judges" some forms of participation.

[60] For allegations of advisory committees creating barriers between government administration and the public, see U.S. Congress, Senate, *Advisory Committees,* Hearings before the Subcommittee on Intergovernmental Relations of the Committee on Government Operations, 92nd Congress, 1st Session, part 2 (Washington, DC: GPO, 1971), p. 497. The FDA's panel on cyclamates offers a well-known example of alleged validation.

[61] Smith, *The Advisers*, p. 122.

[62] U.S. General Accounting Office, *EPA's Science Advisory Board Panels: Improved Policies and Procedures Needed to Ensure Independence and Balance* (Washington, DC: GAO, 2001), p. 2.

[63] Kevin D. Karty, "Closure and Capture in Federal Advisory Committees," *Business and Politics* 4 (2002): 213–238. However, other work suggests that most agencies "rarely close their meetings." See Croley and Funk, "The Federal Advisory Committee Act and Good Government," p. 505. Historically, peer review committees within the National Science Foundation and National Endowment for the Humanities constitute some of the most frequently closed committees.

PARTICIPATORY BUREAUCRACY IN PHARMACEUTICAL
REGULATION AND EDUCATIONAL ASSESSMENTS

Case Selection

This book closely examines public participation in the context of pharmaceutical regulation and federal-level educational assessments. Taking a micro-view of public participation in agency policymaking allows the analysis to demonstrate how participatory bureaucracy works, when it works, when it does not, and when other forms of participation emerge, such as participatory oversight. This micro-view is also essential to assess variation in task-specific expertise. These cases were selected because of important systematic differences in their organizational and institutional forms, which leverage generalizability and are outlined in Table 1.1.

When bureaucrats are in charge of participation, what kinds of participation manifest and to what effect? When does participatory bureaucracy emerge, and when is participation perfunctory as critics allege? Public participation through FDA drug committees enables us to explore these questions. Participation in pharmaceutical regulation is discretionary: the FDA, not Congress, was responsible for creating drug review committees. The FDA's Center for Drug Evaluation and Research decides whether to consult with public committees, on what issues, and when.[64] It is also advisory: decisions about product approval and labeling ultimately rest with the FDA.[65] The agency has historically played a major role in contributing to member selection and choosing "temporary" members who participate at particular meetings even though they are not permanent members.[66] In general, if participatory bureaucracy does not emerge for drug advisory committees, we have little reason to expect it to emerge elsewhere.

What kinds of participation emerge when it is imposed on bureaucrats? Is participatory oversight that comes at the expense of bureaucratic expertise more likely? Public committees associated with educational assessments offer opportunities to explore these questions. The analysis that follows examines different forms of participation for educational assessments, including ad hoc commissions comprised of group representatives, "lay" panels of parents and teachers who review assessment questions, technical review boards linked to

---

[64] The Food and Drug Administration Amendments Act of 2007 added language that the FDA should send new drugs (drugs whose active ingredients have not already been approved) to an advisory committee for review before approving the drug, or explain in the drug's approval letter why the agency did not consult with an advisory committee before approval. P.L. 110–85, Sec.918 (21 USC 355).

[65] Although my analysis focuses on the Center for Drug Evaluation and Research (CDER), I will refer to the FDA throughout this book, to use the agency name familiar to most readers.

[66] Formal appointment authority resides with the Secretary of Health and Human Services, the Assistant Secretary for Health and the FDA Commissioner. 21 CFR 14.80, Revised as of April 1, 2013.

TABLE 1.1. *Institutional and Organizational Attributes of Public Committees*

	FDA Drug Committees	National Assessment Governing Board	Advisory Council on Education Statistics
Institutional Origin	Authorized in statute	Mandated in statute	Mandated in statute
Policy Authority	Advisory	Policymaking	Advisory
Agenda Authority	Agency discretion	Board discretion	Commissioner discretion
Appointments	Several designated positions, rest discretionary; variation in appointment authority	Explicit categories for positions; Secretary appointment authority	Secretary appointment authority
Resources	Agency support	Separate staff and budget	Agency support
Departmental Affiliation	Health and Human Services	Education	Education
Policy Type	Regulatory	Technical	Technical
Participatory Tasks	Discrete policy tasks	Discrete policy tasks	Diffuse tasks

government contracts, and ongoing committees and boards. Among these, the institutional design of National Assessment Governing Board (NAGB) stands in clear contrast to FDA drug advisory committees and is a focal point in the empirical analysis that follows. Congress statutorily created NAGB, mandated specific tasks for the public board to consider, and specified detailed categories for membership. The extent to which similarities appear between FDA drug review committees and NAGB, residing at opposite ends of the participatory spectrum, gives us reason to expect similar patterns to appear in other committees as well.

Key portions of the empirical analysis consider agendas, participation, and outcomes in fifteen FDA drug review committees and in NAGB. I supplement the agenda analyses with a close look at another public committee: the Advisory Council on Education Statistics. The Advisory Council and the Governing Board differ in several important ways. The Council fell fully under the auspices of the Federal Advisory Committee Act, and it was primarily advisory. The National Assessment Governing Board, in contrast, wields policymaking authority over the National Assessment and adheres to only portions of the Federal Advisory Committee Act, such as holding open meetings and making meeting transcripts publicly available, but not others.[67] Historically, the origins

[67] P.L. 103–382. NAGB is separate from ED's hierarchy.

and predecessors of all of these FDA and educational assessment committees began under the auspices of the Department of Health, Education and Welfare in the 1960s and 1970s, allowing systematic variation to occur while holding other institutional variables constant.

This case selection strategy offers room to assess two of the principal allegations that are antithetical to participatory bureaucracy: (1) they are bastions for industry influence; and (2) they are irrelevant. The FDA represents a strong case to test the claim that public participation is really a front for industry influence: just another venue for powerful interests to amass more power. Such allegations have confronted FDA committees since the early 1970s, and a 1972 House Committee study ranked the FDA as one of the worst agencies for public access: none of its committees were open to the public. Educational assessments represent a policy domain conducive to finding federal committee irrelevance because of traditionally weak federal-level authority in the field of education and because of the culture wars that periodically engulf education debate. The more evidence suggests these public committees limit industry influence and contribute substantively to policymaking, the more we should have reason to expect similar or even more robust findings in other agencies.

While the origins of these committees fell under the Department of Health, Education and Welfare umbrella, pharmaceutical regulation and educational assessments embody markedly different policy domains. Pharmaceutical regulation is typically associated with life-or-death regulatory decisions with considerable agency gatekeeping authority to decide which drugs will reach the market and which will not. Educational assessments are typically portrayed as hortatory policies:[68] their potential to bring about change comes through their persuasiveness or through the information they impart. However, both pharmaceutical regulation and educational assessments share a fundamental similarity: they include efforts to use knowledge as a policy instrument.[69] The genesis of the Department of Education, for instance, embodies the allure of influencing educational practice through public information. The Department of Education began in 1867 with a mandate to collect "statistics and facts as shall show the condition and progress of education in the several States and Territories," and the agency's creators expected the information to "shame" states and localities into providing common schools.[70] Nearly one hundred years later, subsequent Office of Education (OE) leadership rekindled the agency's original purpose to use public knowledge to press for educational improvement. In 1962, OE Commissioner Keppel started working to establish

---

[68] Lorraine McDonnell, *Politics, Persuasion and Educational Testing* (Cambridge, MA: Harvard University Press, 2004).

[69] Janet Weiss and Judith Gruber, "Using Knowledge for Control in Fragmented Policy Arenas," *Journal of Policy Analysis and Management* 3 (1984): 225–247.

[70] Harry Kursh, *The United States Office of Education* (Philadelphia: Chilton Company, 1965), pp. 10–11.

a National Assessment of Educational Progress. The underlying purpose was akin to one the agency's founders proposed in 1867: to press states and localities to attend to improved educational practices, consistent with Keppel's "conviction that there were serious weaknesses in [American schools'] curriculum and that they should be exposed."[71] NAEP has since become a highly regarded assessment, grounded in the assumption that performance information – combined with other instruments – will encourage educational improvement.

Knowledge production and use play a vital role in pharmaceutical regulation as well. The FDA's power in pharmaceutical regulation fundamentally arises from gatekeeping: deciding which drugs will reach the U.S. market and which will not. Yet, some of the early roots of American pharmaceutical regulation also stem from an informational foundation: jurisdiction to take action over misbranding drugs. The Pure Food and Drug Act of 1906 made "misbranding" drugs a misdemeanor, gave the FDA's predecessor, the Department of Agriculture's Bureau of Chemistry, the authority to determine if a drug was misbranded, and defined misbranded drugs as having packages or labels that were "false or misleading."[72] FDA's authority over pharmaceutical sales and marketing expanded over the subsequent six decades, with the Food, Drug and Cosmetic Act of 1938 and the Kefauver Amendments of 1962 codifying that expansion.[73] FDA secured significant gatekeeping authority, first through authority to determine if drugs were sufficiently safe, followed by authority to determine if drugs were sufficiently efficacious to be marketed. FDA also retained and expanded its authority to regulate information about pharmaceuticals, especially the claims firms could make about their drugs.[74] Though industry and media reports attend closely to whether public committees vote for a drug's approval, committees devote considerable time to reviewing and debating drugs' informational distribution: what information will be included on labels, what warnings will appear, both before and after a particular drug is approved.

These fifteen drug review committees and the educational assessment committees and their predecessors were selected to address this book's guiding theoretical puzzles about the potential trade-off between expertise and ultimate democratic control. The analyses here are not intended as program evaluations: comprehensive reviews of FDA committees and the National Assessment Governing Board. Rather, this book uses these public bodies as windows into

---

[71] J. A. Hazlett, *A History of the National Assessment of Educational Progress, 1963–1974* (University of Kansas, Doctoral dissertation, 1974), p. 66.

[72] P.L. 59–384, 34 Stat. 768, *Pure Food and Drug Act of 1906*, Sec. 8. The Act specified misbranding in the following way: "if the package fails to bear a statement on the label of the quantity or proportion of any alcohol, morphine, opium, cocaine, heroin, alpha or beta eucaine, chloroform, cannabis indica, chloral hydrate, or acetanilide."

[73] P.L. 75–717, 52 Stat. 1040 *Food, Drug and Cosmetic Act of 1938*; P.L. 87–781, 76 Stat. 780, *Harris Kefauver Act, Drug Amendments of 1962.*

[74] The FDA possesses different types of authority before and after drugs are approved. For further discussion, see Carpenter, *Reputation and Power*, pp. 585–589.

the promise and limits of participatory bureaucracy. Several challenges to generalizability remain, which the conclusion discusses in further detail.

Methodological Approach

I draw on historical, statistical, and comparative case analyses to assess the design and impact of public participation through public committees. Examining the development and use of public committees over sixty years is crucial for explaining both the period before the Federal Advisory Committee Act's passage in 1972 and after. This time span also allows this work to document and examine committee birth, transformation, neglect, termination, and impact. My argument and evidence are grounded in archival material to understand the development of public committees and to illuminate the nuance and variation in committees' origins, uses and trajectories. This archival material includes government agency documents, public committee meeting transcripts and minutes, correspondence, media accounts, and legislative documents including hearings and reports. Some material, such as the legislative documents, is readily available online. Much of the primary source material, however, required searching for and retrieving documents housed in archives, obtaining documents through Freedom of Information Act requests, and reading material available only in government offices or through public officials. To assess both decisions and nondecisions, I used primary source material to derive hundreds of potential agenda items for the committees in my study. When possible, I develop pools of potential participants and actual participants to systematically assess patterns of participation. I approach my observational data cautiously and recognize its limits when assessing the ultimate impact of public participation on agency policymaking.

I have supplemented my statistical work with both participant observation and interviews. I have lurked in the corners of public committee meetings, gaining valuable insight on matters unrecorded in official transcripts or media accounts: the affiliations of the people in the audience, the tone participants use when speaking to each other, the juxtaposition of a smudgy government agency overhead slide against a sleek industry presentation, the hallway chatter, and, on several occasions, participants' tears. I have also used interviews to check myself: to check parts of the story that emerged from my archival review and statistical analysis, to learn where I should look for further evidence (which, on occasion, led to more boxes of original documentary material), and to learn from participants how they perceive the public advising process.

I designed my methodological approach to examine and assess the impact of public participation on bureaucratic administration and democratic accountability. The analyses that follow do not assume that agency leaders are rational actors who have constructed committees to attain specific purposes. This work explains what has happened and explores the effects of what has happened, but does not infer intent from outcomes.

THE PATH FORWARD

Under what conditions does public participation hold promise of supporting bureaucratic administration and democratic accountability? Chapter 2 defines what participatory bureaucracy means, how it operates, and what it entails for government administration and democratic accountability. The chapter's theoretical framework suggests public participation is potentially suited for managing the bureaucracy-democracy tension in the context of interdependent tasks: tasks that depend on multiple implementers inside and outside the agency, commonly referred to as complex tasks. It also specifies the conditions and importance of diverse expertise in managing the tension. This chapter distinguishes participatory bureaucracy, which offers a way to manage both sides of the tension, from strictly oversight forms of public participation that may reinforce the trade-off between expertise and political control.

When do public committees produce relatively public or private participation, closure or openness? Chapter 3 sketches the development of the American advisory committee system and the charges of privilege and secrecy that accompanied its development. Chapters 4 and 5 then situate the development of public committees for educational assessment and pharmaceutical regulation in terms of the broader public committee system. Both educational assessments and pharmaceutical regulation use knowledge as a policy instrument, and both began with public participation that occurred privately, behind closed doors. Despite these closed and private origins, public participation in pharmaceutical regulation and educational assessment laid the foundation for more inclusive, open, and "public" participation.

Given government bureaucrats' legendary appetites for secrecy, when do bureaucrats invite the public to review and discuss agency work? When bureaucrats are in charge of participation, does public engagement focus on interdependent task implementations? When bureaucrats are not in charge of participation, are we more likely to see participatory oversight: public engagement for tasks with more independent implementations? Chapter 6 offers a descriptive overview of venues available for public participation across the federal government using an original dataset that spans from 1974 to 2010. Looking closely at potential agenda items for FDA drug advisory committees, the National Assessment Governing Board (NAGB), and the Advisory Council on Education Statistics (ACES), this chapter examines which topics and tasks reach the public agenda and which do not. It finds support for participatory bureaucracy – agendas focused on interdependent task implementation – in the case of the FDA and, surprisingly, on NAGB agendas as well.

Who enjoys a seat at the public committee table, and is that participation consistent with participatory bureaucracy? Do elites, conventionally defined, dominate, or is there room for something that resembles a public voice? Public participation has long faced accusations of privileging particular interests – such as industry or unions – or giving voice to only technical experts at the

expense of public voice. By design, public committees on pharmaceutical regulation and educational assessments appear well positioned to reinforce both
of these standard critiques. Evidence from both NAGB and FDA committees in
Chapter 7, however, makes clear that they are not wholly owned subsidiaries
of select organized interests. Analysis from both suggests nuance, however: the
potential for bureaucratic administration coupled with fragility that arises in
part from dependence on factors outside of the agency's control, such as trends
in the broader professional community.

How does public participation affect policy implementation and bureaucratic administration? Results from FDA drug committees meet expectations
of participatory bureaucracy. Drugs that received advisory committees reviews
before approval were significantly less likely to encounter post-marketing
safety problems than drugs that did not receive an advisory committee review,
all else being equal; they also were less likely to be subjected to subsequent
legislative scrutiny. Assessing the impact of public participation for educational assessments requires a different analytic approach. Evidence suggests
NAGB supports the distribution of knowledge, consistent with democratic
accountability.

When can public participation support both bureaucratic administration
and democratic accountability? Chapter 9 concludes with a summary of participatory bureaucracy, discusses the ways in which it enhances and departs
from other means of reconciling the bureaucracy-democracy tension, and
considers future work that could advance our understanding of participatory
bureaucracy. Participatory bureaucracy offers a policy process that is public in
the sense of government sponsored, public in the sense of visible, and public
in the sense of resulting from engagement with individuals and groups outside the government's jurisdiction. It can also make policy public by equipping
the governance space beyond the scope of the agency with usable knowledge.
Participatory bureaucracy can yield high-quality policy products and robust
bureaucratic administration. FDA and NAGB provide models for how participatory bureaucracy can manifest in very different agencies, with very different
institutional designs, in very different policy domains, and yet remain faithful
to both participation and bureaucracy. However, along with the potential for
managing the bureaucracy-democracy tension comes vulnerability. The ever-
changing nature of complex tasks renders durable participatory institutionali-
zation difficult to achieve and sustain.

CONCLUSION

Though transparency and public participation are typically cast as ways to
curtail bureaucratic power, bureaucrats may benefit from and seek greater
openness and engagement – and they may do so through public committees.
Scholarship on public committees has helped us understand general committee operations and influence, committees' abilities to balance political and

technical demands, elected officials' abilities to use committees as a way to monitor the bureaucracy, and representation on committees. Missing, however, is an account of public participation from a *bureaucratic perspective*: when public participation transforms into participatory bureaucracy and provides a potential means of managing the tension between democratic accountability and bureaucratic administration.

2

Participatory Bureaucracy in Practice

> Bureaucratic administration means fundamentally the exercise of control on the basis of knowledge ... technical knowledge ... [and] official secrets.
>
> – Max Weber[1]

> Nothing has been discovered which acts in entire isolation.
>
> – John Dewey[2]

Participatory bureaucracy is a systematic process of public engagement that brings diverse expertise to bear on task implementations. When participation is bureaucratic, it is consistent with the core elements of bureaucratic reputation: unique agency expertise and diverse support.[3] When bureaucracy is participatory, the scope of participation is fluid. It enables information to flow in multi-

---

[1] Max Weber, *The Theory of Social and Economic Organizations* (London: Free Press of Glencoe, Collier-Macmillan Ltd., 1947), p. 339.

[2] John Dewey, *The Public and Its Problems* (Athens: Swallow Press/Ohio University Press, 1927), p. 22.

[3] An extensive literature documents bureaucrats' pursuit of expertise, their effort to avoid visible failure, and the cultivation of bureaucratic reputation. On expertise and avoiding visible failure, see Francis E. Rourke *Bureaucracy, Politics and Public Policy*, 2nd ed. (Boston: Little, Brown & Co, 1976), pp. 65–66; Daniel P. Carpenter, *The Forging of Bureaucratic Autonomy: Reputations, Networks, and Policy Innovation in Executive Agencies, 1862–1928* (Princeton, NJ: Princeton University Press, 2001); James D. Thompson, *Organizations in Action: Social Sciences Bases of Administrative Theory* (New York: McGraw-Hill, 1967), p. 33; James Q. Wilson, *Bureaucracy: What Government Agencies Do and Why They Do It* (New York: Basic Books, 1989), pp. 188–192; C. F. Larry Heimann, *Acceptable Risks: Politics, Policy and Risky Technologies* (Ann Arbor: University of Michigan Press, 1997) p. 19. Scholarship suggests visible failure invites more oversight, degrades the agency's "professionalism," and weakens the agency's ability to attract and retain staff. On this point, see Daniel P. Carpenter, "Groups, The Media, Agency Waiting Costs and FDA Drug Approval," *American Journal of Political Science* 46 (2002): 490–505. On reputation, see Daniel P. Carpenter, *Reputation and Power* (Princeton, NJ: Princeton

ple directions – to the agency, from the agency, and beyond the individuals who participate in a particular decision.

Yet, when is participatory bureaucracy likely to arise and add value to bureaucratic administration and democratic accountability? When are we more likely to see participatory oversight that is imposed on bureaucratic administration and that potentially perpetuates the bureaucracy-democracy trade-off, where participation comes at the expense of bureaucratic administration and reputation? The answer resides, in part, in the conditions of the policy task and the design of participation.[4] Scholars have long examined bureaucrats' intentional and active engagement with publics outside agency walls to build supportive coalitions, to gather information, and to facilitate policy implementation.[5] Agencies also intentionally reveal their information to exert regulatory authority, to persuade, to educate other implementers, and to build consensus.[6] Francis Rourke astutely observed more than a half century ago: "Many ... agencies spend a great deal more time in publicizing themselves than they do in concealing information ... their path to power is publicity rather than secrecy."[7] Participatory bureaucracy builds on these insights but embodies a key distinction: it has the potential to manage the tension between bureaucratic administration and democratic accountability. In other words, for participation to be bureaucratic, it must support competent public administration. For bureaucracy to be participatory, it must support aspects of democratic accountability. Not all public engagement supports bureaucratic administration. Not all

University Press, 2010); Patrick Roberts, "FEMA and the Prospects for Reputation-Based Autonomy," *Studies in American Political Development* 20 (2006): 57–87; George A. Krause and J. Kevin Corder, "Explaining Bureaucratic Optimism: Theory and Evidence from U.S. Executive Agency Macroeconomic Forecasts," *American Political Science Review* 101 (2007): 129–142. On bureaucratic preferences, see John Brehm and Scott Gates, *Working, Shirking and Sabotage: Bureaucratic Response to a Democratic Public* (Ann Arbor: University of Michigan Press, 1997); Marissa Martino Golden, *What Motivates Bureaucrats? Politics and Administration During the Reagan Years* (New York: Columbia University Press, 2000); Anthony Downs, *Inside Bureaucracy* (Boston: Little, Brown, 1967).

4 Recall that this work does not aim to provide an optimal strategy for bureaucrats or for elected officials.

5 Rourke, *Bureaucracy, Politics and Public Policy*, pp. 42–43; Herbert Kaufman, *The Administrative Behavior of Federal Bureau Chiefs* (Baltimore, MD: Johns Hopkins University Press, 1981), pp. 24–78; Kenneth J. Meier and John Bohte, *Politics and the Bureaucracy: Policymaking in the Fourth Branch of Government* (Belmont, CA: Thomson Wadsworth, 2007), pp. 53–63; Carpenter, *The Forging of Bureaucratic Autonomy*, pp. 30–32; Herbert A. Simon, Victor A. Thompson, and Donald W. Smithburg, *Public Administration* (New York: Alfred A. Knopf, 1950), p. 415.

6 See Francis E. Rourke, *Secrecy and Publicity: Dilemmas of Democracy* (Baltimore, MD: Johns Hopkins University Press, 1961), p. 127; Deborah Stone, *The Policy Paradox* (New York: W. W. Norton & Company, 2002), pp. 305–323; Janet A. Weiss and Judith Gruber, "Using Knowledge for Control in Fragmented Policy Arenas," *Journal of Policy Analysis and Management* 3 (1984): 225–247; Anne Schneider and Helen Ingram, "Behavioral Assumptions of Policy Tools," *Journal of Politics* 52 (1990): 510–529.

7 Francis E. Rourke, *Bureaucratic Power in National Politics* (Boston: Little, Brown, 1965), p. x.

public engagement supports democratic accountability. Participatory bureaucracy represents a subset of public engagement in which both bureaucracy and democracy have the potential to be better off.

Predominant models of public bureaucracy and delegation theory typically assume that bureaucrats inevitably benefit from and seek monopoly control over information. Given this dominant assumption, they offer little insight on how bureaucrats may weigh trade-offs between closure and openness, when they may choose one over the other, and how bureaucrats' preferences and choices could bear on elected officials' subsequent decisions. As the following discussion makes plain, bureaucrats do indeed have strong incentives to seek closure and to eschew public participation for some kinds of tasks. However, failing to consider public participation from the perspective of bureaucratic administration can overstate the extent of the zero-sum conflict between bureaucrats and elected officials and the perceived trade-off between political control and expertise. From a public policy perspective, neglecting the bureaucratic side of the story omits a vital set of policymakers whose support for public participation can be instrumental to subsequent policy outcomes.

The conditions and potential of participatory bureaucracy begin with characteristics of a policy task – a fundamental unit of bureaucratic work. Recall that Figure 1.1 from Chapter 1 specified two task-specific sources of variation: the degree of bureaucrats' information relative to the task and the degree to which the task entailed interdependence with implementers outside the agency's hierarchy. Though implementation may entail additional dimensions, information and jurisdiction represent two chief features of public bureaucracy. Table 2.1 expands on Figure 1.1.

Instead of asking whether an agency or an organization is an open or closed system, beginning with the policy tasks pivots the question and asks, "When does an organization approach implementation in more or less open/closed ways, depending on the specific task?" A task-specific approach recognizes that bureaucratic expertise and capability are defined by tasks rather than arise from formal structures alone.[8] From the perspective of task implementation – getting the job done – what kinds of tasks are more or less amenable to closed or open policymaking? The first section that follows considers this in terms of tasks that are performed "in-house," within an agency's hierarchical arrangement, yielding primarily opportunities for private agency learning or for participatory oversight that may come at the expense of bureaucratic expertise and authority. The second section considers this in terms of tasks that exceed the scope of an agency's hierarchy, yielding more opportunities for participatory

---

[8] Common measures of bureaucratic capacity that look to budgets, staffing levels, and layers of insulation from the political process overlook the task-specific nature of bureaucratic expertise. Agency expertise for collecting schools and staffing data does not necessarily translate into agency expertise for gathering data on student achievement. Expertise for reviewing drugs to treat hypertension does not necessarily translate into expertise for reviewing drugs to treat pain. Capability depends on knowledge and jurisdictional authority, which vary by task.

TABLE 2.1. *Task Conditions and Contributions of Public Participation*

	High Agency Information Bureaucrats Have Knowledge to Perform Task	Low Agency Information Bureaucrats Lack Knowledge to Perform Task
High Task Independence	**A**	**B**
• Implementation performed in-house • Low external dependence	*Bureaucratic Closure:* • Not share knowledge or decision making in meaningful way *Participatory Oversight:* • Force agency to share private information • Force agency to take other information into consideration	*Private Bureaucratic Learning:* • Seek information from better-informed outsiders behind closed doors • Use closure to hide ignorance *Participatory Oversight:* • Expose agency ignorance through public learning • Force agency to take other information into consideration
Low Task Independence	**C**	**D**
• Interdependent implementation	*Participatory Bureaucracy:* • Distribute information to implementers on whom the agency depends for implementation • Expose outside implementers' information or weaknesses	*Participatory Bureaucracy:* • Create new knowledge • Legitimate knowledge through participatory process

bureaucracy. The final section discusses ways in which participatory bureaucracy builds on but is distinct from other models of public participation.

PARTICIPATION FOR TASKS WITH INDEPENDENT
IMPLEMENTATIONS: AGENDAS, SCOPE, AND IMPLICATIONS

Table 2.1 specifies two general sets of task conditions that characterize conventional bureaucratic organization: (A) for tasks that occur fully within an agency's hierarchy (independent tasks) for which agency bureaucrats have the information they need relative to the task demands; and (B) for tasks that occur fully within an agency's hierarchy, but for which bureaucrats lack the information they need. For tasks that appear in these two conditions, public participation comes with real risks to agency reputation and autonomy built on providing unique services capably. These task conditions, however, are precisely where public participation may be most amenable to elected officials' efforts to oversee federal bureaucracy.

Informed and Independent Tasks: Public Participation in Weberian Bureaucracy

For implementation tasks in Quadrant A, bureaucrats have the information they need to perform the task, and the task occurs in relative independence under the agency's jurisdiction. The Internal Revenue Service (IRS) (in principle) has both the knowledge needed and the authority to issue employer verification numbers. These conditions embody tenets of classic bureaucracy: tasks occur fully inside a bureaucratic hierarchy that links top to bottom, with rules or standard operating procedures governing implementation and technical experts performing the work.[9] Individuals or firms apply for employer identification numbers, the IRS confirms the information provided on the application, and issues a number based on the application review. Such tasks may be "complex," as Weber uses the term, meaning multifaceted, capable of being broken down into discrete assignments, and performed within the hierarchy while taking advantage of bureaucrats' specialized knowledge and skills along the hierarchical chain.[10] For these kinds of tasks, Weber suggests, bureaucrats enjoy more than technical expertise. In the course of performing their tasks routinely, bureaucrats "acquire a special knowledge of facts and have available a store of documentary material peculiar to themselves," which form what Weber calls "official secrets."[11] Together, technical knowledge and "official secrets" form the crux of bureaucratic "control on the basis of knowledge." Put differently, tasks in Quadrant A represent conditions potentially conducive to the unique expertise at the foundation of bureaucratic reputation and autonomy: bureaucrats have the knowledge to do what the task asks and can perform the task in relative independence from other organizations or implementers.

From a bureaucratic perspective, public participation for independent tasks in which bureaucrats enjoy sufficient information comes fraught with risk and little potential value in terms of advancing an agency's image of unique expertise. Public participation for tasks with independent implementations risks

---

[9] Max Weber, *Essays in Sociology*, edited and translated by Hans Heinrich Gerth and C. Wright Mills (New York: Oxford University Press, 1946).

[10] The functionalist account of bureaucratic development suggests bureaucracy exists to manage complex tasks – to break complex tasks into different components and assign those components to specialists equipped to perform that part of the task. Novel, evolving tasks defy this narrow conception of complexity. Evolutionary tasks imply a fluid interdependence that is not conducive to fixed task assignments.

[11] Weber, *The Theory of Social and Economic Organizations*, p. 339. Bureaucratic organization, Weber concludes, manages uncertainty through these two forms of knowledge: technical knowledge and secrecy.

disrupting standard procedures or projecting an image of agency ignorance or incompetence in core agency work. Moreover, it has relatively little value to add in terms of knowledge needed for task performance. Crozier's maintenance workers in *The Bureaucratic Phenomenon* provide a classic example of task information, independence, and subsequent bureaucratic incentives for secrecy. Maintenance workers in Crozier's bureaucracy possess the skills and resources necessary to fix stopped machines independent of other groups (either the production workers or the supervisors). Fixing the machines may be difficult, but it is not complex: it does not depend on others.[12] Crozier's maintainers have what they need to fix the machines, and they prevent others (production workers, supervisors) from learning their skills, their – as Weber would say – "official secrets." From the perspective of Crozier's maintainers, "[m]aintenance and repair problems must be kept secret."[13] The power that bureaucrats can acquire through their specialized knowledge, as Weber suggests, leads bureaucrats to defend their secrecy "fanatically."[14]

Informed, independent task performance is not necessarily inimical to democratic accountability. Elected officials and the public may benefit when bureaucrats perform their tasks competently and display expertise. Individuals may benefit from closure that yields quality policy outcomes, such as safe and effective prescription drugs. Yet, bureaucracy built on specialization, division of labor, standard operating procedures, expertise, and hierarchical authority creates legendary barriers to democratic participation.[15] Bureaucratic closure threatens to levy a double whammy on democracy; both the process and product of bureaucracy can impede democratic expression. Bureaucracy can move decisions out of mass, public hands, denying the public opportunities to engage in government decision making. Even if the public supports the policy outcome, the inability to participate in the process can affect subsequent public political participation.[16] Moreover, bureaucratic knowledge and expertise can crowd out or trump ordinary, usable knowledge and can yield policy outcomes that depart from elected officials' and their constituents' interests, or can yield privilege for particular groups or officials.[17] Given these risks, scholarship has

---

[12] We could imagine how task interdependence that exceeds the scope of the hierarchy could be introduced, but it is not part of Crozier's framework.

[13] Michel Crozier, *The Bureaucratic Phenomenon* (Chicago: University of Chicago Press, 1964), p. 153.

[14] Weber, *The Theory of Social and Economic Organizations*, p. 339; Max Weber, "Essays on Bureaucracy," in *Bureaucratic Power in National Politics* edited by Francis E. Rourke (Boston: Little, Brown and Company, 1965), p. 12.

[15] Emmette S. Redford, *Democracy in the Administrative State* (New York: Oxford University Press, 1969), p. 60.

[16] The danger to democracy thus arises from bureaucracy's impact on public engagement, not just its response to elected officials. On policy feedback and the impact of government on individual political participation, see Joe Soss, "Lessons from Welfare," *American Political Science Review* 93 (1999): 363–380.

[17] Some elected officials and groups may enjoy privileged access to bureaucratic information and use that knowledge to suit their own agendas and to gain advantage over political rivals.

identified a host of procedural means for elected officials to discourage bureaucrats from using their information monopolies in ways elected officials find objectionable.[18] Democratic accountability for independent/informed bureaucratic tasks typically mirrors the hierarchical logic of classic bureaucracy: it strives for bureaucratic agents to respond sincerely and faithfully to democratic principles and to appear at the end of a representative "chain," to use Ansell's term.[19] One such mechanism is public participation, through which elected officials can require agencies to attend to particular sources and kinds of information, give particular interests some measure of policymaking authority, and create opportunities for organized interests to monitor agency operations.[20]

Participatory oversight typically situates interest group advocacy at the center of participation: participation reflects a way for representative groups to advance their interests in the bureaucratic policymaking process.[21] In his classic pluralist view of U.S. government, for instance, David Truman portrayed public advisory committees as a potential portal for interest groups to affect agency policymaking.[22] Both Congress and the president can use public participation to grant groups access to bureaucratic policymaking to monitor and/ or contribute substantively to bureaucratic work.[23] From a bureaucratic view, public participation for independent tasks under conditions of relative information reflects political oversight that can compromise both agency expertise and authority. Public participation, in this context, embodies the potential bureaucracy-democracy trade-off. From a bureaucratic perspective, public participation implies the intrusion of democracy on bureaucracy, with potentially commensurate trade-offs in policy outcomes when political control comes at the expense of expertise.

John Huber and Charles R. Shipan, *Deliberate Discretion: The Institutional Foundations of Bureaucratic Autonomy* (New York: Cambridge University Press, 2002), p. 13.

[18] Matthew McCubbins, Roger Noll, and Barry Weingast, "Administrative Procedures as Instruments of Control," *Journal of Law, Economics and Organization* 3 (1987): 243–277; Matthew McCubbins, Roger Noll, and Barry Weingast, "Structure and Process, Policy and Politics: Administrative Arrangements and the Political Control of Agencies," *Virginia Law Review* 75 (1989): 431–482.

[19] Christopher Ansell, *Pragmatist Democracy: Evolutionary Learning as Public Philosophy* (New York: Oxford University Press, 2011), p. 4.

[20] Steven J. Balla and John R. Wright, "Interest Groups, Advisory Committees, and Congressional Control of the Bureaucracy," *American Journal of Political Science* 45 (2001): 799–812; Petracca argues that access represents a way in which firm and industry interests exercise influence over government agencies, which may or may not be consistent with elected officials' interests: Mark P. Petracca, "Federal Advisory Committees, Interest Groups and the Administrative State," *Congress & The Presidency* 13 (1986): 83–114.

[21] Meier and Bohte, *Politics and the Bureaucracy*, pp. 198–205.

[22] David Truman, *The Governmental Process* (New York: Knopf, 1951), p. 458.

[23] Scholars trace the roots of representative advisory committees to 1911 Wisconsin law that allowed affected groups to participate in state agency decisions related to "industrial safety and workmen's compensation." See Avery Leiserson, *Administrative Regulation – A Study in Representation of Interests* (Chicago: University of Chicago Press, 1942), pp. 160–188.

Delegation theories offer several predictions about when elected officials are more likely to develop and use procedures that, at the expense of expertise, may yield more political control.[24] Notably, inter-branch divisiveness as well as intra-branch divisiveness can encourage legislators to doubt executive branch bureaucrats will attend to majority or enacting coalition wishes. This makes it more likely that legislators will craft procedures or structures amenable to overseeing and guiding executive branch bureaucracy during divided government or congressional divisiveness.[25] The procedures that legislators craft are not neutral but benefit the interests and publics that the elected officials represent. In the course of creating procedures to constrain bureaucratic work, legislators may craft rules to ensure favored interests are represented and have access to bureaucratic work.

Determining the topics on and off the public agenda bears on the broader distribution of power.[26] However, legislative attentiveness to groups could manifest in two different ways. On the one hand, legislators may want to protect groups that already enjoy privileged access to agency policymaking by preventing tasks sensitive to those interests from reaching public participation.[27] On the other hand, legislators may be able to use public participation to enable groups to obtain a place in agency policymaking that they would not otherwise enjoy. Political oversight through agenda setting could manifest in either direction.

Executive-branch leaders benefit from capable bureaucratic administration that is also responsive to executive branch leaders' political preferences: presidents and appointees seek bureaucrats who are both competent and responsive to the administration.[28] Public participation can offer presidents and their appointees ways to circumvent a bureaucracy resistant to presidential policy preferences, and to supplement agency capacity.[29] Presidents' interests in

---

[24] Kathleen Bawn, "Political Control versus Expertise: Congressional Choices about Administrative Procedures," *American Political Science Review* 89 (1995): 62–73.

[25] Epstein and O'Halloran specify that Congress is particularly unlikely to grant discretion in the context of divided government to agencies close to the executive branch. David Epstein and Sharyn O'Halloran, *Delegating Powers: A Transaction Cost Politics Approach to Policy Making under Separate Powers* (New York: Cambridge University Press, 1999), pp. 80–81.

[26] Jack L. Walker, "Setting the Agenda in the U.S. Senate: A Theory of Problem Selection," *British Journal of Political Science* 7 (1977): 423–445.

[27] From this perspective, agency closure would be designed to benefit particular interests. Rourke *Bureaucracy, Politics and Public Policy*, p. 142.

[28] David E. Lewis, *Presidents and the Politics of Agency Design* (Palo Alto, CA: Stanford University Press, 2003), p. 140. Terry M. Moe, "Interests, Institutions and Positive Theory: the Politics of the NLRB," *Studies in American Political Development* 2 (1987): 236–299; and Terry M. Moe, "The Politics of Structural Choice: Toward a Theory of Public Bureaucracy," in *Organization Theory: From Chester Barnard to the Present and Beyond*, edited by Oliver E. Williamson (New York: Oxford University Press, 1990), pp. 116–153.

[29] Thomas Wolanin, *Presidential Advisory Commissions* (Madison: University of Wisconsin Press, 1975); Amy B. Zegart, "Blue Ribbons, Black Boxes: Toward a Better Understanding of Presidential Commissions," *Presidential Studies Quarterly* 34 (2004): 366–393.

executive branch competence create a higher bar for sacrificing agency expertise for political control than does Congress'. Recall, members of Congress may
benefit from some forms of bureaucratic incompetence.[30] Following the same
logic of delegation, presidents would be more likely to sacrifice agency expertise for political control when preferences diverge sharply from the agency's.

Thinking about participation in the context of tasks performed fully within
an agency's hierarchy and over which the agency enjoys suitable implementation information yields several predictions:

- *Bureaucratic Closure:* Bureaucrats are less likely to seek public participation for tasks when the agency enjoys high information and independent
  implementation authority.
- *Participatory Oversight:* Legislators are more likely to impose public participation in conditions of inter-branch or intra-branch divisiveness than
  in conditions of unity.
- *Participatory Oversight:* Presidents are more likely to impose public participation in conditions of inter-branch or intra-branch divisiveness.

Uninformed and Independent Tasks: Private Learning

For task implementations in Quadrant B, bureaucrats lack the information
they need to perform the task, and the task occurs in relative independence.
The United States Air Force, for instance, has authority over the design, development and implementation of the firewall that prevents cyber-attackers from
obtaining access to Air Force logistics information. Yet, the highly technical
nature of the task may mean information technology experts outside the Air
Force may be better informed on some matters of cyber-security than are
civil servants inside the Air Force. Although the task may reside fully within
the bureaucrats' jurisdiction, experts, implementers, and individuals outside
the agency may be better informed than the agency is.[31] Examples of "better
informed" outsiders range from citizens being aware of neighborhood crime
sites that law enforcement was unable to detect on its own,[32] to hedge fund
managers who understand their products better than do SEC regulators, to
medical researchers at the Cleveland Clinic examining the safety risks of widely
used diabetes drugs.[33]

---

[30] Morris P. Fiorina, *Congress: Keystone of the Washington Establishment* (New Haven, CT: Yale
University Press, 1989).

[31] Models of legislative delegation typically assume bureaucratic capability and informational superiority. Huber and McCarty offer a notable exception; John Huber and Nolan McCarty,
"Bureaucratic Capacity, Delegation, and Political Reform," *American Political Science Review*
98 (2004): 481–494.

[32] Archon Fung, *Empowered Participation: Reinventing Urban Democracy* (Princeton, NJ:
Princeton University Press, 2004); Archon Fung, "Varieties of Participation in Complex
Governance," *Public Administration Review* 66 (2006): 66–75.

[33] Weber himself recognized that agencies may find themselves at the uniformed end of an information asymmetry: "The 'secret' as a means of power is," he argued, "more safely hidden

Despite bureaucrats' insatiable appetites for information,[34] visibly learning in public settings poses several serious risks to bureaucratic reputation with implications for the value public participation offers bureaucratic administration. Learning in open, public venues risks signaling some measure of bureaucratic incompetence or lack of expertise, which may hamper the agency's ability to secure political support for staff and resources and may compromise public confidence in the agency, its program, and its underlying science.[35] Learning in public also risks compromising agency uniqueness, a vital component in bureaucratic autonomy.[36] These risks are especially acute for the agency's core tasks – the tasks that fall fully within the agency hierarchy, for which the agency is *supposed* to have sufficient expertise. The logic of bureaucratic reputation suggests bureaucrats would be more likely to seek information privately than publicly for tasks that occur in-house but for which agencies lack implementation information.

Delegation scholars also suggest that, all else being equal, legislators may be less likely to impose structures and procedures, such as public participation, on agencies in the context of complex tasks over which the agency has more specialized expertise than legislators.[37] Quadrant B, however, represents the case when agencies have weak specialized expertise. Legislators may have incentives to not only impose participation for these tasks – to require agencies to learn – but also to require agencies to learn *in public*. While elected officials may share bureaucrats' incentives to learn privately, they may also extract political gains from exposing bureaucrats' ignorance for routine, core bureaucratic work. This is especially likely in conditions of inter-branch or intra-branch divisiveness. From the perspective of either the bureaucracy or elected officials, public participation in Quadrant B positions the agency as the target of the participation: to provide "better" information to the agency, to expose agency weaknesses, and to monitor subsequent bureaucratic actions.

The participatory oversight predictions from Quadrant A (independent/ informed) hold for Quadrant B (independent/uninformed) as well, with an additional prediction:

- *Private Bureaucratic Learning:* Bureaucrats are more likely to seek participation for low information/high independence tasks in *private* than in public.

in the books of an enterpriser than it is in the files of public authorities." Weber, "Essays on Bureaucracy," p. 14.

[34] Kaufman, *The Administrative Behavior of Federal Bureau Chiefs*, pp. 24–45.

[35] Brian Balogh, *Chain Reaction: Expert Debate and Public Participation in American Commercial Nuclear Power, 1945–1975* (New York: Cambridge University Press, 1991).

[36] Carpenter, *The Forging of Bureaucratic Autonomy*, p. 14.

[37] Legislative theories of delegation predict fewer constraints and oversight and more bureaucratic discretion for complex tasks based on the assumption that discretion affords bureaucrats more room to apply their technical knowledge and perform complex tasks successfully. See Epstein and O'Halloran, *Delegating Powers*.

Scope of Participation for Independent Implementation Tasks

Interest group advocacy provides the key mechanism for participatory over-sight: when elected officials construct and use public participation to oversee bureaucratic administration. From the perspective of democratic accountabil-ity, interest group advocacy faces the perennial challenge of developing a par-ticipatory process that reflects all interests instead of giving privileged interests an upper hand.[38] Scholars have long pointed to the privilege that industry enjoys relative to other kinds of interests in participatory processes.[39] Group privilege may be inimical to both democratic accountability and bureaucratic administration.

Elected officials, who are the force behind participatory oversight, can con-tribute to imbalanced interest group representation. While presidents have incentives for executive branch bureaucracy to operate competently, they also seek loyalty.[40] Scholars debate the implications of the pursuit for loyalty rela-tive to the pursuit for competence – whether, when, and where it produces political hacks. Scholars also debate whether Congress constructs public par-ticipation to "stack the deck" – to give privileged interests access to agency pol-icymaking – or to "mirror" the political environment and include both policy supporters and opponents.[41] Mirroring the political environment by including policy "winners and losers" may maximize opportunities for overseeing the bureaucracy and may encourage bureaucrats to attend to the same constella-tion of interests to which legislators' attend.

From a bureaucratic perspective, independent tasks that occur inside the bureaucratic hierarchy are precisely the ones bureaucrats strive to shield from public participation. However, private participation could satisfy the tenets of bureaucratic reputation when it offers agencies knowledge but neither exposes agency ignorance nor usurps agency turf. The scope of participation, from a bureaucratic perspective, would be limited to individuals with knowledge linked to task implementation, without enabling a particular group or interest

---

[38] E. E. Schattsneider, *The Semi-Sovereign People: A Realist's View of Democracy in America* (New York: Thompson Learning, 1960).

[39] Don K. Price, *Government and Science: Their Dynamic Relation in American Democracy* (New York: Oxford University Press, 1962), p. 153; Petracca "Federal Advisory Committees, Interest Groups and the Administrative State," pp. 83–114; Kevin D. Karty, "Closure and Capture in Federal Advisory Committees," *Business and Politics* 4 (2002): 213–238; Jason Webb Yackee and Susan Webb Yackee, "A Bias Toward Business? Assessing Interest Group Influence on the Bureaucracy," *Journal of Politics* 68 (2006): 128–139; Wendy Wagner, "The Participation-Centered Model Meets Administrative Practice," *Wisconsin Law Review* 2 (2013): 671–692.

[40] Richard P. Nathan, *The Administrative Presidency* (New York: MacMillan Publishing Company, 1983); Moe, "The Politics of Structural Choice"; Lewis, *Presidents and the Politics of Agency Design*; David E. Lewis, *The Politics of Presidential Appointments: Political Control and Bureaucratic Performance* (Princeton, NJ: Princeton University Press, 2008).

[41] McNollGast, " The Political Origins of the Administrative Procedures Act," pp. 180–217; Balla and Wright, "Interest Groups, Advisory Committees, and Congressional Control," pp. 799–812; Moe "The Politics of Structural Choice," pp. 116–153.

to dominate. Relevant expertise is central to providing information for task implementation, not group interests, from a bureaucratic perspective. Avoiding single group dominance is central to bureaucratic administration, reputation, and autonomy.

- *Private Bureaucratic Learning:* Bureaucratically initiated participation for high independence/low information tasks (1) limits participation to implementation-specific expertise and (2) avoids single group dominance.
- *Participatory Oversight:* Legislatively initiated participation is more likely to (1) privilege groups salient to the enacting legislative coalition or (2) mirror the political environment by including policy winners and losers.
- *Participatory Oversight:* Presidentially initiated participation is more likely to include public participants who are loyal to the president and his policy positions than it is to include the president's opponents.

Overall, the scope of participation for tasks that are above the horizontal axis in Figure 1.1, Quadrants A and B, reflects the kind of participation that fuels critics of participatory processes. Participatory oversight, private bureaucratic learning, and bureaucratic closure all restrict participation and fail to meet conditions of participatory bureaucracy. From a bureaucratic perspective, participation initiated by elected officials – with either privileged groups or groups that mirror the political environment's supporters and opponents – threaten bureaucratic expertise, bureaucratic turf, or both.

PARTICIPATION FOR TASKS WITH INTERDEPENDENT IMPLEMENTATIONS: AGENDAS, SCOPE, AND IMPLICATIONS

From Weber to Dewey

A significant shift in task conditions occurs when we cross the metaphorical horizontal axis in Figure 1.1 and move from conditions of independence to conditions of interdependence. From a bureaucratic perspective, we could think of tasks appearing in Quadrants A and B as eliciting Weberian implementation. When tasks reside here, knowledge and closure may work in concert. Through closed doors, bureaucrats can protect technical decisions from potentially corrupting political influence and, in the case of private participation, can promote an exchange of ideas, at least among those invited into the room.[42] However, many tasks are not implemented independently within a unified hierarchy connecting the top to the bottom. Instead, interdependent tasks

---

[42] "Secrecy can block the search for truth as well as facilitate it," Harold Wilensky aptly noted. Harold Wilensky, *Organizational Intelligence* (New York: Basic Books, 1969), p. 138. Closed doors can foster sound technical policy by encouraging "honest" debate over policy alternatives and protect a policy or program's technical integrity. See Rourke *Bureaucracy, Politics and Public Policy*, p. 137.

depend on multiple individuals and organizational units, which reside beyond the agency's hierarchical arrangement.[43]

Although American federal bureaucracy wields considerable power, scholars frequently comment how little the American state resembles Weber's hierarchical and technical ideal. Aspects of the United States' patchwork, hollow, and delegated form of bureaucracy lack the kind of closure and muscle Weber imagined.[44] In the United States, given the prevalence of fragmented policy terrains where work depends on implementers outside federal agencies, implementation may reside only partly under bureaucrats' control.[45] Instead of formal hierarchy, aspects of the American administrative state rely on networks of governing authorities and implementers. Instead of isolated and hermetically sealed bureaus, interdependence characterizes many government agencies. Rather than governing through a fixed repertoire of expertise, agencies continue to develop expertise in the process of governing as they perform their policy tasks.[46]

These "failures" of American bureaucracy – its lack of cohesion, expertise, and comprehensiveness – have long been considered evidence of a weak American state and potential impediments to policy implementation. Fractures in American bureaucracy's hierarchy, however, also offer potential portals for democratic action – opportunities for the public to help shape bureaucratic policies, not merely to endure them or oversee them. When appropriately constructed, these portals of participation also create opportunities to ease and

[43] Interdependent tasks share features with formal definitions of complex tasks or Simon's concept of nonprogrammed tasks. Herbert A. Simon, *The Shape of Automation for Men and Management* (New York: Harper & Row, 1965); Scott Page, "Uncertainty, Difficulty and Complexity," *Journal of Theoretical Politics* 20 (2008): 115–149.

[44] Elisabeth Clemens, "Lineages of the Rube Goldberg State: Building and Blurring Public Programs, 1900–1940," in *The Art of the State: Rethinking Political Institutions*, edited by Ian Shapiro, Stephen Skowronek, and Daniel Galvin (New York: New York University Press, 2006), pp. 187–215; Stephen Skowronek, *Building a New American State: The Expansion of National Administrative Capacities, 1877–1920* (New York: Cambridge University Press, 1982); Kimberly J. Morgan and Andrea Louise Campbell, *The Delegated Welfare State: Medicare, Markets and the Governance of Social Policy* (New York: Oxford University Press); H. Brinton Milward and Keith G. Provan, "Governing the Hollow State," *Journal of Public Administration Research and Theory* 10 (2000): 359–380.

[45] Kenneth J. Meier and Laurence J. O'Toole, *Bureaucracy in a Democratic State: A Governance Perspective* (Baltimore, MD: Johns Hopkins University Press, 2006), pp. 48, 58, 122–123. Even before policy is implemented, interdependence pervades the administrative landscape. Describing the period from 1945 to 1975, Brian Balogh argues, "The scope of the debate, regardless of policy area, degree of insulation, or level of expertise, has been inexorably broadened." See Balogh, *Chain Reaction*, p. 326.

[46] Sean Gailmard and John Patty's important work renders expertise endogenous: the result of the incentives and structure of executive branch institutions. Democratic accountability remains feasible in a bureaucratic state through its effects on those structures and incentives. Sean Gailmard and John W. Patty, *Learning While Governing: Expertise and Accountability in the Executive Branch* (Chicago: University of Chicago Press, 2012).

assist bureaucratic administration, not merely monitor government bureaucrats at work.

On this score, we could think of tasks that appear in Quadrants C and D of Figure 1.1 and Table 2.1 as creating incentives for Deweyan implementation. Instead of looking to closure, exclusivity, and fixed hierarchies to manage complex problems, Weber's American contemporary, John Dewey, promoted arrangements that were local, open, evolving, and inclusive. Dewey is known for his normative critiques of elitism in general and of bureaucracy in particular. Yet, Dewey offers a portrayal of American policymaking that is distinguishable from his normative claims. Whereas Weber portrays complexity as a problem to be solved by dividing it into discrete, isolated parts, Dewey portrays complexity as arising from fundamental and ever-evolving interdependence. This interdependence, from Dewey's perspective, enables democratic feedback to emerge, especially at the grassroots level. Whereas Weber portrays the power of knowledge through exclusivity, Dewey portrays its power through its scope and reach – a liquid that flows throughout American society.[47] Thanks to industrialization, to the printing press, and now to the internet, knowledge is difficult to keep within fixed and tidy boundaries.

Dewey did not write specifically about policy implementation. Implicit in his work, however, is the idea that policy is fundamentally dependent on practice and on public knowledge. In his words, "genuinely public policy cannot be generated unless it [is] informed by knowledge."[48] Unlike Weber, the knowledge Dewey deemed necessary for policy resides not only in the hands of economic or technocratic elites. To the contrary, Dewey argued,

> It is impossible for high-brows to secure a monopoly of such knowledge as must be used for the regulation of common affairs. In the degree in which they become a specialized class, they are shut off from knowledge of the needs, which they are supposed to serve.[49]

Bureaucracy, building on this view, cannot do its job – it cannot implement or regulate "common affairs" – without public knowledge, without exchange between policy implementers and policy targets. In this sense, bureaucrats not only make policy as they implement it; they also depend fundamentally on their policy targets for ultimate implementation. Moreover, interdependent implementation challenges the conventional duality between expert and public. Teachers may create mathematics instructional policy through their classroom choices about how to pose questions, who to call on, and how to respond to students. But, teachers ultimately depend on students to learn. Regulators

---

[47] John Dewey, *The School and Society and the Child and the Curriculum*, (Chicago: University of Chicago Press, 1956), p. 30.
[48] Dewey, *The Public and Its Problems*, p. 179.
[49] Dewey, *The Public and Its Problems*, p. 206.

may impose fines, but they ultimately depend on industry to curb pollution. Policy depends on practice.[50]

Policymakers' dependence on policy targets gives rise to a more expansive view of expertise than is commonly attributed to Weber. By blurring the lines between expert and public and by including bureaucrats as part of the public, it also gives rise to a more inclusive view of the public than does Dewey's. Although Dewey keeps his focus on local, mass participation for managing problems, his logic of democratic accountability extends to government bureaucrats' participation. Instead of appearing only at the end of the representative principal-agent chain, government bureaucrats can emerge as one part of the collective problem-managing process.

Although Quadrants C and D both embody interdependence, their informational differences yield different expectations for how public participation can affect bureaucratic administration. From a bureaucratic perspective, the conditions in Quadrant C – where the agency is informed but dependent on others – suggest the audience for the information that public participation generates may not be the agency but instead implementers, elected officials, and other individuals outside the agency's hierarchy. From a bureaucratic perspective, the conditions in Quadrant D – where the agency lacks information and is dependent on others – can enable knowledge arising from public participation to flow in multiple directions: toward the agency, toward other implementers, toward elected officials, and beyond.

Informed and Interdependent: Distributing Knowledge and Allocating Responsibility

For implementation tasks in Quadrant C, bureaucrats have the information they need to perform their part of a task, but task implementation entails fundamental dependence on implementers outside the agency's hierarchical reach. In this case, closure threatens to contribute to implementation failure when it prevents implementers outside the agency from knowing what the policy expects them to do or from learning how to do it. Federal-level bureaucratic administration risks failure when implementers outside the federal agency falter.[51] As Herbert Simon and his colleagues argued long ago, administrative

---

[50] For further discussion of the dependence of policy on practice, see David K. Cohen and Susan L. Moffitt, *The Ordeal of Equality: Did Federal Regulation Fix the Schools?* (Cambridge, MA: Harvard University Press, 2009), pp. 17–44. For a helpful review of Mary Parker Follett's theory of reciprocity between employers and employees, "law of the situation," and "cumulative responsibility," see Ansell, *Pragmatist Democracy*, pp. 69–71.

[51] For discussion of linked reputations, see Susan L. Moffitt, "Promoting Agency Reputation through Public Advice: Advisory Committee Use in the FDA," *Journal of Politics* 72 (2010): 880–893. The FDA's reputation ultimately depends on physicians to prescribe drugs appropriately, where "appropriate" can be contingent and evolutionary. Drugs are rarely "good" or "bad" in general terms, but depend on who takes them, for how long, at what dose, and with what

agencies are unlikely to succeed in their efforts to provide services or regulate the public unless the public is aware of the agencies' programs, understands the terms of regulation, and is willing and able to do what the agencies expect, which encourages agencies to devote resources to public education.[52]

Public participation can impart new knowledge to implementers outside the agency in ways that promote building skills relevant to implementation. Public participation can also yield policy approaches that reflect and include implementers' values in ways that attend to the "will" part of the implementation problem. Interdependent tasks also enhance the value of participation and openness when tasks face a high risk of future implementation failure *because* of external implementers.[53] In the context of tasks that depend on implementers outside the agency, public information can expose external implementers' ignorance, contributions to task implementation, and implementation failure.

To illustrate, consider the case of Propulsid (cisapride), approved for nighttime heartburn in adults.[54] The FDA's internal review of the Propulsid application before the drug was approved raised few initial safety concerns. Most of the drug's apparent side effects appeared minor, and clinical studies suggested that headaches were Propulsid's most common adverse event. Though unexplained cases of seizures appeared in Propulsid users, especially among pediatric patients, those seizures were not attributed to the drug. Moreover, neither the firm nor the FDA linked Propulsid to the cardiac failures in three patients who died within six months of taking Propulsid.[55] The primary issue for the

else. When a doctor makes the decision of "do I prescribe this drug for this particular patient or not," she must simultaneously answer "at what dose, for how long, with what other therapies." For that, she needs complex knowledge, judgment, and adaptation: "call me if you don't feel better, and we'll go from there ..." For a discussion of communication issues in the policy implementation process, see Donald S. Van Meter and Carl E. Van Horn, "The Policy Implementation Process: A Conceptual Framework," *Administration & Society* 6 (1975): 478–480.

[52] Simon, Smithburg and Thompson, *Public Administration*, p. 415.

[53] This expands on Schattschneider's argument that political actors strive to change the scope, venue, and image of conflict in their effort to promote policies consistent with their interests. For more on the scope of conflict, see Frank R. Baumgartner and Bryan D. Jones, *Agendas and Instability in American Politics* (Chicago: University of Chicago Press, 1993), p. 11. Organized groups target government to socialize conflict when disputes erupt between private interests, but government leaders may also *initiate* efforts to shape the scope or venue of conflict. Bureaucrats, in addition to groups, may fashion the scope and character of conflict rather than serve only as the target of appeals for help. This also builds on, but departs from, Weaver's argument that elected officials structure agendas to preclude topics that attract blame. R. Kent Weaver, "The Politics of Blame Avoidance," *Journal of Public Policy* 6 (1986): 371–398. Directing public attention to tasks with high risks of failure is consistent with bureaucratic interests in redistributing blame *when* such publicity makes other implementers' contributions visible.

[54] Food and Drug Administration, *Draft Labeling NDA 20–210*. Documents related to Propulsid are available through the drugs@FDA.gov website: http://www.accessdata.fda.gov/drugsatfda_docs/nda/pre96/020210_S000_CisaprideTOC.cfm.

[55] Food and Drug Administration, "Gastrointestinal Drugs Advisory Committee Meeting Transcript, Propulsid, April 13, 1992."

FDA staff member conducting the medical review of the drug entailed whether or not Propulsid worked: the drug's efficacy appeared marginal.[56]

The FDA approved Propulsid with a narrow indication: for nocturnal heartburn resulting from gastro-esophageal reflux, in adults. Once drugs reach the market, however, physicians could prescribe them however they deemed appropriate – a testament to interdependent implementations. Although Propulsid's sponsor, Janssen, could officially market the drug only to adults, the media reported that the firm underwrote educational seminars that appeared implicitly to promote Propulsid to pediatricians. The cherry-flavored liquid form, ostensibly developed for elderly patients, conveniently worked for off-label pediatric use. Within two years of Propulsid's approval, pediatric patients comprised a sizable proportion of Propulsid users.[57] Troubling evidence began to mount. Not only did ongoing trials fail to improve Propulsid's efficacy profile, but reports of serious adverse events and deaths also became more clearly linked to Propulsid, especially for children. In particular, Propulsid's novel mechanism appeared to result in heart rhythm disorders, which caused heart failure in both adult and pediatric patients.

As evidence of Propulsid's safety risks continued to surface, the FDA had limited regulatory influence. As a condition for Propulsid's approval, the FDA had required Janssen to conduct additional post-marketing trials and surveillance.[58] The firm did not, however, conduct those trials, and the agency lacked follow-up enforcement authority. The FDA pressed the firm to revise Propulsid's label to contraindicate Propulsid for pediatric patients. However the FDA cannot impose label changes; they must be negotiated with sponsoring firms and can take years to revise. Though the FDA can take action when firms falsely brand their products or make unsubstantiated marketing claims, Janssen's marketing practices avoided triggering either.

The FDA, however, could use public venues to make Propulsid's problems and the firm's recalcitrance more visible. In the winter of 2000, the FDA scheduled a public advisory committee meeting to review Propulsid's safety and efficacy profile publicly. The firm swiftly removed the drug from the market before the public meeting could occur. While a host of factors contributed to Janssen's decision, internal firm documents reported that the impending publicity from a public advisory committee review may have been one part of that decision. "Do we want to stand in front of world and admit that we were never able to prove efficacy!" a Janssen executive wrote in internal company documents.[59]

---

[56] FDA, *Division of Gastrointestinal Drug Products Medical Review, NDA 20–210*. Review documents are available at: http://www.accessdata.fda.gov/drugsatfda_docs/nda/pre96/020210_S000_CisaprideTOC.cfm.

[57] Gardiner Harris and Eric Koli, "Lucrative Drug, Danger Signal and the FDA," *New York Times*, June 10, 2005.

[58] Food and Drug Administration, "Approvable letter for NDA 20–210," April 9, 1993.

[59] Quoted in Harris, "Lucrative Drug, Danger Signals and the FDA."

The public meeting offered a potential opportunity for the FDA to make information that the FDA had and that the firm had more visible, including information on the drug's inability to demonstrate efficacy. When the FDA makes itself public through public participation for interdependent task implementations, that interdependence shines light on firms as well. Rather than compromise bureaucratic administration, public participation – or the threat of public participation – can extend bureaucrats' reach, especially when interdependence renders bureaucratic implementation authority incomplete.

Public participation in agency policymaking faces the perennial complaint that government agencies do not "hear anything they could not have anticipated" at public meetings; but, the agency may not be the relevant audience or target of participation.[60] The audience may be implementers outside the agency, elected officials, the media, or even the broader public. Public participation may convey knowledge to others to support the will and skill needed for implementation.[61] It may also make them aware of *other* implementers' weaknesses and responsibilities for potential implementation failure. Other implementers' ignorance, after all, may be intentional. Pharmaceutical companies face more severe legal consequences when they keep drug safety information secret than when they fail to collect drug safety information in the first place.[62] Power can reside in preventing knowledge from ever developing, in addition to keeping that knowledge locked in privileged filing cabinets. Just as there is power in nondecisions as well as in decisions,[63] power can emerge through ignorance as well as through knowledge.

[60] Kaufman, *The Administrative Behavior of Federal Bureau Chiefs*, pp. 39–40. In addition to agency learning and influence, bureaucrats also concern themselves with broader perceptions of the agency that bear on the agency's reputation – to define the boundaries of appropriate action and to present a favorable agency image. Daniel P. Carpenter and George A. Krause, "Reputation and Public Administration," *Public Administration Review* 72 (2012): 26–32; Moshe Maor, Sharon Gilad, and Pazit Ben-Nun Bloom, "Organizational Reputation, Regulatory Talk, and Strategic Silence," *Journal of Public Administration Research and Theory* 23 (2013): 581–608; Moshe Maor, "Organizational Reputation and Jurisdictional Claims: The Case of the US Food and Drug Administration," *Governance* 23 (2010): 133–159.

[61] Sheila Jasanoff, *The Fifth Branch: Science Advisors as Policy Makers* (Cambridge, MA: Harvard University Press, 1990); Stephen Hilgartner, *Science on Stage: Expert Advice as Public Drama* (Stanford, CA: Stanford University Press, 2000). Vertical integration and public participation are not mutually exclusive: agencies can pursue both simultaneously. Yet, participation as a knowledge-based policy instrument represents a different form of control than does expanding agency hierarchy through vertical integration and authority. Charles Lindblom, *Politics and Markets* (New York: Basic Books, 1977); Janet Weiss, "Public Information," in *The Tools of Government: A Guide to the New Governance*, edited by Lester M. Salamon (New York: Oxford University Press, 2002); Janet A. Weiss and Mary Tschirhart, "Public Information Campaigns as Policy Instruments," *Journal of Policy Analysis and Management* 13 (1994): 82–119.

[62] Baram et al. (2000); *Crislip v. TCH Liquidating Co.* 52 Ohio St.3d 251, 257, 556 N.E.2d 1177, 1182–1183, fn. 1 (1990); Grover v. Eli Lilly & Co., 63 Ohio St.3d 756, 760–761, 591 N.E.2d 696, 699–700 (1992).

[63] Peter Bachrach and Morton S. Baratz, "Two Faces of Power," *American Political Science Review* (1962): 947–951.

Bureaucrats who open up the policymaking process in the context of inter-dependent tasks invite visibility and openness into other implementers' parts of the implementation process, including those over whom the agency enjoys little or no hierarchical authority. Even though the agency may have sufficient knowledge for its portion of the implementation – information on drug effi-cacy and safety, for instance – outsiders on whom the implementation depends may jeopardize implementation through their ignorance. Participation offers a way for agencies to distribute knowledge to participants engaged in the imple-mentation and a way to distribute knowledge about responsibility for various parts of the implementation. This stands in contrast to theories of delegation to avoid blame by passing the hard work on to others. In the event of implemen-tation failure, an agency cannot avoid blame, but can strive for responsibility to be apportioned across implementers.

Task interdependence implies that implementation processes are intertwined: when one implementer invites openness into her part of the policy process, she in effect invites some measure of openness into others' parts. When the FDA makes its drug review process publicly accessible, it can make firms' drug research and marketing processes more accessible as well. Public participa-tion for high information–highly interdependent tasks, in other words, creates opportunities to reallocate responsibility in addition to providing substantive information to external implementers. This set of conditions adds another pre-diction, in addition to the ones mentioned earlier:

- *Participatory Bureaucracy:* Bureaucrats are more likely to seek public participation for high information tasks in conditions of task interdepen-dence than in conditions of task independence.

Uninformed and Interdependent: Knowledge Creation and Knowledge Legitimation

Task implementation in Quadrant D embodies fully interdependent tasks where knowledge necessary for implementation emerges and evolves because of that jurisdictional interdependence. Safe and effective use of drugs to treat AIDS in the mid-1980s, for instance, would fall into this category of tasks. Implementers were fundamentally intertwined, since knowledge of how to treat the disease safely and effectively was a moving target.

When we reach full Deweyan interdependence where "nothing ... acts in entire isolation," the tension between knowledge needed for implementation and closure becomes severe.[64] Keeping agency processes closed – shielding them from external inspection and participation – may contribute to agency unique-ness, impede political interference, and provide a way to hide failure. Yet, clo-sure risks eroding bureaucratic administration when it prevents bureaucrats

[64] Dewey, *The Public and Its Problems*, p. 22.

from acquiring needed expertise, from considering helpful alternatives, or from learning from experience and mistakes.[65] Task interdependence involves operational intricacy that includes multiple implementers working in different organizational units, or outside of organizations altogether.[66] These multiple parts that rely on each other create a perpetual sort of novelty, which impedes agencies from developing routines to handle policy because each enactment is dynamic to the extent that the body of knowledge developed for the previous enactment becomes obsolete. Implementing complex, interdependent tasks depends on both knowledge and on implementers beyond the scope of the agency's hierarchy.[67] For bureaucrats to perform their tasks in the context of interdepdendence, they have to think about what other implementers are up to, how they may react, and how to update and revise the agency's approach to the task as implementation unfolds.[68]

Consider the case of Propulsid again, but this time before the drug was initially approved, when the FDA was unsure about both its safety and efficacy. The FDA publicly claims that it is *not* in the business of regulating the practice of medicine: medical care is between doctors and patients. Instead, it regulates firms. Yet, the FDA cannot help but consider the practice of medicine as it regulates firms and their pharmaceutical products. In the course of product regulatory reviews, Food and Drug Administration reviewers may ask: "Will the evidence from clinical trials be replicated when the drug is used outside experimental conditions? How will deviations from experimental conditions bear on drug safety and efficacy, especially in patients who take multiple drug therapies? If pharmaceutical companies market and doctors prescribe the

---

[65] Rourke *Bureaucracy, Politics, and Public Policy*, pp. 137–138.

[66] On complexity, see Heimann *Acceptable Risks*, p. 106. Complex policy tasks are also characterized by their difficulty: they are technically complicated to perform. Task complexity thus is a matter of intricacy and difficulty and presents bureaucracy with not one but two potentially related problems: insufficient knowledge and insufficient authority to use knowledge. See also James G. March, *The Pursuit of Organizational Intelligence* (Malden, MA: Blackwell, 1999), p. 182.

[67] Most agencies experience some degree of interaction with other agencies or implementers. Yet the degree of dependence on implementers outside of the agency is task specific. Nearly any bureaucratic task involves some element of external dependence or uncertainty. Even tasks that entail mainly internal uncertainty, such as regulatory inspections, ultimately depend on firms' willingness to open their doors to inspectors.

[68] Secrecy is not only more risky in the context of interdependent tasks; it is also more costly to achieve. By definition, interdependent tasks consist of multiple parts. Efforts to keep processes and outcomes secret can backfire, leading to political retribution from excluded participants and their elected representatives. Wilson *Bureaucracy*, p. 300; Balogh, *Chain Reaction*, p. 44; Simon, Smithburg, and Thompson, *Public Administration*, p. 466. Moreover, the more parts to the task, the more likely it is that the agency will lack authority over some of those parts. Secrecy would require an agency either to isolate parts of a task from the whole – risking failure – or to incur the costs of expanding agency jurisdiction significantly to move all of the tasks in-house, such as through vertical integration. W. Richard Scott, *Organizations: Rational, Natural, and Open Systems*, 3rd ed. (Englewood Cliffs, NJ: Prentice Hall, 1992).

drug 'off-label' for patient populations and diseases not tested in clinical trials, what effects might the drug have?"[69] To implement its task of ensuring drug safety and efficacy, the FDA depends on an evolving dynamic between disease characteristics, drug characteristics, firms' promotional strategies, physicians' prescription decisions, patients' consumption patterns, and patients' bodies' reactions to the therapies. As an innovative drug, Propulsid presented the FDA with uncertainty about how the drug would be used in practice. The FDA took Propulsid to an advisory committee for review before approving the drug, and asked the committee to consider the drug's efficacy and risk potential if it were to reach practice.

Tasks with emergent knowledge and interdependent implementations create opportunities for public participation to offer value to bureaucratic adminis-tration in terms of the information it brings into agencies *and* in terms of the information it disseminates from agencies.[70] Consider, for instance, the work of the Women's Advisory Committee to the War Manpower Commission, in operation from 1942 to 1945. The committee worked as a portal through which information and learning could flow in multiple directions. Advisory Committee members used their connections with women's organizations to support community-level information campaigns to recruit women into war-time industry work. The Advisory Committee also worked as a channel for communicating problems to the War Manpower Commission on problems for women and communities arising from wartime employment, including the lack of appropriate childcare.[71]

Moreover, the marginal costs of participation appear lower for interdepen-dent tasks compared with tasks that have more independent implementations. Learning from outsiders may help bureaucrats implement their tasks and get their job done. Moreover, the costs and risks of learning *in public* may be less severe for tasks on the more interdependent end of the spectrum. In the perpetually novel conditions that characterize complex, interdependent tasks, there is no "knowledge" to solve the problem: that knowledge is emergent at best. It may not exist at all. In these conditions, public participation can legiti-mize the knowledge that is created in the course of the participatory process.[72] In terms of supporting an agency's unique expertise, public learning may be less risky when "nobody knows." Although agency bureaucrats cannot claim unique abilities, they are not uniquely ignorant.

[69] See Quirk for a discussion of FDA uncertainty over drug use in patient populations. Paul J. Quirk, "Food and Drug Administration," in *The Politics of Regulation*, James Q. Wilson (ed.) (New York: Basic Books, 1980), pp. 205–206.

[70] On government-community collaboration to manage "wicked problems," see Edward P. Weber and Anne Khademian, "Wicked Problems, Knowledge Challenges, and Collaborative Capacity Builders in Network Settings," *Public Administration Review* 68 (2008): 334–349.

[71] U.S. Department of Labor, *Womanpower Committees During World War II, Women's Bureau Bulletin 244* (Washington, DC: U.S. Department of Labor, 1953).

[72] Jasanoff, *The Fifth Branch*; Hilgartner, *Science on Stage*.

In the context of interdependent tasks, public participation can embody a multidirectional flow of information. Including the public in policymaking may bring information into the agency, disseminate information to audiences outside the agency, and create new knowledge that previously did not exist. Participatory bureaucracy includes and yet goes beyond transparency and monitoring by creating opportunities for engaged, collaborative policymaking.[73] Public participation has the potential to align with bureaucratic administration particularly in the context of interdependent tasks – tasks that depend on multiple implementers inside and outside the agency in ways that render knowledge emergent and evolving.[74]

- *Participatory Bureaucracy:* Bureaucrats are more likely to seek public participation for tasks with uncertain and interdependent implementations than for other kinds of tasks.

Scope of Participation

Theories of group decision making point to the value of diverse heuristics built on a foundation of expertise for managing interdependent tasks: diversity can discourage decision makers from getting stuck on a "local maximum" and making "suboptimal" choices.[75] This cognitive approach differs from traditional models of participation in bureaucratic policymaking that frame participation strictly as opportunities for communicating and advocating for particular interests.[76] Managing complex problems requires different perspectives

[73] Public participation may be constructed to be compatible with a range of traditional organizational strategies for managing uncertainty, including buffering the agency's "technical core," diversifying the agency's dependencies, seeking prestige, changing the environment and its demands, anticipating and preparing for fluctuations in the environment, co-opting powerful interests, and vertically integrating suppliers on whom the agency depends. Thompson, *Organizations in Action*, pp. 21–41.

[74] This view of participatory bureaucracy shares the pragmatist view of building competences for problem solving. See Ansell, *Pragmatist Democracy*, chapters 4 and 5.

[75] Page, *The Difference*, pp. 131–174. However, diversity must exceed tokenism. Kristin Kanthak and George A. Krause, *The Diversity Paradox: Political Parties, Legislatures, and the Organizational Foundations of Representation in America* (New York: Oxford University Press, 2012).

[76] Advocates of increased citizen or interest group participation in bureaucratic policymaking processes argue participation can allow interests to be fully expressed and incorporated into agency decisions, reflecting core tenets of pluralism. Redford, *Democracy in the Administrative State*, pp. 63, 69, 152, 197–202; Redford calls participation "the basic requirement of democratic morality," p. 152. Meier and Bohte, *Politics and the Bureaucracy*, pp. 196–205. As Meier and Bohte summarize, this approach is built on pluralist assumptions, namely that all interests will be represented and that policy reflects the aggregation of those preferences. In practice, participatory efforts habitually appear to violate assumptions of full and equal voice in policymaking. For a discussion of conditions consistent with democratic expression that expand opportunities for voice but not necessarily equal voice, see Jane J. Mansbridge, *Beyond Adversary Democracy* (Chicago: University of Chicago Press, 1983), pp. 244–246.

and heuristics, which may or may not align with traditional representations of interests and descriptive identity categories. From the vantage of bureaucratic administration, "suboptimal policy" means policy outcomes that are costly to reverse and/or damaging to agency reputation.[77]

From the perspective of bureaucratic administration, participation that offers *task-specific diverse expertise* holds promise of managing the complexity that manifests for tasks in Quadrants C and D.[78] Expertise for participatory bureaucracy is defined broadly. Scholarship often dichotomizes "experts" and "publics," and with good reason. Decades of research suggest framing issues in technical terms limits participation to individuals with technical training (experts) and excludes those without (the public). Traditional, closed bureaucratic arrangements sharply distinguish between bureaucrats (experts) and individuals outside the organization (mass public, elected officials, excluded experts). Scholarship on public engagement typically classifies individuals who are public officials or professionals as "experts" (teachers, police officers, scientists) and individuals who do not have a government role or professional affiliation, or who are potentially affected by the policy as the "public" (parents, community members, patients, tax payers).

Twenty-first-century conditions of governance, however, challenge sharp distinctions between experts and publics, both in theory and in practice.[79] One limitation comes from the level of inquiry: experts at one level, such as teachers participating in a local advisory committee meeting, may not be considered experts at another, such as teachers participating in a federal-level advisory committee meeting. A second limitation comes from the subject matter of the inquiry: experts on one issue (antidepressant safety and efficacy in adults) may not be expert on another, closely related issue (antidepressant safety and efficacy for children). A third limitation comes from the multiple dimensions of expertise that manifest in any policy: my daughter's teacher may be an expert in teaching mathematics in the classroom, but I may be an expert in cultivating

---

[77] For discussion on costly reversals and agency reputation, see Carpenter, "Groups, The Media, Agency Waiting Costs and FDA Drug Approval," pp. 490–505. For examples of operationalizing policy quality in the context of regulatory agencies, see Daniel P. Carpenter, Jacqueline Chattopadhyay, Susan Moffitt, and Clayton Nall, "The Complications of Controlling Agency Time Discretion: FDA Review Deadlines and Postmarket Safety," *American Journal of Political Science* 56 (2012): 98–114.

[78] Page, *The Difference*, pp. 131–174. As discussed earlier, bureaucrats benefit from diverse support for their programs and policies, instead of support limited to a single dominant group. For additional work on complexity and public committee deliberation, see Miriam Laugesen, "Policy Complexity and Professional Capture In Federal Rulemaking," Paper presented at the Annual Meeting of the American Political Science Association, August 31st – September 2nd, 2013, Chicago, IL; Miriam. J. Laugesen, Roy Wada and Eric M. Chen, "In Setting Doctors' Medicare Fees, CMS Almost Always Accepts The Relative Value Update Panel's Advice On Work Values," *Health Affairs*, 31 (2012): 965–972.

[79] Mark Brown similarly challenges conventional distinctions between expert and lay public. Mark B. Brown, "Fairly Balanced: The Politics of Representation on Government Advisory Committees," *Political Research Quarterly* 61 (2008): 547–560.

mathematical curiosity outside the classroom. A fourth limitation of the dichotomy comes from the expansiveness and ever-evolving nature of knowledge: for instance, some members of the AIDS community acquired medical knowledge that enabled them to display expertise as scientists about the disease and as individuals with the disease. Participatory bureaucracy allows for inclusive definitions of expertise and public.[80]

While participatory bureaucracy may be more inclusive than traditional bureaucracy, participation that occurs in agency settings can bureaucratize participation and put boundaries on the participatory process. For one, the scope of participation is bound by the terms of the policy task. These boundaries connect subsets of policymakers, practitioners, and various publics related to policy implementation. In the context of the FDA, for instance, this includes, among others, government staff responsible for reviewing a drug, a drug's sponsoring firm, the drug's target population and its advocates, the medical community prescribing the drug, and the public that may experience spillover effects from the drug. For another, bureaucratizing the participatory process means providing systematic and predictable opportunities for public engagement. This means having regular public meetings to enable participation. It means having enough structure to the format of participation to allow participants to prepare for the engagement. It means building participation around a platform of diverse perspectives, which are nonetheless grounded in some dimension of expertise.

Despite its task-specific boundaries, participatory bureaucracy remains potentially open in two fundamental senses of the term. It may be open in the sense of being publicly accessible: participatory bureaucracy not only opens policymaking to invited guests but also allows broader publics to observe or engage in policy discussions. It may also be open in the sense of being indeterminate. The course of action in participatory bureaucracy matters to policy design and implementation. In other words, the outcome of FDA public committees – a drug's approval, rejection, labeling, and restrictions – is not foreordained.

- *Public Engagement for Participatory Bureaucracy:* Public participation is more likely to include diverse, task-specific experts and is less likely to abet privileged group dominance.

IMPLICATIONS FOR BUREAUCRACY AND DEMOCRACY

Participatory bureaucracy can support bureaucratic administration in several ways. The flow of knowledge through participation can create opportunities

---

[80] In this sense, it is consistent with Hugh Heclo's issue network argument that "true experts ... are those who are issue-skilled ... regardless of formal professional training." Hugh Heclo, "Issue Networks and the Executive Establishment," in *The New American Political System* edited by Anthony King (Washington, D.C.: American Enterprise Institute, 1978), pp.102–104.

to prevent policy failure or to share responsibility in the event of implementation failures, rather than concentrate blame at the federal level. Building external implementers' knowledge can benefit bureaucrats inside an agency who depend on outsiders for successful implementations. It can benefit bureaucrats who want other implementers to shoulder some responsibility in the event of failure. It can benefit bureaucrats who want their knowledge to shape the course of policy development or implementation. When its conditions are met, participatory bureaucracy offers more expert and more legitimate implementations, satisfying bureaucratic reputation. Support for bureaucratic administration can take several forms: evidence of quality policy outcomes; stable support for the agency and its jurisdiction; bureaucratization of the policy process in terms of clear lines of responsibility; and minimal blame in the event of policy failure.[81]

Participatory bureaucracy differs from co-optation. Recall that the Tennessee Valley Authority participatory processes that Selznik famously studied entailed inviting potential policy opponents to participate in policymaking to temper opposition. Ultimately, agencies lose autonomy when they engage in co-optation:[82] the participatory process shifts the agency away from "getting the job done." In the framework developed here, co-optation is a form of participation that does not meet the criteria of participatory bureaucracy. Instead, co-optation represents a form of participatory oversight, which can also occur for interdependent policy tasks. Task interdependence does not guarantee participatory bureaucracy.

Participatory bureaucracy also differs from pluralism in important ways.[83] Models of participation in government bureaucracy typically portray participants as expressing interests (either individually or through group spokespersons), and then assess policy as a way of aggregating those preferences. Influence flows from participating groups to bureaucratic policy. In participatory bureaucracy, however, information can flow from bureaucrats to outsiders in ways that exceed the scope of a discrete information exchange or policy decision. Although the participatory process may become bureaucratic in systematic, predictable, and expert ways, the products of that process can be indeterminate and take on lives of their own. Ideas and information are non-rivalrous and can defy tidy boundaries: the genie slips out of the bottle. It was in the course of public FDA meetings about Vioxx that reports of possible cardiovascular risks first reached the popular press and appear to have become part of broader

---

[81] Clear lines of responsibility differ from hierarchical authority.

[82] Philip Selznik, *TVA and the Grass Roots: A Study in the Sociology of Formal Organizations* (Berkeley: University of California Press, 1949). On the loss of autonomy, see: Jeffrey Pfeffer and Gerald R. Salancik, *The External Control of Organizations* (New York: Harper and Row, 2003), pp. 110, 164.

[83] Participatory bureaucracy also differs from representative bureaucracy because, to the extent that representation occurs through participation, it manifests through outsiders invited into bureaucratic policymaking, not from the bureaucrats themselves.

discussion and inquiry.[84] Faculty at the Cleveland Clinic, one of whom took part in Vioxx's public review in February 2001, looked more closely at those risks; and through their research they ultimately applied external pressure on Merck to admit to Vioxx's problems.[85] What started as a two-way regulatory process – the FDA regulating the firm – expanded when third parties used the information to apply pressure on the firm from another direction. Participatory bureaucracy's potential contributions to democratic accountability may manifest long after the public meeting ends.

Participatory bureaucracy also differs from principal-agent models that position bureaucracy at the end of a representative chain. For one, participatory bureaucracy can emerge from relative bureaucratic power. The conditions for participatory bureaucracy are consistent with the conditions of bureaucratic autonomy: unique expertise grounded in diverse support. Public participation may emerge not because Congress requires or even induces it, but because bureaucrats construct opportunities for public participation to support bureaucratic administration in the context of interdependent task implementations consistent with tenets of bureaucratic reputation.[86] For another, principal-agent relationships embody hierarchy. As Figure 1.1 suggests, however, hierarchical task implementations represent only a portion of bureaucratic tasks, many of which have implementations that exceed the agency's hierarchy. Learning crucial to task implementation can reside beyond the agency's hierarchical reach.

Participatory bureaucracy expresses a form of administration that has the potential to benefit bureaucratic implementers and elected officials simultaneously. Scholarship suggests elected officials are more likely to grant agencies discretion for complex tasks, with the hope of reaping benefits from agency expertise.[87] When complexity represents a form of interdependence, these tasks

---

[84] This claim is based on author's review of newspaper articles on Lexis-Nexis. Six months after the February 2001 FDA advisory committee meeting on Vioxx, the *Journal of the American Medical Association* published an article that raised "a cautionary flag about the risk of cardiovascular events with COX-2 inhibitors." Debabrata Mukherjee, Steven E. Nissen, and Eric J. Topol, "Risk of Cardiovascular Events Associated With Selective COX-2 Inhibitors," *JAMA* 286 (2001): 954–959. The *New England Journal of Medicine* published an article in 2000, which reported cardiovascular events among Vioxx users relative to Naproxen, but concluded that heart attacks did not achieve statistical significance. Claire Bombardier et al., "Comparison of Upper Gastrointestinal Toxicity of Rofecoxib and Naproxen in Patients with Rheumatoid Arthritis," *New England Journal of Medicine* 343 (2000): 1520–1528.

[85] Dr. Steven J. Nissen, who coauthored the August 2001 article "Risk of Cardiovascular Events Associated with Selective COX-2 Inhibitors," also served on the February 2001 FDA advisory committee.

[86] Political influence thus may manifest indirectly in agency appetites for publicity, rather than through more direct means such as group mobilization.

[87] On deference to experts, see: Anne M. Khademian, *The SEC and Capital Market Regulation: The Politics of Expertise* (Pittsburgh, PA: University of Pittsburgh Press, 1992); William T. Gormley Jr., *The Politics of Public Utility Regulation* (Pittsburgh, PA: University of Pittsburgh Press, 1983).

are precisely the ones *bureaucrats* may be most likely to open up to public participation. Granting discretion for complex tasks may enable elected officials to benefit from bureaucratic expertise *and* take advantage of greater openness and transparency that bureaucrats are likely to offer for such tasks. The extent to which public participation enhances bureaucratic competence can also support some elected officials' interests in policy implementation.[88]

Public participation may nevertheless yield a zero-sum game. Some forms of elite dominance can crowd out the views of ordinary citizens in shaping government policy. Some forms of participation may come at the expense of bureaucratic administration. Yet, in principle, participatory bureaucracy can help reconcile the tension between bureaucratic administration and democratic accountability when used for interdependent task implementations in ways that secrecy ultimately cannot. Gathering and distributing knowledge not only may support bureaucratic administration; it may also provide other policy participants – governors, members of Congress, presidents, physicians and patients, teachers and students – usable knowledge as well.[89] Does this potential play out in practice? When bureaucrats construct public participation, do they do so in ways that appear compatible with bureaucratic administration? Does participatory bureaucracy, in practice, yield potential benefits for democratic accountability as well? The historical and institutional development of public participation through public advisory committees offers a first step toward addressing these puzzles.

---

[88] Access in the context of complex tasks can benefit elected officials who have interests in task implementation as well as in avoiding a place at the uninformed side of an information asymmetry. For legislators' interest in expertise, see Kevin Esterling, *The Political Economy of Expertise* (Ann Arbor: University of Michigan Press, 2004).

[89] In "Closure and Capture," Karty's iron-triangle conception of public advisory committees offers a different way of thinking about how the bureaucracy and elected officials both could "win" through access. Yet, iron triangles hinge on rigid and restrictive policy monopolies and overlook how policy monopolies are "fundamentally unstable," especially under conditions of complexity. On policy monopolies, see Baumgartner and Jones, *Agendas and Instability in American Politics*, p. 5.

3

The Development of Public Committees

This Department and its operating agencies have long been of the view that proper and effective administration requires that meetings of advisory councils, advisory committees, or advisory groups not be open to the press and public. Exclusion of the press and public from the meeting has been deemed necessary primarily to assure the full, unhampered exchange of ideas.

Wilbur Cohen, Secretary of the Department of Health,
Education and Welfare, 1968[1]

The advisory committee is a reminder that the organization is not monolithic in nature, surrounded by walls and a moat, but rather a system which must depend ultimately for its success upon the relationships it has with those not officially a part of it.

David S. Brown, 1970[2]

The loosely stitched terrain of federal committees that developed in the first two-thirds of the twentieth century embodied exclusivity amid profound decentralization. Committees at times reflected the pursuit of "control on the basis of knowledge," to use Weber's term, despite limited knowledge and limited control. Public committees in mid-century America operated at the intersection of agency efforts to control the flow of information in and out of the bureaucracy, group efforts to influence executive branch policymaking, and Congressional

---

[1] Letter from Secretary Wilbur Cohen to Rep. John Moss, August 19, 1968, published in U.S. Congress, Senate, *Advisory Committees*, Hearings on S.3067 before the Subcommittee on Intergovernmental Relations of the Committee on Government Operations, 91st Congress, 2nd Session, October 6 and 7, part 1 (Washington, DC: GPO, 1970), p. 14.

[2] Statement of David S. Brown, U.S. Congress, Senate, *Advisory Committees*, Hearings on S.3067 before the Subcommittee on Intergovernmental Relations of the Committee on Government Operations, 91st Congress, 2nd Session, October 6 and 7, part 1 (Washington, DC: GPO, 1970), p. 33.

attempts to figure out and regulate what agencies and interest groups were up to. These three forces can give rise to classic zero-sum power struggles and iron triangles. In some cases, for some committees, they did. What emerged more broadly, however, were institutions culminating in the Federal Advisory Committee Act (FACA) that both bureaucratized and democratized processes of public participation in executive branch agencies. Some of these guiding institutions arose from agency initiatives. Others trace their roots to Congress. The decentralization and exclusivity that characterized public participation in the period leading up to 1972, expressed in Secretary's Cohen's quote above, gave way to greater centralization and permeable openness after FACA's enactment.[3] Centralization offered agencies added muscle to set some of the key terms of public committees' operations. Procedures for openness also created opportunities for new forms of participation to emerge and to support agency implementation relationships "with those not officially a part of it," in David Brown's words.

This chapter examines the manifestations of public committee decentralization and exclusivity in the pre-FACA period and the opportunities for centralization and openness that FACA created. The development of American federal public committees makes plain that participatory bureaucracy represents only a subset of public participation in agency policymaking. Other forms of participation, including participatory oversight and private learning, appear in American public committees as well. Looking closely at public committees for pharmaceutical regulation and educational assessments, Chapters 4 and 5 subsequently assess implications of committees' institutional development and how those institutions intersected with task implementation conditions.

DECENTRALIZED PARTICIPATION: AGENCY AND INDUSTRY ORIGINS OF AMERICAN PUBLIC COMMITTEES

A sprawling patchwork of venues for participation in agency policymaking developed in the American executive branch long before Congress exerted oversight authority over federal advisory committees through the 1972 FACA. "The advisory committee is not a new device in Government," aptly penned the House of Representatives' Committee on Government Operations in 1956.[4]

---

[3] For reviews of the development of federal advisory committees, see: Steven P. Croley and William F. Funk, "The Federal Advisory Committee Act and Good Government," *Yale Journal on Regulation* 14 (1997): 451–557; Don K. Price, *Government and Science: Their Dynamic Relation in American Democracy* (New York: Oxford University Press, 1962), 154. For an argument that the executive branch restrictions on advisory committees reflect an effort to forestall Congressional action, see Bruce L. R. Smith *The Advisers: Scientists in the Policy Process* (Washington, DC: Brookings Institution Press, 1992), pp. 24–26.

[4] U.S. Congress, House of Representatives Committee Print, *Replies from Executive Departments and Federal Agencies to Inquiry Regarding Use of Advisory Committees,* January 1, 1953–January 1, 1956, Part 3: Department of Health, Education and Welfare, June 5 (Washington, DC: GPO, 1956), preface.

The visible, durable administrative architecture for the late twentieth- and twenty-first-century system of American participatory bureaucracy was largely forged between World War II and the early 1970s, although the practice and habits of public advice began long before.[5] Presidents and agency leaders have periodically convened panels of nongovernmental participants since the early days of the republic, and scholars frequently point to President Washington's use of nongovernmental negotiators to seek a settlement for the Whiskey Rebellion as the earliest example.[6] Nineteenth-century public committees included the Board of Tea Experts, created by the 1897 Tea Act to recommend "legal tea standards for each year,"[7] and public committees flourished in the first half of the twentieth Century.[8] At least eighty-two ongoing public committees were in operation before the start of Word War II, including the Milk and Milk Products Sanitation Advisory Board of the Public Health Service, the Special Advisory Committee on Research of the Soil Conservation Service, the Advisory Committee of the Weather Bureau, and the General Advisory Committee on Maternal and Child Welfare Services.[9] Some estimates suggest 400 temporary public advisory committees arose to support links between government and industry during World War I and nearly twice as many emerged during World War II.[10] Hundreds of additional public committees advised the Office of Price Administration in the 1940s, and another eighty-six defense-

[5] Committees in operation before World War II include the Federal Advisory Committee on Emergency Aid in Education. On the proliferation of committees between World War II and 1957, see U.S. Congress, House of Representatives, House Report 85–576, *Amending the Administrative Expenses Act of 1946, and for Other Purposes,* 85th Congress, 1st session, June 17 (Washington, DC: GPO, 1957), p. 2.

[6] The Federal Advisory Committee Act of 1972 refers to George Washington's public advisers during the Whiskey Rebellion. See also U.S. Congress, House of Representatives, House Report 91–1731, *The Role and Effectiveness of Federal Advisory Committees,* 91st Congress, 2nd Session, 43rd report by the Committee on Government Operations, December 11 (Washington, DC: GPO, 1970), p. 4, referring to President Washington's Sixth Annual Address, November 19, 1794. For a dissenting interpretation of the Whiskey Rebellion, see Thomas Wolanin, *Presidential Advisory Commission: Truman to Nixon* (Madison: University of Wisconsin Press, 1975), p. 5.

[7] The Board of Tea Experts is an example of a congressionally created Board. U.S. Congress, House of Representatives Committee Print, *Replies from Executive Departments and Federal Agencies to Inquiry Regarding Use of Advisory Committees,* January 1, 1953–January 1, 1956, Part 3: Department of Health, Education and Welfare, June 5 (Washington, DC: GPO, 1956), p. 961.

[8] On the development of some kinds of public advice in the late nineteenth and early twentieth centuries, see Harry Garfield, "Recent Political Developments: Progress or Change?" *American Political Science Review* 18 (1924): 1–17.

[9] Norman N. Gill, "Permanent Advisory Committees in the Federal Government," *Journal of Politics* 2 (1940): 411–435.

[10] David S. Brown, *The Public Advisory Board in American Government,* (Doctoral dissertation, Syracuse University, 1954), pp. 28–29. These industry committees were largely disbanded after the wars ended.

related committees appeared in twenty-one agencies including the Office of
Education, the Office of Production Management, and the State Department.[11]
Early twentieth-century committees elicited participation from thousands of
nongovernmental advisers. Estimates suggest that committees advising the War
Production Board and the Office of Price Administration alone included more
than 14,000 members.[12]

The postwar collection of federal-level public committees was so loosely
stitched together, however, that official counts of committees in mid-century
America differed drastically, ranging from 1,500 to 35,000, depending on who
was doing the counting.[13] These committees took several forms. Some were ad
hoc "citizens advisory panels," such as the Citizens' Advisory Committee on the
Food and Drug Administration, which met for a fixed period of time, produced
a formal report, and then dissolved. Other committees, such as the Library
Advisory Committee to the Office of Education, provided ongoing advice to
agency leaders through regular meetings. Industry councils, such as the Business

---

[11] Brown, *The Public Advisory Board in American Government*, pp. 30–35. Non-defense-related
committees also appeared in the Department of Agriculture, such as the National Arboretum
Advisory Council.

[12] Chester Bowles, "OPA Volunteers: Big Democracy in Action," *Public Administration Review* 4
(1945): 350–359, see p. 351; Carl H. Monsees, *Industry-Government Cooperation: A Study of
the Participation of Advisory Committees in Public Administration* (Washington, DC: Public
Affairs Press, 1944), p. 2, cited in Brown, *The Public Advisory Board in American Government*,
p. 29.

[13] See U.S. Congress, House of Representatives, House Report 85–576, *Amending the
Administrative Expenses Act of 1946, and for Other Purposes,* 85th Congress, 1st session, June
17 (Washington, D.: GPO, 1957), p. 3. The number of public committees in operation in the
1950s is a matter of dispute. Estimates typically excluded 31,000 Agricultural Stabilization and
Conservation county and state committees, as well as 3,000 Farmers' Home Administration
county and state committees, and "several thousand local committees concerned with the use of
public lands for grazing purposes and local groups enlisted by the Treasury Department to assist
in the promotion of the sale of savings bonds" (p. 4). Including these other kinds of committees
yielded totals of more than 35,000 advisory committees in operation in 1955–56 (p. 2). The
Department of Justice reported 5,400 advisory committees in operation throughout the federal
government in 1956. On committee variation, see U.S. General Accounting Office, "Statement
of Elmer B. Staats before the House Committee on Government Operations in Connection with
a Study of the Utilization and Operations of Interagency and Public Advisory Committees in
the Federal Service," March 12, 1970, p. 1. Committees that appeared in *Congressional Record*
debate in 1956 and 1957 include: The Stamp Advisory Committee; the Advisory Board for the
Post Office Department; The Advisory Committee on Energy Supplies and Resources Policy;
International Development Advisory Board; Advisory Council on Social Security; National
Advisory Council on International Monetary and Financial Problems; Advisory Committee
on Reactor Safeguards; The President's Advisory Committee on Government Operations;
The Advisory Committee on Weather Control; The Rubber Advisory Committee; The Debt
Management Advisory Committee; and Advisory Committee on Energy Supplies and Resources
Policy. For recent examples, see Robert Steinbrook, "Science, Politics and Federal Advisory
Committees," *New England Journal of Medicine* 350 (2004): 1454–1460.

Advisory Council to the Department of Commerce, were created and funded by private industry but were housed inside government agencies.[14]

Public committees from Theodore Roosevelt's through Richard Nixon's administrations emerged primarily from executive branch initiative and were regulated, to the extent they were regulated, by individual agencies, the Department of Justice, and the Bureau of the Budget.[15] Although public boards and committees appeared throughout the federal government, twelve agencies stood out as housing the lion's share of public committees in the period leading up to the 1972 FACA, with the Department of Health Education and Welfare leading the pack.[16]

The language of complexity permeates the historical record as a justification for the development and use of public committees,[17] along with rhetoric that committees supported agency leaders,[18] supported democracy by enabling public officials to receive "the advice of the governed,"[19] and supported a two-way flow of information between the agency and public participants.[20] Some committees emerged in conjunction with the development and implementation

---

[14] Presidential commissions also manifested in the period leading up to FACA, such as the Hoover Commission. Presidential committees, however, are largely outside the scope of this study.

[15] Norman N. Gill's 1940 study identified eighty-two federal advisory committees in operation in 1939, most of which were created in the 1930s. He found that the "majority" of these committees arose from agencies exerting their discretion under the "general purpose" clause of the act that created the agency. He noted that Congress created only sixteen of the eighty-two committees in operation in 1940, one of which included the Board of Visitors of the Bureau of Standards, which had been in operation since 1901, the oldest of the committees he found. Gill notes indirect Congressional involvement through restrictions on appropriations codified in 1909 through Section 9 of 35 Stat. 1027. Gill, "Permanent Advisory Committees in the Federal Government," pp. 411–435.

[16] The First Annual Report of the President on advisory committees listed the following agencies as housing the greatest number of advisory committees: Health, Education and Welfare; Agriculture; Interior; Defense; Commerce; Small Business Administration; Transportation; Commission on Civil Rights; Federal Power Commission; Labor; State; National Science Foundation. White House, "Federal Advisory Committees: First Annual Report of the President, 1973," p. 2.

[17] Garfield, "Recent Political Developments," p. 3.

[18] In his 1970 testimony before Congress, the General Accounting Office Comptroller General referred to public advisory committees as, "appointed by the head of an agency purely for his own guidance in a certain area." U.S. General Accounting Office, "Statement of Elmer B. Staats before the House Committee on Government Operations in Connection with a Study of the Utilization and Operations of Interagency and Public Advisory Committees in the Federal Service," p. 2.

[19] U.S. Congress, House of Representatives Committee Print, *Replies from Executive Departments and Federal Agencies to Inquiry Regarding Use of Advisory Committees,* January 1, 1953–January 1, 1956, Part 3: Department of Health, Education and Welfare, June 5 (Washington, DC: GPO, 1956), preface. Very similar language appears in the following Congressional Report: U.S. Congress, House of Representatives, House Report No. 91–1731, *The Role and Effectiveness of Federal Advisory Committees,* Committee on Government Operations, 43rd Report, 91st Congress, 2nd Session, December 11 (Washington, DC: GPO, 1970).

[20] On "informal communication to and from the Board," see the statement of Secor D. Browne, U.S. Congress, Senate, *Advisory Committees,* Hearings before the Subcommittee on

of new federal policy. For instance, the Office of Price Administration, which set price ceilings and rationed scarce products during World War II, created and consulted with consumer advisory committees, industry advisory committees, and labor advisory committees at both the national and district levels to develop policy and support grassroots implementation. In the words of the agency's top administrator, implementation required both federal level continuity (in the form of standard ration books) and local discretion, because "mothers even in the most remote villages had to be able to replace their children's scuffed out shoes quickly with extra coupons obtained from their local war price and rationing boards."[21] Public committees, in his view, offered potential support for this mix of centralized and decentralized policymaking and implementation by serving as conduits for communication and by engaging "tens of thousands" of individuals who served on more than 700 federal and district committees, in addition to the 236,000 volunteers who worked on the 5,556 local rationing boards.[22]

While the committees advising the Office of Price Administration were temporary, like the agency itself, other committees were ongoing. The Library Advisory Committee, for instance, was created in 1941 to "identify problems in the college, university, school and public library fields; and to make recommendations to solve them."[23] To support this mission, the committee consisted of eleven individuals who were appointed by the Commissioner of Education and who were affiliated with different kinds of libraries including public libraries, school libraries, university libraries, federal government libraries, and one corporate library. Library Advisory Committee members' travel expenses were reimbursed, but they received no other remuneration. The Library Advisory Committee was convened, on average, once per year by the Commissioner of Education, followed an agenda created by the Office of Education, and met in

Intergovernmental Relations of the Committee on Government Operations, 92nd Congress, 1st Session, June 10–11, part 1 (Washington, DC: GPO, 1971), p. 15.

[21] On the two-way flow of information, see: Gill, "Advisory Committees in Federal Government," pp. 421–422; Avery Leiserson, *Administrative Regulation: A Study of Representation of Interests* (Chicago: University of Chicago Press, 1942), pp. 160–188.

[22] Bowles, "OPA Volunteers," pp. 350–359. A 1943 Office of Price Administration directive required the agency to consult specifically with industry advisory committees before issuing new regulations or significant policy changes. Committee members were selected by the agency on the basis of geographic representation. For a review of procedures governing industry advisory committees associated with the war effort, see Carl Henry Monsees, "Industry Advisory Committees in the War Agencies," *Public Administration Review* 3 (1943): 254–262. On petroleum-specific industry advisory committees during World War II, see William H. Newman, "Government-Industry Cooperation that Works," *Public Administration Review* 6 (1946): 240–248.

[23] U.S. Congress, House of Representatives Committee Print, *Replies from Executive Departments and Federal Agencies to Inquiry Regarding Use of Advisory Committees*, January 1, 1953–January 1, 1956, Part 3: Department of Health, Education and Welfare, June 5 (Washington, DC: GPO, 1956), pp. 1007–1008.

the Office of Education. The Library Advisory Committee kept minutes of its meetings, which were available for public inspection in the Office of Education, but the committee did not publicly advertise its meetings.

The mid-century development of centralized rules to govern federal public committees, however, emerged from concern about committees that bore little resemblance to the Library Advisory Committee. Starting with 1944 Department of Justice reviews of industry advisory councils, executive branch procedures for regulating public committees reflected concerns that public committees could give private industry privileged and potentially undemocratic access to agency policymaking. Unlike the Library Advisory Committee, industry advisory councils were formed and funded by industries such as energy producers and manufacturers; and their membership comprised primarily of industry leaders who "advised" government agencies on policies relevant to industry. The Business Advisory Council, created in 1933 to "submit to the Secretary of Commerce a constructive point of view on matters of public policy affecting the business interests of the country," consisted of sixty members, who in 1955 included the chairman of the board of the Ford Motor Company, the president of Detroit Edison, the president of General Electric, the president of the New York Stock Exchange, among other notable captains of industry.[24] While the Secretary of Commerce formally "invited" members to the Council, a panel of existing Business Council members was in charge of nominating new members and selecting officers. Unlike the Library Advisory Committee, which was convened only by the Commissioner of Education, either the Council Chairman *or* the Secretary of Commerce could convene the Business Council and set its agenda. The Business Council had office space within the Commerce Department, but its finances were outside of the General Accounting Office's purview, including the dues that members paid to fund the Council's Executive Director and other staff. Council meetings convened in "swank" resort locations, and, unlike the Library Advisory Committee, Business Council records were not publicly available.[25] Critics claimed industry committees such as the Business Council in effect set policy, not merely advised the government; and they highlighted personal gain committee members accrued from advising agencies. Members of the councils advising the Department of Agriculture's Commodity Credit Corporation, for instance, held financial stakes in the Corporation's decisions.[26]

---

[24] U.S. Congress, House of Representatives Committee Print, *Replies from Executive Departments and Federal Agencies to Inquiry Regarding Use of Advisory Committees,* January 1, 1953–January 1, 1956, part 2, Department of Commerce (Washington, DC: GPO, 1956), pp. 912–921.

[25] For discussion of the Business Advisory Council from the Commerce Department, see the statement from Rep. Celler (D-NY) from the antitrust subcommittee of the Committee on the Judiciary, *Congressional Record – House* July 10, 1957, p. 11257.

[26] Statement of Representative Lawrence H. Fountain (D-NC), *Congressional Record – House* July 10, 1957, p. 11260. These committees included: Dairy Industry Task Committee, the Cotton

In 1944, the Department of Justice ruled that when industry committees acted in an advisory capacity but did not make policy, they did not breech antitrust requirements.[27] Yet, concerns about industry councils persisted. In a letter to the Secretary of the Interior on February 16, 1951, for instance, the Department of Justice summarized the Petroleum Advisory Council in the following way:

> This intermingling of Government functions with those of industry advisory committees resulted in complete delegation to such committees of functions which properly must reside exclusively in Government officials.[28]

Department of Justice guidelines established in 1950 set terms for public committees under its jurisdiction.[29] These guidelines offered means of protecting and bolstering agency authority relative to public committees, with industry advisory councils in mind. The Department of Justice guidelines emphasized that committees should be advisory and specified terms for committee creation, requiring committees to be authorized in statute or arise from an "administrative finding." Industry alone could not create them. The guidelines also required government agency officials – not private citizens – to convene meetings and set meeting agendas; and they required committees to keep minutes.[30]

Even though the roots of the Department of Justice provisions emerged from concerns over excessive industry influence through industry councils, the Department of Justice recommended that its standards apply to public committees throughout the federal government.[31] Concern that the procedures could

Export Advisory Committee, the Seed Advisory Committee, and the Advisory Committee on Grain Exports.

[27] U.S. Congress, House Committee on the Judiciary, Antitrust Subcommittee (Subcommittee No. 5), *WOC's [Without Compensation Government Employees] and Government Advisory Groups,* Hearings, 84th Congress, 1st session, August 4, Part 1 (Washington, DC: GPO, 1955), pp. 585–586, cited in Wendy R. Ginsberg, *Advisory Committees: A Primer* (Washington, DC: U.S. Congressional Research Service, 2010), p. 3.

[28] *Congressional Record – House* July 10, 1957, p. 11254. The Antitrust Subcommittee of the Judiciary Committee also conducted investigations of advisory committees.

[29] Peyton Ford, Deputy Attorney General, to the Office of the Attorney General, October 19, 1950, published in U.S. Congress, House of Representatives, House Report 85-576, *Amending the Administrative Expenses Act of 1946, and for Other Purposes,* 85th Congress, 1st session, June 17 (Washington, DC: GPO, 1957), p. 15. Recall that one of the earliest recorded forms of congressional advisory committee oversight appeared in 1842 with congressional efforts to control advisory committee appropriations. On Department of Justice guidelines, see Croley Funk, "The Federal Advisory Committee Act and Good Government," p. 453, fn10.

[30] Peyton Ford, Deputy Attorney General, "Letter to All Agencies Regarding Advisory Committees," (U.S. Department of Justice: GPO, October 19, 1950), available in U.S. Congress, House Committee on the Judiciary, Antitrust Subcommittee (Subcommittee No. 5), *WOC's [Without Compensation Government Employees] and Government Advisory Groups,* Hearings, 84th Congress, 1st session, August 4, part 1 (Washington, DC: GPO, 1955), pp. 586–587, cited in Ginsberg, *Advisory Committees: A Primer,* pp. 3–4.

[31] The DOJ noted that statutorily created committees would be governed by the terms specified in their authorizing statute. Testimony submitted by the Department of Justice suggested that

produce bureaucratic authority at the expense of democratic expression did not appear in the public record. Instead, the underlying logic implied a strong bureaucracy was necessary to support a strong democracy and keep industry in check. House of Representatives' efforts to pass legislation in 1957 that would have applied many of the Department of Justice guidelines across government agencies reflected concerns about making sure government agencies remained in charge of committees. In the words of Representative Dante Fascell (D-FL), "we do not want [a] committee in any way, directly or indirectly, to usurp the function of the department head. We want him to exercise the judgment, the managerial capacity, the executive capability, and not the committee."[32] While legislative efforts to establish some guiding standards across committees failed to make it past the House, Bureau of Budget standards and procedures adopted the Department of Justice guidelines in 1959. These Bureau of Budget standards later provided the foundation for President Kennedy's 1962 Executive Order 11007, which extended the basic Department of Justice standards for establishing committees, keeping minutes, and setting meeting agendas.[33]

Some estimates suggested about half of the committees in operation in 1957 followed Department of Justice guidelines.[34] The centralization glass could appear either half full – half of the committees adhered to rudimentary centralized guidance – or half empty, since more than 1,000 committees *did not* adhere to centralized guidelines. Either interpretation, however, leaves room for significant variation across committees and agencies,[35] including room for agencies to develop their own systematic public committee procedures. Years before President Kennedy's Executive Order 11007 and before the 1972 FACA, the Department of Health Education and Welfare (HEW) – the agency with the most advisory committees – began developing its own procedures for advisory

---

1,393 committees were not governed by statutes and of those about 615 were in compliance with Department of Justice standards. U.S. Congress, House of Representatives, House Report 85–576, *Amending the Administrative Expenses Act of 1946, and for Other Purposes,* 85th Congress, 1st session, June 17 (Washington, DC: GPO, 1957), p. 3.

[32] *Congressional Record – House,* July 10, 1957, p. 11253.

[33] Issued on February 26, 1962. Executive Order 11007 appears in the *Federal Register* Wednesday February 28, 1962, pp. 1875–1877.

[34] Representative Dante Fascell (D-FL) estimated that approximately 50 percent of the "thousands" of advisory committees in operation followed the DOJ guidelines voluntarily by 1957. *Congressional Record – House* July 10, 1957, p. 11254. In their review of advisory committee oversight, Croley and Funk assert the DOJ guidelines were "largely ignored"; Croley and Funk, "The Federal Advisory Committee Act and Good Government," p. 459. For discussion on variation in DOJ guideline adherence among Department of Agriculture committees, see the statement of Representative Lawrence H. Fountain (D-NC), *Congressional Record – House* July 10, 1957, p. 11260.

[35] On the vast variation in Advisory Committee operations in 1971, see the opening statement of Senator Lee Metcalf (D-MT), U.S. Congress, Senate, *Advisory Committees,* Hearings before the Subcommittee on Intergovernmental Relations of the Committee on Government Operations, US Senate, 92nd Congress, 1st Session, June 10–11, part 1 (Washington, DC: GPO, 1971), p. 1. For more on CAB committees, see p. 40 of same hearing.

committee management. HEW kept a full accounting of its public committees, and in 1959 it commissioned and released "A Guide to the Use of Advisory Committees."[36] A decade later, in 1969, HEW conducted a review of all existing advisory committees, eliminated forty of them, and prevented new committees from forming until the review was complete. HEW also developed a more centralized model for overseeing committees and their appointments,[37] and it developed policies for recruiting women, underrepresented minorities, and lay participants to committees and councils before the passage of the FACA.[38] Other agencies, such as the Department of Transportation, also developed extensive agency-specific procedures for committee creation, operation, and review.[39]

While congressional allegations that advisory committees constituted a "fifth branch" of government may have overstated the pervasiveness of committee independence from executive branch oversight, concerns about industry power on some prominent committees set the tone for legislative inquiry in the 1950s, 1970s, and beyond. Industry-oriented committees persisted throughout the mid-century, and allegations that public committees gave industry an open pipeline to influence government policy dominated congressional oversight hearings in the mid-1950s and early 1970s. For instance, industry committees

---

[36] U.S. Department of Health Education and Welfare, *A Guide to the Use of Federal Advisory Committees* (Washington, D.C.: GPO, 1959), cited in Gerald Kluempke, *A Descriptive Analysis of the Attitudes, Make-Up, Function, and Utilization of Advisory Councils of the U.S. Department of Education* (George Washington University, Doctoral dissertation, 1976), p. 43. For a list of HEW committees in operation between 1953 and 1956, see U.S. Congress, House of Representatives Committee Print, *Replies from Executive Departments and Federal Agencies to Inquiry Regarding Use of Advisory Committees*, January 1, 1953–January 1, 1956, Part 3: Department of Health, Education and Welfare, June 5 (Washington, DC: GPO, 1956).

[37] See the testimony of Dr. Rodney H. Brady, Assistant Secretary of HEW, U.S. Congress, Senate, *Advisory Committees*, Hearings before the Subcommittee on Intergovernmental Relations of the Committee on Government Operations, 92nd Congress, 1st Session, part 3 (Washington, DC: GPO, 1971), p. 952.

[38] U.S. Congress, Senate, *Advisory Committees*, Hearings before the Subcommittee on Intergovernmental Relations of the Committee on Government Operations, 92nd Congress, 1st Session, part 3 (Washington, DC: GPO, 1971), pp. 953, 958. For a critique of the NIH grant review process, the lack of female scientist inclusion on committees, the inclusion of individuals tied to industry, and insufficiently applied conflict of interest guidelines, see the comments of Dr. Julia Apter, pp. 1041–1043.

[39] See, for instance, "The Department of Transportation Order 1120.3, August 11, 1970, Committee Management Policy and Procedures," printed in U.S. Congress, Senate, *Advisory Committees*, Hearings on S.1637, S.1964, and S.2064 before the Subcommittee on Intergovernmental Relations of the Committee on Government Operations, 92nd Congress, 1st Session, October 6, 7, 8, and 11, part 3 (Washington, DC: GPO, 1971), pp. 735–771. Starting in 1963, consistent with EO 11007, the Bureau of the Budget began reporting to the U.S. Attorney General a list of its committees and members, as well as providing minutes of committee meetings. U.S. Congress, Senate, *Advisory Committees*, Hearings before the Subcommittee on Intergovernmental Relations of the Committee on Government Operations, 91st Congress, 2nd Session on S.3067 October 8 and 9, part 2 (Washington, DC; GPO, 1970), p. 174.

that fell under the umbrella of the Bureau of the Budget's Advisory Council on Federal Reports, constituted after the 1942 Federal Reports Act and aimed at reducing paperwork burden on businesses, received repeated congressional scrutiny and criticism.[40] Critics claimed that industry influence on the reports committees prevented the Bureau of the Budget from gathering information potentially hostile to industry interests, including questionnaires designed to help enforce antipollution laws.[41] The lack of a centralized, government-wide process for accounting and managing committees made it difficult to assess the proportion of committees that industry established or controlled and the extent of the "fifth-branch" problem.

EXCLUSIVE PARTICIPATION

Alongside the public critique that public committees lacked sufficient executive branch oversight resided the companion concern that this lack of centralized oversight abetted exclusivity. The mid-century portrait of public committees suggests a quasi-bureaucratized process for inviting select members of the public to participate in agency policymaking and to be part of a limited flow of information: between the agency and invited participants, and between the committee and anyone who subsequently read the committee's report. On the one hand, public committees broke with rigid bureaucratic hierarchy by including nongovernmental participants in the policymaking process. On the other hand, federal public committees expressed classic Weberian closure by limiting the flow of information and participation. Although variation appeared across agencies and committees in terms of public and press access to committee deliberations, critics alleged barriers to general public participation arose from the lack of a systematic meeting notification process, and from refusals to allow the public to attend or participate at meetings.[42]

---

[40] The Senate Report accompanying the 1972 Federal Advisory Committee highlighted the OMB's Council on Federal Reports as foundational to congressional investigations and concerns about federal advisory committees. U.S. Congress, Senate, Senate Report No. 92–1098, *Federal Advisory Committee Act*, Committee on Government Operations, 92nd Congress, 2nd Session, September 7 (Washington, DC: GPO, 1972). For a critique of these committees, see the comments of Charles F. Wheatley Jr., General Manager and General Counsel for the American Public Gas Association, representing municipal utilities excluded from the BOB/OMB committees, U.S. Congress, Senate, *Advisory Committees*, Hearings on S.1637, S.1964, and S.2064 before the Subcommittee on Intergovernmental Relations of the Committee on Government Operations, 92nd Congress, 1st Session, October 6, 7, 8, and 11, part 3 (Washington, DC: GPO, 1971), pp. 584–594.

[41] U.S. Congress, Senate, *Advisory Committees*, Hearings on S. 3067 before the Subcommittee on Intergovernmental Relations of the Committee on Government Operations of the United States, 91st Congress, 2nd Session, December 8, 10, 17, part 3 (Washington, DC: GPO, 1970), p. 505.

[42] For a detailed account of which committees announced meetings, opened meetings, and kept records, see the various volumes of U.S. Congress, House of Representatives Committee Print, *Replies from Executive Departments and Federal Agencies to Inquiry Regarding Use of Advisory*

A systematic review of federal advisory committees in 1939 found that "nearly all" of the eighty-two committees in operation kept "some form of record of the discussions and recommendations of their committees," and that "[i]n most cases the minutes of meetings are open to the inspection of persons with legitimate reasons for wanting to see them."[43] Long before the Department of Justice Guidelines, Presidential Executive Orders, and the Federal Advisory Committee Act, agencies were keeping minutes and making them publicly available, according to Gill's report. The extent of committee transparency and public access, however, appears to have varied by committee and by agency. The FDA's mid-1950s account of its advisory committees suggests verbatim minutes were rarely kept and meetings were rarely publicized, except at times in trade publications.[44] Closure was not unique to the FDA, but appeared elsewhere in HEW. While the barriers to public access that emerged in HEW stemmed in part from the preponderance of its grant review committees and norms of closure in the peer review process, closure characterized non-grant review committees as well.[45]

Systematic steps toward greater openness began with the 1962 Executive Order 11007, which specified that industry committees should keep full transcripts of meeting deliberations and that other kinds of public committees, such as the Library Advisory Committee noted earlier, needed to keep meeting minutes. Executive Order 11007, however, permitted agency leaders to waive the transcript requirement, and it did not require committees to allow the general public or media to attend committee meetings.[46] A congressional study conducted before the passage of the 1972 FACA reported that of the 1,940

Committees, January 1, 1953–January 1, 1956, Department of Health, Education and Welfare, June 5 (Washington, DC: GPO, 1956). On refusal to allow the public to attend, see the discussion of the CAB Labor Advisory Committee, U.S. Congress, Senate, *Advisory Committees,* Hearings before the Subcommittee on Intergovernmental Relations of the Committee on Government Operations, 92nd Congress, 1st Session, June 10–11, part 1, (Washington, DC: GPO, 1971), p. 67. For barriers to access on the DOD Industrial Advisory Council and lack of minutes and transcripts, see U.S. Congress, Senate, *Advisory Committees,* Hearings before the Subcommittee on Intergovernmental Relations of the Committee on Government Operations, 92nd Congress, 1st Session, June 15, 17, 22 and July 13, 27, 28, part 2 (Washington, DC: GPO, 1971), pp. 314–318.

[43] Gill, "Permanent Advisory Committees in the Federal Government," p. 415.

[44] U.S. Congress, House of Representatives Committee Print, *Replies from Executive Departments and Federal Agencies to Inquiry Regarding Use of Advisory Committees,* January 1, 1953–January 1, 1956, part 3: Department of Health, Education and Welfare, June 5 (Washington, DC: GPO, 1956), pp. 960–995.

[45] U.S. Congress, Senate, *Advisory Committees,* Hearings before the Subcommittee on Intergovernmental Relations of the Committee on Government Operations, 92nd Congress, 1st Session, part 3 (Washington, DC: GPO, 1971), p. 953. For discussion on variation in FDA access to minutes and transcripts, see p. 975; and for general closure to the public and the press, see p. 976.

[46] For discussion on problems in advisory committee record keeping practice, see Croley and Funk, "The Federal Advisory Committee Act and Good Government," pp. 460–463.

advisory committees it reviewed, slightly more than half (996) allowed members of the public to attend meetings,[47] that meeting minutes were recorded for 1,375 committees (71 percent of committees), but only 789 of these committees made the minutes publicly available. Transcripts of meetings were kept for 599 committees, and the vast majority of those committees (496) made their minutes available to the public. The report crowned the Department of Labor's Wage and Hour Division (100 percent open), Interior's Land Management (100 percent open), the Interstate Commerce Commission (98 percent open), the Environmental Protection Agency (85 percent open), and the Department of Agriculture's Forest Service (84 percent open) as having the best transparency records (the most open meetings). The National Institute of Health, the FDA, the National Science Foundation, and the National Endowment for the Arts were identified as having the worst transparency records: they convened no open meetings, which was partly attributable to the prevalence of grant review committees in these agencies.[48]

Variation also appeared in terms of the extent and nature of diversity among committee members. President Kennedy's Executive Order 11007 called for representative membership on industry-related committees (i.e., including large *and* small business owners), but the requirement did not apply to all committees, nor was representation defined in detail. Provisions for categories of members appeared in some committees' authorizations, and some agencies argued they strived to tap diverse expertise.[49] The extent of committee bias

---

[47] Statement of Alan Chvotkin, U.S. Congress, House of Representatives, *US Government Information Policies and Practices – Public Access to Information from Executive Branch Advisory Groups*, Hearings before the Subcommittee of the Committee on Government Operations, 92nd Congress, 2nd Session, June 6, 8, and 19, 1972, part 9 (Washington, DC: GPO, 1972), p. 3423. The estimates come from a survey of agencies conducted in October 1971. OMB had different estimates of committee totals: 1,104 advisory committees and 620 interagency committees in 1971; see p. 3439.

[48] Statement of Alan Chvotkin, U.S. Congress, *US Government Information Policies and Practices*, p. 3425. The authors of the study interpret their results and the justifications that agencies gave for closing meetings, including EO 11007, the 1789 "housekeeping" statute for Title 5 U.S.C. 301, and the Freedom of Information Act to suggest "that as the Federal bureaucracy has grown, it has lost touch with the public," p. 3427. For more discussion of closing peer review meetings and court cases supporting such closure, see Michael H. Cardozo, "The Federal Advisory Committee Act in Operation," *Administrative Law Review* 33 (1981): 42–46. For agency estimates of the cost of requiring transcripts, see U.S. Congress, *Advisory Committees*, Hearings before the Subcommittee on Intergovernmental Relations of the Committee on Government Operations, 92nd Congress, 1st Session, part 3 (Washington, DC: GPO, 1971), pp. 815–825. Estimates ranged from no cost (Civil Aeronautics Board) to $491,621 (DOD) to $1.7 million (HEW).

[49] For an example of how the CAB justified its committee member selection, see the testimony of CAB Chairman Secor D. Browne in U.S. Congress, Senate, *Advisory Committees*, Hearings before the Subcommittee on Intergovernmental Relations of the Committee on Government Operations, 92nd Congress, 1st Session, June 10–11, part 1 (Washington, DC: GPO, 1971), p. 16.

and privilege was not systematically documented, and membership bias was
not an issue the General Accounting Office raised in its 1970 review of public
committees. Much of the rhetoric in the public record, however, portrays both
closed bureaucracy and closed interest group dynamics,[50] with committees
comprised primarily of scientific experts and conventionally defined elites.[51]
Critics of public committees pointed to instances in which industry leaders
filled slots designated for "public" representatives.[52] "Public" members on the
Advisory Council on Federal Reports that advised the Bureau of the Budget,
for instance, included stockbrokers and corporate lawyers.[53] Other leading
examples came from the National Railroad Passenger Corporation Financial
Investment Advisory Committee, which in 1970 failed to contain any members
of the general public despite statutory language calling for seven public members. Instead, the committee included representatives from railroads, utilities,
banks, investment firms, law firms, and a mining company.[54] Other committees
that failed to include public representatives or appeared to favor big business
during this era included the Industrial Pollution Control Council, the General
Advisory Committee of the Federal National Mortgage Association, and

---

[50] On the scarcity of consumer representation on BOB/OMB Reports advisory committees in the
1970s, see House Report 92-1017, *Federal Advisory Committee Standards Act*, Committee
on Government Operations, 92nd Congress, 2nd Session, April 25 (Washington, DC: GPO,
1972), p. 6. See also the statement of Erma Angevine, Consumer Federation of America, U.S.
Congress, Senate, *Advisory Committees*, Hearings on S.3067 before the Subcommittee on
Intergovernmental Relations of the Committee on Government Operations, 91st Congress, 2nd
Session October 6 and 7, 1970, part 1 (Washington, DC: GPO, 1970), p. 73. On the secrecy
of decision making, see U.S. Congress, Senate, *Advisory Committees*, Hearings on S.3067
before the Subcommittee on Intergovernmental Relations of the Committee on Government
Operations, 91st Congress, 2nd Session October 6 and 7, part 2 (Washington, DC: GPO, 1970),
pp. 179–180 and see p. 249 on the lack of *Federal Register* meeting notification.

[51] For 1971 EPA committee rosters, see U.S. Congress, Senate, *Advisory Committees*,
Hearings before the Subcommittee on Intergovernmental Relations of the Committee on
Government Operations, 92nd Congress, 1st Session, part 3 (Washington, DC: GPO, 1971),
pp. 848–876.

[52] See U.S. Congress, Senate, *Advisory Committees*, Hearings before the Subcommittee on
Intergovernmental Relations of the Committee on Government Operations, 92nd Congress, 1st
Session, June 15, 17, and 22 and July 13, 27, and 28 (Washington, DC: GPO, 1971), pp. 359–
360. For discussion on the difficulty of securing representation of unorganized interests, see
Leiserson, *Administrative Regulation*, p. 172.

[53] For efforts to include labor, consumer, and small business members on the Advisory Council
on Federal Reports, see U.S. Congress, Senate, *Advisory Committees*, Hearings before the
Subcommittee on Intergovernmental Relations of the Committee on Government Operations,
S.3067, 91st Congress, 2nd Session, October 6 and 7, part 1 (Washington, DC: GPO, 1970),
p. 2. For a brief review of the Advisory Council on Federal Reports, see Cardozo "The Federal
Advisory Committee Act in Operation," p. 8.

[54] U.S. Congress, Senate, *Advisory Committees*, Hearings on S. 3067 before the Subcommittee
on Intergovernmental Relations of the Committee on Government Operations, 91st Congress,
second session, December 8, 10, and 17, part 3 (Washington, DC: GPO, 1970), p. 497. See also
the statements of Senator Lee Metcalf (D-MT), pp. 602–628.

committees reporting to the Interstate Commerce Commission.[55] Other commentators warned of perfunctory participation or participation in appearance only.[56] Some commentators noted the difference between industry committees and scientific committees, though both presented opportunities for exclusion.[57] Both parties took advantage of committee exclusivity, and allegations of partisanship surfaced across administrations.[58] Neither the Bureau of the Budget nor the General Accounting Office, however, documented the extent to which committee membership systematically privileged particular voices over others.

Beneath the calls for greater openness and critiques of committee closure resided concerns that closure, exclusivity, and secrecy enabled agency power, unchecked industry influence on agency policymaking, or both.[59] Although visible congressional oversight of public committees was relatively rare, the congressional mid-century critique juxtaposed allegations of insufficient agency muscle – letting private industry call the shots – and exclusive agency control – using committees to promote agency policies. In the words of William Dawson (D-IL), chairman of the Committee on Government Operations, greater openness would "protect the Government by making it difficult for representatives of special interests to insinuate themselves on advisory committees, and, under a veil of secrecy, gain a venal or flagitious advantage."[60] Advocates in the early 1970s, such as Ralph Nader, characterized advisory committees, and the National Business Council on Consumer Affairs in particular, as means of "formalizing the lobbying process" that led to "severely imbalancing the right

---

[55] U.S. Congress, Senate, *Advisory Committees*, Hearings on S. 3067 before the Subcommittee on Intergovernmental Relations of the Committee on Government Operations, 91st Congress, second session, December 8, 10, and 17, part 3 (Washington, DC: GPO, 1970), pp. 501, 505.

[56] U.S. Congress, Senate, *Advisory Committees*, Hearings before the Subcommittee on Intergovernmental Relations of the Committee on Government Operations, U.S. Senate, 92nd Congress, 1st Session, part 3 (Washington, DC: GPO, 1971), p. 788.

[57] On the topic of scientific exclusion or inclusion, see Martin Perl, "The Scientific Advisory System," *Science*, September 24, 1971, reprinted in U.S. Congress, Senate, *Advisory Committees*, Hearings before the Subcommittee on Intergovernmental Relations of the Committee on Government Operations, 92nd Congress, 1st Session, part 3 (Washington, DC: GPO, 1971), p. 779.

[58] U.S. Congress, Senate, *Advisory Committees*, Hearings before the Subcommittee on Intergovernmental Relations of the Committee on Government Operations, 92nd Congress, 1st Session, part 3 (Washington, DC: GPO, 1971), p. 877.

[59] See the statement of William H. Rogers Jr., U.S. Congress, Senate, *Advisory Committees*, Hearings on S.3067 before the Subcommittee on Intergovernmental Relations of the Committee on Government Operations, 91st Congress, 2nd Session October 6 and 7, part 1 (Washington, DC: GPO, 1970), p. 19.

[60] U.S. Congress, House of Representatives, House Report 85–576, *Amending the Administrative Expenses Act of 1946, and for Other Purposes*, 85th Congress, 1st session, June 17 (Washington, DC: GPO, 1957), p. 22. For a contrary view, see the comments of Representative Clare Hoffman (R-MI), who wrote the minority portion of the Committee report, *Congressional Record – House* July 10, 1957, p. 11256.

of unorganized citizens or citizen groups to have relatively equivalent access."[61] Other critics argued that advisory committees, such as the National Industrial Pollution Control Council, provided a venue for well-resourced campaign donors to gain access to agency policymaking.[62] Even when closure did not yield corruption, critics alleged that the inaccessibility of committee documents and minutes risked fostering feelings of alienation and exclusion.[63]

Some members of Congress also worried about committee secrecy as a means of augmenting agency power. In its 1957 report, the Committee on Government Operations wrote that secrecy allowed committees to "be channeled into a convenient and effective source of support for established programs or policies."[64] Committees singled out for rebuke included the Citizen's Advisory Council of the Post Office and Civil Service Committee.[65] The House committee report warned that such secrecy could allow the executive branch to use public advice to promote executive branch policies and to lobby indirectly, even illegally. Instead of offering government agencies advice, public committees could work as a possible mouthpiece for executive branch propaganda, critics suggested. The House committee report cautioned:

> Under the ostensible objective of seeking advice and counsel, the real purpose may be in many instances to enlist support of the regulated in the process of regulation.... A selling campaign may be subtly initiated by encouraging favorable public statements by committee members and the interest groups from which they come.[66]

[61] U.S. Congress, Senate, *Advisory Committees*, Hearings before the Subcommittee on Intergovernmental Relations of the Committee on Government Operations, 92nd Congress, 1st Session, part 3 (Washington, DC: GPO, 1971), p. 984.

[62] Statement of William H. Rogers, U.S. Congress, Senate, *Advisory Committees*, Oversight Hearings before the Subcommittee on Budgeting, Management and Expenditures of the Committee on Government Operations, 93rd Congress, 1st and 2nd Sessions on P.L. 92–463, November 29, December 13, 1973; February 5, 1974 (Washington, DC: GPO, 1973–1974), p. 80.

[63] See the statement of David S. Brown, U.S. Congress, Senate, *Advisory Committees*, Hearings on S.3067 before the Subcommittee on Intergovernmental Relations of the Committee on Government Operations, 91st Congress, 2nd Session, October 6 and 7, part 1 (Washington, DC: GPO, 1970), pp. 32–33.

[64] U.S. Congress, House of Representatives, House Report 85–576, *Amending the Administrative Expenses Act of 1946, and for Other Purposes*, 85th Congress, 1st session, June 17 (Washington, DC: GPO, 1957). Debate on the bill suggested that "many" committees did not keep or provide minutes of their proceedings, but that "over half" of then-operating committees were already meeting the House bill proposal to record the names of people attending and summarize "matters discussed at such meetings." See the statement of Representative Dante Fascell (D-FL), *Congressional Record – House*, July 10, 1957, p. 11253.

[65] Remarks of Representative August Johansen (R-MI), *Congressional Record* July 10, 1957, p. 11255.

[66] U.S. Congress, House of Representatives, House Report 85–576, *Amending the Administrative Expenses Act of 1946, and for Other Purposes*, 85th Congress, 1st session, June 17 (Washington, DC: GPO, 1957), p. 5.

Amid legislative calls for greater openness in 1957[67] and 1971,[68] agencies largely responded in Weberian bureaucratic fashion, with justifications for why the agency should be able to maintain control over the flow of information. Yet, agency opposition also highlighted agency reliance on external expertise, in sharp contrast to closed models of bureaucracy that assume information sufficient for task implementation resides fully inside bureaucratic hierarchy. Opposition arose from agencies arguing that legislative "inflexibility" would "straightjacket" the agencies and discourage "the free exchange of ideas between Government executives and their advisers from the public at large" and "citizens' rights to confer with their government."[69] Agency bureaucrats claimed secrecy, not openness, enabled information exchanges between the agency, experts, implementers, and the public.[70] The Post Office Department, for instance, took specific issue with provisions to require full and complete minutes, arguing such minutes would

> result in reluctance on the part of committee members to express fully their views on the various subjects under discussion if they knew that their remarks were being made a matter of public record and might be cited to their embarrassment at some future date.[71]

---

[67] Opposition to HR 7390 emerged from: the Department of Agriculture, the Bureau of the Budget, the Commerce Department, the Department of Defense, the General Services Administration, the Department of Health, Education and Welfare, the Department of Interior, the Department of Justice, the Department of Labor, the Post Office, and the Treasury Department. *Congressional Record – House*, July 10, 1957, p. 11255. The Minority Report on HR 7390 asserted that executive departments opposed the legislation "with few exceptions," U.S. Congress, House of Representatives, *Advisory Committees, House Report, Minority Report on HR 7390*, June 17 (Washington, DC: GPO, 1957), p. 13.

[68] OMB supported much of the spirit of the legislative effort, but asserted that it could handle the oversight itself and through new Executive Orders. Comments from Arnold Weber, Associate Director of OMB, U.S. Congress, Senate, *Advisory Committees*, Hearings before the Subcommittee on Intergovernmental Relations of the Committee on Government Operations, 92nd Congress, 1st Session, part 2 (Washington, DC: GPO, 1971), pp. 533–534. FTC supported the advisory committee bill, citing its experience with industry-dominated BOB/OMB reports committees, and calling for more consumer and small-business representation on the committees. U.S. Congress, Senate, *Advisory Committees*, Hearings on S.1637, S.1964, and S.2064 before the Subcommittee on Intergovernmental Relations of the Committee on Government Operations, 92nd Congress, 1st Session October 6, 7, 8, and 11, part 3 (Washington, DC: GPO, 1971), p. 557.

[69] U.S. Congress, House of Representatives, *Interim report of the Antitrust Subcommittee of the House Judiciary Committee on the Business Advisory Council*, 84th Congress, 1st session (Washington, DC: GPO, 1955), pp. 34–35.

[70] For a discussion on this point and the potential advantages of informal over formal processes, see Cary Coglianese, Richard Zeckhauser, and Edward Parson, "Seeking Truth for Power: Informational Strategy and Regulatory Policymaking," *Minnesota Law Review* 89 (2004): 277–341, including footnotes 152–157.

[71] Letter from Maurice H. Stans, Deputy Postmaster General to Representative William L. Dawson, Chairman, Committee on Government Operations, April 4, 1957. Reprinted in, U.S. Congress, House of Representatives, House Report 85–576, *Amending the Administrative Expenses Act*

Some agencies argued that public access could have negative effects on financial markets and product safety.[72] The FDA resisted making minutes or transcripts publicly available throughout the 1950s, 1960s, and into the early 1970s, asserting the deleterious effects publicity could have on both debate and product markets. In justifying his opposition to keeping formal minutes of committee proceedings, FDA Deputy Commissioner John Harvey wrote in 1957 that such minutes:

> would necessarily restrict the scientific discussions that scientists must engage in in order to make sound recommendations ... because favorable opinions, no matter how well qualified, could give rise to false or premature hopes as to the efficacy of a medicine, and unfavorable comments could become a source of misunderstanding and unjust harm to the reputations of individuals and organizations engaged in experimental and developmental projects if such comments were made a matter of record before full evaluation of a drug had been completed.[73]

Others justified committee exclusivity on the basis of the highly specific knowledge needed for committee deliberations. Department of Transportation Undersecretary James H. Beggs' testimony illustrates a prominent rationale for conventionally defined expert committee participation:

> [W]hen you are dealing with subjects such as pipeline safety standards, which are highly technical – they involve an understanding of corrosion activity on pipelines, they involve an understanding of construction methods and standards and so forth – it is difficult to get an ordinary private citizen deeply involved in these problems.[74]

Other agency officials charged that if they were to lose control over committee membership, more open, more diverse committees would degenerate into "a babble of conflict and controversy."[75]

While critics of public committees pointed to their exclusivity, agency advocates pointed to their inclusion: their ability to engage public participation in agency policymaking that would otherwise not occur. The Department of

---

of 1946, and for Other Purposes, 85th Congress, 1st session, June 17 (Washington, DC: GPO, 1957), pp. 17–18.

[72] Statement of Arnold Weber, Associate Director of OMB, U.S. Congress, Senate, *Advisory Committees,* Hearings before the Subcommittee on Intergovernmental Relations of the Committee on Government Operations, 92nd Congress, 1st Session, part 2 (Washington, DC: GPO, 1971), pp. 521–522.

[73] Letter from FDA Deputy Commissioner John Harvey to Representative John Bell Williams, dated July 9, 1957, reprinted in *Congressional Record – House,* July 10, 1957, p. 11262.

[74] James H. Beggs, Undersecretary of Transportation, Department of Transportation U.S. Congress, Senate, *Advisory Committees,* Hearings on S.1637, S.1964, and S.2064 before the Subcommittee on Intergovernmental Relations of the Committee on Government Operations, 92nd Congress, 1st Session, October 6, 7, 8, and 11, part 3 (Washington, DC: GPO, 1971), pp. 629–632.

[75] See the comments of the Chair of the Industrial Pollution Control Council, U.S. Congress, Senate, *Advisory Committees,* Hearings before the Subcommittee on Intergovernmental Relations of the Committee on Government Operations, 92nd Congress, 1st Session, part 2 (Washington, DC: GPO, 1971), p. 405.

Health, Education and Welfare and the Department of Transportation vigorously defended their committees' contributions and their ability to include "individuals who would otherwise never be involved in Government activity."[76] Along with vocal critiques of public advisory committees came caution to recognize the variation across committees and relative rarity of business dominance: that "the total advisory committee structure is by no means dominated by the business community."[77] Even one of the staunchest supporters of legislation to formalize procedures for more openness on committees, Senator Metcalf, argued:

> I do not want the fact that we have criticized some of these people to take away from the fine public service that 99 ½ percent of the members of the various advisory committees all over the United States have contributed in their own time and in the public interest.[78]

During the first two-thirds of the twentieth century, however, participation on and access to public committees and councils were primarily by invitation only. These invitations were extended to tens of thousands of individuals who participated yearly on public committees, councils, and boards in the pre-FACA period. The decentralized terrain of public committee afforded differing degrees of exclusivity, access, and openness, depending on the agency and on the task. Some forms of participation – such as item reviews for the National Assessment of Education Progress – allowed hundreds of educators and parents to participate in reviewing assessment questions.[79] Others – such as the National Academy of Sciences committees convened to help the FDA review drugs for efficacy that had been approved before the 1962 Kefauver amendments, were tightly constrained to the point that meeting locations and participant lists were kept secret. In general, procedures for openness such as widely distributed meeting announcements, public availability of meeting transcripts, and opportunities for the press and anyone else to attend were rare in the pre-FACA era. On the one hand, participation on public committees and published committee reports offered portals of access to government decision making. On the other, knowledge trickled rather than flowed from some corners of agency policymaking. Restricted information exchanges appeared to prevail in

---

[76] James H. Beggs, Undersecretary of Transportation, Department of Transportation, U.S. Congress, Senate, *Advisory Committees*, Hearings on S.1637, S.1964, and S.2064 before the Subcommittee on Intergovernmental Relations of the Committee on Government Operations, 92nd Congress, 1st Session, October 6, 7, 8, and 11, part 3 (Washington, DC: GPO, 1971), pp. 629–630.

[77] See the statement of Charles Stewart, U.S. Congress, Senate, *Advisory Committees*, Hearings on S.3067 before the Subcommittee on Intergovernmental Relations of the Committee on Government Operations, 91st Congress, 2nd Session, October 6 and 7, part 1 (Washington, DC: GPO, 1970), p. 37.

[78] U.S. Congress, Senate, *Advisory Committees*, Hearings on S.1637, S.1964, and S.2064 before the Subcommittee on Intergovernmental Relations of the Committee on Government Operations, 92nd Congress, 1st Session, October 6, 7, 8, and 11, part 3 (Washington, DC: GPO, 1971), p. 633.

[79] These item review panels were not designated "federal advisory committees," but reveal a related and important source of public participation.

the varied and decentralized terrain of American public committees before the passage of the FACA.

CONTINUITY AND TRANSFORMATION: BUREAUCRATIZING AND DEMOCRATIZING THROUGH THE FEDERAL ADVISORY COMMITTEE ACT OF 1972

The 1972 FACA in many ways codified governing procedures that the executive branch established in the 1950s, 1960s, and early 1970s. Yet, FACA also bureaucratized and democratized public committees in new ways. It put the vast terrain of American public committees under the centralized auspices of the Office of Management and Budget (and later the General Services Administration), and created common procedures to justify committee creation and maintenance. FACA juxtaposed greater committee centralization with new procedures for transparency and openness, including public meeting announcements and publicly available transcripts. By opening new frontiers for both bureaucracy and democracy, FACA expressed the tension between bureaucratic administration and democratic accountability while laying the potential foundation for both to develop simultaneously.

Though occasional congressional involvement in public committees appeared over the course of the nineteenth and first half of the twentieth centuries through appropriation riders and hearings,[80] the development and use of advisory committees occurred primarily under the auspices of the executive branch.[81] As of 1970, the General Accounting Office had conducted only one report of agency advisory committees: a 1960 review of committees affiliated with the Department of Agriculture.[82] Congressional attentiveness to

---

[80] U.S. Congress, House of Representatives, House Report 91–1731, *The Role and Effectiveness of Federal Advisory Committees*, Committee on Government Operations, December 11, (Washington, DC: GPO, 1970), p. 6. In 1842 and 1909, Congress expressed some authority over commissions, boards, and council through appropriations. See 5 Stat. 533. (1842) and 35 Stat. 1027. (1909). Referenced in Ginsberg, *Advisory Committees* p. 2 fn9. An example of post-FACA congressional intervention through appropriations arose when Congress stopped funding the National Industrial Pollution Control Council in 1974. Statement of David R. Obey, U.S. Congress, Senate, *Advisory Committees*, Oversight Hearings before the Subcommittee on Budgeting, Management and Expenditures of the Committee on Government Operations, 93rd Congress, 1st and 2nd Sessions on P.L. 92–463, November 29, December 13, 1973, and February 5, 1974 (Washington, DC: GPO, 1973–1974), p. 48.

[81] On Congressional unawareness of public advisory committees, see the statement of Senator Lee Metcalf (D-MT), U.S. Congress, Senate, *Advisory Committees*, Hearings before the Subcommittee on Intergovernmental Relations of the Committee on Government Operations, 92nd Congress, 1st Session, part 2 (Washington, DC: GPO, 1971), p. 439.

[82] U.S. General Accounting Office, "Statement of Elmer B. Staats before the House Committee on Government Operations in Connection with a Study of the Utilization and Operations of Interagency and Public Advisory Committees in the Federal Service," March 12, 1970, p. 10. The main conclusion was "that the department should provide for periodic, objective reviews of committee activities so as to maintain closer control" even though "we found no great deficiencies in management."

TABLE 3.1. *Major Formal Policies and Initiatives Guiding Public Committees,* *1950–1993*

Policy	Date	Key Provisions
Department of Justice Guidelines	10/19/1950	Specified that committees should: advise, not set policy; be authorized in statute or arise from an administrative finding; be convened and have agendas set by agency officials; should keep minutes.
HR 7390	1957	Proposed to extend DOJ guidelines across government agencies.
Bureau of the Budget Report	1959	Set forth "Standards and Procedures for the Utilization of Public Advisory Committees by Government Departments and Agencies."
Executive Order 11007	2/26/1962	Codified BOB rules on agenda setting; required minutes for non-industry committees; required transcripts for industry committees; established committee sunset provisions.
BOB Circular A-63	3/2/1964	Extended guidelines for advisory committees by building on EO 11007; focused on Inter-agency committees.
Executive Order 11671	6/5/1972	Required agencies to provide systematic committee information that would be compiled in an annual report to Congress, to open meetings to the public, to announce meetings in the *Federal* Register, and to keep detailed, public records of meeting proceedings.
Federal Advisory Committee Act	1972	Codified major elements of EO 11007. Required: meetings to be announced in *Federal Register*; meetings to be open to the public (with exceptions); balanced membership on Congressionally created committees; centralized executive branch annual review of committees.
Executive Order 11686	10/7/1972	Established Committee Management Secretariat in OMB; developed federal advisory committee implementation guidelines.
OMB Circular A-63	3/27/1974[83]	Provided guidelines on operation of advisory committees including process for creating advisory committees, renewing advisory committees, terminating committees, public participation, and closing meetings.
FACA Amendments	1977	Brought Sunshine Act provisions to bear on federal advisory committees.

(cont.)

TABLE 3.1. *(cont.)*

Policy	Date	Key Provisions
Executive Order 12024	12/1/1977	Transferred advisory committee oversight responsibility from the OMB to the GSA.
Executive Order 12838	2/10/1993	Limited the number of advisory committees and required agencies to eliminate at least one-third of all nonstatutory committees.

federal advisory committees gathered steam in the early 1970s. Rhetoric in the 1970s continued two themes raised in the mid 1950s – waste[84] and potential corruption[85] – and legislative proposals focused on two remedies – greater centralization and greater openness.[86]

Despite President Kennedy's 1962 Executive Order 11007 and the Bureau of the Budget's 1964 Circular A-63, the House Committee on Government Operations asserted that committees lacked centralized oversight and systematic review. The decentralized terrain left too much to individual agency discretion, the House Committee claimed, and even prevented Congress from knowing how many committees were in operation.[87] Reports on the number of committees in operation in 1970 and 1971 varied from 1,200 to as many as 3,200 committees.[88] Congressional advocates alleged that the lack of centralized

[83] Published in the *Federal Register* on April 5, 1974, effective May 1, 1974.

[84] On waste, see U.S. Congress, House of Representatives, House Report No. 91–1731, *The Role and Effectiveness of Federal Advisory Committees,* Committee on Government Operations, 43rd Report, 91st Congress, 2nd Session, December 11 (Washington, DC: GPO, 1970); U.S. Congress, Senate, *Advisory Committees,* Hearings on S.1964 and S.2064 Before the Subcommittee on Intergovernmental Relations of the Senate Committee on Government Operations, 92nd Congress, 1st session (Washington, DC: GPO, 1971). Some of the allegations of wastefulness focused on presidential advisory committees. For a general discussion of themes raised in FACA, see Croley and Funk, "The Federal Advisory Committee Act and Good Government," pp. 461–463.

[85] Croley and Funk note that Senate concerns about capture focused on several advisory committees, including the National Industrial Pollution Control Council, the Council on Environmental Quality, and the Advisory Council on Federal Reports. Croley and Funk, "The Federal Advisory Committee Act and Good Government," pp. 462–463.

[86] On 1957 proposals, see *Congressional Record – House,* July 10, 1957 on Amending the Administrative Expenses Act of 1946, pp. 11247.

[87] U.S. Congress, House of Representatives, House Report 91–1731, *The Role and Effectiveness of Federal Advisory Committees,* Committee on Government Operations, December 11 (Washington, DC: GPO, 1970), pp. 6, 9. On the inability to account for all committees, see pp. 13–14.

[88] Different counts of the number of federal advisory committees appear in the following: U.S. Congress, Senate, *Journal of the Senate,* 92nd Congress, 1st session, May 26, 1971 (Washington, DC: GPO, 1971), p. 381, cited in Ginsberg, *Advisory Committees,* p.6 fn28. Statement from Arnold Weber, Associate Director of OMB, U.S. Congress, Senate, *Advisory Committees,* Hearings before the Subcommittee on Intergovernmental Relations of the Committee on

oversight enabled committee irrelevance and waste. Congress pointed to examples, such as the Marine Corps Memorial Commission, which accomplished little between 1947 and 1970,[89] or the Advisory Committee on 2, 4, 5 T, which received subsequent public and scientific rebuke, to support its claims of committee uselessness lurking in the sprawling federal advisory committee terrain.[90] Waste – or committees outliving their usefulness – was also a primary critique raised in the General Accounting Office's 1970 review.[91] Beneath calls for greater efficiency came mounting legislative attention to the potential for agencies to use public advice to promote agency decisions,[92] such as the FDA use of advisors to justify an agency decision regarding cyclamates.[93]

Key provisions of the 1972 FACA codified prevailing executive branch policy. Executive branch agencies largely retained authority over setting committee agendas, calling meetings and selecting committee members, all of which comprise important sources of conventional policymaking power. Yet the Act also laid the foundation for more broadly exerting centralized authority over advisory committee operations. The Act's provisions for greater centralization through the Office of Management and Budget[94] and later the General

Government Operations, 92nd Congress, 1st Session, part 2 (Washington, DC: GPO, 1971), pp. 530, 702–736. The First Annual Report of the President on federal advisory committees reported 1,439 committees in operation in 1972. White House, "Federal Advisory Committees: First Annual Report of the President, March 1973," p. 4. The OMB repeated the 1,439 estimate in congressional testimony. U.S. Congress, Senate, *Advisory Committees*, Oversight Hearings before the Subcommittee on Budgeting, Management and Expenditures of the Committee on Government Operations, 93rd Congress, 1st and 2nd Sessions on P.L. 92–463, November 29, December 13, 1973, and February 5, 1974 (Washington, DC: GPO, 1973–1974), p. 2.

[89] U.S. Congress, House of Representatives, House Report 91–1731, *The Role and Effectiveness of Federal Advisory Committees*, Committee on Government Operations, December 11 (Washington, DC: GPO, 1970), p. 8.

[90] U.S. Congress, Senate, *Advisory Committees*, Hearings before the Subcommittee on Intergovernmental Relations of the Committee on Government Operations, 92nd Congress, 1st Session, part 3 (Washington, DC: GPO, 1971), pp. 792–806.

[91] U.S. General Accounting Office, "Statement of Elmer B. Staats before the House Committee on Government Operations in Connection with a Study of the Utilization and Operations of Interagency and Public Advisory Committees in the Federal Service, March 12, 1970," p. 15.

[92] For more on agency use of public committees to "sell" agency decisions or programs, among other uses, see Brown, *The Public Advisory Board in the Federal Government*, pp. 449–454.

[93] U.S. Congress, House of Representatives, House Report 91–1731, *The Role and Effectiveness of Federal Advisory Committees*, Committee on Government Operations, December 11 (Washington, DC: GPO, 1970), fn 105, p. 17. See also U.S. Congress, House of Representatives, *House Report No. 91–1595*, Committee on Government Operations of House of Representatives, October 8 (Washington, D.C.: GPO, 1970), pp. 7–13, 16.

[94] For a summary of OMB administrative actions in the years following the FACA, see the statement of Frederic Malek, Deputy Director of the OMB, U.S. Congress, Senate, *Advisory Committees*, Oversight Hearings before the Subcommittee on Budgeting, Management and Expenditures of the Committee on Government Operations, 93rd Congress, 1st and 2nd Sessions on P.L. 92–463, November 29, December 13, 1973, and February 5, 1974 (Washington, DC: GPO, 1973–1974), pp. 98–99.

Services Administration enabled Congress to access a more predictable stream of information about public committees.[95] Developing common committee reporting procedures also supported subsequent presidential efforts to reduce the overall number of agency committees.[96]

FACA also enabled new means for public engagement and for Congressional oversight of federal advisory committees through its reporting and transparency provisions.[97] Statements about the potential to use committees as Congressional watchdogs – a form of participatory oversight – began to appear in the 1970s.[98] The Act brought more openness to public committees in several ways. It ended industry-only committees and created "balanced membership" requirements for committees created by Congress. The Act also required committees and their sponsoring agencies to notify the public through the *Federal Register* of upcoming meetings, to allow the public to attend the meetings, to allow the public to participate in meetings by submitting comments, to record meeting minutes that contained details about committee participants, documents and conclusions, and to develop systematic procedures for making those minutes publicly available.[99]

FACA transparency provisions are nevertheless limited in several respects. Congress, for one, can exempt committees and boards from falling under FACA's purview. For instance, the Commission on Online Child Protection is exempt from FACA,[100] as are committees advising the Central Intelligence Agency and the Federal Reserve Board.[101] For another, commentators note that FACA does little to prevent agencies from closing meetings to public participation and that the act offered little guidance or legal muscle for obtaining balanced committee membership.[102]

Legislative rhetoric surrounding FACA cast government agencies in familiar bureaucratic terms. Legislators issued familiar warnings of bureaucratic secrecy

---

[95] For a list of committees and members in 1973, see U.S. Congress, Senate, Committee Print, *Federal Advisory Committees: Report of the President to the Congress Including Data on Individual Committees*, March 1973, Subcommittee on Budgeting, Management and Expenditures of the Committee on Government Operations, Part 5, Index, January 7 (Washington, DC: GPO, 1974).

[96] 58 *Federal Register* 28, February 10, 1993; Ginsberg, *Advisory Committees: A Primer*.

[97] Subsequent amendments in 1977 brought Sunshine Act (P.L. 94-4) provisions to bear on federal advisory committees. For more on this point, see Ginsberg, *Advisory Committees: A Primer*, p. 9.

[98] U.S. Congress, Senate, *Advisory Committees*, Hearings on S.3067 before the Subcommittee on Intergovernmental Relations of the Committee on Government Operations, 91st Congress, 2nd Session, October 8 and 9, part 2, (Washington, DC: GPO, 1970), p. 208.

[99] Reviewed in Croley and Funk, "The Federal Advisory Committee Act and Good Government," p. 464.

[100] Wendy R. Ginsberg, *Advisory Committees: A Primer* (Washington, DC: U.S. Congressional Research Service, 2008), p. CRS-10.

[101] Cardozo, "The Federal Advisory Committee Act," p. 12.

[102] Cardozo, "The Federal Advisory Committee Act," p. 11.

inimical to democratic governance. Agency leaders offered familiar bureaucratic justifications for discretion: to apply and develop their expertise. Even though some agency officials testified to their willingness to open meetings,[103] legislative provisions related to greater openness met stiff resistance from federal agencies including the National Institutes of Health and NASA, especially a proposal to reserve one-third of membership slots for the general public.[104] The one-third provision was removed from the ultimate 1972 FACA, but provisions for public meeting notices, meeting transcripts, and opportunities for the public to attend and make statements at committee meetings remained.[105]

Beneath these familiar arguments resided a significant challenge facing bureaucratic administration: implementing complex policy in America's loosely jointed, fragmented state. In the words of Senator William Roth (R-DE), "as the function of Government has become more complex and the decisions more difficult, numerous advisory committee have sprung up to advise the President and other decision-makers in the Federal Agencies and the Congress."[106] Agency leaders echoed this point. Noting that the HEW was tasked with implementing 300 programs in 1975, Assistant Secretary John D. Young stated, "Usually the more amorphous the program given us to carry out, the more useful the advice from an advisory committee."[107]

[103] See the statement of Arnold Weber, Associate Director of OMB, U.S. Congress, *Advisory Committees*, Hearings before the Subcommittee on Intergovernmental Relations of the Committee on Government Operations, 92nd Congress, 1st Session, part 2 (Washington, DC: GPO, 1971), p. 521.

[104] For opposition to the House proposals for meeting announcements, transcript requirements, and for one-third of committee members to be members of the public, alleging it would transform committees to "debating clubs" and "destroy their use to the Department," see the testimony of Larry Jobe, Assistant Secretary of Commerce, U.S. Congress, Senate, *Advisory Committees*, Hearings before the Subcommittee on Intergovernmental Relations of the Committee on Government Operations, 92nd Congress, 1st Session, part 2 (Washington, DC: GPO, 1971), pp. 389–397. For more reaction to congressional openness and transparency procedures from the Departments of Agriculture, Interior, and State, see U.S. Congress, Senate, *Advisory Committees*, Hearings before the Subcommittee on Intergovernmental Relations of the Committee on Government Operations, 92nd Congress, 1st Session, June 10–11, part 1 (Washington, DC: GPO, 1971), pp. 126, 129, 131, 132. On reaction from the Department of Transportation, Treasury, and the Federal Power Commission to membership and transcript proposals, see U.S. Congress, Senate, *Advisory Committees*, Hearings before the Subcommittee on Intergovernmental Relations of the Committee on Government Operations, 92nd Congress, 1st Session, part 2 (Washington, DC: GPO, 1971), pp. 598, 600, 606, 608–610.

[105] U.S. Congress, Senate, Senate Report No. 92–1098, *Federal Advisory Committee Act*, Committee on Government Operations, 92nd Congress, 2nd Session, September 7 (Washington, D.C.: GPO, 1972), p. 16.

[106] See, for instance, U.S. Congress, Senate, *Journal of the Senate*, 92nd Congress, 1st session, May 26, 1971 (Washington, DC: GPO, 1971), p. 381. Cited in Ginsberg, *Advisory Committees: A Primer*, (2010), p. 6 fn28.

[107] Letter from Assistant Secretary Young to GAO Comptroller General Ahart, November 30, 1976, included in U.S. General Accounting Office, *Better Evaluations Needed to Weed Out Useless Federal Advisory Committees*, April 7, 1977 (Washington, DC: GAO, 1977), p. 66.

The 1957 House Committee Report criticized agencies for using advisory committees to "enlist support of the regulated in the process of regulation."[108] Yet, as noted in Chapter 2, Herbert Simon and his colleagues famously observed in the same era as the 1957 House committee report, "If the people to be regulated do not know what they are supposed to do, they *cannot* do it; and if they do not agree with what they are supposed to do, many of them *will* not do it."[109] Insufficient information exchange risks yielding policy failure, which bureaucrats strive to avoid and which bureaucratic administration is, in principle, supposed to discourage. Beyond drumming up political support or privileging particular interests, public participation through public committees offered agencies a potential venue for creating and exchanging knowledge potentially vital for policy implementation and bureaucratic administration.[110] "[T]he organization is not monolithic," public administration scholar David Brown reminded Congress in his 1970 testimony.[111] Public committees offer agencies a means of managing their interdependence.

CONCLUSION

The rhetoric surrounding the development of FACA expresses the multiple potential manifestations of public participation specified in Chapter 2: to promote decisions that have already been made, to support internal agency learning, to cultivate privileged interests, to oversee government agencies, to enable implementation, and to develop new knowledge where none currently exists. Did early efforts at public participation for pharmaceutical regulation and education assessments manage the tension between bureaucratic administration and democratic accountability through participatory bureaucracy; and, if so, when? We turn to these questions next.

The institutional pillars created through agency guidelines, through Executive Order 11007 and through FACA standardized aspects of public participation in agency policymaking. The degree to which public participation supports bureaucratic administration and/or democratic accountability, however,

---

[108] U.S. Congress, House of Representatives, House Report 85–576, *Amending the Administrative Expenses Act of 1946, and for Other Purposes*, 85th Congress, 1st session, June 17 (Washington, DC: GPO, 1957), p. 5.

[109] Herbert A. Simon, Victor A. Thompson, and Donald W. Smithburg, *Public Administration* (New York: Alfred A. Knopf, 1950), p. 415.

[110] For thoughtful analysis of efforts to use public committees to generate public and political demand for agency programs and policy preferences, as well as how experts' public disagreement undermined policy support, see Brian Balogh, *Chain Reaction: Expert Debate and Public Participation in American Commercial Nuclear Power, 1945–1975* (New York: Cambridge University Press, 1991).

[111] Statement of David S. Brown, U.S. Congress, Senate, *Advisory Committees*, Hearings on S.3067 before the Subcommittee on Intergovernmental Relations of the Committee on Government Operations, 91st Congress, 2nd Session, October 6 and 7, part 1 (Washington, D.C.: GPO, 1970), p. 33.

ultimately depends on the task and specific participatory arrangement. In the account of public committees' development for pharmaceutical regulation and educational assessments that follows, we see agencies grapple with problems that Dewey identified: the fundamental interdependence of the public, policy-makers, grassroots practice, and emergent problems. Public committees' pre-FACA existence is a testament to government agencies' efforts to reach beyond government hierarchy to gather and distribute information. Public committees' post-FACA endurance is a testament to agencies' continued pursuit of public engagement, even when participation facilitates congressional scrutiny, fluid participation, and knowledge that agencies cannot control.

4

Making Educational Performance Public

Reporting on the Progress of Education

> If it could be published annually from this capital through every school district of the United States that there are states in the Union that have no system of common schools ... It would shame out of their delinquency all the delinquent states.
>
> Representative James Garfield, (R-OH), 1866[1]

> The purpose of this letter is to invite you to a small unpublicized conference on methods for assessing the level of educational attainment in the United States. This conference is being sponsored by the Carnegie Corporation with the cooperation of the United States Office of Education.
>
> Letter to Ralph Tyler from John W. Gardner, November 7, 1963[2]

Within the vast terrain of federal level public committees, when do different forms of participation emerge, and what are their implications for bureaucratic administration and democratic accountability? The themes of decentralization and exclusivity that characterized debate over the development of public committees in the twentieth century manifested in participatory processes related to the collection and use of educational statistics and assessments. Looking closely at the development of public committees for educational assessments also reveals variation in the conditions yielding different kinds of participation, as expected. The field of education statistics and assessments allows us to look at a wide spectrum of public participation – from unpublicized participation in nongovernmental venues to commissions composed of nationally prominent individuals to panels of parents and educators to committees consisting of conventionally defined technical experts. Some of these committees have

---

[1] Speech of James A. Garfield, U.S. House of Representatives, June 8, 1866, on a bill "To Establish a National Bureau of Education." Harry Kursh, *The United States Office of Education* (Philadelphia: Chilton Company, 1965), pp. 10–11.
[2] Carnegie Corporation of New York Archives, Columbia University, Box 516.3.

offered only advice. Others have been empowered to make policy. Through this variation, the field of education statistics and assessments gives witness to the limits of the Federal Advisory Committee Act. Not all venues for participation in operation after 1972 fall under the auspices of FACA: institutional explanations take us only part of the way in understanding the emergence, use, and impact of participatory processes.

Reflecting the general terrain of American federal public committees, public committees for education statistics and assessments emerged initially from executive branch initiative, though they have not always been under executive branch control. As task conditions vary – more/less agency task expertise, more/less agency task jurisdiction – so too have the forms that participation has taken, ranging from private learning, to promoting executive branch policy, to public educating, to developing new knowledge.

THE DEVELOPMENT OF EDUCATIONAL STATISTICS AND ASSESSMENTS

On a general level, the field of education statistics and assessments expresses the collision of the Weberian ideal of "control on the basis of knowledge" with the Deweyan reality of fundamental interdependence. Since the earliest days of the original U.S. Department of Education, the federal government has attempted to use knowledge as a policy instrument: to deploy statistics and assessments to push states and localities to change their educational practices.

The federal government largely stayed out of the business of American public education for most of the nation's first 100 years, leaving authority over children's education primarily in local and state hands.[3] When elected officials initiated a departmental-level federal role in education, they did so with an eye toward gathering and distributing knowledge: the Department of Education began with a mandate to collect and distribute education statistics. From the perspective of Congressman James Garfield (R-OH), collecting and disseminating information on basic school information could work as a policy instrument and propel states to provide common schools. Congressman Garfield, who sponsored the bill to create a Bureau of Education, argued that a federal education agency would be able to, in his words, "use that power, so effective in this country, of letting in light on subjects and holding them up to the verdict of public opinion." While common schools – the American foundation to current traditional public schools – flourished in northeastern and midwestern states in the second half of the nineteenth century, they were slow to take root in southern states. Congressman Garfield argued that if school records from systems that did not offer common schools could be publicly compared with the records of states that did have common schools, "the mere statement of the

---

[3] Early federal involvement in education traces to the 1862 Morrill Act, which established land grant schools.

fact would rouse their energies, and compel them for shame to educate their children."[4]

Publicizing previously unrecorded state and local practices, the Department of Education's proponents claimed, would induce states and localities to expand common schools. The federal agency would not keep this information to itself, but "[diffuse] such information respecting the organization and management of schools and school systems, and methods of teaching."[5] Making federal data collections open and public offered opportunities to make locally controlled American schools potentially more visible as well. Knowledge, it seemed, could be liquefied.

The federal education agency[6] implemented its task for its first 100 years by describing levels of school enrollment, attendance, salaries, graduation rates, basic school expenditures, and other conventional school resources.[7] The federal agency[8] created surveys, distributed them to the known universe of schools, compiled the results, and released biennial or annual comprehensive volumes of descriptive data.[9] Through a twenty-first-century lens, descriptive data on school expenditures appears relatively modest: such data are ill equipped to explain differences in children's achievement, for instance. In late nineteenth-century America, descriptive data marked a bold and controversial expansion of federal authority that sparked controversy as well as state

---

[4] Speech of James A. Garfield, U.S. House of Representatives, June 8, 1866, on a bill "To Establish a National Bureau of Education" cited in Kursh, *The United States Office of Education*, pp. 10–11.

[5] 14 Stat. 434. *An Act to Establish a Department of Education*, March 2, 1867.

[6] The Department of Education moved into the Department of the Interior in 1869 and changed its name to the Office of Education. It moved from Interior to the Federal Security Agency in 1939. It then moved under the auspices of the Department of Health Education and Welfare in 1953. It reemerged as the Department of Education in 1980. W. Vance Grant, "Statistics in the US Department of Education: Highlights from the past 120 years," in *120 Years of American Education: A Statistical Portrait*, edited by Thomas D. Snyder (Washington, DC: National Center for Education Statistics, 1993), p. 1.

[7] U.S. General Accounting Office, *The National Assessment of Educational Progress: Its Results Need to be Made More Useful* (Washington, DC: GPO, 1976), pp. 2–3; Dorothy Gilford, "NAEP and the US Office of Education, 1971–1974," in *The Nation's Report Card: Evolution and Perspectives*, edited by Lyle V. Jones and Ingram Olkin (Bloomington, IN: Phi Delta Kappa Educational Foundation, 2004), p. 166; Grant, "Statistics in the US Department of Education," pp. 1–5. Grant describes how the information the department collected expanded from enrollment information to more detailed descriptions of expenditures. Gilford describes these kinds of data as educational "inputs."

[8] Grant, "The Statistics in the US Department of Education," p. 1. Like the Department of Education, the National Center for Education Statistics has had a number of different names and homes since 1870. For clarity, it is referred to as the National Center of Education Statistics here, even though its names have included the Research and Statistical Services Branch, the Educational Statistics Branch, and the Division of Educational Statistics, among others.

[9] Grant, "The Statistics in the US Department of Education," p. 2. This came to include both private and public schools, colleges, and universities.

and local opposition.[10] Gathering data could bring more transparency to state and local educational operations, which could threaten existing state and local authority. The emerging federal agency's pursuit of transparency collided with state and local interests in secrecy: in preventing knowledge from developing. Congress demoted the fledgling Department to an Office, cast it over to the Department of Interior – whose secretary opposed a federal role in education – and significantly reduced the commissioner's salary, all within the agency's first two years.[11]

Opposition aside, developing the knowledge and capacity to collect descriptive education data was no small matter. American schooling has always entailed a sprawling, loosely coordinated enterprise, not only nationally but also within states.[12] No centralized hierarchy linked local school districts to state administrators to federal officials. When the federal education agency received its original mandate to gather and distribute education statistics, no "authentic list" of schools and colleges existed.[13] Moreover, the Department of Education consisted initially of only the commissioner and three clerks.[14] Even with ample staff and complete lists, collecting reliable data on enrollment, staffing, and school finances posed operational challenges. Student mobility can frustrate accurate enrollment counts. Variation in states' and schools' definitions of students, staff, schools, and finances can frustrate efforts to aggregate and compare results. Federal dependence on states and localities further complicated data collection. Neither in 1867 nor in 1967 did federal officials march into classrooms, count bodies, review school ledgers, and collect the data themselves. Instead, federal leadership relied on state and local officials to complete forms accurately and return them to the federal agency, originally with the help of only a few field agents to encourage data submissions from non-respondents.[15] Collecting data entails an inherent degree of mutual dependence among survey designers, data collectors, respondents, analysts, and report writers.

---

[10] Kursh, *The United States Office of Education*, p. 10.
[11] Kursh, *The United States Office of Education*, pp. 13–16.
[12] Although states have constitutional authority over education, they largely passed that authority on to localities for much of the nation's first 200 years. David K. Cohen, "Policy and Organization: The Impact of State and Federal Educational Policy on School Governance," *Harvard Educational Review* 52 (1982): 474–499; David K. Cohen and James P. Spillane, "Policy and Practice: The Relations Between Governance and Instruction," in *The Future of Education: Perspectives on National Standards in Education*, edited by Nina Cobb (New York: College Entrance Examination Board, 1994), pp. 112–113.
[13] Grant, "Statistics in the US Department of Education," p. 1.
[14] Grant, "Statistics in the US Department of Education," p.1. Congress authorized the department to hire a statistician in 1872. Capability in state departments of education was similarly modest.
[15] Grant, "Statistics in the US Department of Education," p. 2. The department used field agents from 1923 to 1962, but managed to achieve workable response rates.

By 1875, the federal education agency managed to compile "complete" lists of "nearly all grades of schools," which developed into an architecture for collecting descriptive data.[16] Over the next 100 years, the federal agency shuffled between departmental homes, enjoyed few financial and personnel resources, generated low visibility, and produced little in the way of knowledge to "shame" states and localities to improve educational practices.[17] Every other year, and then every year, the agency would release volumes of descriptive data.[18] These arrangements enabled a modest public information infrastructure to take shape,[19] and left much about state and local practice unobserved.

School data did occasionally emerge in political debates. The commissioner of education in 1934, George F. Zook, for instance, used descriptive data to make his case for federal school support during the Great Depression. In a pamphlet entitled, "The Crisis in Education," Commissioner Zook used basic descriptive information – including the number of children affected by closed schools, the number of teachers receiving less than the minimum wage, reductions in school services, increasing student-teacher ratios, and shortened school years – to portray dire conditions in public schools and justify his call for financial aid.[20]

In addition to releasing statistics such as these in the Department of Interior's pamphlet, Commissioner Zook invited public participation, albeit on a limited scale. The commissioner convened a Federal Advisory Committee on Emergency Aid in Education, chaired by James H. Richmond, Kentucky's superintendent of public education, and included representatives from twenty organizations, including the American Federation of Teachers. Thinking about task conditions that vary in terms of information and interdependence, school finance represented a case where the federal government had information on local educational financial needs, but lacked jurisdiction. In conditions of relatively high government agency information, we expect the audience for agency-initiated

---

[16] Grant, "Statistics in the US Department of Education," p. 1.

[17] From 1870 through 1917, results appeared in *The Annual Report of the Commissioner of Education*. From 1917 through 1958, these results appeared in *The Biennial Survey of Education in the United States* and in *The Digest of Education Statistics* starting in 1962. Grant, "Statistics in the US Department of Education," p. 3.

[18] Results from 1953–1954, for instance, were reported in the following way: "In 1953–54, enrollment in public elementary and secondary schools reached a new peak, 28,836,052 pupils. Of these, 22,545,807 (78.2 percent) were enrolled in kindergarten through grade 8 inclusive; and 6,290245 (21.8 percent) were in grades 9–12 and postgraduate work." U.S. Office of Education, U.S. Department of Health, Education and Welfare, *Biennial Survey of Education in the United States: Statistical Summary of Education 1953–54* (Washington, DC: GPO, 1958), p. 23.

[19] On the development of state capacity and an information infrastructure, see Tracy Steffes, *School, Society and the State: A New Education to Govern Modern America, 1890–1940* (Chicago: University of Chicago Press, 2012).

[20] Reported in the *Congressional Record*, House of Representatives, January 15, 1934, pp. 657–659. See the comments of Comments of Representative Ernest Lundeen (Farmer-Labor Party, MN).

public participation to be outward-oriented rather than inward-oriented, to educate outsiders rather than teach the agency. The committee concluded that "only through liberal Federal aid can the Nation's schools be rescued from unsanitary and unsafe buildings and over-crowded conditions,"[21] consistent with the commissioner's position. A second forum, the federal Advisory Committee on Education, established in 1937, revisited the issue of federal funding for public and private schools. The committee's invited participants included unions, Catholic organizations, business interests, administrators, and teachers.[22] Once again, the Office of Education wove together both education statistics and limited public participation to press for an extended federal role in education. In conditions of relatively high agency information but low jurisdiction, the participatory audience once again appeared outward-oriented rather than inward-oriented (Quadrant C from Figure 1.1). This form of participation could be understood as a way to distribute knowledge, or, as congressional critics later charged, a way to engage in a "selling campaign" that issued "favorable public statements by committee members and the interest groups."[23]

While significant federal financial support for local schools would not materialize until the 1965 Elementary and Secondary Education Act, the intersection of education statistics and public participation offered federal officials an additional pathway for potentially influencing aspects of American public education.

LETTING IN LIGHT: THE NATIONAL ASSESSMENT OF
EDUCATION PROGRESS

Nearly 100 years after the federal education agency began, subsequent Office of Education leadership rekindled the agency's original purpose to use public knowledge to press for educational improvement. In 1962, Commissioner of Education Francis (Frank) Keppel initiated steps toward conducting an assessment that would help reveal and possibly explain levels of student achievement across the United States. In subsequent testimony to Congress, Commissioner Keppel advocated collecting very different kinds of data to implement the task of reporting on the condition and progress of education: information on student achievement as well as on the conventional resources schools and states

[21] Comments of Representative Ernest Lundeen (Farmer-Labor Party, MN), *Congressional Record*, House of Representatives, January 15, 1934, p. 659. Report of the Federal Advisory Committee on Emergency Aid in Education, published in the *Congressional Record*, January 15, 1934, p. 658.

[22] See Ann Marie Ryan, "Keeping Every Catholic Child in a Catholic School During the Great Depression, 1933–1939," *Catholic Education* 11 (2007): 157–175, see pp. 168–170.

[23] U.S. Congress, House of Representatives, House Report 85-576, *Amending the Administrative Expenses Act of 1946, and for Other Purposes*, 85th Congress, 1st session, June 17 (Washington, DC: GPO, 1957), p. 5.

applied to education.[24] He called for a national assessment of educational progress.

Similar to Congressman Garfield's call to let in the light from one hundred years earlier, agency leaders, including Commissioner Keppel, pitched the assessment as consistent with the charge to "show the condition and progress of education." The underlying purpose was akin to one the Department's founders proposed in 1867: to press states and localities to attend to improved educational practice, consistent with Keppel's "conviction that there were serious weaknesses in [American schools'] curriculum and that they should be exposed."[25] Reflecting on the condition of education in the early 1960s, Keppel claimed:

> There was an information problem ... no data existed to supply ... facts on the quality and condition of what children learned. The nation could find out about school buildings or discover how many years children stayed in school; it had no satisfactory way of assessing whether the time spent in school was effective.[26]

Reporting on the condition of education, from Keppel's perspective, was not merely a means of updating Congress, but an opportunity to produce new knowledge that might provoke improvements in American schooling. Keppel's vision would expand tasks beyond merely collecting data to reporting data in ways that might promote school improvement at the local level.

Keppel's tenure as commissioner coincided with a period of tremendous pressure on American schools stemming from burgeoning enrollments, concern about links between education and the economy,[27] and complicated issues of poverty, race, and civil rights. In this context, Keppel advocated expanding the federal role in American schooling.[28] Yet, the federal government had few means – little knowledge, limited funds, and limited authority – to affect change in America's schools. As commissioner of education, Keppel filled the top federal education post, but he enjoyed limited formal capacity to govern states and localities. He could not command states and localities to make curricular changes, engage in particular instructional practices, or devote funds to particular programs or students. Even with the Progressive reforms of the early

---

[24] J. A. Hazlett, *A History of the National Assessment of Educational Progress, 1963–1974* (Doctoral dissertation. University of Kansas, 1974), pp. 352–353. Keppel's 1963 testimony included, "It has often been pointed out that America lacks standards by which it can measure educational results, and stimulate its students to greater accomplishment ... we have no reliable means by which to judge the vast output of some 33,000 heterogeneous school districts." Quoted in Hazlett, *A History of the National Assessment of Educational Progress*, p. 353.

[25] Hazlett, *A History of the National Assessment*, p. 66. OE's routine data collections did not assess curricula, instructional practice, and student achievement in the period before NAEP.

[26] Francis Keppel, *The Necessary Revolution in American Education* (New York: Harper & Row, Publishers, 1966), pp. 108–109.

[27] Keppel wrote about the emergence of "the idea that education is a factor in economic growth." Keppel, *The Necessary Revolution in American Education*, p. 50.

[28] Keppel, *The Necessary Revolution in American Education*, pp. 108–109.

twentieth century, American public schooling lacked the hierarchical cohesiveness embodied in its Western European cousins. In the early 1960s, observers described Congress as a "graveyard for federal aid to education" legislation: Commissioner Keppel could not shape schooling by infusing federal funds into local programs.[29] Keppel did, however, have authority to report on the condition and progress of American schools. Generating and distributing knowledge on American schooling constituted one of the primary policy instruments at Keppel's disposal to approach his task.

Reporting on the progress of education, from a bureaucratic perspective, offered Keppel a way to capitalize on the fundamental interconnectedness of American schooling, the upside of weak federal hierarchical authority. The interdependence of national, state, and local contributions to American schooling meant that making data from one level more visible had the potential to spill visibility over into the others. A *national* assessment of educational progress could provide both a national picture of student achievement and a picture of what states and localities were up to: it could open multiple points of visibility. The potential power of national achievement information, in this sense, could open new frontiers of public governance.[30] Augmenting the information at federal officials' disposal could augment information for policymakers and practitioners elsewhere in the disparate nooks of America's loosely connected educational system. Keppel could not order state and local changes, but getting information into the hands of multiple political actors – state officials, organized interests, educators, parents – offered avenues for affecting change that extended well beyond the Office of Education's limited hierarchical capacity and authority.

In 1962, however, nobody had the comparative data on educational achievement Keppel wanted. The issue entailed producing new kinds of data. Collecting national-level data on, in Keppel's words, "whether children were learning well enough to adjust to the changing economy" departed markedly from practice both inside and outside government; the knowledge and authority to conduct

---

[29] Julie Roy Jeffrey, *Education for Children of the Poor: A Study of the Origins and Implementation of the Elementary and Secondary Education Act of 1965*, (Columbus: Ohio State University Press, 1978), p. 62. After repeated failures to pass legislation that would provide federal aid to schools, politicians and academics alike declared federal aid to schools a dead issue. See Hazlett, *A History of the National Assessment of Educational Progress*, p. 312; Frank J. Munger and Richard F. Fenno, *National Politics and Federal Aid to Education* (Syracuse, NY: Syracuse University Press, 1962). After Kennedy's assassination, the passage of the 1964 Civil Rights Act, and an influx of new Democratic members to Congress, however, Congress passed federal aid to education legislation in 1965: the Elementary and Secondary Education Act. On the ESEA, see David Cohen and Susan Moffitt, *The Ordeal of Equality* (Cambridge, MA: Harvard University Press, 2009), pp. 2–3; John F. Jennings, "Chapter 1: A View from Congress," *Educational Evaluation and Policy Analysis* 13 (1991): 335–338.

[30] See Cohen, "Policy and Organization," for a discussion of how the expansion of state and federal policy translated into organizational expansion across all levels and domains of educational practice.

such an assessment was not housed inside the Office of Education.[31] At the time, norm-referenced standardized tests based on multiple-choice questions dominated the field of commercially available assessments.[32] Measuring educational performance, from Keppel's perspective, would, in contrast, entail assessing achievement relative to particular learning objectives and reporting the educational equivalent of an unemployment rate – "a census … of knowledge, skills, understandings, and attitudes" of American students.[33] Measuring *progress* in student achievement, moreover, was not only novel but also technically difficult. It would entail measuring how successive populations of students performed at successive points in time. This would require developing comparable samples across time and space, which depended on securing both test takers' and administrators' participation. It also required stability in the assessment's instruments, which hinged on not only using the same questions repeatedly but also having those same questions measure or reflect the same concepts from one point in time to the next.[34]

When he assumed his post as commissioner of education, Keppel did not wait to follow Congress's lead on education policy: Congress remained deadlocked in debate over the scope of government, race, and religion in education throughout the early 1960s, failing repeatedly to produce legislation to address pressures facing the nation's schools.[35] He could not command states and localities to change. Instead, Keppel sought a new kind of knowledge, a new kind of visibility, that created room to expand federal influence as well as influence from myriad other sources: an assessment that would provide a

---

[31] Quote from Keppel, *The Necessary Revolution in American Education*, p. 109.

[32] GAO, *The National Assessment of Educational Progress*, pp. 8–10; Wayne Martin, "NAEP from Three Different Perspectives," in *The Nation's Report Card: Evolution and Perspectives*, edited by Lyle V. Jones and Ingram Olkin (Bloomington, IN: Phi Delta Kappa Educational Foundation, 2004), p. 309. Norm-referenced tests report student performance relative to other student scores, such as whether the student performed at the 10th percentile or the 90th percentile, relative to other test takers.

[33] William Greenbaum, Michael S. Garet, and Ellen R. Solomon, *Measuring Educational Progress: A Study of the National Assessment* (New York: McGraw-Hill Book Company, 1977), pp. 5, 115, 199; Frank Womer, *What Is National Assessment?* (Denver, CO: Education Commission of the States, 1968), p. 1. This would require first determining learning objectives, such as deciding which math skills should be tested for particular age or grade levels, and then reporting performance relative to those established objectives. This has taken a number of different forms throughout NAEP's history: x percent of students performed this exercise correctly; x percent of students received a score of 500 or more; x percent of students achieved at the basic math level.

[34] Questions about computer use from the 1970s, for instance, face validity problems when asked in 2004. See Michelle Galley, "Governing Board Considers Scrapping Long-Term NAEP," *Education Week* 21 (2001): 22. Science questions from the 1960s face similar problems.

[35] Nor did Congress participate in – or even know about – Keppel's earliest discussion with technical experts and foundation representatives, which laid the groundwork for the national assessment. See Hazlett, *A History of the National Assessment of Educational Progress*, p. 352.

window into educational achievement, capitalize on the interdependence of America's educational system, and potentially expose weaknesses in schooling.[36] A national assessment offered the federal agency a promising way to promote change despite weak federal authority, capacity, and knowledge. Yet, a national assessment itself posed authority, knowledge, and capacity problems: it would require capabilities that exceeded the agency's traditional practice and capacity to gather state and local data.

Putting this back into our schematic terms of reference from Figure 1.1, the task conditions facing Keppel approached a total lack of information and jurisdiction, creating task conditions conducive to participatory bureaucracy (Quadrant D). Indeed, Keppel approached this condition of fundamental interdependence and uncertainty by seeking public participation to develop a national educational assessment. At first, however, he did so privately, behind closed doors. Yet the participatory processes for the development and implementation of a national education assessment soon expanded well beyond the original conference room.

DEVELOPING KNOWLEDGE AND CAPABILITY THROUGH MULTIPLE FORMS OF PARTICIPATION

Private Participation

In 1962 and 1963, the Office of Education had little to lose, from a bureaucratic perspective, by including nongovernmental participants in federal policymaking, either in terms of what a national assessment might reveal or in the process of developing and administering that assessment. To the extent that a national assessment might reveal weak student performance, that weakness was unlikely to reflect failure on the part of the federal government: responsibility for American schools rested squarely on state and local shoulders.[37] Moreover, looking outside the federal government to develop a national assessment did not risk disrupting extant federal data collection routines and procedures: the

---

[36] Keppel promoted the assessment as a way to produce data to encourage states and localities to improve educational practices. Record of Interview 10/3/63 with Francis Keppel, Carnegie Corporation of New York Archives, Columbia University, Box 516.3.

[37] During the first half of the twentieth century, federal funding for education came from disparate agencies and served disparate purposes. The Department of Agriculture provided funds for school lunch programs. The Department of the Interior funded programs for Native American education. Various departments, including the Department of Commerce, Department of Defense, and Department of Treasury, provided funds for postsecondary institutions, such as military academies. See U.S. Office of Education, *Biennial Survey of Education in the United States: Statistical Summary of Education 1953–54* (Washington, DC: GPO, 1959). The federal government also funded Impact Aid for districts that housed government installations and vocational education aid. In the 1950s and 1960s, the National Science Foundation and the Office of Education sponsored curriculum development projects and NDEA fellowships. Peter B. Dow, *Schoolhouse Politics: Lessons from the Sputnik Era* (Cambridge, MA: Harvard University Press, 1991).

Office of Education,[38] at the time, had no standard operating procedures for collecting national student achievement data.[39]

Similar to the resistance that emerged in response to nineteenth-century efforts to collect national education data, Commissioner Keppel faced stiff opposition from some state and local administrators and teachers for an assessment that would compare relative state educational performance. Given the political intractability of initiating an effort to expose state and local educational weakness from within the Office of Education, Commissioner Keppel sought help from the Carnegie Corporation of New York to convene a panel of advisors and to hold exploratory meetings outside the federal government, with few traces of federal fingerprints.[40] For technical help Keppel called on Ralph Tyler, director of the Center for Advanced Study in the Behavioral Sciences at Stanford University, to develop a set of guiding principles on how a national assessment might be designed and administered. Using Tyler's design as a framework, Keppel helped arrange exploratory meetings outside the federal government within a private foundation and with a foundation president as the meeting's chair to discuss developing a national assessment.[41] The early meetings were private, unpublicized affairs.[42]

Group-Based Participation

After sketching a general architecture for an assessment program, proponents of the national assessment broadened participation in the assessment development

---

[38] Alexander Mood is credited with organizing the National Center for Educational Statistics (which later became the National Center for Education Statistics) while Assistant Commissioner of Education. He joined the Office of Education in 1964.

[39] Some organizations outside of the Office of Education had expertise to conduct educational assessments. In addition to norm-referenced standardized tests such as the Stanford Tests of Achievement, the American Institute of Research conducted the Project Talent study of educational achievement as part of a federal grant during the same time period as the National Assessment's development. Letter from Lorne H. Woollatt to Commissioner James E. Allen, Jr., December 5, 1963, Carnegie Corporation of New York Archives, Columbia University, Box 516.3. However, assessment architects worried that "competent technical manpower in the testing field is in short supply." "Summary Report: Two Conferences on a National Assessment of Educational Attainment, December 18/19 1963, January 27/28 1964, The Carnegie Corporation" prepared by David A. Goslin, Carnegie Corporation of New York Archives, Columbia University, Box 516.3.

[40] Agencies across the federal government looked to private foundations for expertise during this time period. See Brian Balogh, *Chain Reaction* (New York: Cambridge University Press, 1991), pp. 6–7, 22.

[41] For reviews of the early development of the national assessment, see: Hazlett, *A History of the National Assessment of Educational Progress*; Greenbaum, *Measuring Educational Progress*; Irvin J. Lehmann, "The Genesis of NAEP," in *The Nation's Report Card: Evolution and Perspectives*, edited by Lyle V. Jones and Ingram Olkin (Bloomington, IN: Phi Delta Kappa Educational Foundation, 2004), pp. 25–92.

[42] Letter from John Gardner to AP, 9/11/1963. Gardner wrote, "I feel sure that this should not be discussed outside the office at the present time." Carnegie Corporation of New York archives, Columbia University, Box 516.3.

process. With Carnegie Corporation funding, the exploratory meetings turned into an official exploratory committee, which turned into a foundation funded and incorporated Committee for the Assessment of Progress in Education (CAPE) devoted to developing a national assessment.[43] Committee members including Ralph Tyler and Princeton's John Tukey became both key architects and spokesmen for the national assessment.[44] Even though the exploratory committee did not contain official members from the federal government, committee members consulted with Commissioner Keppel throughout the assessment development process, especially with respect to membership on the assessment's public committee.[45]

The subsequent product of Commissioner Keppel's efforts, the National Assessment of Educational Progress, was designed to reveal educational performance rather than to catalog educational inputs. It provoked fierce yet familiar state and local opposition from some administrators, principals, and teachers whose practice and routines a national assessment might expose or disrupt. Collecting and distributing information on the progress of education risked revealing a part of American schooling that had never before been systematically visible: what came out of American schools, in addition to what went in. Its novelty meant that no one knew what a national assessment would find or how those findings would be used. A national assessment could offer local officials and educators new information they could use to shape practice, but such information could be risky for established local authority and jurisdiction. Achievement information would not necessarily come at local educators' expense, but it could invite federal, state, interest group, or parent inspection of local routines. Comparisons between schools, districts, and states could accompany such inspections and lead to judgments about their relative performance. An analysis of public reactions to the proposed national assessment revealed "a problem associated with public understanding of the difference between assessment and national testing" – a misunderstanding, the analysis concluded, that contributed to professional and public fear of the assessment.[46]

---

[43] Lehmann, "The Genesis of NAEP," pp. 29–43.

[44] Lloyd Morrisett, "An Interview with Lloyd Morrisett," in *The Nation's Report Card: Evolution and Perspectives*, edited by Lyle V. Jones and Ingram Olkin (Bloomington, IN: Phi Delta Kappa Educational Foundation, 2004), p. 129. However, Keppel was also part of publicizing the assessment. See CCNY Record of Interview, Roy Larsen and LM, 9/28/65. Carnegie Corporation of New York Archives, Columbia University, Box 516.6.

[45] Carnegie Corporation of New York archives, Columbia University, Box 516.3, Folder 516.4, Box 516.5. In particular, see CCNY Record of Interview, National Education Assessment, Frank Keppel and LM 5/18/64; CCNY Record of Interview, National Educational Assessment, 6/4/64; CCNY Record of Interview, National Educational Assessment, 6/25/64, Frank Keppel and LM, in Folder 516.4. Hazlett concluded in his study: "It is quite evident from letters and memoranda that Morrisett and his associates at Carnegie kept in close touch with Keppel, both to provide information and to secure his reaction to plans in the making." Hazlett, *A History of the National Assessment of Educational Progress*, p. 307.

[46] Letter from William A. Miler to Lloyd Morrisett, Februrary 24, 1966. Additional discussion of the lack of public understanding of the assessment proposal appears in: CCNY Record of

This novelty, moreover, occurred in the context of an educational statistics community that lagged behind its labor, health, and agricultural compatriots both inside and outside government.[47] Squads of educational statisticians would not be on hand to greet the educational equivalent of an unemployment rate with varying but predictable interpretations, similar to economists responding to data releases from the Bureau of Labor Statistics. Interpretation and use would be left to the government or to a professional field with little infrastructure at the time for approaching such interpretation.[48] No one might interpret or use the results,[49] or policy participants might link the results with any number of policy arguments, which might or might not be grounded in theory and explicit assumptions.

Once the assessment's architects made their plans public, opposition to those plans mobilized. The American Association of School Administrators (AASA) instructed its members to refuse to participate in any national assessment effort.[50] One of the nation's largest teachers' unions, the National Education Association (NEA), followed suit.[51] For an assessment to occur, administrators have to agree to let the assessment in the schoolhouse door, teachers have to know how to conduct it, parents have to agree to let their children sit for it,

Interview, H. Thomas James and LM, February 17, 1966. Ralph Tyler gave speeches, including one to the American Association of School Administrators on February 12, 1966, to clarify the assessment was "not an effort to impose national standards" and that it was "not a national testing program." The speech clarified that sampling would occur by region and that no child would take the entire test. Carnegie Corporation of New York archives, Columbia University, Box 516.7.

[47] Interview 1104, conducted by Susan Moffitt, November 2004.

[48] Thinking about how to distinguish separate home and school effects on student learning, for instance, Ralph Tyler warned, "I don't think, even with the most sophisticated data at the present we can tell, in Scarsdale, how much of that [student achievement] was due to the home and to the school." John Tukey concurred, "I will take it one statement further – that is to say, I don't think this question is answerable." Both quotes appear in Greenbaum, *Measuring Educational Progress*, p. 119.

[49] Surveys conducted by the GAO in 1975 revealed that few federal, state, or local officials reported using NAEP data. GAO, *The National Assessment of Educational Progress*, p. 24.

[50] Memo from the Executive Committee of the AASA to Members of the AASA, January 9, 1967. The memo noted on p. 3: "It is the prerogative of any school system to determine whether it will or will not participate in the field tryouts of test items and test batteries or the application of the final instruments for the NAEP project. If you share the concerns of the Executive Committee ... you and your board can help ... by refusing to participate in either." Carnegie Corporation of New York archives, Columbia University, Box 517.4.

[51] "Resolutions of the National Education Association, July 5–7, 1967, Minneapolis, MN." The NEA concluded: "The National Education Association calls on its members and affiliates to withhold cooperation from the national assessment." Carnegie Corporation of New York archives, Columbia University, Box 517.3. The Association for Supervision and Curriculum Development submitted a resolution for its members to consider that stood "firmly against the development of a national testing program." "Resolution for consideration of the Members of the Association for Supervision and Curriculum Development, March 2, 1965," Carnegie Corporation of New York archives, Columbia University, Box 516.6. For additional discussion, see Hazlett, *A History of the National Assessment of Educational Progress*, pp. 177, 195.

students have to agree to take it, and the broader community has to know how to make sense of the results. Without state, local, professional and parental consent, active participation and knowledge, a national assessment would be impossible.

The National Assessment's architects anticipated state and local opposition,[52] and they planned to expand the assessment's public committee framework and solicit greater public participation in assessment design, including participation from well-known assessment opponents. The National Assessment's leadership broadened the reconstituted Exploratory Committee for the Assessment of Progress in Education membership to "develop understanding" of the assessment, to mobilize support from potential sympathizers[53] *and* to mollify assessment opponents such as school administrators.[54] The committee doubled its original membership to include members representing key state and local interests.[55]

This expansion could suggest several different kinds of participation. For one, it appears akin to participatory oversight that elected officials might seek, including supporters and opponents to enhance monitoring. For another, it could resemble an installment of Selznik-like co-optation – by including interests to acquire their assent, only to risk subverting the policy in the process.[56]

---

[52] See, for instance, "A Report on the Second Conference of a National Assessment of Educational Progress," January 27/28, 1964, prepared by Margot Viscusi, Carnegie Corporation of New York archives, Columbia University, Box 516.5. However, Irvin Lehmann argued, "Tyler did not realize the magnitude of the opposition that would confront the assessment" in 1967. Lehmann, "The Genesis of NAEP," p. 44.

[53] The Corson report 4/14/64, entitled "Launching A National Educational Assessment," by McKinsey & Company, Inc., wrote "The Interim Commission should devise ways of expanding consensus as to the desirability of a periodic assessment. To accomplish this end it is proposed that it hold a two or three-day conference ... to bring together forty or fifty individuals not previously involved in the consideration of the idea, but who might be expected to be sympathetic with the objective. Such a conference should be designed to test the validity of such periodic assessments, and importantly, to develop understanding of the objective and to gain support for the undertaking" (p. 13), Carnegie Corporation of New York Archives, Columbia University, Box 516.5.

[54] Lehmann, "The Genesis of NAEP," p. 44; Hazlett, *A History of the National Assessment of Educational Progress*, p. 110; Frederic A. Mosher, "An Age of Innocence," in *The Nation's Report Card: Evolution and Perspectives*, edited by Lyle V. Jones and Ingram Olkin (Bloomington, IN: Phi Delta Kappa Educational Foundation, 2004), p. 110; Lee Cronbach, "An Interview with Lee Cronbach," in *The Nation's Report Card: Evolution and Perspectives*, edited by Lyle V. Jones and Ingram Olkin (Bloomington, IN: Phi Delta Kappa Educational Foundation, 2004).

[55] These interests included the American Association of School Administrators, the Chief State School Officers, the National Association of Secondary School Principals, the Department of Elementary School Principals, the National Education Association, the American Federation of Teachers, the National Congress of Parents and Teachers, the National Association of State Boards of Education, and the National School Boards Association. For a general discussion, see Greenbaum, *Measuring Educational Progress*, p. 18.

[56] Inclusion of opponents can represent a strategy for co-optation. See Philip Selznik, *TVA and the Grass Roots: A Study in the Sociology of Formal Organizations* (Berkeley: University of

From a bureaucratic perspective, however, the committee's expansion and incorporation of opponents occurred after the boundaries of the task had already been defined, after key aspects of the design were already in place, and after the issue of whether the assessment should occur at all was essentially off the table.[57] Participation, in other words, was focused on task implementation. Key aspects of the assessment and its implementation remained to be defined and developed.

Teacher, Parent, and "Lay" Participation

Participatory democracy would be unlikely to see the national assessment's restricted, implementation-focused participation as democratic expression. From the perspective of bureaucratic administration, however, hundreds of public participants engaged in various aspects of assessment development and implementation would not have manifested in a closed bureaucracy. Beyond the Exploratory Committee itself, the National Assessment's architects recruited educators and other lay participants to review the assessment's objectives (i.e., what content areas a science assessment for ten-year-olds should include) and the proposed test questions that contractors developed. These reviews, some foundation staff perceived, offered a way to create "local salespeople" for the assessment, or, at a minimum, to blunt their opposition.[58] Yet, these panels also created room for meaningful grassroots participation in the National Assessment's development. Estimates suggest that about 1,300 education practitioners ranked the 10 subject-matter objectives that 230 people developed for the National Assessment to assess.[59] The Exploratory Committee for the Assessment of Progress in Education selected "lay" participants from a pool of nominations from groups ranging from NAACP to the Chamber of Commerce to various educational associations and parent-teacher organizations, seeking diversity in terms of region, race, gender, religion, and socioeconomic status.[60] The panels were asked to consider "Is this something important for people to

California Press, 1949). In the event of co-optation, however, the program's purpose changes as a result of including opponents, and many of the assessment design principles that the original architects planned have remained in place.

[57] Hazlett, *A History of the National Assessment of Educational Progress*, p. 110.

[58] Morrisett, "An Interview with Lloyd Morrisett," p. 129. This review process was extensive and entailed multiple levels. See Hazlett, *A History of the National Assessment of Educational Progress*; GAO, *The National Assessment of Educational Progress*, pp. 11–12.

[59] Lehmann, "The Genesis of NAEP," p. 63.

[60] See Part V, "The Committee on Assessing the Progress of Education," p. V.9, Carnegie Corporation of New York archives, Columbia University, Box 516.8. For a discussion of opposition to "lay committees" from representatives of the American Association of School Administrators, see the letter from Alex M. Mood, Assistant Commissioner for Educational Statistics, to Ralph Tyler, January 25, 1966, Carnegie Corporation of New York archives, Columbia University, 516.7.

learn today?" and "Is this something I would like to have my children learn?" as they judged assessment objectives.[61]

Subsequent evaluations of the conferences in which the lay educators reviewed and discussed the assessment objectives concluded that, "in general, there was good agreement not only among the lay panels but also between the lay and professional judgments regarding the objectives."[62] The evaluation noted this was not surprising, given that the National Assessment did not propose creating new objectives from scratch. Instead, evaluators concluded the Assessment "represented a reorganization, restatement, and something of a summarization of objectives which frequently had appeared in print in the last quarter century."[63]

The National Assessment also included professional and lay participants to review exercises that the assessment would administer. The National Assessment's contractors developed the test questions and then submitted them to lay panels to consider:

1. Would you object to having the exercise used with your child?
2. In your opinion, would any important group in your community object to the use of the exercise?[64]

The lay panels concluded about 60 percent of the exercises were "acceptable as written," with the remaining 40 percent either removed or revised.[65] Subjects such as citizenship and literature proved more controversial than math and science.[66] After the lay review, the Exploratory Committee for the Assessment of Progress in Education sent the exercises to subject matter specialists from

---

[61] Part V, "The Committee on Assessing the Progress of Education," p. V.9, Carnegie Corporation of New York archives, Columbia University, Box 516.8.

[62] Lehmann, "The Genesis of NAEP," p. 64.

[63] J. C. Merwin and F. B. Womer, "Evaluation in Assessing the Progress of Education to Provide Bases of Public Understanding and Public Policy," in *National Society for the Study of Education Yearbook, Educational Evaluation: New Roles, New Means*, edited by R. W. Tyler (Chicago: University of Chicago Press, 1969), p. 316, cited in Lehmann, "The Genesis of NAEP," pp. 64–65.

[64] Part V, "The Committee on Assessing the Progress of Education," p. V.14, Carnegie Corporation of New York archives, Columbia University, Box 516.8.

[65] Some issues flagged by lay panels included questions that were "too general" or that "seem to reinforce misconceptions." Part V, "The Committee on Assessing the Progress of Education," p. V.16, Carnegie Corporation of New York archives, Columbia University, Box 516.8. Other types of exercises that lay panelists noted as potentially offensive included references that contained sexual themes, violence, cast authority figures in "unfavorable light," were demeaning to minority groups, called for "interpretation of Darwinian theory," discussed religious issues, or were "in any way connected with family financing," among others. Jack C. Merwin, "Conference on the Development of Instrumentation for Assessment of the Progress of Education in the United States," Project OE 5-99-251, 1967, pp. 8–9. See p. 15 for a discussion of the number of individuals who participated, Carnegie Corporation of New York archives, Columbia University, Box 517.3.

[66] Lehmann, "The Genesis of NAEP," p. 67.

various professional organizations to assess the items in terms of their validity, reliability, and rigor.[67]

The National Assessment's contractors revised about 25 percent of the assessment's exercises and eliminated about 1 percent based on the comments received from the subject-matter professional reviews.[68] The Exploratory Committee for the Assessment of Progress in Education followed these initial reviews with two subject-matter review conferences, one in 1967 and one in 1968. The panels, organized by subject matter and by assessment age group, included "at least one person with experience in working with low socio-economic children, one person with a measurement background in the subject, and two or more who were subject experts at either the appropriate teaching level or at colleges of education with specialization in the specific subject area."[69]

When experts open their policymaking processes to mobilize demand for their program or services, they risk losing their scientific authority.[70] There is little evidence that including thousands of "lay" and professional reviewers in the National Assessment's development impaired the assessment's technical rigor, nor did broadened participation prevent the assessment from occurring. However, the National Assessment's ultimate 1969 design made a significant concession to states and localities. The assessment was designed to reveal national and regional student performance: it would be unable to reveal comparable state or local performance.[71] Assessment results would not report school, district, or state performance: they would compare only regions and offer a national portrait of student achievement. This meant that the Southeast could be compared with the Northeast, but Florida's student achievement would not

---

[67] C. J. Finley and F. S. Berdie, *The National Assessment Approach to Exercise Development* (Denver, CO: National Assessment of Educational Progress, 1970), p. 48, cited in Lehmann, "The Genesis of NAEP," p. 68.

[68] Lehmann, "The Genesis of NAEP," p. 68.

[69] Finley and Berdie, *The National Assessment Approach to Exercise Development*, p. 71, cited in Lehmann, "The Genesis of NAEP," p. 70.

[70] Balogh, *Chain Reaction*, pp. 56–58.

[71] Recall Congressman Garfield justified the development of national educational statistics and assessments in 1866 as a way to compare states. Some accounts suggest some of NAEP's architects did not consider changing the assessment to report by region rather than by state as problematic. On this point, see Mosher, "An Age of Innocence," p. 110. The assessment's design – its sampling and reporting mechanisms in particular – aimed to assuage state and local concerns: Morrisett, "An Interview with Lloyd Morrisett," p. 124. Tyler's original proposal, which became the foundation for NAEP, relied on matrix sampling. This sampling technique would give parts of the assessment to samples of students in samples of schools and then link those samples: no student would take the entire test. This would reduce the assessment's burden on assessment administrators and test takers. It also made it impossible to report individual student scores. Instead, the assessment would report results by group, using broad categories such as age, gender, and race. In addition to reporting NAEP results by group, NAEP's architects also resolved to report results by each NAEP exercise, reasoning that this reporting arrangement would make "the results comprehensible to teachers in terms that they could put to use in their teaching": Cronbach, "An Interview with Lee Cronbach," p. 147.

be compared with New York's. Limiting the assessment to regional comparisons limited its potential strength and salience to influence and provoke state or local educational improvement. But reporting results by region rather than by state, a primary evaluation concluded, was "not concessions that particularly offended Ralph Tyler's sense of what the design could or should be."[72] The assessment's architects also agreed to house assessment administration in the Education Commission of the States (ECS) – a consortium of state leaders with strong ties to the AASA – and fund the assessment through a loosely specified federal grant. From the perspective of the former AASA president, this arrangement would allow the assessment to be administered by an "on-going body, which is legally responsible and responsive to the electorate of the states."[73]

Participatory Bureaucracy?

This account of the development of the National Assessment offers ample room for conventional critiques of participation. NAEP's participatory processes could be portrayed: as a channel for private influence, such as philanthropic foundations; as a channel for powerful groups to co-opt the government and exert undue influence, such as the AASA; and as a channel for the government to manipulate opponents or the general public through deliberate efforts to win support for the fledgling assessment from groups and the grassroots.

What about from a bureaucratic perspective? Participation supports bureaucratic administration when it offers a systematic process that focuses on task implementation and is consistent with the core elements of bureaucratic reputation: unique agency expertise and diverse support. This account supports some of these elements. Both the policy and the pursuit of the initial private participation through the Carnegie Corporation arose from executive branch initiative through Commissioner Keppel. The various participatory processes were implementation-oriented: what the design should entail, what the assessment frameworks would include, what questions would look like. Moreover, public participation for the National Assessment's development did little to threaten the agency's unique expertise, and instead offered some promise of enhancing it in the long run. From the perspective of federal-level executive branch bureaucracy, opening up the National Assessment development process to public participation was relatively low risk. The federal level agency had little if any unique expertise or jurisdiction to protect at the time. The new assessment did not violate or interfere with existing *federal* bureaucratic routines: few existed in this emerging field. If NAEP worked, it could represent a big addition to the agency's portfolio. If it did not get off the ground, the agency had little to lose: the agency had few resources invested in the earliest stages of NAEP.

---

[72] Mosher, "An Age of Innocence," p. 110.
[73] Lehman, "The Genesis of NAEP," p. 56.

However, the participatory processes did not actively build federal bureaucracy. Fundamental aspects of the National Assessment's operation – the development of test items, assessment administration, and analysis – became the responsibility of the assessment's grantee, the Education Commission of the States, not the federal agency. The assessment's public participation and governing structure also reported to the National Assessment's grantee, not to the National Center for Education Statistics. The participatory processes did not jeopardize federal turf, nor did they significantly expand it initially. While the decision to include NAEP opponents such as the AASA late in the process could appear on one level as a form of public manipulation, it could be understood as a means of enabling diverse support as opposed to single group domination. Including the AASA later meant theirs was one of many voices at the table, not the only one calling the shots.

Does the lack of full and free participation mean the absence of meaningful democratic accountability? Clearly, this case does not present ideal participatory democracy. Yet, participation displayed elements of breadth and fluidity engaging teachers and parents in addition to traditional group representatives. This was not a one-time in-house process or one that resembled the industry councils that populated other parts of the executive branch during this era. The original group that met at the Carnegie conferences, including Commissioner Keppel, was instrumental in establishing the architecture for the National Assessment. One evaluation critical of the National Assessment concluded that, "in essence, when all the participatory processes were done, virtually all the most important decisions that had been made were basically unaltered versions of those made by Tyler and Tukey from September 1963 to January 1964."[74] First-mover agenda-setters may have durable influence, no doubt, and technical experts can dominate lay participants. Yet, the outcome was not perfunctory or rubber-stamped in meaningful ways. The design did change to preclude state-by-state comparisons. Panels of lay participants did reject assessment items. The Education Commission of the States obtained the grant to conduct the National Assessment. The National Assessment was not delivered from the initial Carnegie conferences a *fait accompli*.

The National Assessment represented the long-term potential of enabling information to flow in multiple directions: creating new knowledge that third parties could use in various ways for *future* democratic accountability. It represented a way to create new knowledge that parents, teachers, administrators, officials, and groups could use to encourage educational performance, at least in principle. Yet, in terms of fluid information flows, the participatory processes for the National Assessment resembled the limits of other participatory venues from this era. Like other forms of public participation in the pre-1972

---

[74] Greenbaum, *Measuring Educational Progress*, p. 12. The evaluation goes on to offer a critical assessment of the impact of "lay" people on the development of objectives, consistent with critiques of lay domination by experts. See p. 55.

FACA period, meetings were not announced in the *Federal Register* or widely open, beyond invited participants.

Though one alternative is no bureaucracy at all, participatory bureaucracy assumes there is some form of bureaucracy, but it can manifest in forms more or less inimical to democratic accountability. From this perspective, consider two alternative bureaucratic arrangements different than the one that took shape. If we put American politics aside for a moment, the executive branch bureaucracy could have, in principle, developed a national exam entirely within the confines of the federal education agency, as many industrialized nations do. The Commissioner of Education lacked authority over much of American education, but he had statutory authority to assess the progress of education in the states. Models of managerial responsibility remind us that hierarchical bureaucratic expressions of authority can be consistent with democracy, as democracy depends on bureaucratic competence. In the United States in 1963, however, the federal agency lacked meaningful in-house technical capacity to design such an assessment at the time, let alone administer it. The feasibility of meeting the conditions of managerial responsibility in this case is a far stretch at best. A closed hierarchical bureaucratic approach not only would discourage active democratic oversight, but it was also unlikely to produce competent administration.

Alternatively, bureaucratic administration could have remained in local hands. Recall that even though the federal government began expressing new authority through the Elementary and Secondary Education Act of 1965, control over schools from 1962 to 1969 was fundamentally local. In the words of the late civil rights advocate Phyllis McClure, reflecting on this period, "there was a conspiracy of silence" at the state and local levels.[75] Local-level administrators, some proponents of the National Assessment claimed, systematically pursued strategic ignorance: the absence of educational achievement data precluded comparisons that could reveal profound inequalities along racial and socioeconomic lines. Leaving educational assessment to local-level bureaucracy in the 1960s would have offered one extreme form of control on the basis of knowledge: one where little knowledge existed that could flow anywhere.

Compared with these other bureaucratic alternatives – a closed, hierarchically constructed and imposed assessment developed by an agency with relatively little technical capacity; or no assessment and continued local administrator exclusive control over (nonexistent) educational achievement information – NAEP's various, limited, imperfect participatory processes offered multiple potential points of access and oversight. In 1969, the National Assessment conducted its first series of assessments in science, civics, and writing. Commissioner Keppel went "public," and the effort resulted in an assessment equipped to report on the progress of education in the United States, albeit four years after he left his post.

---

[75] Personal communication, December 1996.

DEVELOPING PORTALS FOR TECHNICAL ADVICE

Not long after the assessment went into production, federal agency leaders at the National Center for Education Statistics began exploring and developing additional venues for receiving public advice, including technical advice. In 1970, the federal government assumed primary financial responsibility for the National Assessment.[76] Along with federal purse strings came new federal supervision: the National Center for Education Statistics began overseeing the National Assessment in 1971.[77] The assistant commissioner for education statistics in 1971, Dorothy Gilford, described the National Assessment as "a welcome addition" to the Center's statistical program.[78] Both Gilford and her predecessor, Commissioner Alex Mood, had advocated for the National Assessment's creation, as well as for extending the Center's statistical program beyond collecting resource information.[79] Expanding the Center's statistical program meant, in part, gathering data that might help explain differences in student achievement, advancing the more complex vision of the federal role in education that Keppel had advocated: providing information to press for improvement. To this end, the agency contracted with the National Opinion Research Center to conduct the first longitudinal study of American students.[80] Commissioner Gilford looked to the National Assessment as another source for *explaining* student achievement.[81] She approached the National Assessment's grantee, the Education Commission of the States, and its public committee to consider expanding the background information the National Assessment would collect on students taking the assessment.

[76] Hazlett, *A History of the National Assessment of Educational Progress*, p. 255; Lyle V. Jones and Ingram Olkin, *The Nation's Report Card: Evolution and Perspectives* (Bloomington, IN: Phi Delta Kappa Press, 2004), pp. 1–2.

[77] Jones and Olkin, *The Nation's Report Card*, p. 14. The Memorandum of Understanding, forged between the Office of Education and ECS in June 1969, specified a minimal federal role, particularly with respect of the assessment's budget. "OE recognizes that ECS must have considerable flexibility in developing its grant budget, both because of the nature of the Assessment and because of the uncertainties inherent in the initial assumption of responsibility for the Assessment": Dorothy Gilford, "NAEP and the US Office of Education," in *The Nation's Report Card: Evolution and Perspectives*, edited by Lyle V. Jones and Ingram Olkin (Bloomington, IN: Phi Delta Kappa Press, 2004), p. 180.

[78] Gilford, "NAEP and the US Office of Education," p. 166.

[79] On support for the development of a national assessment, see the reference to the Letter from Alexander Mood to Dr. Wayne O. Reed, May 2, 1966, noting "the Office has a strong interest in the sound development of the Carnegie [national assessment] program," contained in the memo from Harold Howe II to August Steinhilber, August 24, 1966, Carnegie Corporation of New York archives, Columbia University, Box 516.8. Gilford, "NAEP and the US Office of Education," pp. 166–167. Hazlett, however, reports ways in which NCES Commissioner Mood's perception of what NAEP would ultimately provide (i.e., "basic data for evaluation of the US educational system and its elements") differed from the ECAPE design: Hazlett, *A History of the National Assessment of Educational Progress*, pp. 311–312.

[80] Interview 1104, conducted by Susan Moffitt, November 2004.

[81] Gilford, "NAEP and the US Office of Education," pp. 169–170.

The Education Commission of the States continued the National Assessment's tradition of using public committees for both governing decisions and advice.[82] The committees' meeting content and participation remained under the jurisdiction of the Education Commission of the States: the federal government lacked official jurisdiction over who was invited to participate or what they discussed at their meetings. Commissioner Gilford approached the chair of the National Assessment's Analysis Advisory Committee to discuss expanding the background variables the National Assessment collected. The committee's chair, the National Assessment architect John Tukey, refused to put the topic on the committee's agenda.

Using the schema from Figure 1.1, the task of adding background variables to the National Assessment invoked elements of Quadrants B from the perspective of the National Center for Education Statistics, but straddles the line with Quadrant D. The agency lacked complete in-house expertise and full jurisdiction, though the agency enjoyed more authority over the task once the agency assumed budgetary oversight and perhaps even more so when funding for NAEP and ECS switched from a grant to a contract in FY1974. Commissioner Gilford could not command the assessment's Analysis Advisory Committee to consider adding background variables to the National Assessment: the committee's agenda-setting authority resided in the hands of the Education Commission of the States (the grantee) and its committee leaders. Nor could Gilford replace the Analysis Advisory Committee chairman with someone more closely aligned with her preferences: the Education Commission of the States determined committee membership.[83]

Despite committee resistance to gathering more background information through NAEP, the FY1974 budget request devoted funds to research on back-

---

[82] The Assessment Policy Committee, composed of Tyler, Tukey, the former president of the AASA, a school superintendent, and a state legislator, had authority for NAEP operations and expanded its membership in 1970: Hazlett, *A History of the National Assessment of Educational Progress*, p. 280. The Policy Committee received advice from three advisory committees: the National Assessment Advisory Committee, which drew its membership from state government, school administration, business, higher education, and the statistics/measurement community; the Technical Advisory Committee, later named the Analysis Advisory Committee, chaired by NAEP architect John Tukey; and the Operations Advisory committee: Lehman, "The Genesis of NAEP," p. 58. Lay panels to review assessment exercises also continued. Gilford, "NAEP and the US Office of Education," p. 169.

[83] When Tukey finished his term as chair of the Analysis Advisory Committee, the Education Commission of the States replaced him with Harvard's Frederick Mosteller, who proposed "that the massive NAEP national sample and administrative operation be turned to the complex measurement of input factors affecting educational achievement": Greenbaum, *Measuring Educational Progress*, p. 125. This is not to suggest that NCES influenced the advisory committee or its chairman selection, but rather that the agency and NAEP's advisors worked in the same professional community.

ground questions.[84] Commissioner Gilford also sought new forms of advice, but from a group other than the one selected by the ECS.[85] She recalled,

> Although it would be difficult to name a more outstanding group of specialists than those on the Analysis Advisory Committee, NCES staff thought it would be desirable to obtain the views of a group of individuals who had not been closely involved in the project.[86]

The Center developed "annual project site reviews," using its own group of evaluation, testing, and statistics experts to review aspects of the National Assessment. The Commissioner recalled, "Recommendations made at these reviews provided the basis for pushing the project to include data relevant to national policy concerns, including information on student background characteristics."[87]

The Center's decision to consult with advisors other than the National Assessment's official committees expanded beyond the background variable issue. External reviews became part of the assessment's grant review process, in Commissioner Gilford's words, "to take advantage of expertise not available in NCES and to get a broader perspective on the merit of the activities proposed by NAEP."[88] Gilford recalled that "top-level ECS and NAEP staff were quite irate about this procedure."[89] Yet, the reviews persisted, and National Assessment staff ultimately "adopted some of the suggested improvements."[90]

Housed outside the federal agency and under the auspices of the Education Commission of the States, the Assessment Policy Committee and the Analysis Advisory Committee provided a check on the executive branch's influence over assessment design. The Center faced incomplete knowledge and incomplete authority for the National Assessment's development, and it created new channels of advisors. Together these forms of participation suggest a combination of participatory oversight (through the ECS) and private learning (through technical review panels), consistent with Quadrant B from Figure 1.1. Although lay panels continued to review assessment exercises, the participation portrayed in Commissioner Gilford's account appears to have been largely removed from general public engagement. These forms of participation may have supported

---

[84] Gilford, "NAEP and the US Office of Education," p. 170.

[85] For examples of creating parallel committees in the context of nuclear energy, see Balogh, *Chain Reaction*, p. 129.

[86] Gilford, "NAEP and the US Office of Education," pp. 170–171.

[87] Gilford, "NAEP and the US Office of Education," pp. 170–171. A 1976 critique of NAEP's usefulness asserted that the assessment continued to collect too few background variables: GAO, *The National Assessment of Educational Progress*, p. 35. A significant expansion in the number and kind of background variables that NAEP collected did not occur until NAEP switched contractors in the early 1980s.

[88] Gilford, "NAEP and the US Office of Education," p. 177.

[89] Gilford, "NAEP and the US Office of Education," p. 177.

[90] Gilford, "NAEP and the US Office of Education," p. 177.

democratic accountability through enhanced bureaucratic competence and through ECS's connection to states. There is little evidence to suggest they contributed directly to the flow of knowledge beyond the agency.

NEW OPPORTUNITIES FOR LIQUEFYING KNOWLEDGE: THE NATIONAL ASSESSMENT GOVERNING BOARD AND STATE NAEP

Despite Keppel's vision, the National Assessment offered little data the federal government could use to press for state or local educational improvements.[91] The information the assessment provided – difficult-to-understand test scores, reported by region – was not readily usable by the public, parents, educators, or officials. Changes to the National Assessment proposed by a "blue-ribbon" commission appointed by Secretary Bennett and codified in law in 1988 redesigned the National Assessment, its public board, and the scope of the information it provided. Changes in the National Assessment's interest group and implementation landscape supported these shifts. In 1867 and in 1967, local-level administrators forged common cause with state officials and "fought hard" to prevent federal officials from exposing relative state and local educational performance.[92] Yet, by the mid-1970s, opposition to reporting state-level National Assessments results showed signs of softening.[93] The early-1980s publication of *A Nation at Risk* – a report released by President Reagan's first Secretary of Education Terrell Bell – furthered fractured state-local alliances opposed to educational assessments. The report detailed dismal academic performance by American students and warned of devastating economic implications. Following the report, the Department of Education began issuing what became known as "The Wall Chart," which compared states' educational performance using SAT scores and an assortment of state-produced data. Using justifications similar to Congressman Garfield's in 1866 and Commissioner Keppel's in 1962, federal officials sought to gather and distribute knowledge to nudge states and localities toward attending to student performance.

In the words of one federal official, the Wall Chart "galvanized" some chief state school officers and governors to join Reagan administration officials in advocating for data collection that would enable systematic cross-state comparisons.[94] By the early 1980s, the Southern Regional Education Board (SREB)

[91] GAO, *The National Assessment of Educational Progress*, p. 35.

[92] John Gardner, "An Interview with John Gardner," in *The Nation's Report Card: Evolution and Perspectives*, edited by Lyle V. Jones and Ingram Olkin (Bloomington, IN: Phi Delta Kappa Educational Foundation, 2004), pp. 118–119.

[93] U.S. General Accounting Office, *The National Assessment of Educational Progress*, p. 33. Some states sought state-level assessments as early as 1969. Lehmann, "The Genesis of NAEP," p. 87.

[94] Interview with Emerson Elliott, conducted by Susan Moffitt on November 4, 2004.

conducted versions of the National Assessment in eight southern states to allow cross-state comparisons of student achievement.[95] The Council of Chief State School Officers, the national group representing the state-level public officials who lead state departments of elementary and secondary education, began exploring assessment alternatives that would permit cross-state comparisons.[96] Still, many state officials remained opposed to state-level educational comparisons. A resolution by the Council of Chief State School Officers to explore the possibility of systematic state-by-state comparisons passed by only one vote. The nation's top state school officials were almost evenly divided on the issue.

Some federal and state officials looked to the National Assessment as a possible alternative to the Wall Chart. In 1983, responsibility for administering the National Assessment shifted from the Education Commission of the States to the Educational Testing Service amid mounting concern that ECS lacked the technical capabilities to administer such a complex assessment.[97] Yet, the assessment continued to report results by region rather than by state, hampering its effectiveness at revealing relative educational performance. President Reagan's second secretary of education, William Bennett, established a "blue-ribbon" panel composed of nationally renowned members to consider whether the National Assessment could replace the patchwork Wall Chart as a means of comparing states' educational performance. From the perspective of one participant, "we all knew what the agenda was": to advance a major expansion of the National Assessment to allow for systematic state-level comparisons of student achievement and for state results to be compared with national results.[98]

The National Assessment continued to receive policy direction from its Assessment Policy Committee. After a decade of National Assessment operations, Congress statutorily codified the Assessment Policy Committee in 1978, marking the first official Congressional involvement into NAEP's structure for public participation.[99] The mandate, however, largely codified extant practice. Consistent with the National Assessment's tradition, the mandate gave the Assessment Policy Committee broad policy authority and specified general categories of stakeholders to serve on the committee. It left authority over the Assessment Policy Committee's agenda, member selection, and

---

[95] Emerson Elliott and Gary Phillips, "A View from the NCES," in *The Nation's Report Card: Evolution and Perspectives*, edited by Lyle V. Jones and Ingram Olkin (Bloomington, IN: Phi Delta Kappa Educational Foundation, 2004), pp. 243–244.

[96] Ramsay Selden, "Making NAEP State-By-State," in *The Nation's Report Card: Evolution and Perspectives*, edited by Lyle V. Jones and Ingram Olkin (Bloomington, IN: Phi Delta Kappa Educational Foundation, 2004), p. 196.

[97] NAEP started as a grant to ECS, changed to a contract to ECS in 1974, changed to a grant to ETS in 1983, and then changed to a contract to ETS in 1988. Lyle V. Jones and Ingram Olkin (eds.), *The Nation's Report Card: Evolution and Perspectives* (Bloomington, IN: Phi Delta Kappa Press, 2004), pp. 14–17; P.L. 100–297.

[98] Interview 1104, conducted by Susan Moffitt, November 2004. Results from the special NAEP eight-state SREB study were released the first day the Alexander-James panel convened, "setting the tone" for what was to come.

[99] P.L. 95–561.

whether to adhere to the committee's recommendations up to the assessment's grantee;[100] and the public committee remained separated from federal officials. While under the jurisdiction of the Education Commission of the States, the committee provoked criticism for meeting infrequently, for consisting of members who lacked "high visibility or great knowledge of the issues," and for failing to take an active role in policy development.[101] After winning the 1983 National Assessment grant, the Educational Testing Service stated that it would "[increase] the role of the assessment's policymaking committee."[102]

The Alexander-James panel nonetheless recommended significantly reconfiguring the National Assessment's public governing board.[103] In the words of then–Assistant Secretary Finn, the Assessment Policy Committee "was just a horse and buggy structure for an airborne age, and it wasn't up to the task."[104] He continued,

> The president of ETS took [the Assessment Policy Committee] seriously ... [but] It was the contractor's decision whether to take it seriously ... the policy decisions for NAEP in those days ... were not actually made by the representatives of the public.[105]

---

[100] P.L. 95–561, Sec. 1242 (3); Robert L. Linn, "The Influence of External Evaluations," in *The Nation's Report Card: Evolution and Perspectives*, edited by Lyle V. Jones and Ingram Olkin (Bloomington, IN: Phi Delta Kappa Educational Foundation, 2004), p. 299. Congress specified that NAEP's Assessment Policy Committee would consist of three public representatives, two business representatives, one chief state school officer, two state legislators, two district superintendents, one state board of education chairman, one local school board chairman, one governor, and four teachers. Federal officials would participate as ex officio and nonvoting members. P.L. 95–561, Sec. 1242 (2) (A).

[101] Eileen White, "Better Proposal Said to Win Assessment Project for ETS," *Education Week*, March 2, 1983.

[102] Eileen White, "Better Proposal Said to Win Assessment Project for ETS."

[103] Lamar Alexander and H. Thomas James, *The Nation's Report Card: Improving the Assessment of Student Achievement* (Washington, DC: National Academy of Education, 1987), pp. 8–9; Michael Kirst, "Roles, Governance and Multiple Uses for a New NAEP," (Paper Commissioned by The Study Group on the National Assessment of Student Achievement, 1986), p. 7. In addition to recommendations on NAEP's governance, the Alexander-James panel made a series of recommendations, which included expanding NAEP to allow for cross-state comparisons, expanding NAEP samples especially for private school students, and expanding NAEP's budget. Similar to NAEP's original design, structural aspects of state NAEP's ultimate design attended to state-level concerns over expanding the knowledge that would be collected and distributed about state schooling. State NAEP would remain voluntary and the content of State NAEP assessment would be based on "objectives" derived through a consensus process led by the Council for Chief State School Officers.

[104] Interview with Chester E. Finn Jr., conducted by Susan Moffitt, August 20, 2003. Minutes from the January 17, 1987 Assessment Policy Committee meeting contain discussion from Alexander-James panel vice-chair, Tom James, on ways in which responsiveness to state interests figured into the Policy Board's reorganization. Many of the additions to the Board's membership, however, were not state representatives. In addition to a governor and a chief state school officer, the board added two measurement experts, one business representative, and three members of the general public, among others. See PL 100–297 and PL 95–561.

[105] Interview with Chester E. Finn Jr., conducted by Susan Moffitt, August 20, 2003.

The blue-ribbon Alexander-James panel proposed separating the assessment's policy body from the assessment's contractor and creating more and different categories of board members.[106]

The report became the backbone of the ultimate legislation, which authorized expanding the National Assessment to assess state-level student performance and restructuring the assessment's administration.[107] The Augustus F. Hawkins–Robert T. Stafford Elementary and Secondary School Improvement Amendments of 1988 authorized NAEP to conduct an assessment in 1990 that would produce comparable state-level achievement results in mathematics, but only on a trial basis and only for states and localities that were willing to participate.[108] The act also reconfigured the National Assessment's public board, giving the board its own line item for budget and staff.[109] With that staff would come the potential for the Board to develop its own in-house expertise instead of relying on either the agency or the contractor for that expertise. The amendments also expanded the Secretary's authority over the National Assessment and its governing board by giving the Secretary the authority to appoint National Assessment Governing Board members, taking that responsibility away from the Assessment's contractor.[110] The reconstituted governing

---

[106] Alexander and James, *The Nation's Report Card*, p. 33; Kirst, "Roles, Governance and Multiple Uses for a New NAEP," p. 7. In addition to promoting NAEP access through a reconstituted governing board, the Alexander-James panel also explored expanding NAEP's accessibility in terms of the ways in which NAEP results and data were presented and disseminated. Darrell R. Bock, "Designing the National Assessment of Educational Progress to Serve a Wider Community of Users: A Position Paper" (Paper Commissioned by The Study Group on the National Assessment of Student Achievement, 1986).

[107] Congress authorized state-level NAEP on a trial basis. PL 100–297, Sec 3403. The legislation also changed the assessment's administration from a grant to contract, giving the agency oversight authority for that contract. In doing so, the legislation granted the agency new opportunities to specify the terms of NAEP's tasks and engage more systematically in operations.

[108] PL 100–297, Sec 3403. Congress codified the Assessment Policy Committee in 1978 amendments, leading to the committee's formal classification as "created by Congress." The 1988 law changed the name of NAEP's public board from the Assessment Policy Committee to the National Assessment Governing Board.

[109] Under the APC arrangement, the committee used ETS staff to support its work. Under NAGB, the Board would hire its own staff. PL 100–297.

[110] The Assessment Policy Council issued a response to the Alexander-James panel's recommendation for a reconstituted NAEP board. Their statement asserted that "This change in governance, when combined with concerns expressed about the possible standardizing effects of a system of state comparisons, may create an unintended impression of considerably increased federal influence over education." See Assessment Policy Committee, "Comments of the Assessment Policy Committee on the Nation's Report Card: Improving the Assessment of Student Achievement," Chester E. Finn, Jr. Archive Collection, Box 73, Hoover Institution. For a thoughtful discussion of NAGB's independence and intradepartmental tensions surrounding that independence, see "An Interview with Marshall S. Smith. What NAEP Really Could Do," in *The Nation's Report Card: Evolution and Perspectives*, edited by Lyle V. Jones and Ingram Olkin (Bloomington, IN: Phi Delta Kappa Educational Foundation, 2004). Former Undersecretary Smith concluded, "I have always been impressed by [NAGB's] independence." Smith, "Interview," p. 269.

TABLE 4.1. *Membership Categories for NAEP's Public Committees*

1978: Assessment Policy Council	19 Members

Statutory Authority: PL 95–561
Appointment Authority: NAEP Grantee/
    Contractor
	1 governor of a state
	2 state legislators
	1 chief state school officer
	2 school district superintendents
	1 chairman of a state board of education
	1 chairman of a local school board
	4 classroom teachers
	2 representatives of business and industry
	3 representatives of the general public
	Director of the National Institute of Education:
	    ex officio member
	National Council on Education Research:
	    nonvoting member

1988: National Assessment Governing Board	**24 Members**

Statutory Authority: PL 100–297
Appointment authority: Secretary of
    Education
Diversity: "The Secretary and the Board
    shall ensure at all times that the
    membership of the Board reflects
    regional, racial, gender and cultural
    balance and diversity and that it
    exercises its independent judgment,
    free from inappropriate influences and
    special interests."
	2 governors (or former governors) from different
	    political parties
	2 state legislators, from different political parties
	2 chief state school officers
	1 superintendent of a local educational agency
	1 member of a state board of education
	1 member of a local board of education
	3 classroom teachers representing the grade
	    levels at which the National Assessment is
	    conducted
	1 representative of business or industry
	2 curriculum specialists
	2 testing and measurement experts
	1 nonpublic school administrator or
	    policymaker
	2 school principals (1 elementary and 1 secondary)
	3 representatives of the general public, including
	    parents
	The Assistant Secretary for Educational Research
	    and Improvement: ex officio nonvoting member

1994: National Assessment Governing Board	**26 Members**

Statutory Authority: PL 103–382
Appointment Authority: Secretary of
    Education
Diversity: "The Secretary and the Board
    shall ensure at all times that the
    membership of the Board reflects
    regional, racial, gender, and cultural
    balance and diversity and that the
    Board exercises its independent
    judgment, free from inappropriate
    influences and special interests."
	Same membership criteria as the 1988
	    amendments, PLUS 1 additional testing
	    and measurement expert and 1 additional
	    representative of the general public

board for the National Assessment, called the National Assessment Governing Board, expanded Board membership, and offered additional categories of members described in Table 4.1.

The Alexander-James panel's recommendations for a reconfigured National Assessment mapped closely onto what the Secretary and Assistant Secretary advocated: Assistant Secretary Finn described himself as a ghostwriter for the report produced by the Alexander-James panel.[111] Its closeness to the Secretary and Assistant Secretary provides an illustration of participatory oversight rather than participatory bureaucracy, consistent with scholarship on presidents and their appointees. The Board's membership authority, its policymaking authority, and its distance from the agency, however, suggested new opportunities for expanded public participation in the National Assessment's subsequent development.

CONCLUSION

The development of the National Assessment reveals task conditions that illustrate all four quadrants of Figure 1.1. However, like many typologies, the bright lines blur in practice. If we take the view of state and local school bureaucrats in the 1860s or 1960s, we may find ourselves in Quadrant A. Information about and authority over public education resided firmly in state and local hands.[112] Federal efforts to liquefy knowledge and authority through data collection and/or participatory processes met stiff state and local resistance, consistent with Weberian predictions. Secrecy – or in Phyllis McClure's words, "a conspiracy of silence" – prevailed until federal officials sought to impose various forms of sunlight and participation.

If we take the view of assessment implementers housed in the Education Commission of the States or the National Center for Education Statistics in the early 1970s, we find ourselves more in Quadrant B, depending on the task. Though ECS and NCES each enjoyed authority over parts of task implementation, knowledge and expertise did not reside fully in house. Both looked to participation from technical experts through venues that largely reflected private learning and limited information exchanges.

If we take the view of Commissioner Zook in 1934 or Commissioner Keppel in 1964, we may find ourselves in Quadrant C. Federal agency leaders had information they wanted to distribute to broader audiences for issues over which they lacked jurisdiction: information on desperate school financial conditions in the case of Commissioner Zook and information on how the national assessment would differ from a national test in the case of Commissioner Keppel. Quadrant C, however, treads a fine and ambiguous line between what we might think of as participatory bureaucracy (increasing the flow of knowledge

---

[111] Finn, "An Interview," p. 252.
[112] That is, to the extent that knowledge existed at all.

to support task implementation) and participatory advocacy (using participation as part of a "selling campaign."

If we take the view of National Assessment developers in the mid-1960s, we may find ourselves in Quadrant D. The knowledge for developing the assessment was emergent and authority to do so was profoundly interdependent. Here we see elements of participatory bureaucracy, woven together with aspects of participatory oversight.

The development of the National Assessment also highlights the limits of FACA when it came to defining fully the terms of public participation in agency policymaking. Public participation flourished long before FACA, and important sources of participation occurred and remain outside of FACA's purview. Public committees with decision-making authority, like NAEP's Assessment Policy Committee and subsequent National Assessment Governing Board, do not fall fully under the auspices of FACA. Groups that are convened by contractors, such as some forms of technical review panels or lay panels, do not necessarily trigger FACA.[113] Subcommittees that do not provide official recommendations, which have appeared as part of NAEP boards and committees, also do not invoke FACA.[114] Focusing exclusively on FACA as a binding institution would miss vital portions of the participatory story. Participation emerges in part from task conditions that exceed FACA's reach.

---

[113] *Byrd v. United States Environmental. Protection. Agency*, 174 F.3d 239, 246–47 (D.C. Cir. 1999); *Food Chemical News v. Young*, 900 F.2d 328, 333 (D.C. Cir. 1990).

[114] National Anti-Hunger Coalition v. Executive Committee of the President's Private Sector Survey of Cost Control, 711 F.2d 1071, 1075-6 (D.C. Cir 1983).

5

Private Knowledge for Public Problems

Regulating Pharmaceutical Information

> Almost every package insert submitted to the FDA for approval is initially burdened with fiction, ranging from vague soft-sell language to outright false claims.... Nothing is more frustratingly prolonged and tortured than controversy over labeling.
>
> J. Richard Crout, 1974[1]

> [F]orces were operating to keep those of us who want openness ... to not have our say.
>
> Testimony of Dr. Julia Apter to Senate Hearings, Member of the Cardiovascular and Renal Drugs Advisory Committee, 1974[2]

In the era before the passage of the Federal Advisory Committee Act, public participation in the FDA took a range of forms including: the 1955 Citizens' Advisory Committee on the Food and Drug Administration; the Medical Advisory Panel on the Accidental Ingestion of Salicylate Preparations that was staffed through a contract with the National Academy of Sciences; informal engagement with professional societies such as the American Academy of Pediatrics; and industry committees that consulted with the American Drug Manufacturers Association and American Pharmaceutical Manufacturers Association.[3] Each of these venues offered a vivid juxtaposition of agency-

---

[1] J. Richard Crout, "In Praise of the Lowly Package Insert," *Food & Drug Commission Law Journal* 29 (1974): 139–145.

[2] Testimony of Julia Apter, U.S. Congress, Senate, *Examination of the Pharmaceutical Industry* 73–74, Joint Hearings before the Subcommittee on Health of the Committee on Labor and Public Welfare and the Subcommittee on Administrative Practice and Procedure of the Committee on the Judiciary, 93rd Congress, 1st and 2nd Sessions, Part 7, August 15 (Washington, DC: GPO, 1974), p. 2883.

[3] U.S. Congress, House of Representatives Committee Print, *Replies from Executive Departments and Federal Agencies to Inquiry Regarding Use of Advisory Committees, January 1, 1953–January*

initiated public participation and relatively closed participatory processes, which ultimately earned the FDA the label of having one of the worst advisory committee transparency records among all government agencies.[4] Participatory bureaucracy for educational assessments faced the challenge of producing "bureaucracy" given long-standing American antipathy toward federal government involvement in public education. Participatory bureaucracy in pharmaceutical regulation faced the challenge of mobilizing participation in ways conducive to democratic accountability: allegations of industry dominance or scientific exclusivity have confronted FDA participatory processes for over half a century.

The passage of the Federal Advisory Committee Act appeared peripheral to the participatory processes for educational assessments. For the FDA, FACA procedures brought more openness than had existed before. Before FACA, the FDA established a range of venues for gathering information from conventionally defined experts. Consistent with expectations for bureaucratic administration, the agency sought this form of advice – for low information/high independence tasks – privately. "Public" access came from the particular information exchanges, between the parties in the room. The FDA also experienced periodic participatory oversight: reviews and reports of the agency delivered to external audiences. When HEW requested these reviews, the reports largely promoted the agency instead of offering accounts that impugned the agency's expertise.

While FACA made it more challenging for the FDA to learn privately, it also opened opportunities for the FDA to distribute information about firms and products. In the words of a former FDA staffer,

> ... don't forget, the FDA is prohibited from releasing any data in a new drug application ... that's a trade secret, and so the advisory committee basically provides an override ... in that it enables them to disclose data publicly and to release those data.[5]

While FACA shone light on the FDA in ways the agency may have preferred to avoid, it also gave the agency new ways to shine light on firms and distribute information in ways that supported bureaucratic administration.

1, 1956, Part 3: Department of Health, Education and Welfare, June 5 (Washington, DC, 1956), pp. 959, 962.

[4] U.S. Congress, House of Representatives, *Use of Advisory Committees by the Food and Drug Administration*, Hearings before the Committee of Government Operations, 93rd Congress, 2nd Session, March 6, 7, 8, 12, 13; April 30; May 21 (Washington, DC: GPO, 1974); U.S. Congress, House of Representatives, *Use of Advisory Committees by the Food and Drug Administration Part 2*, Hearings before the Committee of Government Operations, 94th Congress, 1st Session, April 23, May 9 and 12 (Washington, DC: GPO, 1975).

[5] Interview 112204, conducted by Susan Moffitt on November 22, 2004. This quote also appears in: Susan L. Moffitt, "Promoting Agency Reputation through Public Advice: Advisory Committee Use in the FDA," *Journal of Politics* 72 (2010): 880–893.

REGULATING PRACTICE THROUGH INFORMATION: THE
COMPLEXITY OF DRUG LABELS

Like educational assessments, early twentieth-century pharmaceutical regulation attempted to use information to influence practice: the 1906 Pure Food
and Drugs Act took steps to discourage the interstate sale of "misbranded or
adultered food and drugs."[6] Drug producers and sellers did not need to prove
their chemicals were effective or safe. Nor, according to the Supreme Court,
did they have to make therapeutically accurate claims.[7] Producers could not,
however, provide "false or fraudulent" information to the public about drug
ingredients or properties.[8] The burden of proving that drug claims "intended to
defraud" the consumer rested with the federal agency. That burden was steep
and constrained the federal agency's regulatory authority.[9]

The subsequent 1938 Food, Drug and Cosmetic Act wove together a range
of regulatory policy instruments including requirements for firms to demonstrate new drugs' safety to the FDA before releasing the drugs on the market, to create new criteria for appropriate drug labels, to impose limits on the
amount of poison contained in drugs, and to permit inspection of pharmaceutical factories.[10] Although the FDA's formal regulatory jurisdiction continued to
expand, labeling remained an important source of regulatory leverage.[11] The
law continued to prohibit the sale of misbranded drugs, which included labels
that were "false or misleading," that failed to disclose that a drug was "habit-
forming," or that failed to disclose the drug's active ingredients.[12] By mid-century, drug labels needed to include information on drug indications (what the
drug treated), recommended dosage levels, information on drug effects and

---

[6] Earlier legislation included the 1848 Drug Importation Act.

[7] *U.S. v. Johnson* (1911). The drug in question was Johnson's Mild Combination Treatment
for Cancer. Given the Supreme Court's ruling, Congress followed with the 1912 Sherley
Amendment, which forbade "labeling medicines with false therapeutic claims intended to defraud the purchaser."

[8] Paul J. Quirk, "Food and Drug Administration," in *The Politics of Regulation*, edited by James
Q. Wilson (New York: Basic Books), p. 194.

[9] Authority for overseeing drug labeling rested with the Bureau of Chemistry in the Department
of Agriculture, renamed the Food, Drug and Insecticide Administration in 1927, which was then
"shortened" to the Food and Drug Administration in 1930. A Department of Agriculture appropriations bill shortened the name. The agency moved from the Department of Agriculture to
the Federal Security Agency in 1940, which became the Department of Health, Education and
Welfare in 1953.

[10] Jurisdiction for regulating drug advertising fell to the Federal Trade Commission under the
Wheeler-Lea Act. The act also created the architecture for violations to carry "legal ramifications." The 1914 Harrison Narcotics Act offered some grounds to regulate the content of pharmaceuticals, such as limiting the amount of opium and cocaine in drug products.

[11] The U.S. Court of Appeals affirmed that drug labels must specify the drug's purpose or indication in *Alberty Food Products Co. v. U.S.*, 1950.

[12] For more on the definition of misbranded drugs, see the Citizens' Advisory Committee "Report
to the Secretary of Health, Education and Welfare, June 1955," p. 53.

side effects, as well as contraindications, precautions, and warnings.[13] FDA influence over drug labeling expanded even in the absence of new legislative authority. The FDA began to consider new drug applications as "incomplete," and thus ineligible for FDA review and subsequent marketing, if the firm did not guarantee it "would not go beyond the labeling in the original NDA [New Drug Application]"; and the agency increasingly recalled drugs from the market for "labeling issues."[14] Influence over public information through labels spilled over to influence over firms' drug development and testing processes.[15]

The FDA amassed impressive regulatory power in the period between the 1906 Pure Food and Drugs Act and the 1962 Kefauver amendments, skillfully developing its authority even before that authority was codified in law.[16] Yet key aspects of pharmaceutical research, development, production, and promotion – as well as medical practice – remained outside the FDA's jurisdiction. Though FDA Commissioner George P. Larrick asserted in 1960 Congressional testimony that the FDA did not allow drug applications to become "effective" until drug manufacturers provided labels that were "as sound and informative for all aspects of safe use as can be achieved by competent medical scientists on the basis of the available information," misleading information nevertheless made its way to practicing physicians. Commissioner Larrick noted that "pharmaceutical manufacturers usually promote their products to the medical profession through the distribution of great quantities of literature by direct mail and by personal 'detailing.'" Though the FDA oversaw some aspects of product labeling, other aspects of promotion and detailing exceeded the FDA's regulatory authority and were not "precleared" by the agency.[17] Commissioner Larrick went on to specify two impediments to regulating misleading information: insufficient agency staff and insufficient formal regulatory authority over drugs' efficiency.[18]

Regulating pharmaceutical practice thus embodied both technical difficulty and implementation interdependence. The FDA could not command safe drug

---

[13] Statement of George P. Larrick, Commissioner of Food and Drugs, U.S. Department of Health, Education and Welfare, prepared for the Senate Subcommittee on Antitrust & Monopoly of the Senate Committee on the Judiciary, June 1960. See p. 28 of his prepared testimony.

[14] Daniel P. Carpenter, *Reputation and Power: Organizational Image and Pharmaceutical Regulation at the FDA* (Princeton, NJ: Princeton University Press, 2010), pp. 167–171.

[15] As Daniel Carpenter discusses, some FDA staffers "proposed new rules to require 'not for pediatric use' labels upon all drugs where the clinical tests did not explicitly examine and support the safety of pediatric dosages." Carpenter, *Reputation and Power*, pp. 167–171.

[16] Carpenter, *Reputation and Power*, pp. 149–156.

[17] Statement of George P. Larrick, Commissioner of Food and Drugs, U.S. Department of Health, Education and Welfare, Before the Senate Subcommittee on Antitrust & Monopoly of the Senate Committee on the Judiciary, June 1960. See p. 28 of his testimony for discussion of promotions and detailing not being precleared.

[18] Statement of George P. Larrick, Commissioner of Food and Drugs, U.S. Department of Health, Education and Welfare, Before the Senate Subcommittee on Antitrust & Monopoly of the Senate Committee on the Judiciary, June 1960. See p. 29 of his prepared testimony.

use, which depended on the complex interplay between firms' development, manufacturing, and promotion and physician and patient practice. Nor could the agency even dictate label and promotional materials' content, which was the product of negotiations between the FDA and an individual firm. Through its authority to require firms to demonstrate safety, the FDA implicitly pressed firms to demonstrate pharmaceutical efficacy by requiring them to demonstrate the drug's safety relative to the drug's proven benefits.[19] Still, significant gaps in FDA authority – over both drug promotion and drug efficacy – remained. Like federal education officials, the FDA looked to public committees, especially when lacking either implementation authority and/or information.

PROMOTING AGENCIES AND POLICIES

One type of venue for participation that appeared in the FDA before FACA involved examining agency operations and reporting to external audiences. A second type of venue focused on task-specific questions and reported directly to the agency, privately. While the first kind of venue offered the potential for participatory oversight in principle, in practice it served primarily to promote the agency.

A mid-century manifestation of the former arose from a Health, Education and Welfare request "to have FDA activities reviewed by a representative citizens advisory group ... whose general purpose would be to assess objectively the present enforcement and certification policies and programs of FDA."[20] The Secretary of HEW appointed the committee's members, including academics, industry leaders, and representatives from various union and women's organizations.[21] "Citizens," in this case, did not mean average pharmaceutical consumers or family doctors.[22] A press release announced the committee and its purpose but did not issue an open invitation. The committee kept minutes, which the FDA retained and did not classify. The committee met twice in its entirety and convened a series of subcommittee meetings before issuing its findings and recommendations, which were summarized in a subsequent press

---

[19] Carpenter, *Reputation and Power*, pp. 149–156.

[20] This request arose during 1954 appropriations hearings. Citizens' Advisory Committee, "Report to the Secretary of Health, Education and Welfare, June 1955."

[21] The information in this account comes from: U.S. Congress, House of Representatives Committee Print, *Replies from Executive Departments and Federal Agencies to Inquiry Regarding Use of Advisory Committees, January 1, 1953–January 1, 1956, Part 3: Department of Health, Education and Welfare*, June 5 (Washington, DC: GPO, 1956), pp. 957–958. Also see Citizens' Advisory Committee, "Report to the Secretary of Health, Education and Welfare, June 1955," p. 1. See Carpenter for a review of the corporatist structure of the committee: Carpenter, *Reputation and Power*, pp. 167–171.

[22] When describing the sources of information used to develop the report, the committee mentions consumers once and never mentions physicians. The committee collected information from visits to district offices, FDA documents, interviews with FDA staff, a study of FDA laws and

release. Rather than shine a critical light on FDA operations or blame the FDA for problems in pharmaceutical regulation, the subsequent Citizens' Advisory committee praised FDA staff:

> The personnel responsible for the administration of the FDA and its various divisions are able and experienced officials. A high proportion of the staff is composed of professional persons, highly trained in various fields of science ... a very capable group, with high devotion to the public service ... the returns on the money appropriated to the FDA are high in terms of the protection of public health and other consumer interests, with due regard to the legitimate interests of the industries concerned.[23]

The report's careful language warned of future threats and risks to public safety given the agency's meager resources. The FDA's workload had increased and had become more complex, the report argued, noting drops in the ratio of FDA enforcement staff relative to the population over the fourteen-year span from 1941 to 1955.[24] The Committee concluded, "The Food and Drug Administration now has insufficient funds, staff, and facilities to meet its essential responsibility of protecting public health," and it went on to recommend more generous appropriations, more personnel, and updated technology.[25] Public participation through the Citizens' Advisory Committee did little that appeared to jeopardize the FDA's developing bureaucratic administration. From an agency point of view, the report did not expose or criticize core FDA routines or activities, impugn the expertise of FDA staff, or threaten the FDA's existing jurisdiction. If anything, the report turned the spotlight on Congress, the agency's authorizing statute and its appropriations, not on the agency or on industry.[26] More so than educational assessment committees in the Office of Education, FDA public committees explicitly supported expanding the FDA's hierarchical authority over pharmaceutical regulation while building unique internal agency expertise. The Office of Education deliberately stayed in the shadows during part of the National Assessment's development. National

---

regulations, and "Memoranda from consumers, industry and retailers affected by FDA activities." Citizens' Advisory Committee "Report to the Secretary of Health, Education and Welfare, June 1955," p. 5.

[23] Citizens' Advisory Committee, "Report to the Secretary of Health, Education and Welfare, June 1955," pp. 12–13.

[24] Citizens' Advisory Committee, "Report to the Secretary of Health, Education and Welfare, June 1955," p. 2.

[25] Citizens' Advisory Committee, "Report to the Secretary of Health, Education and Welfare, June 1955," p. 6. Even though agency resources increased after the Committee issued its report, funds were largely directed at areas such as pharmacology and toxicology, which the agency had been trying to build well before the committee convened and issued its report. For further discussion, see Carpenter, *Reputation and Power*, pp. 167–171.

[26] In *Reputation and Power*, pp. 195–196, Carpenter concludes: "The other legacy of the Committee report was the echo it provided about the underlying strength and benevolence of the Administration. Whatever problems existed with US pharmaceutical regulation were

Assessment public committees were careful to avoid claims of extending federal authority, although the federal agency ultimately enjoyed spillover effects from the design and implementation of the National Assessment. The Citizens' Committee report, in sharp contrast, advocated for expanding FDA resources and authority.

The National Academy of Sciences (NAS) and its National Research Council (NRC) also conducted reviews of FDA operations.[27] This included closed NAS/NRC reviews of the FDA's relationship with industry: "to review the policies and procedures used by the Food and Drug Administration" and "present such recommendations as it might consider desirable for the protection of the public health through the functions of the FDA."[28] The NAS review known as the Bronk Committee was commissioned on the heels of controversy, shortly after allegations that the FDA Director of the Division of Antibiotics had "an improper relationship with the pharmaceutical industry."[29] Its eight committee members were all medical professionals who held MDs: an even more limited subsection of the public than the Citizens' Committee. A key part of the committee's mandate entailed reviewing decisions made while Dr. Henry Welch was director, to assess the "integrity of the scientific decisions."[30] The committee affirmed the FDA's decisions, "found no evidence of disregard for the public health," and qualified any concerns by pointing to the FDA's limited authority and resources.[31] Similar to the Citizens' Advisory Committee Report, the NAS/NRC Bronk Committee shone light on problems with the FDA's authorizing

weaknesses in the law, not weaknesses in the 'public protector' charged with enforcing it. Put differently, the fault of weak food and drug regulation lay with Congress, not with the FDA."

[27] Consultations with the National Academy of Sciences were part of the FDA's practice for more than drug reviews. The Pesticide Chemicals Amendment of the Food, Drug, and Cosmetic Act, for instance, specified that the NAS should appoint members to committees developed to advise the agency on "tolerances for pesticide chemical residues." Letter from FDA Deputy Commission Harvey to Representative John Bell Williams, printed in *The Congressional Record – House*, July 10, 1957, p. 11262. Looking to the NAS/NRC for advice was not unique to the FDA and HEW, but occurred in agencies throughout the executive branch during this time period.

[28] National Academy of Sciences – National Research Council, "Report of Special Committee Advisory to the Secretary of Health, Education and Welfare to Review the Policies, Procedures, and Decisions of the Division of Antibiotics and the New Drug Branch of the Food and Drug Administration, Committee Report, September 27, 1960," p. 1.

[29] Peter Barton Hutt, "Investigations and Reports Respecting FDA Regulation of New Drugs (Part 1)," *Clinical Pharmacology and Therapeutics* 33 (1983): 539–540. The report of impropriety appeared in the popular press and was followed by congressional hearings.

[30] Hutt, "Investigations and Reports," pp. 539–540.

[31] NAS/NRC, "Report of Special Committee," p. 1. HEW also conducted an internal investigation following the allegations against Dr. Welch, yielding a report that made a series of recommendations for ensuring scientific rigor and appropriate agency-industry interaction. See "Report of the Special Investigative Unit of the Food and Drug Administration," (Washington DC, U.S. Department of Health, Education and Welfare, December 23, 1960). On the guidelines

statute and resources, not on agency administration. The committee's report concluded that "certain weaknesses inherent in the existing law and current staffing and budgetary support hamper the FDA in its task of protecting the public health."[32]

The Committee report went on to recommend granting the FDA formal authority to require firms to demonstrate drug efficacy in their drug applications, expanding the FDA's authority over drug labeling, consistent with the FDA commissioner's own recommendations.[33] Both of these of public reviews appear high risk from a bureaucratic perspective: investigating core agency procedures over which the agency enjoys expertise and independent authority. Like the Citizens' Committee, however, the Bronk Committee process, report, and recommendations appeared consistent with bureaucratic administration, advocating for greater agency authority and pressing for greater agency resources without impugning the agency's expertise.

The second form of public engagement came from participation that was restricted and private in ways that differed from the Citizens' Committee exclusivity. In the 1950s, for instance, the FDA would consult informally with medical experts on drug reviews under FDA consideration – such as new treatment for diabetes – during professional meetings that experts attended.[34] More systematic private advice came from NAS/NRC panels that supported FDA efficacy reviews of drugs approved before 1962. In addition to granting the FDA formal authority over requiring firms to demonstrate a drug's safety *and* efficacy in new drug applications, the 1962 Kefauver Amendments granted the FDA authority to revisit drugs that went on the market between 1938 and 1962 to determine whether they met efficacy standards. Reviewing twenty-four years' worth of drugs for efficacy presented a monumental increase in the FDA's workload, and the FDA sought NAS/NRC help reviewing roughly 3,000 drugs on the basis of efficacy.[35] In 1966, FDA Commissioner James L. Goddard pointed to the NAS's expertise to justify their participation in the reviews:

for "proper relationships with industry" that Deputy Commissioner Harvey issued on January 16, 1961, see Peter Barton Hutt, "Investigations and Reports," pp. 539–540.

[32] NAS/NRC, "Report of Special Committee," p. 2.

[33] The report specified, "The Committee believes that the information supplied to physicians concerning drugs should not only be accurate, but also complete, and that the date of such information is essential to its prior evaluation. It therefore endorses the proposed amendments to present labeling requirements published by the Commissioner in the Federal Register for 22 July 1960." "Bronk Committee Report," September 27 1960, p. 2.

[34] Letter from FDA Deputy Commissioner Harvey to Representative John Bell Williams, printed in *The Congressional Record – House*, July 10, 1957, p. 11262.

[35] Two reports offer conflicting numbers (3,637 or 2,824), but the estimate of 2,800 drug reviews is generally considered accurate. R. Keith Cannan, "Status of the Drug Efficacy Study of the National Academy of Sciences-National Research Council," *Food, Drug and Cosmetic Law Journal* (January 1968): 32–35; Warren E. Whyte, "Effectiveness of the NAS-NRC Drug Effectiveness Study," *Food, Drug, Cosmetic Law Journal* (February 1970): 91–100.

Recommendations from the most expert sources are essential if the Administration is to suppress flagrant claims, eliminate worthless products and at the same time protect the physician's therapeutic resources.[36]

The subsequent press release announcing the use of NAS panels to review drugs also pointed to supplementing FDA capacity, noting, "The FDA itself does not have sufficient medical personnel to carry out a project of this scope."[37] On the one hand, efficacy reviews fell under the FDA's full jurisdiction, raising the risk that participation could jeopardize the agency's image of providing unique expertise. The NAS/NRC reviews, however, assisted ostensibly new – not established – formal regulatory authority (determining drug efficacy) and were billed as temporary operations geared toward helping the agency deal with a temporary backlog of work. Both of these features rendered them more amenable – and less threatening – to bureaucratic administration. Also consistent with bureaucratic administration, the NAS/NRC committees advised the FDA but did not obligate it to accept their recommendations, though FDA decisions were "often" consistent with the committees' recommendations.[38] The committees' reviews were kept confidential, meetings were not publicly announced, and meeting locations were not publicly revealed.[39] Using the terms of reference from the schema for participation in Figure 1.1, reviewing drug efficacy presented a general task condition of relatively high independent authority and low information in Quadrant B: the agency sought private learning from select, conventionally defined experts.

THE DEVELOPMENT OF PARTICIPATORY BUREAUCRACY IN THE FDA

A third form of participation in the FDA before the passage of FACA came from a system of ongoing committees with whom the FDA periodically met to discuss specific drug reviews. FDA Bureau of Medicine leadership created a series of committees along general therapeutic lines, including committees for anti-infective agents, cardiovascular and renal disorders, dermatology, endocrinology and metabolism, hematology, dental products, neuropharmacology, oncology, obstetrics and gynecology, radioactive drug products, and respiratory

---

[36] Memorandum from James L. Goddard, MD, Commissioner of Food and Drugs, to Dr. Keith Cannan, Division of Medical Science, National Academy of Sciences–National Research Council (NAS-NRC), "Efficacy Review of Pre-1962 Drugs," March 31, 1966, NAS-NRC Archives. Quoted in Richard Rettig, Laurence E. Earley, and Richard A. Merrill (eds.), *Food and Drug Administration Advisory Committees* (Washington, DC: National Academy Press, 1992), p. 50.

[37] Quoted in Rettig, *Food and Drug Administration Advisory Committees*, p. 51.

[38] Firms could challenge or respond to the FDA decision and take the agency to court to contest a drug withdrawal. Rettig, *Food and Drug Administration Advisory Committees*, p. 51.

[39] The FDA also did not select NAS panel members. Rettig, *Food and Drug Administration Advisory Committees*, p. 56.

and anesthetic drug products.[40] The FDA dissolved the original 1967 committees but reestablished them in the early 1970s.[41] By 1974, the FDA consulted with fifteen public committees.[42]

Since FDA standing committees existed through agency discretion, the FDA could have disbanded its committees in light of FACA requirements for greater committee openness and permeability. Once they fell under the auspices of the 1972 Act, FDA committees needed to justify closing meetings to members of the general public not serving on the committee. While the agency kept minutes of early meetings, FACA specified the agency should keep verbatim transcripts and ensure that minutes and transcripts were publicly available. Instead of dissolving its committees and relying exclusively on alternate forms of participation that would not trigger FACA, new FDA policies governing its public advisory committees emerged during the early 1970s. These policies both interpreted FACA and went beyond the Act to establish systematic FDA advisory committee practice. Addressing members of the Gastrointestinal Drugs Advisory Committee, Director of the Bureau of Drugs J. Richard Crout specified guidelines for committee operations that afforded greater committee openness than in the past through open-access to meetings and publicly available transcripts of open sessions. Crout noted, "All meetings are open unless they are closed ... [that statement] always brings a smile ... but it's a reversal of past policies within regulatory agencies."[43]

---

[40] Carpenter, *Reputation and Power*, p. 314, table 5.5.

[41] The Public Health Services Act authorized the Secretary of Health and Human Services to, "from time to time, appoint such advisory councils or committees ... for such periods of time, as he deems desirable ... for the purpose of advising him in connection with any of his functions" (21 USC 394). This statutory authorization effectively leaves advisory committee creation for the FDA in the hands of the executive branch.

[42] Testimony of Commissioner Schmidt, U.S. Congress, Senate, *Examination of the Pharmaceutical Industry 73–74*, Joint Hearings before the Subcommittee on Health of the Committee on Labor and Public Welfare and the Subcommittee on Administrative Practice and Procedure of the Committee on the Judiciary, 93rd Congress, 1st and 2nd Sessions, Part 7, August 16 (Washington, DC: GPO, 1974), p. 25 of submitted testimony, p. 3071 of Committee hearing transcript. J. Richard Crout credits himself, Charles Edwards, and Marion Finkel with establishing and solidifying the FDA's advisory committee system in the early 1970s. Transcript of J. Richard Crout, Oral History, History of the Food and Drug Administration, Interview, November 12, 1997, p. 23. He argued, "We started the system, we picked the people, we wrote the regs, we did a lot of the initial thinking of how to do this." See Carpenter, *Reputation and Power*, p. 314, table 5.5 for a list of committees from 1897 to 1967.

[43] Quoted in *FDC Reports* (1974) 36 (35), p. 6. Internal memoranda specified that transcripts would not be destroyed. Memo to the FDA Commissioner from Ernest L. Brisson, October 29, 1974, Subject "Clarification for the Record: Minutes of the Commissioner's Staff Meeting with the Bureau of Drugs, November 30, 1972." Brisson wrote (p. 2), "Presently, the decision regarding what means may be utilized for keeping records of panel meetings is still left to the individual panels. All panels, however, have been advised that no tape recordings or transcripts may be destroyed pending a specific policy decision by the Commissioner. Insofar as standing technical advisory committees are concerned, present policy is to retain any verbatim transcript or tape that may be prepared." On meeting openness, see Testimony of Commissioner Schmidt, U.S.

Along with greater openness came greater scrutiny. FDA public committees amassed critics both inside and outside the agency. Reflecting on the early days of public advisory committees, former director Crout argued that the added openness, "scrutiny," and "participation" that accompanied the advisory committee system were, "to some extent ... a threat to the FDA review culture at the time, and certainly it was a threat to the people in the bureau who liked the notion of total power – and there were some."[44] As the system of ongoing advisory committees emerged, it provided fodder for congressional oversight. Senator Edward Kennedy (D-MA) used the advisory committee process in his efforts to expose possible weaknesses in FDA regulatory activity and called on an advisory committee member, Dr. Julia Apter of the Cardiovascular and Renal Drugs Advisory Committee. Dr. Apter testified that the committee's chairman and executive secretary made her "feel uncomfortable" after she requested the committee keep a transcript of the proceedings, in accordance with PL 92-463.[45] Lack of openness, her testimony suggested, was abetted through relationships between committee members and the firms whose drugs they were charged to review.

FDA Commissioner Alexander M. Schmidt responded to allegations of agency secrecy by noting that, "Very often there is no request for anyone from the outside to come and nobody from the outside is there, and then really the issue of openness is moot."[46] He also defended maintaining secrecy while the agency was in the process of considering alternatives, in part out of concern for stock market fluctuations based on "speculation" of future FDA actions and potential damage to the "public good" that could arise from public discussion that fueled such speculation.[47]

Congressional criticism of FDA advisory committees persisted and followed themes of more general congressional critiques of federal advisory committees overall. The House Committee on Government Operations, chaired

Congress, Senate, *Examination of the Pharmaceutical Industry 73–74,* Joint Hearings before the Subcommittee on Health of the Committee on Labor and Public Welfare and the Subcommittee on Administrative Practice and Procedure of the Committee on the Judiciary, 93rd Congress, 1st and 2nd Sessions, Part 7, August 16 (Washington, DC: GPO, 1974), p. 2983.

[44] Transcript of J. Richard Crout, Oral History, History of the Food and Drug Administration, Interview, November 12, 1997, p. 22.

[45] Testimony of Dr. Julia Apter, U.S. Congress, Senate, *Examination of the Pharmaceutical Industry 73–74,* Joint Hearings before the Subcommittee on Health of the Committee on Labor and Public Welfare and the Subcommittee on Administrative Practice and Procedure of the Committee on the Judiciary, 93rd Congress, 1st and 2nd Sessions, Part 7, August 15 (Washington, DC: GPO, 1974), p. 2883.

[46] Testimony of Commissioner Schmidt, U.S. Congress, Senate, *Examination of the Pharmaceutical Industry 73–74,* Joint Hearings before the Subcommittee on Health of the Committee on Labor and Public Welfare and the Subcommittee on Administrative Practice and Procedure of the Committee on the Judiciary, 93rd Congress, 1st and 2nd Sessions, Part 7, August 16 (Washington, DC: GPO, 1974), p. 2983.

[47] Testimony of Commissioner Schmidt, *Examination of the Pharmaceutical Industry 73–74,* p. 2983.

by Representative Lawrence H. Fountain (D-NC), levied a series of harsh allegations against FDA advisory committees in 1976, alleging

> Non-essential use of advisory committees ... Improper closing of advisory committee meetings ... Inadequate and incomplete minutes of meetings ... Premature destruction of verbatim transcripts ... Holding of advisory committees in locations that tend to discourage public attendance and participation ... Lack of balance in the composition of advisory committees.[48]

Linked to these allegations of waste and secrecy came charges that the FDA used advisory committees "to short-circuit intensive and critical examination of NDA data by its own medical and scientific staff" and "to gain support in the medical community for regulatory decisions thought desirable by the agency's leadership," citing "the selective providing or withholding of data from FDA files" as evidence.[49] FDA leadership disputed these claims and carried on with its committee system, though Bureau of Drugs Director Crout later validated some of the criticisms:

> We did make mistakes in implementation at the beginning. We got some people on advisory committees who were not ideal, and some were poorly staffed. We asked people who already had a job to do, out of their side pocket, to also manage an advisory committee; it was extra work for them. We had a number of complaints by advisory committee members that they weren't well educated into their role and mission – quite true. Some said that they didn't receive packages for review in time – quite true. All of the difficulties of getting the program up to speed were there to pick at.[50]

The federal bureaucracy – on its own initiative – laid a foundation for public engagement through public committees. It was, however, a narrow foundation in terms of the public the FDA invited to participate as formal committee members and in terms of the public who was attentive enough to watch, attend, follow, and participate in the committee's deliberations.

Getting Up to Speed: The Case of Propranolol

As the FDA got its public advisory committees "up to speed" administratively, drug labeling emerged as an important domain for public participation. The

---

[48] U.S. Congress, House of Representatives, Committee on Government Operations, House Report No 94–787, *Use of Advisory Committees by the Food and Drug Administration*, 94th Congress, 2nd Session, January 26 (Washington, DC: GPO, 1976), p. 12.

[49] U.S. Congress, House of Representatives, Committee on Government Operations, House Report No 94–787, *Use of Advisory Committees by the Food and Drug Administration*, 94th Congress, 2nd Session, January 26 (Washington, DC: GPO, 1976), pp. 5–8. Using public committees to support decisions already made represents a long-standing criticism of public committees. Thomas A. Wolanin, *Presidential Advisory Committees: Truman to Nixon* (Madison: University of Wisconsin Press, 1975), pp. 15–20.

[50] Transcript of J. Richard Crout, Oral History, History of the Food and Drug Administration, Interview, November 12, 1997, p. 23.

controversial case of the drug Inderal (Propranolol) for treatment of angina (chest pain resulting from insufficient blood flow to the heart) illustrates the challenges facing the FDA and the relationship between advisory committee operations and bureaucratic administration.

The FDA approved Propranolol in 1967 for cardiac arrhythmias (abnormal heart rate or rhythm), but did not approve subsequent applications from the drug's sponsor, Ayerst, in 1968 and again in 1969 for angina indications.[51] Reports suggested, however, that doctors prescribed Propranolol for angina, even though the FDA had not approved the drug for the angina indication. The FDA faced competing pressures. Propranolol became a sort of symbol for what FDA critics called the "drug lag": an argument that other countries had approved Propranolol for angina and that the FDA's failure to extend the drug's approved indications was costing lives.[52] Yet, medical reviewers inside the FDA found that the trials submitted as part of the Propranolol applications did not meet FDA criteria for safety and efficacy. The FDA took the Proporanol issue to an ad hoc committee of experts for external review in 1970. The committee agreed with the FDA reviewers that Ayerst's application had not satisfied FDA criteria for safety and efficacy.

When the FDA took Propranolol to its Cardiovascular and Renal Drugs Advisory Committee for review in 1973, the terms of the conversation shifted somewhat. The FDA noted that doctors were prescribing Propranolol to patients to treat angina, which was entirely legal: doctors were not prohibited from using drugs for off-label purposes. Doctors' prescription practices remain beyond the FDA's regulatory reach, underscoring the underlying interdependence of implementing drug safety and efficacy. The advisory committee debated whether Propranolol's label should include instructions for safe and effective use for angina, even though the drug was not approved for that indication. If doctors were prescribing the drug anyway for angina, they should know how to do so as safely and as effectively as possible, the committee reasoned. The committee voted 4 to 1 to revise the drug's label to include instructions for use in angina patients.

More controversy followed when FDA Bureau of Drugs Director Crout sent a letter to Ayerst stating that Propranolol was approvable for angina, referring to the advisory committee and suggesting the advisory committee recommended its approval. Advisory committee member, Dr. Apter, later charged that the FDA had grossly misrepresented the advisory committee's position. "We have gone specifically on record as not recommending the Propanolol for

---

[51] Ayerst withdrew its application in 1968, and the FDA deemed Inderal "not approvable" for angina in 1969. See U.S. Congress, House of Representatives, Committee on Government Operations, House Report No 94–787, *Use of Advisory Committees by the Food and Drug Administration*, 94th Congress, 2nd Session, January 26 (Washington, DC: GPO, 1976), p. 18.

[52] For more on allegations of the drug lag, see Carpenter, *Reputation and Power*, pp. 374–380.

angina," Dr. Apter asserted at 1974 Senate hearings.[53] Dr. Apter argued that the vote reflected the committee's views on how the package insert should be written, not on whether the drug was safe and effective for approval for a new indication. Crout responded that "labeling and efficacy are two halves of the same coin": by voting to change the package label, the committee must have been implicitly stating that it was possible to specify efficacious drug use. Dr. Apter, backed by Senator Kennedy, disagreed. Crout's interpretation appeared consistent with the FDA's pre-Kefauver amendment practice of regulating drug efficacy before the agency had formal jurisdiction to do so: to use the drug label to regulate how drugs could be promoted.

The Propranolol controversy emerged at the intersection of competing pressures on the FDA, competing perceptions of the agency, and competing roles for public advice. Along with critics that the FDA was too slow approving drugs that other countries had approved came critics, like Dr. Apter, charging that the FDA was neglecting science to accommodate industry. Alongside accusations that the FDA was endangering public health by failing to approve promising therapies were accusations that the FDA was endangering public health through insufficient rigor in its regulatory and approval processes. Alongside claims that the FDA was using public committees to justify positions the FDA had already reached came claims that the committees were influencing the agency to defer to industry wishes.

Media coverage of Propranolol appeared both in trade publications and in the popular press, including coverage on Propranolol's reputed effectiveness for angina several years before the drug was approved in the United States for that indication.[54] The public review of Propranolol along with subsequent congressional hearings shone light on the FDA's drug review process as well as on the drug's characteristics.[55] The Cardiovascular and Renal Drugs Advisory

---

[53] Testimony of Dr. Julia Apter, U.S. Congress, Senate, *Examination of the Pharmaceutical Industry* 73–74, Joint Hearings before the Subcommittee on Health of the Committee on Labor and Public Welfare and the Subcommittee on Administrative Practice and Procedure of the Committee on the Judiciary, 93rd Congress, 1st and 2nd Sessions, Part 7, August 15 (Washington, DC: GPO, 1974), p. 2886. Dr. Crout disputed Dr. Apter's interpretation of the committee position. He testified, "The Cardiovascular and Renal Advisory Committee voted 4 to 1 to approve propranolol for angina pectoris. The one was Dr. Apter, dissenting." U.S. Congress, Senate, *Examination of the Pharmaceutical Industry* 73–74, Joint Hearings before the Subcommittee on Health of the Committee on Labor and Public Welfare and the Subcommittee on Administrative Practice and Procedure of the Committee on the Judiciary, 93rd Congress, 1st and 2nd Sessions, Part 7, August 16 (Washington, DC: GPO, 1974), p. 2955.

[54] These references include: Ruby Abramson, "Exciting New Treatment for Angina Described," *Boston Globe*, February 17, 1967, p. 40; Herbert Black, "New Hope of a Million Victims of Angina," *Boston Globe*, October 19, 1969, p. A-20; *The New York Times*, August 5, 1974; Gail Bronson, *Wall Street Journal*, March 7, 1977; *FDC Reports* (August 19, 1974) 36 (33); *FDC Reports* (August 26, 1974); *FDC Reports* (September 2, 1974) 36 (35).

[55] Congressional review and hearings may impugn an agency but may also provide the agency with an opportunity to refute its critics' claims. See Carpenter, *Reputation and Power*, p. 344.

Committee convened and deliberated on Propranolol's label and effectiveness, but it did so in a closed meeting. It was not until the Senate committee hearings that minutes and transcripts from the closed meeting enjoyed a broader audience. Bureaucratically initiated participation for private learning collided with congressional appetites for oversight. Propranolol offers a glimpse into how the passage of FACA and its requirements for openness layered awkwardly, at times, on existing closed participatory arrangements.

Unlike the ad hoc public committees of the 1950s and 1960s, which carefully presented the agency in favorable terms while advocating for expanding agency authority and resources, and unlike the NAS/NRC review panels, which conducted their specific drug reviews behind closed doors, FDA public advice in the 1970s edged toward more open, more participatory, and more indeterminate policymaking, with new opportunities for broader access to the discussion and for public dissent. Much about the FDA's early venues for public participation supported bureaucratic administration but was modestly participatory, at best.[56] Yet, an agency-initiated platform for participatory bureaucracy began to take shape.[57]

FACA AND THE FOUNDATION FOR PARTICIPATORY BUREAUCRACY

The implementation of FACA lurched and varied across the federal government in terms of committee openness, access, and contributions. A 1977 review by the General Accounting Office asserted that the Office of Management and Budget struggled to provide sufficient advisory committee oversight and management. The GAO documented agency uncertainty over what counted as an advisory committee, different financial reporting practices, and inconsistent criteria for judging committee effectiveness. Implementation continued to vary by agency.[58]

---

[56] The FDA's advisory committee system has faced a series of external reviews and critiques. For instance, the 1976 Fountain Report – emerging amid allegations that committees were promotional devices, not essential to the substantive drug review process, and a waste of agency resources – accused the agency of "seeking recommendations from advisory committees on matters that have already been decided." Rettig, *Food and Drug Administration Advisory Committees*, p. 102. The counterpoint to these allegations claimed the agency was still getting up to speed and working out the kinks in its advisory committee development process, and that the allegations reflected the views of staffers who worried advisory committees may encroach on agency review turf and practice. See J. Richard Crout, Oral History. Other external reviews occurred in the Dorsen Report (1977), the MacMahon Report (1982), and the Lasagna Committee Report (1990). See Rettig, *Food and Drug Administration Advisory Committees*, pp. 101–107 for a review.

[57] The FDA retains a range of ways to obtain private advice that does not fall under the auspices of FACA. 21 CFR 14.1(b)(4, 5 & 7), 1991. For a review, see Rettig, *Food and Drug Administration Advisory Committees*, p. 47.

[58] U.S. General Accounting Office, *Better Evaluations Needed to Weed Out Useless Federal Advisory Committees* (Washington, DC: GAO, 1977).

Neither the FDA nor the Office of Education constructed public participation in the pre-FACA and post-FACA periods in ways that fully reflect either bureaucratic or democratic ideals. Yet, both agencies took significant steps *before* FACA passed in 1972 to construct ongoing processes for public participation in agency policymaking. The National Assessment model emphasized aspects of "participatory" more than "bureaucracy." Public committees that developed around the National Assessment enjoyed formal policymaking authority and were housed separately from the federal agency. Other aspects of assessment development invited participation from grassroots "lay" reviewers. The National Assessment and its participatory bodies owe their origins to Office of Education Commissioner Frank Keppel, and they enjoyed the support of National Center for Education Statistics bureaucrats. Still, the federal bureaucracy set few of the terms for the assessment's public participation, and public participation largely occurred with the federal bureaucracy at arm's length.

The institutional origins of public participation appeared more bureaucratic for pharmaceutical regulation than for educational assessments. FDA public committees largely arose from bureaucratic initiatives and offered expert extensions to bureaucratic work. The committees were public in the sense of consisting of nongovernmental participants. And they became public in the sense of providing meeting minutes and public access to committee meetings after FACA. For the National Assessment committees, diversely expert participation meant including teachers, administrators, academics, and "lay" assessment reviewers, among others, in the policymaking process. For pharmaceutical regulation, diversely expert participation in the 1960s and 1970s largely meant including MDs *and* PhDs.

FACA augmented opportunities for openness through its meeting notification, open meeting requirements, and record keeping procedures. Did public participation in pharmaceutical regulation and educational assessments capitalize on these opportunities in ways conducive to bureaucratic administration, democratic accountability, or both? The general lack of federal-level authority over of the terrain of American schooling created general conditions of interdependence for the federal agency, coupled with generally low expertise. These conditions lend themselves to potential participatory bureaucracy, and some aspects of the participation that ensued supported elements of bureaucratic administration and accountability. The FDA faced conditions of greater independent authority for task implementation in general, consistent with predictions that agencies seek private information in conditions of relatively high independence but low information. Interdependent implementations, however, can vary within an agency depending on the task. Some FDA drug reviews present more implementation interdependence than others, as do some educational assessment tasks. The next chapter looks more closely at variation in task-specific interdependence and uncertainty to assess how both agencies used their participatory venues in the post-FACA period.

6

Setting the Public Agenda

> FDA has come to realize that safe and effective use of drugs does not mean safe
> and effective theoretically as in the label, but safe and effective in the real world.
> FDA is concerned about how drugs are actually used; how physicians use the
> drugs; how the public uses them; if the medical community understands risks and
> benefits of the drug, and how to improve this understanding and actual safe and
> appropriate use of the drugs. This problem is a complex problem that is not solved
> by government, not solved by FDA alone, and not solved for just one drug
>
> > Former FDA Office Director, Florence Houn,
> > before the Gastrointestinal Drugs Advisory Committee[1]

The development of public committees for national educational assessments
and pharmaceutical regulation suggests potential portals for public engagement in agency policymaking. When does that engagement reflect the criteria
of participatory bureaucracy consistent with bureaucratic reputation for cultivating unique expertise and diverse support? When does engagement reflect
participatory oversight or group dominance? Looking closely at committee
agendas allows us to assess task-specific conditions for public advice along the
continuum of task uncertainty and interdependent implementations.

Agenda setting embodies a source of political power[2] by determining which
issues are open for participation and which are not. Agendas affect who is
included in the discussion and who is excluded, and they can confer privilege
through the sequence of topics under consideration. Examining agendas on
public committees offers opportunities to discern potential sources of privilege and power in agency policymaking. When they succeed at liquefying

---

[1] Food and Drug Administration, "Gastrointestinal Drugs Advisory Committee Meeting Transcript:
Lotronex, June 27, 2000."
[2] Peter Bachrach and Morton S. Baratz, "Two Faces of Power," *American Political Science Review*
(1962): 947–951; Jack L. Walker, "Setting the Agenda in the U.S. Senate: A Theory of Problem
Selection," *British Journal of Political Science* 7 (1977): 423–445.

FIGURE 6.1. Total Number of Federal Public Advisory Committees, 1972–2010.

knowledge, public committees' agendas may contribute to a broader public agenda as well.

Public committee existence represents a precursor to agenda setting by providing potential venues for public engagement. Descriptive estimates depicted in Figure 6.1 suggest the number of public committees in operation in the federal government has hovered around 1,000 committees since the beginning of the twenty-first century.

The total number of agency-initiated committees declined in the last quarter of the twentieth century, reflecting presidential initiatives more than agency abandonment of public participation in the post-FACA period. Presidents and their political appointees have a reputation for "cleaning house" after assuming office by purging public committees established by predecessors.[3] A bird's eye view of the American federal advisory committee system suggests the executive branch has actively contributed to the creation and dissolution of public committees over the past forty years.

Figure 6.2 reports the number of public committees that were eliminated or combined with other committees between 1972 and 2010.[4] Descriptively, three sizable spikes appear. A significant reduction in public committees appears

[3] One of the architects of the FDA's advisory committee system, J. Richard Crout, argued that "we will always see advisory committees come under pressure whenever the administration changes." Transcript of J. Richard Crout, Oral History, History of the Food and Drug Administration, Interview, November 12, 1997, pp. 23–24.

[4] Data for figures 6.1, 6.2, and 6.3 come from the Annual Reports of the President to Congress on advisory committees from 1972 through 1998, when the requirement to submit an annual report ended. Reports may be accessed at http://www.fido.gov/facadatabase/PrintedAnnualReports.asp.

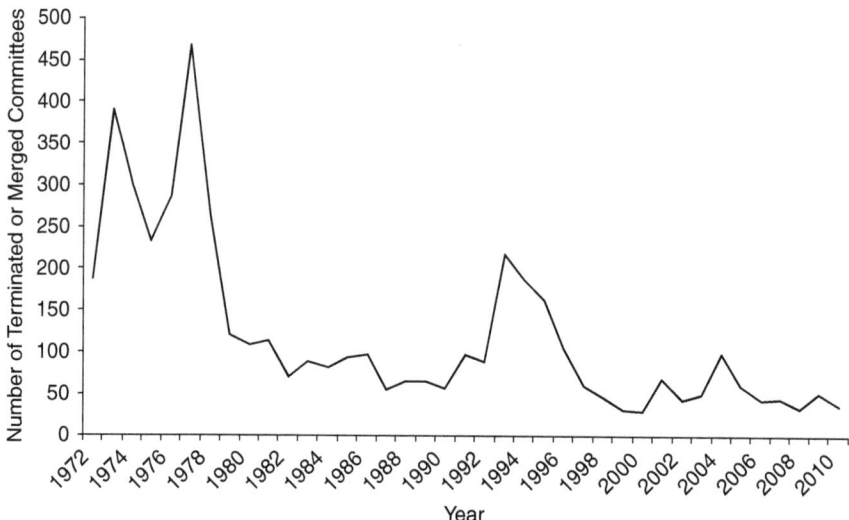

FIGURE 6.2. Count of Federal Public Advisory Committees Terminated or Merged, 1972–2010.

after the passage of the 1972 FACA. A second large reduction appears after President Carter assumed office and actively terminated committees, and a third appears toward the beginning of President Clinton's first term, consistent with his Executive Order 12838 calling for agencies to reduce discretionary committees by one-third.[5] Although some Congressional rhetoric charged that the American advisory committee system was rife with an excess of committees that offered too little value, the lion's share of committee termination has arisen from executive branch discretion. Before the Carter administration reductions, nearly twice as many executive branch committees as congressionally mandated committees were in operation. By the end of the Clinton administration, committees created by Congress and executive-branch-created committees were roughly equal in number.[6]

Within this landscape of committees – potential portals of public engagement – which tasks appear on public agendas and when? FACA grants government agencies general authority over setting public committees' agendas,

Data from 1998 through 2010 come from General Service Administration records, which are publicly available for the 1997–2010 period at http://facadatabase1997–2013.fido.gov/.

[5] See U.S. General Accounting Office, *Federal Advisory Committee Act: Overview of Advisory Committees Since 1993, Statement of L. Nye Stevens* (Washington, DC: GAO, 1997), p. 1. See Figure 1.2 in Chapter 1 for disaggregated committee origins over time.

[6] Looking more closely at the period from 1997 through 2010, my supplemental analysis suggests that advisory committees in cabinet agencies were more likely to be terminated or not used: all else being equal, about two more committees were terminated in cabinet agencies compared with other types of agencies.

and doing so appeared relatively uncontroversial in legislative debate in the 1950s and 1970s.[7] Congress and executive branch appointees, however, enjoy various ways to influence public committees' agendas. Congress may mandate topics for public committees, for instance, or exempt topics or committees from all or part of FACA. All applications to the FDA's Center for Device and Radiologic Health, for instance, receive a public advisory committee review before approval. Committees advising the Central Intelligence Agency are exempt from FACA.

Peering into specific committee operations suggests the extent to which these potential portals for participation support participatory bureaucracy by producing agendas that focus on tasks with uncertain and interdependent implementations as opposed to tasks over which agencies enjoy more information and independent implementation authority. Putting tasks over which bureaucrats enjoy expertise and implementation authority on public agendas risks compromising bureaucratic turf and uniqueness. Doing so, however, may suit elected officials concerned with overseeing government agencies, bypassing resistant agencies, exposing agency incompetence, or promoting preferred policies. Public committees associated with drug reviews and educational assessments provide systematically different institutional venues for assessing whether and when public participation reflects participatory bureaucracy, oversight, and/or group dominance. Recall some of the predictions developed in Chapter 2.

- *Participatory Bureaucracy:* Bureaucrats are more likely to seek public participation for tasks with uncertain and interdependent implementations than for other kinds of tasks.
- *Participatory Oversight:* Legislators are more likely to impose public participation in conditions of inter-branch or intra-branch divisiveness than in conditions of unity.
- *Participatory Oversight:* Presidents are more likely to impose public participation in conditions of inter-branch or intra-branch divisiveness than in conditions of unity.

The analysis of public committee agenda setting for pharmaceutical regulation and educational statistics and assessments in this chapter looks across committee institutional origin (agency-created vs. congressionally mandated), across committee authority (advisory vs. policymaking), across agenda setting

---

[7] Congressional support for agencies' agenda-setting authority dates back at least to 1957. U.S. Congress, House of Representatives, House Report 85–576, *Amending the Administrative Expenses Act of 1946, and for Other Purposes,* 85th Congress, 1st session, June 17 (Washington, DC: GPO, 1957), p. 6 proposed legislation that "requires that the agenda for each advisory committee shall be formulated or approved by a full-time officer or employee of the Government." The justification argued the provision "will prevent the committees from acting on their own initiative and giving advice on matters without having been request to do so by the department involved."

TABLE 6.1. *Institutional and Organizational Attributes of Public Committees: Agenda Setting*

	FDA Drug Committees	National Assessment Governing Board	Advisory Council on Education Statistics
Institutional Origin	Authorized in statute	Mandated in statute	Mandated in statute
Policy Authority	Advisory	Policymaking	Advisory
Agenda Authority	Agency discretion	Board discretion	Commissioner discretion
Resources	Agency support	Separate staff and budget	Agency support
Departmental Affiliation	Health and Human Services	Education	Education
Policy Type	Regulatory	Technical	Technical
Tasks	Discrete policy tasks	Discrete policy tasks	Diffuse tasks

authority (agency discretion vs. congressional mandate), and across forms of committee resources (reliance on agency for staff support vs. separate committee staff). Table 6.1 summarizes key sources of systematic variation across public committees.

The results developed and explained in this chapter suggest that across institutional forms, public committees associated with drug reviews and educational statistics and assessments display an increased likelihood of putting tasks with greater implementation interdependence and uncertainty on their public agendas. The FDA offers the most robust illustration of participatory bureaucracy: agenda setting that focuses on tasks with uncertain and interdependent implementations but that does not confer discernible privilege to well-resourced groups such as large firms. The FDA is also the case with the most agency institutional authority: the committees are created through agency discretion, the agency has agenda setting authority for committee meetings, and the agency supports the committee through agency staff resources.

Relative to FDA drug review committees, the institutional design of the National Assessment Governing Board sits at the opposite end of the continuum of agency discretion. The Board can make policy, has congressionally mandated agenda items, and enjoys its own staff and resources. The Board represents the institutional design where we least expect participatory bureaucracy and its cultivation of unique agency expertise. Indeed, the Board's pattern of agenda setting suggests attentiveness to its political environment and mixed attentiveness to interdependent tasks. Yet, even in this case, elements of participatory bureaucracy emerge through the Board's systematic process of public participation focused on task implementation.

The Advisory Council on Education Statistics (ACES) offers a nuanced story. Like FDA committees and NAGB, agenda setting on ACES during the time period studied did not appear to confer discernible privilege on well-organized interests. The extent to which the Council focused on uncertain or interdependent tasks, however, appears more mixed. Even though it shares key organizational and institutional features with FDA committees or with NAGB, ACES was not a unique source of advice or engagement for NCES: the agency continued the tradition of receiving advice from technical review panels affiliated with survey and assessment contracts. While the Council displayed agenda-setting patterns consistent with aspects of agency reputation, analysis suggests that most of ACES's agenda items did not focus on task implementation, but instead focused on general administrative issues such as the agency budget, committee administration, and methodological procedures. Lacking a durable, systematic process keyed to task implementation, the Council struggled to offer public agenda setting consistent with participatory bureaucracy.

THE BUREAUCRATIC ROOTS OF PUBLIC ADVICE: SETTING AGENDAS FOR FDA DRUG ADVISORY COMMITTEES

From the 1970s through the early twenty-first century, setting the agenda for public participation in drug reviews resided largely in FDA staffers' hands. The agency has been responsible for creating its committees, determining when and how frequently they will convene, and deciding whether the meetings will be opened or closed to general public participation.[8] FDA staff typically determine which drugs to bring to an advisory committee for review, what specific questions to ask its public advisors, and whether the timing of those reviews should be before the approval decision, after the approval decision, or both. FDA meetings follow a predictable format, with portions of the meeting allocated for firm presentations, FDA presentations, open comments from public members of the audience, and committee participation. Committee meetings have a topic – a specific drug to review – along with a set of questions the FDA prepares and submits to the committee for consideration. The vast majority of

---

[8] As mentioned in Chapter 1, The Food and Drug Administration Amendments Act of 2007 specifies that the FDA should send new drugs (drugs whose active ingredients have not already been approved) to an advisory committee for review before approving the drug, or explain in the drug's approval letter why the agency did not consult with an advisory committee before approval. P.L. 110-85, Sec.918 (21 USC 355). The FDA continues to send some drugs to public committees for review, but not others, and justifies its choice in approval letters. Some evidence suggests the FDA used its Drug Safety and Risk Management Committee more frequently after the passage of the Food and Drug Administration Amendments Act of 2007. Elaine H. Morrato and S. Ling, "The FDA Drug Safety and Risk Management Advisory Committee: A Case Study Evaluation of Meeting Frequency, Content and Outcomes Before and After FDAAA," *Medical Care* (November 2012): 970–986.

meetings reviewing new drugs[9] ask for a series of committee votes on the drug's approvability (in terms of efficacy and safety), as well as formal committee recommendations on drug dosage levels and labeling considerations. Most – but not all – of the FDA's drug review committees meet consistently, between two and four times per year. Moreover, most FDA public meetings reviewing New Molecular Entities have been open to the public during the 1985–2010 period. In contrast to committee meetings in the 1960s and early 1970s, the FDA rarely meets with its public committees behind closed doors for new drug reviews.

This routinized process for public participation does not mean that the outcome of participation is preordained or that it operates tightly under the agency's control to promote or advocate for the agency. Rather, the meetings' predictable format lets members of the general public or organized interests – such as groups representing the HIV/AIDS community or consumer groups such as Public Citizen – know how to use the open public portion of the meeting to raise their concerns. Even though the FDA provides the committee with specific questions to discuss, committee members have added votes and topics the FDA did not request.[10] Does participation, however, focus on tasks with uncertain or interdependent implementations, key components of participatory bureaucracy?

Drug efficacy and safety, in general, present the FDA with interdependent and uncertain task implementations, as Director Houn's opening quote suggests. Drug safety and efficacy depend on a collection of processes involving implementers who work beyond the FDA's hierarchical reach. These processes include the design and implementation of clinical trials, firm and FDA analyses, drug labeling, firm marketing, physician practice, patient use, and post-marketing monitoring. Specific drug approval tasks, however, vary in the degree to which they present uncertain and/or interdependent implementation problems (how can we ensure safe and effective drug use in practice?), which is a matter of adaptation that cannot be revealed fully inside the FDA review process. The more experience the FDA has with therapies in practice, the better equipped it is to manage potential implementation problems, check firms' claims, and predict how the therapy might behave in patients' bodies. Novel therapies, in contrast, exacerbate FDA uncertainty and dependence on implementers outside the agency, creating greater potential room for public participation to support bureaucratic administration. The cases of the drugs Colazal and Lotronex illustrate variation in the challenge of implementation that arises from drug reviews that are relatively more uncertain and interdependent, as well as the incentives these challenges create for agencies to seek public engagement.

---

[9] By "new drugs" I mean New Molecular Entities specifically.
[10] The FDA's Drug Safety and Risk Management Advisory Committee, for instance, went beyond the FDA's request for discussion of alternatives for studying heart risks associated with ADHD stimulant drugs and called for a vote on whether ADHD drugs should carry a boxed warning. The committee voted 8–7 in favor of the warning. Steven E. Nissen, "ADHD Drugs and Cardiovascular Risk," *New England Journal of Medicine* 354 (2006): 1445–1448.

The Case of Colazal

For the review of the drug Colazal (balsalazide) to treat the symptoms of ulcerative colitis,[11] the FDA relied on experience with other ulcerative colitis therapies along with supplemental internal agency analyses to understand the drug's mechanism and to predict its likely use in practice. The FDA, as well as the broader field of medical research, faces uncertainty with respect to treating ulcerative colitis, for the deadly disease's cause and cure remain elusive.[12] Yet, because Colazal's basic pharmaceutical properties were similar to the drug mesalamine, already approved for ulcerative colitis, the FDA could apply its knowledge of mesalamine to the Colazal review.

The FDA's experience with mesalamine, for one, helped the agency assesses Colazal's safety risks. Studies submitted to the FDA as part of Colazal's application revealed two cases of infants born with birth defects to women who had taken Colazal early in their pregnancies, leading the division charged with the drug's review, the Gastrointestinal Drug Products Division, to request an internal, *private* FDA review to assess Colazal's teratogenicity or its potential to cause fetal malformations.[13] The reviewer based her conclusions on her knowledge of other mesalamine drugs:

> Biochemically, balsalazide seems to be similar to the other medications. It contains the same active moiety.... If ... mesalamine is truly non-teratogenic, as the other studies seem to report, then it is likely that balsalazide is equally non-teratogenic.[14]

Experience suggested mesalamine was not associated with impaired fetal development, and so the special reviewer concluded that Colazal did not pose a greater risk than other similar and already approved drugs.[15]

---

[11] Colazal is the drug's trade name. Balsalazide is the drug's generic name. Ulcerative colitis is a form of inflammatory bowel disease that affects the lining of the colon.

[12] The only cure is surgery to remove the damaged organ. Some prevailing theory suggests that it originates from an immune system's response to a bacterium or virus.

[13] Food and Drug Administration, "Colazal (NDA 20-610) Drug Review Package." Drug reviewers worried, considering that more than half of potential Colazal patients would be women of childbearing age, about more fetal development side effects appearing when patients started using the drug outside of tightly controlled clinical trials.

[14] Within the NDA 20-610 review package, see the Administrative Documents, SGE Evaluator's review for more details. Drug review materials are available from the FDA at http://www.accessdata.fda.gov/drugsatfda_docs/nda/2000/20-610_Colazal.cfm.

[15] The review concluded: "Balsalazide meets three of the five criteria for the establishment of a pregnancy registry and, as such, could be monitored in that fashion. However, balsalazide has close similarity to other widely used and apparently non-teratogenic medications. The active medication is only minimally absorbed and the carrier molecule is a common amino acid. If balsalazide is considered to meet other requirements for Food and Drug Administration approval, it would be reasonable to encourage provider reports of adverse pregnancy outcomes rather than pursuing formal pregnancy registration." See NDA 20–610 review package. For more details, see Administrative Documents, SGE Evaluator's review.

The FDA's experience with mesalamine also enabled the FDA to detect an area where the pharmaceutical company sponsoring the drug had not fully revealed its information. Careful inspection of the Colazal application revealed that the company's two pivotal clinical trials, which had occurred in the United Kingdom, had compared Colazal against a formulation of mesalamine that was not identical to the form of mesalamine that had been approved for use in the United States.[16] The FDA, therefore, had to decide whether Colazal could be marketed as more effective than mesalamine.[17] The Gastrointestinal Drug Division asked for *internal* FDA bioequivalence tests to determine whether the different formulations were comparable enough to support the firm's comparative efficacy claim; they ultimately concluded that the two forms of mesalamine were bioequivalent.[18] With these additional internal FDA reviews, the Medical Officer and the Gastrointestinal Drug Division leadership concluded the drug was safe and effective; they approved the drug in July 2000 without seeking public engagement through an advisory committee.[19]

From the perspective of bureaucratic administration, broadening participation and inviting public engagement for the Colazal review by taking the drug to an advisory committee offered relatively little administrative or implementation benefit. The FDA had substantive knowledge to bring to bear on the review: the agency could summon decades of experience with other ulcerative colitis drugs and mesalamine products to check the company's claims of bioequivalence and fetal safety. Moreover, FDA reviewers' experience suggested how mesalamine drugs performed as a class in the broader population, how doctors prescribe them, and how patients use them, attenuating the uncer-

---

[16] The FDA noted that the firm did not make this deviation plain in its initial application.

[17] NDA 20–610 review package. In a March memo to Salix, the firm sponsoring Colazal, the Acting Director of the Office of Drug Evaluation III asserted: "If the formulation of Asacol [mesalamine] used in the pivotal studies was not identical to the one approved for use in the United States, the labeling which accompanied the approvable letter [claiming efficacy relative to mesalamine] may be both false and misleading, thus rendering any product associated with it as misbranded under sec. 502(a) of the Food, Drug and Cosmetic Act." See NDA 20–610, Administrative Documents, Raczkowski memo, March 16 1999, p. 2 for more details. The issue for the FDA was not whether Colazal was effective: they concluded that it was, based on a dose comparison study. "The Salix pivotal US study ... includes two doses of balsalazide.... The high balsalazide dose was significantly superior to the low dose in improving symptomatology.... According to regulation, this dose-comparison should suffice to accept efficacy of balsalazide, since the active compound of balsalazide ... has been proven to be an effective drug in ulcerative colitis." See NDA 20–610, March 2000 Medical Review for more details.

[18] A July 2000 memo from the Division Director to the Office Director implies that the agency may have changed its mind on bioequivalence. NDA 20–610 review package.

[19] In his March 2000 review, Medical Officer Prizont concluded, "Balsalazide is, essentially, a relatively safe drug. Most of the AEs reported were recurrences of the acute ulcerative colitis due to treatment failure. This statement is supported by the following brief report from the two year post-marketing experience in the UK.... As with other mesalamine preparations (Asacol) balsalazide may cause some kidney damage." See NDA 20–610, March 2000 Medical Review.

tainty in implementation after the drug's approval. The FDA approved Colazal without first consulting with its public committee for a review.

The Case of Lotronex

From the perspective of bureaucratic administration, more novel therapies, especially those that will be used in a broad or diverse population, exacerbate the agency's dependence on implementers outside the agency. During the same time period as the Colazal review, the Gastrointestinal Drug Products Division reviewed Lotronex (alosetron), sponsored by Glaxo-Wellcome, for the treatment of the signs and symptoms of irritable bowel syndrome (IBS).[20] Like ulcerative colitis, IBS is chronic, its cause is undetermined, and it has no known cure. Two aspects of the Lotronex review, however, heightened FDA dependence on external implementers.

For one, at the time of the Lotronex review, there were no other treatments approved for IBS, which meant that FDA reviewers could not bring their practical experience to bear on the review. Lotronex shared chemical properties with three other marketed drugs – Kytril, Zofran, and Anzemet – which the FDA approved to prevent nausea in patients undergoing chemotherapy or anesthesia. Treatment for nausea, however, typically occurs on a relatively short-term basis. IBS is chronic, meaning experience with Kytril, Zofran, and Anzemet offered the FDA little knowledge about Lotronex's safety if used continuously and indefinitely.[21]

For another, IBS is considerably more prevalent. Some estimates suggest that as many as one in five adults may suffer from some form of IBS, and that IBS is a common diagnosis.[22] Moreover, it presents in markedly different forms, with different degrees of severity. Its prevalence and variability, coupled with the agency's lack of practical experience, exposed FDA's dependence on outside implementers – on the firm marketing the drug, on doctors prescribing the drug, and on patients taking the drug – for it would be difficult to predict and manage drug use once it reached the market.

The FDA's review of Lotronex highlighted several problems facing the drug's implementation: after the clinical trials, uncertainty about the drug, the disease, and the effect of the drug on the disease remained. The FDA's safety reviewer concluded:

---

[20] Lotronex is the drug's trade name. Alosetron is the drug's generic name. Glaxo-Wellcome later became Glaxo-SmithKline (GSK). The reviewer who reviewed Colazal was also in charge of Lotronex's efficacy review. Irritable bowel syndrome's most common symptoms include severe abdominal cramping, and pain. Drug review materials for Lotronex are available at http://www.accessdata.fda.gov/drugsatfda_docs/nda/2000/21107a_Lotronex.cfm.

[21] Food and Drug Administration, "Lotronex (NDA 21-107) Drug Review Package." See NDA 21-107 Medical Safety review, pp. 4–13 for more details.

[22] This claim comes from public NIH information, http://digestive.niddk.nih.gov/ddiseases/pubs/ibs/#3 (accessed November 28, 2012).

> A great many studies were done, but unfortunately they were planned and exe-
> cuted before the sponsor discovered the appropriate gender and dose, so that
> no conclusions can be drawn with any confidence about the pharmacodynamic
> effects of alosetron in the patients to be treated in the dose to be used.[23]

In the course of analyzing the results from the clinical trials, Glaxo discovered
that Lotronex appeared significantly more effective in women than in men.
Yet, the trials had been designed to overrepresent men, leaving too few female
participants to allow Glaxo to draw conclusions about what was happening
within this particular population that contributed to the drug's efficacy. Glaxo-
Wellcome had collected information; it just had not collected information that
allowed the FDA to understand the drug's mechanism.

From a bureaucratic administration perspective, the knowledge problem
that Lotronex posed (how does this drug work?) combined with the implementation problem (how will this drug behave in the bodies of the millions of
people who might take this drug?) and was exacerbated further by inconclusive but troubling evidence from Glaxo's clinical studies about the drug's risks.
Several serious, life-threatening adverse events had appeared in the Lotronex
treatment group. Although scant knowledge on some of Lotronex's properties
precluded conclusions that Lotronex caused life-threatening adverse events,
a staff member who was overseeing the drug's review for the FDA's Gastro-
Intestinal Drug Division asserted:

> One will have to wonder what will happen if one approved this compound when
> the conditions are no longer controlled, and so one will have to raise potential
> additional risks, such as uncontrolled settings, such as the drug being taken by
> sicker patients, longer use, other medications, concurrent diseases such as liver
> disease, variable follow ups, and other risk factors such as, for example, acet-
> aminophen or the intake of alcohol.[24]

Once approved and marketed in a field where no other therapies existed, where
one in five adults might seek relief for IBS symptoms, Lotronex would be used
in conditions decidedly different from those in the clinical trials. Clinical trials excluded patients with other underlying health problems, they monitored
Lotronex use for a limited period of time, and they prevented participants
from taking other drugs. All of these conditions would change in practice.
The FDA staffer overseeing the Lotronex review feared that if a handful of
life-threatening adverse events appeared in tightly controlled conditions, more
could appear once those conditions were relaxed.

From the perspective of the FDA's safety reviewer, weak knowledge about
Lotronex's effects in the context of what would likely be widespread Lotronex
use underscored the need to communicate carefully with physicians and

---

[23] FDA, "Lotronex (NDA 21-107) Drug Review Package." See NDA 21-107 Medical Safety
Review, p. 9 from October 22, 1999 for more details.
[24] Food and Drug Administration, "Gastrointestinal Drugs Advisory Committee Meeting
Transcript: Lotronex, November 16, 1999."

patients. The reviewer noted that the lack of knowledge about the disease and the drug made it difficult to attribute causality for adverse events. However, he took serious issue with what he considered Glaxo-Wellcome's effort to bury potentially serious side effects in the "fine print" of Lotronex's proposed label. Regarding Glaxo's proposed label for Lotronex, the FDA reviewer asserted:

> It is very disturbing that the applicant has chosen to downplay so strongly the important issue of constipation induced commonly and predictably by alosetron [Lotronex], and has totally ignored the potentially very serious although uncommon problems of ischemic colitis[25] .... The applicant has a duty to recognize, admit and publicize the constipation problem, and to investigate it much more thoroughly.... This will have to be dealt with in the labeling, in the instructions to physicians and patients as to how best to use this new agent, and in the advertising and promotion of the product if it is approved for prescribed clinical use and marketing. The serious clinical adverse event of ischemic colitis cannot be ignored. It must be dealt with constructively and thoroughly.... The index of suspicion among physicians and patients needs to be raised to deal with this uncommon but potentially very serious adverse effect of alosetron [Lotronex].[26]

The safety reviewer's conclusion noted the importance of collecting more information: Glaxo has a "duty" "to investigate [the side effect] much more thoroughly." But, he also emphasized communicating existing information to physicians. The serious adverse events, he asserted, should be publicized not only on the label but also in instructions to physicians and through product advertisement and marketing. At the end of his review, the FDA safety reviewer made five recommendations, one of which focused on gathering new information to manage the knowledge problem. The other four focused on communicating the risks to doctors and patients.[27]

---

[25] Ischemic colitis entails blocked blood flow to the large intestine, which causes inflammation that can result in death.

[26] FDA, "Lotronex (NDA 21-107) Drug Review Package." See the NDA 21-107 Medical Safety review, p. 62 for more details.

[27] FDA, "Lotronex (NDA 21-107) Drug Review Package." The five recommendations were: "1. The frequent problem of alosetron-induced constipation must be recognized much more clearly by Glaxo Wellcome, and the labeling revised to recognize it. Further, precautions to be taken when prescribing alosetron should be specified, and instructions written as to how the problem of constipation should be handled by adjustments of the treatment regimen. 2. The infrequent but serious problem of alosetron-induced ischemic colitis must also be much more clearly recognized and addressed in the labeling, including a warning to physicians that it may occur with an incidence of about 1:300 patients. 3. The rare but also potentially serious problem of alosetron-induced hepatitis, or idiosyncratic hepatotoxicity, must be recognized and addressed in revised labeling. 4. A post-marketing prospective study of sufficient patients on the approved regimen of alosetron 1 mg b.i.d. should be a condition for approval. The study should be powered to detect ischemic colitis ... 5. The term 'diahrrea-predominant' as a defining subtype of the IBS patients is probably not appropriate, and should be called 'non-constipated' IBS to emphasize the concern that the drug should not be given to constipated patients, and may produce constipation frequently if given to patients with IBS who are not constipated previously." See NDA 21-107 Medical Safety review, p. 64 for details.

Lotronex presented the FDA with not only an information gathering problem (how can we learn about how this drug works) but also a problem of communicating with other implementers (how can we help physicians and patients understand how to use Lotronex safely and effectively, especially when we do not really know what it is doing) in the context of pharmaceutical industry incentives to maximize sales and in an implementation context where the FDA enjoys little authority over prescription practices. Public participation offered the FDA a means of addressing the drug's implementation uncertainty. Unlike Colazal, the FDA broadened public participation in the Lotronex review: it took the drug to its Gastrointestinal Drugs Advisory Committee for review both before and after the drug was approved. The FDA's decision to seek public participation for Lotronex appears consistent with bureaucratic administration's practice of seeking public participation in the context of greater task uncertainty and implementation interdependence.

Participatory oversight, however, might interpret this narrative differently and highlight different aspects of the cases. Patient demand for Lotronex was high, particularly in the absence of other therapies to treat IBS; and the prevalence of IBS implies an extensive group of potential stakeholders. Taking Lotronex to a public advisory committee could offer the FDA a way to gather information from potential Lotronex users on the intensity of their demand and the likelihood that their demand could spill into other political arenas such as Congress. Or, if public participation worked as an oversight mechanism, committee reviews may focus on the same interests and issues that receive Congress's attention. Topics or groups or firms that generate congressional attention could be more likely to appear in the agency's public deliberations as well. In this sense, agenda setting could privilege particular groups or industries by configuring participation in ways that offer advantages to some groups or companies relative to others.

Colazal and Lotronex also differed in terms of their sponsoring firms' sizes. A relatively small firm, Salix, sponsored Colazal. Pharmaceutical giant Glaxo-Wellcome sponsored Lotronex. Theories of company influence through public participation advance two predictions based on conflicting assumptions. One assumes that companies enjoy little access to the FDA review process and that advisory committees offer companies access they would not otherwise enjoy. This perspective implies that advisory committees could work to companies' advantage, and it expects that firms with more resources would press for this kind of public participation. The second assumes that companies enjoy inherent access to the drug approval process. Public meetings risk delaying product approval[28] or opening the firm and its product to more public scrutiny than it would otherwise face. If so, firms with more resources may be less likely to seek advisory committee participation. Public participation that advances

---

[28] Kenneth I. Kaitin, Ann Melville, and Betsy Morris, "FDA Advisory Committees and the New Drug Approval Process," *Journal of Clinical Pharmacology* 29 (1989): 886–890.

group oversight or privilege suggests a systematic relationship could appear between companies' strength and advisory committee agenda setting, albeit in either direction.

From the perspective of bureaucratic administration, companies' interests are built into any drug review process. The FDA may request particular kinds of information and particular trials, but firms are the ones that produce the data and make choices about revealing that information to the FDA. Moreover, when an advisory committee reviews a drug, the drug's sponsor has an automatic seat at the public table: any advisory committee meeting reviewing a drug includes the firm who sponsors the drug and the firm's squad of spokespersons. Thus, the question for the FDA is not whether to incorporate companies' interests but when to expand participation beyond the company to include the broader public in the agency's policymaking process. Similarly, public participation that supports bureaucratic administration does not claim that elected officials' interests do not matter. Rather, public participation that supports bureaucratic administration may yield by-products that also enhance democratic governance, by revealing information – especially company information – that might otherwise not be revealed. Public participation may also support democratic accountability through competent administration: safe and effective pharmaceutical use and implementation.

Choosing Public Participation: FDA Advisory Committee Agenda Setting, 1986–2006

The Colazal and Lotronex cases suggest public participation's potential to work in ways that support bureaucratic administration by inviting public participation for tasks with uncertain and interdependent implementations. This agenda-setting pattern emerges systematically for drugs approved by the FDA between 1986 and 2006.[29] The results suggest that the FDA is more likely to

---

[29] Descriptive statistics each of the measures are presented in appendix Table A.1. The unit of analysis is the drug, with the primary sample consisting of all new molecular entities submitted for review between 1985 and 2005 and later approved within the 1986–2006 time frame. Drugs submitted before 1985 or after 2005 were not included in the sample. For each drug, public advice is evaluated as a dichotomous choice. Of the 520 approved drugs in the primary sample, data for all included variables was available for 474 drugs. One hundred ninety-eight of the 474 drugs went to an advisory committee for review. The primary sample was restricted to NMEs to limit the scope of the inquiry to a comparable group of policy tasks, consistent with prevailing scholarship: Daniel P. Carpenter, "Groups, the Media, Agency Waiting Costs and FDA Drug Approval," *American Journal of Political Science* 46 (2002): 490–505. For related work on FDA advisory committee agenda setting, see: Susan L. Moffitt, "Promoting Agency Reputation through Public Advice: Advisory Committee Use in the FDA," *Journal of Politics* 72 (2010): 880–893; Stéphane Lavertu and David L. Weimer, "Federal Advisory Committees, Policy Expertise, and the Approval of Drugs and Medical Devices at the FDA," *Journal of Public Administration Research and Theory* 21 (2011): 211–237; Philippe Urfalino, "Secret-Public Voting in FDA Advisory Committees," in *Private Public Debate and Voting* edited by Jon Elster (New York: Cambridge University Press, Forthcoming).

invite public participation for several measures of drug uncertainty and interdependence, consistent with participatory bureaucracy. One measure comes from the drug's *priority status*. A drug's designation as a priority review reflects its innovation – its potential contributions to effectiveness, compliance, and safety. With innovation, however, comes potential uncertainty: the drug formulation is new and has not been tested in practice outside experimental conditions or in unrestricted patient populations who take multiple therapies. Priority drugs represent the potential for greater drug safety, greater drug efficacy, and yet greater risk as they are introduced to the market.[30] The results in Table 6.2 suggest priority status increased the odds of a drug appearing on an advisory committee agenda by a factor of four, holding all other variables constant. Converting the coefficients from Table 6.2 to changes in predicted probabilities reveals that changing from a standard drug to a priority drug increases the predicted probability of an advisory committee review by 33 percent.[31]

Another manifestation of implementation uncertainty and interdependence comes from whether the drug treats a *lethal disease*. The FDA distinguishes between drugs that treat lethal diseases and those that do not; the agency is more willing to let drugs that treat lethal diseases in the market even if those drugs come with high risks of serious side effects. Uncertainty in this case is not a matter of the drug: the agency knows about the side effects. Uncertainty and FDA dependence on implementers, however, manifest through risk communication: whether a company's information will adequately convey risk, and whether physicians and patients will heed those warnings.[32] Treating a lethal disease increased the odds of a drug appearing on an advisory committee agenda by a factor of 1.5, holding all other variables constant. In other words, the change from a drug that treats a nonlethal disease to a drug that treats a lethal disease is associated with a 10 percent increase in the predicted probability of an advisory committee review. This result, however, is significant at the 90 percent confidence level.

Another measure of implementation interdependence comes from the drug's *pharmacological complexity*, measured through a count of the number of words

---

[30] A drug's priority status is a dichotomous measure, coded 1 if the drug is a priority review. To illustrate: FDA division director Solomon Sobel asked the Metabolism and Endocrine Drugs Advisory Committee in 1996 about the novel, *priority* diabetes drug, Rezulin, "Are we justified at this point in accepting known risks and hypothetical risks?" Data on drugs' priority status is publicly available at http://www.accessdata.fda.gov/Scripts/cder/drugsatfda/index.cfm.

[31] The predicted probabilities in this model are calculated for the baseline case of a priority drug, a lethal disease, in divided government, with all other variables held at their respective means. The change in predicted probabilities is calculated by bootstrapping. The 95 percent confidence interval around the change in the predicted probability, going from a standard drug to a priority drug, ranges from 0.236 to 0.452.

[32] This dichotomous measure of disease is coded 1 if the disease is lethal. The designation of "lethal" was based on CDC General Mortality Tables, available at http://www.cdc.gov/nchs/deaths. htm. The 95 percent confidence interval around the change in predicted probability ranges from −0.007 to 0.218.

TABLE 6.2. *FDA Advisory Committee Agenda Setting 1986–2006, Approved NMEs, Logistic Regression*

Variable	Coefficient (SE)	Odds Ratio (SE)
Implementation Interdependence and Uncertainty		
Drug Priority Classification (Priority = 1)	**1.394 (0.230)**	**4.033 (0.927)**
Drug for Lethal Disease (Lethal = 1)	0.444+ (0.236)	1.558+ (0.368)
Drug Pharmacological Complexity, Natural Log of Label Word Count	**0.826 (0.178)**	**2.285 (0.406)**
Political Oversight		
Demand for Therapy: Order of Drug Entry to the Market, Natural Log	−0.032 (0.101)	0.968 (0.097)
Elite Disease Attention: NEJM Disease Attention, Rolling Ave. 3 Years Prior	−0.010 (0.036)	0.990 (0.035)
Public Disease Attention: Media Disease Attention, Rolling Ave. 3 Years Prior	0.000 (0.001)	1.001 (0.001)
Firm Experience: Number of Previous Firm NME Submissions	−0.002 (0.009)	0.997 (0.009)
Congress: Average Cong. Committee Disease Attention, Rolling Ave. 3 Years Prior	0.391+ (0.200)	1.479+ (0.296)
Divided: Divided Government (Divided = 1)	**0.935 (0.257)**	**2.548 (0.654)**
Constant	**−7.830 (1.250)**	0.000 (0.000)
	N = 474	

Boldface indicates significance at the p<.05 level; + indicates significance at the p<.1 level; all tests two-tailed.

on each drug's published label that deal specifically and solely with the drug's chemical and pharmacological properties. This measure captures the complexity of the drug, and describing these properties is standard on drug labels, which enables cross-drug comparisons.[33] A one-standard-deviation increase in the log of the pharmacological complexity is associated with a 10 percent increase in the predicted probability of an advisory committee review.

Table 6.2 offers little evidence that FDA public participation reflects traditional forms of political oversight. One form of political oversight comes from groups' demand for new therapies, measured through a count of the number of

---

[33] Label information was obtained from *The Physician's Desk Reference*. The label information was retrieved electronically and the word count of the drug's chemical and pharmacological properties was calculated using Microsoft Word. This part of the label does not typically appear as part of advisory committee deliberations, although committees may discuss drugs' pharmacological properties. Other parts of drug labels routinely come before advisory committees for review, such as whether to include a boxed warning on the label. Including a full count of the words that appear on a drug label could present endogeneity. The 95 percent confidence interval around the change in the predicted probability ranges from 0.061 to 0.152.

previous drugs approved to treat the disease represented in each drug's primary indication, with a higher count representing lower drug demand. A second form comes from potential company strength and influence, measured through the count of the number of drugs each company previously submitted to the FDA.[34] Firms and groups may use public participation to obtain a place in agency policymaking they would not otherwise enjoy.[35] Alternatively, firms and groups that already enjoy privileged access to agency policymaking may induce agencies to keep tasks sensitive to those interests away from broader, more inclusive public participation. If powerful firms or groups shape public advisory committee agendas, systematic patterns could emerge in either direction. A third measure of group mobilization comes from a lagged, average measure of *Washington Post* attention to disease during the three years before a drug's approval, included to assess potential group mobilization and interest.[36] The models supplement the *Washington Post* measure with a similar lagged, average measure of the number of *New England Journal of Medicine* articles discussing the disease each drug is indicated to treat. This latter measure is aimed at gauging elites' attentiveness to disease. *None* of these political oversight measures reaches standard levels of statistical significance.

From a political oversight perspective, public participation may reflect the same constellation of interests and issues that are salient to Congress. The models thus also include a measure of the lagged, average number of disease-specific references made in House and Senate oversight committees.[37] Higher

[34] These measures are consistent with prevailing scholarship: Carpenter, "Groups, the Media, Agency Waiting Costs." Specifically, both measures are based on a count of NMEs. Because capture arguments focus on the advantage of larger and more established firms, the measure of drug submissions is designed to reflect firm establishment. See Daniel P. Carpenter, "Protection without Capture: Product Approval by a Politically Responsive, Learning Regulator," *American Political Science Review* 98 (2004): 613–631.

[35] In the words of an industry consultant, the FDA advisory committee system serves several purposes: "[F]rom the companies' standpoint, it helps them explain to Wall Street what they're doing, it provides an endorsement, it provides a marketing platform for them, it provides one or two days of free publicity – not free publicity, it's not free, but it's an opportunity for publicity in an FDA setting which has a lot of credibility." Interview 112204, conducted by Susan Moffitt on November 22, 2004.

[36] This measure is also consistent with prevailing scholarship. See Carpenter, "Groups, the Media, Agency Waiting Costs." To conduct the media searches, the author composed a list of 316 disease search terms. The author and her research assistants searched electronic versions of *The Washington Post* and *The New England Journal of Medicine* for each term, excluding obituaries. Articles were retrieved, checked for accuracy, and counted for each year. The measure included in this model is based on the average number of disease references in the three years before the drug was approved.

[37] This measure is based on the average number of disease references in congressional oversight subcommittee hearings for the three years before the drug's approval. To conduct the hearing searches, the author used the same list of 316 disease search terms that had been compiled for the media searches. The author and her research assistants searched electronic versions of congressional hearings using *Lexis Nexis Congressional* (which later changed to *Proquest Congressional*).

levels of congressional disease-specific attention are associated with a greater likelihood of drugs linked to that disease appearing on an FDA advisory committee agenda at the 90 percent confidence level. Another measure of general political conflict – a control for divided government – suggests divided government increased the odds of a drug appearing on an FDA public advisory committee agenda by a factor of 2.5, consistent with participatory oversight.[38] In other words, reviewing a drug during divided government instead of unified government is associated with a 22 percent increase in the predicted probability of an advisory committee review.

Lotronex's appearance on an FDA public advisory committee agenda appears to be part of a systematic trend. Twenty years of FDA advisory committee experience suggest the agency chooses to invite public participation for drugs with the most uncertain and interdependent implementation profiles consistent with participatory bureaucracy. The FDA enjoys considerable discretion over meeting timing and topics. Moreover, the topics selected for public participation often relate to tasks that exceed the scope of the agency's implementation jurisdiction, and they carry a high risk of implementation failure not necessarily because of the agency's actions, but because of the agency's dependence on implementers outside of the agency. The results also suggest elements of participatory oversight, notably a greater likelihood of committee use in periods of divided government. Participatory bureaucracy and participatory oversight may coexist, but others measures of participatory oversight were inconclusive.

MANDATED PARTICIPATION: SETTING AGENDAS FOR THE NATIONAL ASSESSMENT OF EDUCATIONAL PROGRESS

Like the FDA's public committees, the National Assessment of Educational Progress's public board, the National Assessment Governing Board, has developed a systematic process for public participation.[39] This systematic process, however, does not directly contribute to the authority of federal agency that helps administer NAEP: the National Center for Education Statistics. Unlike the FDA, NCES does not set NAGB's agenda. The agency's lack of agenda setting authority has yielded participation that has, at times, frustrated agency bureaucrats and constrained aspects of the federal agency's bureaucratic administration and expansion. The federal agency has nonetheless enjoyed spillover

[38] The models include a dichotomous measure of divided government, consistent with scholarship suggesting greater political oversight and greater agency risk aversion during divided government. George A. Krause, "Coping with Uncertainty: Analyzing Risk Propensities of SEC Budgetary Decisions, 1949–1997," *American Political Science Review* 97 (2003): 171–188.

[39] Recall that, unlike the FDA committees, NAGB enjoys policymaking authority. FDA committees are entirely advisory. Portions of FACA, such as the open meetings and publicly accessible meeting minutes requirements, apply to NAGB.

effects from the Governing Board's routinization, suggesting the Governing Board offers public participation that supports bureaucratic administration without actively building federal bureaucracy.

Authoritative and administrative distance between NAEP's public committees and its affiliated federal agency, NCES, has existed since the assessment's earliest days.[40] In the words of former undersecretary of education, Marshall (Mike) Smith, "[The NCES] always wanted to exert more authority over NAEP than they ended up being able to exert."[41] Unlike the FDA's committees, public participation for the National Assessment became codified in statute: a 1978 law gave the assessment's public board authority to oversee the design and administration of the assessment, including

> the selection of the learning areas to be assessed, the development and selection of goal statements and assessment items, the assessment methodology, the form and content of the reporting and dissemination of assessment results, and studies to evaluate and improve the form and utilization of the National Assessment.[42]

By mandating responsibilities to the National Assessment's public governing body, the statute fashioned the contours of the board's public agenda. The National Assessment's grantee – the Education Commission of the States from 1969 to 1983 and the Educational Testing Service from 1983 to 1988 – filled in the details of the public agenda: responsibility for National Assessment committees' agendas and operations rested in the grantee's hands.[43] Reflecting on the Assessment Policy Committee, in operation between 1982 and 1988, former NCES Commissioner Elliott recalled,

> [T]he grantee was responsible for creating [The Assessment Policy Committee]. So the government was supposed to keep hands off ... When [Assistant Secretary] Checker [Finn] and I would go to their meetings, we were there as government representatives, but the meetings were run by the president of ETS and the people on the board were responding to him, not to us. If we had problems we would take them up some other way.[44]

---

[40] The 1978 Education Amendments (P.L. 95–561) granted the National Institute of Education administrative authority for NAEP in 1978. Administrative authority returned to NCES in 1985.

[41] Marshall Smith, "An Interview with Marshall Smith," in *The Nation's Report Card: Evolution and Perspectives*, edited by Lyle V. Jones and Ingram Olkin (Bloomington, IN: Phi Delta Kappa Educational Foundation), p. 270.

[42] P.L. 95–561, 92 STAT. 2353. The law also specified that the National Institute of Education should issue a federal grant to a nonprofit education organization that would be "responsible for overall management of the National Assessment." The grantee would then "delegate authority to design and supervise the conduct of the National Assessment to an Assessment Policy Committee established by such organization."

[43] NAEP started as a grant to ECS, changed to a contract to ECS in 1974, changed to a grant to ETS in 1983, and then changed to a contract to ETS in 1988. ETS has remained one of NAEP's contractors. Lyle V. Jones and Ingram Olkin (eds.), *The Nation's Report Card: Evolution and Perspectives* (Bloomington, IN: Phi Delta Kappa Press, 2004), pp. 14–17; P.L. 100–297.

[44] Interview with Emerson Elliott, conducted by Susan Moffitt on November 4, 2004.

The Assessment Policy Committee's meetings, under the auspices of the National Assessment's grantee, created visibility and public access in a couple of respects. Meeting notices appeared in the *Federal Register*, and the meetings were open to the public. In other respects, the meetings discouraged participation by meeting relatively inconsistently from 1979 through 1988 – sometimes once per year, sometimes up to three times per year.[45] Even though the meetings were open to the public, they did not necessarily have consistent or easily accessible meeting locations.[46]

Although the Educational Testing Service advanced a plan for increasing "the role of the assessment's policymaking committee" upon receiving the National Assessment grant,[47] the 1988 legislation ushered in new responsibilities for both the National Assessment and in its public board. In addition to the responsibilities spelled out in the 1978 statute, the committee's responsibilities expanded in 1988 to include "developing standards and procedures for interstate, regional and national comparisons." Adding interstate comparisons to the National Assessment represented a bold and significant addition. State comparisons had been part of Commissioner Keppel's original vision, but they took more than twenty years to come to fruition. The Improving America's Schools Act of 1994 elaborated further, charging the newly constituted National Assessment Governing Board "to develop assessment objectives and test specifications through a national consensus approach which includes the active participation of teachers, curriculum specialists, local school administrators, parents, and concerned members of the public." It also specified that the Governing Board would design the methodology of the assessment "in consultation with appropriate technical experts."[48] The 1994 statute offered more opportunities for more and different kinds of public participation.

---

[45] Claim based on search of *Federal Register* meeting notices listed in the *Federal Register Index* for each year. The *Federal Register* reports the following meeting dates: February 8–9, 1980 (Denver, CO – open); June 13–14, 1980 (Denver, CO – open); September 24–25, 1980 (DC – open); June 12–13, 1981 (Denver, CO – open); February 12–13, 1982 (Denver, CO – open); June 11–12, 1982 (Denver, CO – open); August 17–18, 1982 (Portland OR – open); February 25–26, 1983 (Denver, CO – open); July 16–17, 1983 (Princeton, NJ – open); October 13, 1984 (New Orleans, LA – open); January 25, 1985 (Phoenix, AZ – open); June 1, 1985 (Princeton, NJ – open); October 19, 1985 (DC – open); February 1, 1986 (Hilton Head, SC – open); May 31, 1986 (Princeton, NJ – open); January 17, 1987 (Tampa, FL – open); November 18–19, 1988 (DC – partially closed to discuss qualification of potential members); December 16, 1988 (DC – subgroup meeting, no mention if closed); January 5, 1989 (Rosemont, IL – partially closed); January 11, 1989 (DC – no mention if closed).

[46] When the Education Commission of the States held the National Assessment contract, meetings often convened in Denver, CO, the city where the Education Commission of the States was headquartered. After the Educational Testing Service assumed the contract, more meetings occurred in contractor's home base, Princeton, NJ, with other meetings held in locations such as Hilton Head, Tampa, Phoenix, and New Orleans.

[47] Eileen White, "Better Proposal Said to Win Assessment Project for ETS," *Education Week*, March 2, 1983.

[48] P.L. 103–382, October 20. 1994, 108 STAT. 4041.

Even though the 1988 and 1994 amendments moved the National Assessment into NCES, to "report directly to the Commissioner for Educational Statistics," much about NAEP's Governing Board reflected the earlier distance between the federal agency and the assessment's public committee. The 1988 statute specified that the Governing Board would be "independent of the Secretary and the other offices and officers of the Department of Education."[49] To this end, the statute enabled the Governing Board to hire its own staff separate from the Department of Education, gave the Governing Board its own budget line item, and allowed the Governing Board to be housed outside and away from the Department.[50] Agenda setting authority for board meetings rested with Governing Board staff and committee members.[51] One former member recalled,

> [NAGB] staff members would work with the respective committee chairs to develop the agendas for the particular meetings. There have been times when ... committee chairs ... have requested that time be set aside ... to meet jointly [to] ... negotiate whether we need additional committee meetings between the NAGB meetings.[52]

In the years immediately following the 1988 amendments, the Governing Board and NCES negotiated the terms of their roles and responsibilities, which the statute had left ambiguous. In a 1992 Memorandum of Understanding between the Governing Board and the Department of Education, the Department agreed to "make every reasonable attempt to implement the policy-setting actions" of the Governing Board but qualified that

> if [the Governing Board's] direction conflicts with the commissioner's statutory quality-assurance responsibilities, the commissioner may legitimately inform [the Policy Board] that he or she cannot follow its instructions and may refuse to accept as satisfactory a solution that is not technically sound.[53]

Palpable tension sometimes spilled into public participation. NAGB Chairman Finn wrote to Commissioner Elliott:

---

[49] 102 STAT. 347.

[50] 102 STAT. 347.

[51] The amendments granted the Secretary of Education appointment authority over board members. The act, however, gave the board some authority over nominations: "(iii) As vacancies occur, new members of the Board shall be appointed by the Secretary from among individuals who are nominated by the Board after consultation with representatives of the groups listed in subparagraph (B). For each vacancy the Board shall nominate at least 3 individuals who, by reason of experience or training, are qualified in that particular Board vacancy." This was modified in 1994 under PL 103–382: "The Secretary shall appoint new members to fill vacancies on the Board from among individuals who are nominated by organizations representing the type of individuals described in subsection (b)(1) with respect to which the vacancy exists." 108 STAT. 4040.

[52] Interview 82103, conducted by Susan Moffitt on August 21, 2003.

[53] U.S. General Accounting Office, *Educational Achievement Standards: NAGB's Approach Yields Misleading Interpretations* (Washington, DC: GAO, 1993), p. 62.

As I said (in public) at the December 1989 Board meeting, it is my personal opinion that you find NAGB inconvenient and wish it would go away. I'm well aware that it does not fit tidily into the standard NCES modus operandi and that it has occasionally developed views of its own, some of them at variance with NAEP custom.[54]

Public boards that deviate from agency "custom" or that intervene in routine agency practices represent participation amenable to discouraging bureaucratic administration – the kind of public participation traditional bureaucracy would strive to avoid. The federal agency and the Governing Board jockeyed over their respective responsibilities, as the NCES's initiative to collect more reliable socioeconomic data through the National Assessment illustrates.

The Case of Background Questions

Gathering background data on assessment participants has provoked periodic controversy for the National Assessment since the assessment's inception. Some of the National Assessment's original proponents argued for a design that not only would report levels of achievement but also attempt to explain what contributed to that achievement.[55] In contrast, the National Assessment's principal architects specifically sought to limit the number and type of background variables the assessment would include.[56] Ralph Tyler, together with his colleague John Tukey, argued against using the National Assessment to explain student achievement. They asserted that including noncognitive measures, such as measures of students' home and school environments, could distract the assessment from its central purpose of depicting changes in educational achievement over time.[57] This conflict continued in the early 1970s, and Commissioner Gilford

---

[54] Letter from Checker Finn to Emerson Elliott, dated June 28, 1990. Finn Archives, Hoover Institution, Box 99.

[55] At the first meeting convened to discuss the feasibility of a national assessment, some conferees implied there was little point to conducting a national assessment that could not distinguish the varying impact of "television and the school system" on student achievement. William Greenbaum, Michael S. Garet, and Ellen R. Solomon, *Measuring Educational Progress: A Study of the National Assessment* (New York: McGraw-Hill Book Company, 1977), p. 109.

[56] Greenbaum, *Measuring Educational Progress*, pp. 109–116.

[57] Ralph Tyler argued to fellow NAEP architects that "additional data that you can build into it [NAEP], that will not make the thing so complex that it fails in the early stage ... I'm all for that, but I realize that you are on touchy questions when you get into trying to find out about the family, the notion of many of the Congress that this is – that this is privacy; that is nobody's business.... Let's be sure we get a defensible level of education for different age groups that we are talking about and as much else as we can feed into it that might have legitimate use in analysis. This is my view of it – but not to demand that unless you can pick out how much of that was due to the school and how much to the home, that you wouldn't have anything to do with it." Cited in Greenbaum, *Measuring Educational Progress*, p. 112; see also Irvin J. Lehmann, "The Genesis of NAEP," in *The Nation's Report Card: Evolution and Perspectives*, edited by Lyle V. Jones and Ingram Olkin (Bloomington, IN: Phi Delta Kappa Educational Foundation, 2004), p. 27.

cited conflict over the inclusion of background measures as part of her rationale for creating separate, Center-sponsored review panels.[58] By the late twentieth century, the National Assessment gathered socioeconomic data on assessment participants in part by asking students – such as fourth graders – to report on their families' socioeconomic characteristics. Assessment analysts and administrators began to realize that this produced unreliable data: fourth graders are ill-equipped to evaluate their families' material and social conditions. Center staff proposed a new survey of households to gather the data more reliably, consistent with Center's perceived authority to select such noncognitive items as the ones that a parent survey would include. Yet, the parent survey risked provoking problems for the National Assessment and its implementation. It was a novel survey, and using the National Assessment to delve more deeply into family issues risked triggering privacy concerns and a backlash against the larger assessment. This sort of novelty and interdependence suggests the type of task potentially consistent with participatory bureaucracy. NAGB put the parent survey issue on its agenda.

At the time, however, ambiguity and conflict over who had jurisdiction for ultimately choosing the noncognitive items that could be included on the assessment were part of the public debate. Before the Governing Board meeting at which the parent survey would appear as an agenda item, Governing Board staff provided board members with preparatory materials including the full parent survey and highlighted portions of the legislation through which the Governing Board could infer its jurisdiction over noncognitive or background variables.[59] At the subsequent Governing Board meeting, the Board asserted that the proposed Educational Testing Service/NCES parent survey indeed fell under the Governing Board's jurisdiction. Stressing that the survey "would not appropriately contribute to NAEP data collection and reporting," and "could threaten NAEP's future viability," board members opposed its development and administration.[60]

The addition of separate staff to support NAGB offered the board more room to push back against the agency's request. Former NCES commissioner, Emerson Elliott, who led NCES from 1984 through 1995, recalled,

> I remember something that [a former NAGB member] wrote one time to two of the members of NAGB about the need for them to be having their own staff, and he said, "Well, you know, [Emerson Elliott] will just go right on doing whatever he … pleases until we have staff.[61]

[58] Dorothy Gilford, "NAEP and the US Office of Education, 1971–1974," in *The Nation's Report Card: Evolution and Perspectives*, edited by Lyle V. Jones and Ingram Olkin (Bloomington, IN: Phi Delta Kappa Educational Foundation, 2004), p. 170.

[59] National Assessment Governing Board, "Briefing on NAEP Background Questionnaires, 7/27/94," in August 1994 NAGB Briefing Book, Attachment 1.

[60] National Assessment Governing Board, "Report of the Reporting and Dissemination Committee, August 1994 Meeting Minutes," p. 22.

[61] Interview with Emerson Elliott, conducted by Susan Moffitt on November 4, 2004.

Having its own staff offered the Governing Board resources to become intimately involved in the National Assessment's core functions. One NAGB staff member recalled, "Initially, the board was in no position to change any of the analytical techniques already in use by the operations contractor, ETS. However, the board made every effort to learn about the policy ramifications of each technical issue."[62] To this end, Governing Board staff members were involved in the background variable issue. At the Board's request, the Board's staff examined whether information on free and reduced-priced lunches could be used as a socioeconomic status measure for the National Assessment. The Board's staff also provided the Board with "an analysis of the appropriate role of the Governing Board in regard to NAEP background items," which included considering the option of "establishing a mechanism for formal consultation with state officials on the nature and content of NAEP background questionnaires."[63] The Board's involvement thus expanded from the particular parent survey to a broader policy on background variables, with Board staff providing the Board with special technical knowledge.

The Educational Testing Service and the Center did not administer the parent survey, but nonetheless included some related items on the 1995 student survey that some Governing Board members considered "too intrusive."[64] The Governing Board went on to issue a policy that, among other things, "required a board review of all background questions to be used in either field testing or operational NAEP," whether for novel survey instruments or for routine questions that had been asked for a decade.[65] What started with a novel issue that risked implementation difficulty – a new parent survey to help manage the problem of depending on nine-year-olds to report on family socioeconomic status – seeped into core functions agency leaders perceived as falling under agency jurisdiction: the general collection of background variables. Moreover, it did so in the heat of the limelight. *Education Week*, whose audience includes education policymakers and practitioners, reported on the parent survey disagreements four times over a ten-month period.[66] Not only had the collection

[62] Bourque, Mary Lyn, "A History of the National Assessment Governing Board," in *The Nation's Report Card: Evolution and Perspectives*, edited by Lyle V. Jones and Ingram Olkin (Bloomington, IN: Phi Delta Kappa Educational Foundation, 2004), p. 219.

[63] National Assessment Governing Board, "Resolution of the Ad Hoc Committee on Design and Reporting of NAEP Data Analyses, October 20, 1994," Attachment 3a, in the November 1994 NAGB Briefing Book. National Assessment Governing Board, Letter from Larry Feinberg to Roy Truby: NAEP Background Questionnaire and SES Data – Role for the Governing Board and Policy Issues, in November 1994 NAGB Briefing Book, Attachment 3b. National Assessment Governing Board, Letter from Steve Gorman to Roy Truby: Status of Parent Questionnaire Issues, in November 1994 NAGB Briefing Book, Attachment 3c.

[64] Bourque, "A History of the National Assessment Governing Board," p. 211.

[65] Bourque, "A History of the National Assessment Governing Board," p. 211. The Governing Board obtained formal authority over background variables in 2002 through statutory provisions in the No Child Left Behind Act.

[66] *Education Week* articles on the parent survey disagreement appeared on September 7, 1994, November 30, 1994, March 15, 1995, and May 24, 1995.

of background variables become public; media attention further broadened scrutiny of core agency tasks, precisely the kind of publicity agency bureaucrats typically strive to avoid and that can interfere with bureaucratic administration. Along with NAGB came more visibility overall. *Education Week* reported on the Assessment Policy Committee's meetings, members, and decisions approximately seven times between 1983 and 1988, its first six years under the Educational Testing Service's jurisdiction.[67] It reported on NAGB 102 times during the board's first six years.[68] Yet, as the agency and the Governing Board formalized their relationship, a more routine, less adversarial relationship appeared to emerge.[69]

Public boards that operate largely beyond an agency's reach can appear inimical to bureaucratic administration by potentially injecting more "politics" – more particular group influence, more patronage, more sympathy for the president and his appointees' agendas – into policy decisions by interfering with core agency tasks and by disrupting established lines of authority and hierarchy. Conflict over background variables persisted during the consideration and passage of the No Child Left Behind Act, with several sets of considerations. As one former board member recalled,

> [There] was a concern on the part of some members that NAEP was asking intrusive questions. Part of it comes from a concern on the part of NCES and NAGB themselves that as they are asking states and schools to participate in NAEP more often, that they need to reduce the burden. And so they were feeling a need to shorten the amount of time that people spent on background questionnaires and to make sure that they were really getting sort of essential stuff.... And then most recently part of the concern has come from the new Institute for Educational Sciences ... concerned that NAEP not be putting out correlational data that people assign causality to, and so pushing to limit the background questionnaire for that reason as well.[70]

Yet, the National Assessment's narrative offers glimpses of how public participation through the Governing Board could, nevertheless, support bureaucratic administration. The Governing Board's institutional design offered buffers from the surrounding political context, and NAEP's reputation offered spillover benefits for the agency, especially as it continued to develop as a statistics agency in the late twentieth century. In these senses, a public committee like the Governing Board offered the potential to support bureaucratic administration by supporting the implementation of the prized educational assessment.

---

[67] This figure may undercount the number of *Education Week* articles reporting on the Assessment Policy Committee because of inconsistent availability of 1986 *Education Week* articles at the time the data were collected by the author.

[68] These counts are based on searches of the *Education Week* online databases.

[69] This claim based on systematic reviews of media articles and transcript reviews. Conflict, however, does still emerge over issues such as excluding students from the assessment.

[70] Interview 92603, conducted by Susan Moffitt on September 26, 2003.

Setting the Public Agenda for the National Assessment of Educational Progress

In the case of FDA committees – when the federal agency sets the public committee's agenda – topics with uncertain and interdependent implementations, especially implementations at risk of complications stemming from the agency's dependence on firms, doctors, and patients outside of the agency's regulatory reach, were more likely to appear on committee agendas, consistent with participatory bureaucracy. NCES lacked the agenda setting authority for the National Assessment's public boards, and a mixed portrait for participatory bureaucracy emerges from the public boards' agendas.[71]

The analysis presented in Table 6.3 assesses a broad pool of potential National Assessment agenda items considered from 1989 to 2000. Public participation consistent with bureaucratic administration would focus on tasks with uncertain and interdependent implementations, whereas participation consistent with political oversight would be more likely to appear for routine tasks and for tasks that mapped on to elected officials' or their constituents' interests.

---

[71] NAEP constitutes not just a single task, a single assessment, but a collection of assessments and tasks. Certain NAEP math, science, reading, and writing assessments are given routinely to track student educational progress over time. Other assessments, in these subjects and others, are given only once. For each subject matter assessment, specific tasks include, among many others, setting the assessment's content objectives, choosing items for that assessment, administering the assessment, analyzing the results, linking the results with other, non-NAEP assessment instruments, and reporting the results. Some of these tasks occur habitually, others do not. Some of these tasks fall under the agency or contractor's jurisdiction, others fall under the Board's jurisdiction, and some cross jurisdictions. All of these kinds of tasks, for all kinds of NAEP assessments, constitute potential NAGB agenda items. A comprehensive list of NAEP tasks was compiled to derive the potential pool of NAGB agenda items. Sources for this list included: NAEP design documents from 1969 to 2000, NAEP published reports, internal agency memoranda and correspondence, interviews, NAGB minutes, and media reports. The complete list was stratified in three ways. Tasks were first divided in terms of assessment-specific tasks, such as designing the 1990 mathematics assessment, and organizational or administrative tasks, such as committee staff support. This produced a small subset of administrative tasks and a much larger group of assessment-specific tasks. The assessment-specific tasks were then divided along five general dimensions, commensurate with the way that NCES and NAGB divide the tasks: assessment design (designing instruments, selecting questions), assessment schedule and administration (time frame for each assessment, administration policies), methods and analysis (BIB-spiraling), reporting and dissemination, and special projects. Again, commensurate with the way that NCES and NAGB approach the tasks, assessment design, schedule, and reporting were then divided along disciplinary lines: reading, mathematics, U.S. history, and writing, among others. This approach aimed both to ensure that potential as well as actual agenda items were included and to ensure that each unit of analysis was similarly calibrated. Based on board meeting minutes and agendas, the appearance of these tasks on the public agenda was measured as a dichotomous variable (1 for agenda appearance, 0 for no appearance) indicating whether the task appeared on NAGB's agenda in each of the time periods when it would have been possible for the topic to appear.

TABLE 6.3. *National Assessment Governing Board Agenda Setting, 1989–2000 Random Effects Logistic Regression Panel Model*

Variable	Coefficient (SE)	Odds Ratio (SE)
Implementation Uncertainty and Interdependence		
Novel Tasks: First Time or Special Project Task (1 = Novel)	**–1.277 (0.331)**	**0.279 (0.094)**
NAEP Mandated Tasks, Ambiguous Authority (1 = NAEP Mandate)	**0.730 (0.213)**	**2.076 (0.511)**
Technical Tasks: Moving Average of Process Publications	0.057 (0.242)	1.059 (0.308)
Political Oversight		
Statutorily Mandated NAGB Task (1 = Mandate)	**0.926 (0.245)**	**2.524 (0.574)**
Congress: Lagged Moving Average Cong. Committee Attention, 3 Years Prior	0.101 (0.898)	1.106 (1.209)
Profession: Lagged Moving Average *Education Week* Attention, 3 Years Prior	**0.240 (0.059)**	**1.272 (0.058)**
Divided Government (1 = Divided)	–0.062 (0.227)	0.940 (0.204)
Internal Capacity		
Agency Resources: NCES Staff/Budget Ratio	**0.315 (0.081)**	**1.370 (0.107)**
Control		
Previous Board Attention: Lagged Task Frequency, Previous Year	**0.589 (0.087)**	**1.803 (0.136)**
Constant	**–2.035 (0.416)**	**0.131 (0.053)**
Number of observations	1,404	1,404
Number of groups	117	117

Boldface indicates significance at the p<.05 level; all tests two-tailed.

One measure of potential uncertainty, *novel* tasks – such as special studies on the effects that varying state accommodations and exclusion rules for Limited English Proficient (LEP) students have on National Assessment results – were significantly less likely to appear on the Governing Board's agenda, in contrast to participatory bureaucracy predictions.[72] A measure of task interdependence, whether an item was a *core NAEP task* but not specifically assigned to the public board, increased the odds of appearance on the Board's agenda by a factor of two.[73] These tasks represented jurisdictional

---

[72] Task novelty is a dichotomous measure indicating whether the task was a one-time, first-time, or special NAEP project (1 for novel, 0 for not).

[73] This is a dichotomous measure based on statutory requirements, 1 for NAEP mandate, 0 otherwise. Some tasks are both NAEP mandated and NAGB mandated, because of the scope of the task.

ambiguity and could be more likely to encounter implementation trouble. No clear pattern emerged for technical tasks: technical tasks failed to yield a systematic relationship with the Board's agenda setting.[74] Considered from the lens of federal bureaucrats, these are the tasks we would expect bureaucrats to want to keep off the public agenda. Some of the tasks at the higher end of the scale included National Assessment analysis tasks (processes for statistical weighting, computational procedures, and dimensionality analysis). Topics at the lower end of the scale included using the National Assessment as a model for other assessments. Board encroachment on core agency technical responsibilities – illustrated in the background variable case presented earlier in the chapter – does not seem to reproduce systematically across agenda topics and over time.[75]

NAEP's public boards have, at times, been labeled political. Yet several of the measures of political influence included here do a poor job of explaining the Governing Board's agenda setting. Political overseers may seek public participation to circumvent the federal agency or to expose its incompetence, yielding predictions that agency fragility should be associated with more public participation. One typical way to capture potential workload stress or possible incompetence is through the *staff/budget ratio*.[76] The results suggest a higher ratio – more agency staff relative to the workload – is positively associated with agenda setting, the opposite of what political oversight would expect. Moreover, the impact of the political context – measured through *hearings* and *divided government* – appear to be inconclusive.[77] Topics salient to NAGB and NCES's professional audience, reflected in the publication *Education Week*, were more likely to appear on the public

---

[74] This is measured as the three-year lagged moving average of the number of reports on NAEP processes for each task. By NAEP processes I mean reports on gathering NAEP data rather than reports on NAEP results. For instance, *Use of Person-Fit Statistics in Reporting and Analyzing National Assessment of Educational Progress Results* was counted as a process report. The 1996 *Mathematics Report Card for the Nation and the States*, which focused on reporting math achievement results rather than the processes that underlie those producing those results, was not. Sources included *The Directory of NAEP Publications*, as well as ERIC searches. This count deliberately excludes NAGB/APC publications and takes the three-year average prior to the "at risk" year to avoid potential endogeneity.

[75] However, other examples of the Board preventing NCES initiatives exist. This includes the Board setting aside a special study in reading that NCES staff devised, but that the Board did not ask for and that departed from the Reading Framework.

[76] Basic measures of budgets and staffing levels, however, are not equipped to reveal whether those resources are sufficiently abundant and appropriately targeted to accomplish particular tasks. Nor are these measures able to speak to the state or quality of knowledge in the agency's larger professional field, that is, whether "better knowledge" exists "out there."

[77] To construct this measure, I searched Congressional hearings' summaries available through *Lexis-Nexis/Proquest Congressional*, using each of the potential agenda item described in footnote 71 as search terms. I restricted searches to NAEP's authorizing committees. Results were tallied for each year. The measure was then constructed using a lagged three-year moving average of the authorizing committees' attention to NAEP tasks.

agenda, suggesting agenda setting was attuned to the general concerns of the educational community.[78]

The significance of *legislatively mandated tasks*, however, represents an important vehicle for participatory oversight. Table 6.3 suggests that topics related to the Governing Board's mandated responsibilities increased the odds of appearing on the Governing Board's public agenda by a factor of 2.5. Examples of mandated tasks include developing frameworks and objectives for the National Assessment. Board members noted that they had room to put items on the agenda, and that board members relied on staff members to develop the agenda, sometimes in ways that related to legislative concerns. One member recalled,

> The [NAGB] executive director … was always vigilant and had people watching the legislative process on the Hill. He knew what was happening with the appropriations, he knew what changes he was going to try to get into the language of appropriations.[79]

Part of that vigilance entailed redirecting, focusing, or preventing particular forms of congressional action that board members thought would compromise the integrity of the assessment. Two notable examples come from the board's opposition to efforts to have NAEP linked with the Clinton administration's Voluntary National Test effort and to the Bush administration's attempts to involve NAEP more directly in the accountability provisions of the No Child Left Behind Act. Attention to the political environment may have enabled the Governing Board to buffer the assessment from key forms of political volatility.

Public participation in the National Assessment appears to both bureaucratize and democratize, supporting elements of participatory bureaucracy and elements of participatory oversight. The governing board's institutional features represent a design of public participation where we least expect to find participatory bureaucracy. To this end, there appears to be little room for agency-initiated agenda setting, and potentially novel tasks were unlikely to obtain agenda space. However, consistent with participatory bureaucracy, the public agenda systematically included items with ambiguous jurisdictions, and a systematic relationship with core agency technical tasks did not appear. Moreover, NAGB has helped bureaucratize the participatory process in significant ways.

---

[78] This entails a measure of each task's lagged, moving average *Education Week* coverage. The process for developing a measure of *Education Week* coverage parallels the process for measuring congressional committee attention, described in footnote 77. The list of potential agenda items served as search terms for the online *Education Week* database. To guard against endogeneity, the measure excluded articles that reported on Board meetings or decisions. The models also include controls for divided government and staff/budget ratios in NCES, as well as a lagged measure of previous Board or Committee attention to the topic. The budget was measured in constant 2000 dollars. Information on NCES staffing was obtained through a FOIA request.

[79] Interview 82103, conducted by Susan Moffitt on August 21, 2003.

NAGB routinized its meeting process, convening at least four times per year as a full board, with some subgroup meetings occurring in between. A portion of each board meeting was closed to the public, specifically parts covering issues such as member selection, budgets, and not-yet-releasable results. The majority of the board meetings have been open to the public, however; and the board has kept faithful records and transcripts, made easily accessible. The systematic form of public participation offered through NAGB stands in contrast to another public council: the Advisory Council on Education Statistics (ACES).

PARALLEL PUBLIC ADVICE: THE ADVISORY COUNCIL ON EDUCATION STATISTICS

NCES oversees a range of surveys and assessments in addition to NAEP.[80] The Center continues a distant cousin of the data collection effort the federal education agency began in 1867, gathering descriptive information on the universe of American elementary, secondary, and postsecondary schools.[81] It also administers surveys and assessments – on longitudinal educational outcomes, on international comparisons, on colleges and universities, and on vocational education, among others – that gather and distribute information on American schooling.

Beyond the technical review panels Commissioner Gilford initiated to oversee the National Assessment discussed in Chapter 4, NCES has convened public committees, such as ACES, since the early 1970s.[82] The 1974 legislation that moved the Center from a staff office within the Office of Education to a separate statutory entity created ACES and charged the Council to "review general policies for the operation of [NCES]."[83] With the exception of reviewing the

---

[80] The National Institute for Education assumed sponsorship responsibilities for NAEP in 1978. NAEP reverted back to NCES sponsorship in the early 1980s.

[81] This data collection effort now goes under the name of the Common Core of Data program.

[82] One review suggests that in 1975, the Office of Education operated 16 advisory councils consisting of 244 members appointed by the Commissioner, Secretary, or president. See Gerald Kluempke, *A Descriptive Analysis of the Attitudes, Make-Up, Function, and Utilization of Advisory Councils of the U.S. Department of Education* (Doctoral dissertation, George Washington University, 1976), p. 1. This did not include the Advisory Council on Education Statistics.

[83] P.L. 93–380, Sec.406; 88 STAT 556–558. See also Levine 1986, p. 6. The council's charge includes: "to establish ... statistical standards to insure that the statistics and analyses disseminated by the Center are of high quality and not subject to political influence" (P.L. 93–380, Sec. 406). ACES's original authorizing legislation granted the Council the authority to set statistical standards for NCES. NCES did not, however, have formal statistical standards until the mid-1980s. Although ACES participated in setting those standards, the Council supported changing its authorizing legislation to underscore the Council's advisory, rather than policymaking, authority. Advisory Council for Education Statistics, "Response to the National Academy of Sciences' Evaluation of the Center for Education Statistics, 1986," p. 6. Legislation passed in 1988 clarified that ACES's responsibilities were advisory PL 100–297. NCES also builds task-

Center's statistical standards, the authorizing statute and subsequent amendments remained largely silent on the Council's duties, affording agency leadership considerable discretion on committee agendas and operations.[84]

Analysis of ACES, mandated by Congress but over which NCES enjoyed agenda setting authority, suggests that both participatory bureaucracy and participatory oversight depend on more than formal agenda setting authority or statutory origins. Much of the Advisory Council's nearly thirty-year history mirrored the shifting circumstances facing NCES and its home department, with the Council lurching from advocate for the federal agency to its adversary, from periods of vibrant engagement to languishing with few meaningful opportunities for participation.

Agency discretion over public participation, the ACES account suggests, represents only the potential for participatory bureaucracy, not its guarantor. The statistical analysis that follows shows some systematic Council attention to interdependent tasks in the period between 1989 and 1999. The historical analysis, however, suggests that, unlike FDA committees or NAGB, the Council struggled over its lifetime to develop a systematic process for offering advice on task implementations. Recall the predictable format found in FDA meetings, with deliberation focused around a series of decisions and recommendations but with room for information to flow in multiple directions – to and from the agency, advisors, firms, and broader public audiences. ACES meetings, in contrast, developed a reputation for presenting NCES projects to the Council but not necessarily eliciting specific policymaking decisions or participation. The ad hoc structure of the meetings lent themselves, at times, to the sort of advocacy that appeared through the Citizens' Advisory Committee on the FDA, or to its opposite – adversarial oversight. Even though its authorizing statute called for four meetings per year, the Council failed to meet at all in 2000 and 2001. The Council met briefly in 2002 and then dissolved entirely, bearing witness to the fragility of participation in agency policymaking.

The Advisory Council for Education Statistics: Advocate and Adversary

The 1970s and 1980s brought organizational tumult to NCES. This tumult included the creation of the National Institute for Education, which assumed

specific technical assistance into its contracts through Technical Review Panels. Unlike NAEP's Assessment Policy Council authorization, ACES's original mandate did not specify particular categories for council membership (P.L. 93–380).

[84] The law specified that no more than four of ACES's members could come from the same political party and that the Director of the Census and the Commissioner of Labor Statistics should serve as ex officio members. It otherwise left ACES's membership entirely up to the Secretary. The statutory backbone for ACES granted departmental political appointees jurisdiction over key institutional components of public participation: it gave the Secretary of Health, Education and Welfare, later the Department of Education, appointment authority for ACES's seven members; and it designated the Assistant Secretary as ACES's presiding officer. This meant that a departmental political appointee would run ACES's meetings.

some of Center's former responsibilities during this time frame, and the Office of Education's elevation to the Department of Education in 1980. Some scholarship suggests that the president and his appointees sometimes purge agency advisory committees to be more consistent with a new administration's policy positions. To this end, Donald Senese, Assistant Secretary for Educational Research and Improvement, who had jurisdiction over the Center from 1981 through 1985, wrote that the ACES had operated as a "special interest lobbying body" that advanced the agendas of Chief State School Officers. Assistant Secretary Senese sought to transform the Council into an "oversight group."[85]

One manifestation of oversight appeared in an Advisory Council resolution that passed in December 1983 requesting the National Academy of Sciences to review the content, quality, and timeliness of the Center's statistical programs and agency operations.[86] Concerns about the quality of the Center's data collection system arose from the Office of Management and Budget, as well as from the Advisory Council. During the same month as the Advisory Council's resolution to seek the NAS review, the Office of Management and Budget refused to allow the Center to continue collecting data for its massive yet fledgling congressionally mandated Vocational Education Data System (VEDS), citing quality concerns.

The VEDS's well-publicized troubles figured into the subsequent NAS review, but the 1986 NAS report asserted that the problems facing the vocational education data including "within-state discrepancies ... variability in collection methodologies ... a lack of uniform reporting ... duplicated counts ... differential response rates ... missing data," all of which compromised the integrity of the results, appeared in other statistical programs at the Center as well.[87] In particular, it charged that these problems appeared in traditional, bread-and-butter Center tasks, such as the Common Core of Data collection. Overall,

---

[85] Memo from Donald Senese to William Bennett, 4/18/85, Finn Archives, Hoover Institution, Box 78. The 1986 NAS evaluation of NCES concluded that "ACES has had a checkered past. In its early incarnation, its members indeed were technically oriented and extremely competent to review operating policies and commenting on how the center carried out its mission. Later, the membership changed to reflect a broad variety of experience, but not in the collection of education data or in topics necessarily related to the concerns of the center." Daniel B. Levine, *Creating a Center for Education Statistics: A Time for Action* (Washington, DC: National Academy Press, 1986), pp. 32–33.

[86] U.S. Department of Education, "Statement of Work for *An Evaluation of the National Center for Education Statistics by the National Academy of Sciences*," no date. ACES passed the resolution requesting the NAS review in December 1983. The Department of Education signed the agreement with NAS on September 29, 1984. Just twelve days earlier, on September 17, Emerson Elliott arrived at NCES as the new director for the Center. Interview with Emerson Elliott, conducted by Susan Moffitt on November 4, 2004.

[87] Levine, *Creating a Center for Education Statistics*, pp. 16–22. Concerns about NCES's statistical program emerged during this period from sources other than the NAS report. U.S. General Accounting Office, *The Condition of Information on Education* (Washington, DC: GAO, 1986); Marshall S. Smith, "Improving the Quality and Usefulness of NCES Data," (Washington, DC: Resources in Education, 1985).

the NAS report severely criticized the Center – going straight to the agency's "heart and soul," in the words Emerson Elliott, who was the Center's director at the time.[88] The NAS review made several dozen recommendations and went so far as to assert that if the Center did not change in the recommended ways, "serious consideration should be given to the more drastic alternatives of abolishing the center and finding other means to obtain and disseminate education data."[89] From the perspective of agency careerists, the NAS report "impugned their integrity, their professional competence and expertise."[90] In marked contrast to the ad hoc reviews and commissions that assessed the FDA's programs in the 1950s and 1960s, the Advisory Council and its NAS collaborators exposed the agency's bureaucratic administration to damning public scrutiny.

Yet, along with "impugning" the Center's reputation, the NAS report also made plain that part of the Center's data collection trouble stemmed from the agency's dependence on states and localities and on problems with subnational data collection systems. The National Academy report asserted:

> The poor quality of the data is generally attributed to the fact that the data are collected, in large part, from administrative records maintained at the local level, which records 'official' rather than 'real' behavior; that the data are the product of diverse record-keeping systems that lack comparability in definitions and time periods; that the data provided to the center are at such gross levels of aggregation – such as for a state as a whole – as to seriously limit anyone's ability to check them for accuracy, consistency and reasonableness ... [91]

Problems facing data collection efforts at state and local levels reverberated to the federal level in 1986, just as they did in 1867. Part of the challenge for

---

[88] In his December 1986 remarks to the NAS, Emerson Elliott described the subsequent NAS report's message as bearing on "the heart and soul of a Government statistical agency." Emerson J. Elliott, "A Time for Action: The Way to Start. The Director's Response to the Report of the National Academy of Sciences, 1986," p. 4.

[89] Levine, *Creating a Center for Education Statistics*, p. 4; Eileen White, "Reagan Weighing Much Deeper Education Cuts And Faster Dismantling of Federal Department," *Education Week*, September 28, 1981.

[90] Interview with Emerson Elliott, conducted by Susan Moffitt on November 4, 2004. A survey by the government employees' union conducted shortly after the report revealed low NCES staff morale. The union conducted the survey in the fall of 1987; 66 percent of the staff responded to the survey; 82 percent of those who responded "felt there was a relatively low sense of mutual trust between management and staff." Emerson J. Elliott, "The Condition of the Center: Report," (prepared for the Advisory Council on Education Statistics, 1988), p. 9. Causes for mistrust were not specified.

[91] Levine, *Creating a Center for Education Statistics*, p. 15. Critics charged that NCES should "be more systematic and persistent about following up and [expeditiously] processing [the] data that had been returned." Emerson J. Elliott and Charles D. Cowan, "Redesigning the Collection of National Education Statistics, 1987," p. 4. Elliot and Cowan (p. 4) noted that even though states used different definitions for their reports to the Center, critics also charged that some of the questions the agency asked "did not elicit full or accurate information."

the agency entailed building the capacity of state and local data collectors over whom the agency lacked hierarchical authority. Weaknesses in state and local data collections bubbled their way up to national-level weaknesses.

After assuming his post in 1984, Director Emerson Elliott developed channels of broader public engagement that enabled the agency to gather and distribute knowledge.[92] The federal agency created ad hoc technical review panels, or created such panels through its survey contracts, to enable the agency to gather technical knowledge privately. It also conducted "annual training programs" for states and collaborated with Chief State School Officers to facilitate communication with state data collectors on data definitions and deadlines.[93] The agency also expanded its authority over the Advisory Council.

During President Reagan's second term, Department of Education appointees and the Center found common cause in strengthening federal educational data collection. Former Assistant Secretary Finn recalled that he and Secretary Bennett considered collecting education data "arguably the most important thing" the Department of Education's Office of Educational Research and Improvement did.[94] With this view of education research, departmental political leadership reallocated staff resources to the NCES and set out to move the Center toward an arrangement that more closely paralleled other statistical agencies. This included modifying the flow of information in and out of the Center, including opportunities for participation.

With Secretary Bennett and Assistant Secretary Finn's tenures in the Education Department came two changes to ACES. For one, Secretary Bennett and Assistant Secretary Finn chose one of the Council's members to serve as the Council's presiding officer instead of the Assistant Secretary, ending the practice of having a political appointee run the Council's meetings. For another, NCES's top administrator became involved in selecting the Council's members and creating the agenda for the Council's meetings.[95] These changes offered more room for the Center's director to shape which parts of the Center's work became publicly accessible through the Council.

The Advisory Council and Assistant Secretary Finn, along with Director Elliott, presented themselves on the same side of some notable issues, including

---

[92] Interview with Emerson Elliott, conducted by Susan Moffitt on November 4, 2004. Emerson Elliott was officially NCES's director in 1984. The position changed from director to commissioner after the passage of the 1988 Hawkins-Stafford Amendments.

[93] Commissioner Elliott noted the Center ran training sessions for state staff on how to fulfil data requests. Interview with Emerson Elliott, conducted by Susan Moffitt on November 4, 2004.

[94] Chester E. Finn Jr., "An Interview with Chester E. Finn, Jr." in *The Nation's Report Card: Evolution and Perspectives*, edited by Lyle V. Jones and Ingram Olkin (Bloomington, IN: Phi Delta Kappa Educational Foundation, 2004), p. 252. The Heritage Foundation issued a report in 1984 that advocated ending the federal role in education with the exception of gathering statistics. Levine, *Creating a Center for Education Statistics*, p. 12.

[95] Interview with Emerson Elliott, conducted by Susan Moffitt on November 4, 2004.

advocating for higher budget and staffing levels for the Center,[96] but they diverged over the Center's ultimate position and authority within the department: the Advisory Council went on record advocating for more distance between the Center and the rest of the department's political hierarchy. Noting that the NAS report had similarly argued for the Center to become "quasi-independent" with respect to the Department of Education, the Advisory Council stated that it supported changing the Center's structure to provide it with its own budget line item.[97] Appointed agency leadership disagreed and asserted that the Center benefited from its position in the Office of Educational Research and Improvement, which allowed the Assistant Secretary to "slosh" some other Office program funds to the Center.[98]

The House of Representatives took up this issue of greater Center independence from the Office of Educational Research and Improvement as part of the 1988 Hawkins-Stafford amendments. Advisory Council minutes assert that the House

'carefully considered' and agreed with the Council's recommendation for a 'quasi-independent status for the Center within the Department' and a separate line-item budget for personnel and operations.[99]

[96] Advisory Council on Education Statistics, "Response to the National Academy of Sciences' Evaluation of the Center for Education Statistics, 1986," p. 7. Reductions during the first Regan administration lowered NCES's staffing and budget levels significantly. NCES's staff dropped from 173 in 1980 to 111 in 1986; its inflation-adjusted budget fell 28 percent. Levine, *Creating a Center for Education Statistics*, pp. 15–22, 44–45. Even at 170 employees, NCES's staffing levels were much lower than many other government statistics agencies. Moreover, NCES had to fill fourteen of its few positions with employees who had been "RIF-ed" from elsewhere in the department. Levine, *Creating a Center for Education Statistics*, p. 44. Assistant Secretary Finn moved funds from other OERI programs to NCES and pressed department officials to secure financial support for NCES. Interview with Chester E. Finn Jr., conducted by Susan Moffitt, August 20, 2003. See memo from OERI Assistant Secretary Finn to William Kristol, Chief of Staff to Secretary Bennett, in January 1987, Finn Archives, Box 67, Hoover Institution. During Finn's tenure, NCES's budget grew from $17.1 million to $28.1 million in constant dollars. The agency also added thirty-two new staff members. See Emerson J. Elliott, "A Time for Action: The Way to Start. The Director's Response to the Report of the National Academy of Sciences, 1986," attachment A.

[97] Advisory Council for Education Statistics, "Response to the National Academy of Sciences' Evaluation, 1986," pp. 2–3.

[98] Finn, handwritten notes on ACES 1986 response to the NAS report, Finn Collection Box 70, Hoover Institution. Finn discussed this more in an April 1987 memo to the Assistant Secretary for Legislation, Frances Norris, "The separate appropriation authorization would make it difficult, perhaps impossible to transfer general OERI funds … into statistics.… Such a transfer was made this year to the substantial benefit of statistics programs at the expense of other OERI activities." Chester E. Finn Jr., Memo from Chester E. Finn, Jr. to Frances Norris: Visclosky Amendment, April 10, 1987, p. 2, Finn Archives, Box 70, Hoover Institution.

[99] Advisory Council on Education Statistics, "Minutes from the Advisory Council on Education Statistics, May 24, 1988," p. 5.

Congress proposed and approved not only a separate budget line for NCES but also changed Center leadership to a presidentially appointed commissioner at the same level as the Office of Educational Research and Improvement Assistant Secretary. In response to the congressionally proposed and subsequently approved changes, Assistant Secretary Finn wrote that this structural change would "virtually destroy the balanced OERI organization [the Reagan Administration] sought to achieve."[100] The transformed Advisory Council's advocacy appeared consistent with advancing Center autonomy, similar to the 1957 FDA Citizens' Advisory Committee's advocacy for FDA expansion.

Following the NAS report and after Commissioner Elliott assumed his post, some efforts to routinize the Advisory Council emerged. The Advisory Council took an active role in helping the agency develop statistical standards and "developed an agenda format, which include[d] a topical presentation by NCES staff members (or others) and an ACES member as discussant or discussion leader."[101] But, unlike the FDA's committees and NAGB, NCES struggled to transform its public council into a systematic venue for public participation focused on task implementation. Some participants perceived that meetings felt like "show-and-tells by NCES staff to a generally passive committee.... The staff undoubtedly spent many hours preparing for the presentations, but the committee members ... did not often react."[102] In the words of a former Advisory Council member who served on the Council throughout the early 1990s, "basically we would meet and it would be ... perfunctory ... meaning we never did anything ... it was a small and very low-key group."[103] In the words of another Council member,

[T]he committee saw one of its roles to be to say things that perhaps the Commissioner could not say about how they needed some assistance or why this staffing issue was so critical and really needed reevaluation. I mean that wouldn't

[100] Chester E. Finn Jr., Memo from Chester E. Finn, Jr. to Frances Norris: Visclosky Amendment, April 10, 1987, p. 2. The full quote reads, "The Presidentially appointed Commissioner would reestablish the conflicting authority that existed when the Presidentially appointed NIE director was in place. This one provision alone would virtually destroy the balanced OERI organization we sought to achieve." Secretary Bennett wrote a letter to Representative Hawkins opposing proposals for NCES leadership to change to a presidentially appointed commissioner of education statistics, as well as for a separate NCES budget line item. For some additional context and discussion of this time period, see Maris Vinovskis, *Overseeing the Nation's Report Card: The Creation and Evolution of the National Assessment Governing Board* (Washington, DC: National Assessment Governing Board, 1998).

[101] Marie D. Eldridge, "The Status of Advisory Committees to the Federal Statistical Agencies," *The American Statistician* 44 (1990): 154–162. See p. 160.

[102] Eldridge, "The Status of Advisory Committees to the Federal Statistical Agencies," p. 160.

[103] Interview 81203, conducted by Susan Moffitt, August 21, 2003. Former commissioner Forgione offered a similar interpretation: "They'd bring them in for a day and they'd run presentation after presentation by them, and at the end of the day you had a giant notebook," Interview with Pascal Forgione, conducted by Susan Moffitt, November 19, 2004.

be something that a commissioner could take a strong and public on in the way that the committee could.[104]

The Council enjoyed a burst of revitalization following 1994 amendments that increased the number of Council members and gave the Council new responsibility "to advise NAGB as well as NCES." The Council began to meet more frequently and organized into subcommittees that worked between full Council meetings with staff support from NCES.[105]

Advisory Council members described a "collegial" relationship with Center staff and "consensus" within the council.[106] While no mention of conflict between Center staff and the public Advisory Council appeared in media reports, Council transcripts, or meeting minutes, committee members recalled, "The staff could occasionally get defensive, but in the main I thought it was very well received."[107] From one Council member's perspective,

> I think the NCES staff used to get really nervous when we used to talk about ... one of your clients ... [is] teachers in public schools ... a lot of their products ... are very far removed from an individual teacher's classroom, and to try to think about their work being more friendly to teachers is a daunting task for them.[108]

The Council tried to help the agency forge links with schools, teachers, and potential data users far outside the agency's jurisdiction: one manifestation of interdependent tasks, the kinds of tasks that participatory bureaucracy can help agencies manage.

Agenda Setting for Education Statistics

Did ACES systematically focus on uncertain and interdependent task implementations, consistent with participatory bureaucracy? The results presented here are mixed and suggest that the Council may have instead focused on building agency reputation in ways that differed from task implementation. The model that follows examines whether each survey or assessment reported in the *Federal Register* between 1986 and 2000 appeared on the agenda of the agency's ACES. Looking across the Center's survey and assessment products,[109] Table 6.4 suggests that two measures of task uncertainty and interdependence – *new* survey

[104] Interview 7901, conducted by Susan Moffitt, July 9, 2001.
[105] Interview 81203, conducted by Susan Moffitt, August 21, 2003. Interview with Pascal Forgione, conducted by Susan Moffitt, November 19, 2004.
[106] Interview 81203, conducted by Susan Moffitt, August 21, 2003. Interview 7901, conducted by Susan Moffitt, July 9, 2001.
[107] Interview 81203, conducted by Susan Moffitt, August 21, 2003.
[108] Interview 7901, conducted by Susan Moffitt, July 9, 2001.
[109] Agenda status is measured as a dichotomous choice for each of the Council's meetings, during the time frame when the survey or assessment was viable. Each observation reflects a separate *Federal Register* information collection request. However, multiple requests may appear as part of a larger survey or assessment program. Separate notices, for instance, appeared for the 1985 Foundations of Literacy assessment conducted by NAEP (which entailed a special assessment that focused on literature and U.S. history) and for the 1985 National Assessment for Math,

tasks[110] and surveys with a broader *scope*,[111] attempting to reach more respondents – fail to produce systematic relationships with Advisory Council agendas in the 1989–2000 period.

The results in Table 6.4 also display little support for a political oversight account of the Advisory Council's agenda setting, even though the Council was created in statute and even though the agency faced political tumult during this time period. Measures of *divided government*,[112] the impact of the survey or assessment on *groups* or other levels of *government*,[113] and agency *capacity*[114] fail to achieve standard levels of statistical significance. The results also suggest that topics salient to *Congress*[115] or that impacted *for-profit interests* were systematically less likely to be put on the Council's agenda. Converting

Science and Reading. These were not the same assessment, making it inappropriate to combine separate notices. Yet, because both notices reflected data collection efforts that occurred under the National Assessment umbrella, they might not represent fully independent tasks. Logistic models with standard errors clustered by broader survey program for NCES provide the framework for assessing which NCES tasks appeared on public agendas. Standard error calculations for NCES cluster observations according to whether each is part of an umbrella survey or assessment program (like NAEP).

[110] This may result from problems with the measure's validity. In practice, the measure reflects, among other things, requests from the Secretary or other political actors for data on timely issues. Each small-scale, nonrecurring NCES sample survey is classified as new. For instance, the Survey of Undergraduate Institutional Reporting Capabilities and the Survey on Advanced Telecommunications in U.S. Public Schools were some of the new notices that stemmed from Secretaries' requests for data to prepare for congressional testimony. Regrettably, data on which surveys were Secretary-initiated is not consistently available.

[111] Required response time and number of respondents appear systematically in the *Federal Register*'s proposed information data collection notices. Since the measure ranges from 1 respondent to 1,440,000 respondents, the model uses the natural log. The number of hours a survey requires is highly correlated with the number of survey respondents.

[112] A dichotomous measure of divided government is included here to reflect general divisiveness.

[113] Groups may use public participation to obtain a place in agency policymaking they would not otherwise enjoy. Alternatively, groups that already enjoy privileged access to agency policymaking may induce agencies to keep tasks sensitive to those interests away from broader, more inclusive public participation. If powerful groups determine public participation, systematic patterns of publicity could emerge in either direction. For NCES, group measures come from the *Federal Register*'s information collection notices indicating whom the government data collection process affect: *State and Local Governments* (such as state officials who are asked to report on state school enrollment levels), *For-Profit Firms* (such as businesses who participate in vocational education programs), *Non-Profits* (such as teacher unions), and *Individuals* (such as the member of the household who answers the phone). These are not mutually exclusive categories. Some surveys affect only one category. Others affect multiple categories. A majority of the surveys affected "individuals."

[114] NCES's staffing levels increased during some of the periods of budget expansion, but not all, and the rate of programmatic budget increases far surpassed the agency's staffing levels, leaving the agency with more work than staff. Congress determines agency appropriations for programmatic areas. However, NCES staffing levels were determined at the time by the Department of Education. The budget was measured in constant 2000 dollars. Information on NCES staffing was obtained through a FOIA request.

[115] The models include a measure of the lagged, average number of agenda-specific references or survey topic references made in House and Senate oversight committees, to represent

TABLE 6.4. *Advisory Council on Education Statistics Agenda Setting, 1985–2000, Logistic Regression*

Variable	Coefficient (SE)	Odds Ratio (SE)
Implementation Uncertainty and Interdependence		
Survey Scope: Natural Log of Assessment of Respondents	–0.096 (0.073)	0.908 (.066)
Task Novelty: First Time or Expedited Data Collection (1 = Novel)	–0.205 (0.394)	0.815 (0.321)
Internal Capability		
Technical Review Panel in Contract (1 = Technical Panel)	**1.194 (0.457)**	**3.301 (1.508)**
Agency Resources: NCES Staff/Budget Ratio	0.111 (0.107)	1.118 (0.119)
Political Oversight		
Profession: Lagged Moving Ave. *Education Week* Attention, 3 Years Prior	**0.143 (0.052)**	**1.153 (0.060)**
Congressionally Mandated Survey/Assessment (1 = Mandated)	0.171 (0.433)	1.186 (0.513)
Congress: Lagged Moving Ave. Cong Committee Attention, 3 Years Prior	**–1.099 (0.434)**	**0.333 (0.145)**
Divided Government (1 = Divided)	0.311 (0.465)	1.365 (0.635)
Survey Impact on State/Local Govts (1 = Government)	–0.378 (0.384)	0.685 (0.263)
Survey Impact on For-Profits (1 = For-Profit)	–0.549+ (0.317)	0.578+ (0.183)
Survey Impact on Non-Profits (1 = Non-Profit)	0.080 (0.378)	1.083 (0.410)
Survey Impact on Individuals (1 = Individuals)	0.408 (0.366)	1.503 (0.550)
Control		
Previous Board Attention: Frequency on Agenda in Previous Year	0.064+ (0.036)	1.066+ (0.038)
Constant	–1.458+ (0.836)	0.233+ (0.195)
	N = 262	N = 262

Boldface indicates significance at the p<.05 level; + indicates significance at the p<.1 level; all tests two-tailed.

Congressional Attentiveness. This measure is based on the average number of survey references in congressional oversight subcommittee hearings for the three years before the survey's administration. Data came from Lexis-Nexis Congressional, using the survey or assessment name as the search term. The model also includes a dichotomous measure of whether the survey was statutorily *Mandated* (1 for mandate, 0 for not mandated). Data for the technical review panel measure come from agency published and unpublished documents indicating whether or not a technical panel was part of the survey/assessment process (1 for technical review panel, 0 for not). Sources included ACES minutes (such as ACES minutes from 3/11/93) and personal interviews. I was unable to obtain a comprehensive list from ED on technical review panels, and my multiple-source approach may underreport the panels used for some survey or assessment programs.

the coefficients from Table 6.4 to predicted probabilities indicates that a one-standard-deviation increase in congressional attention is associated with a 7 percent decrease in the predicted probability of ACES agenda attention.

However, notice that survey topics that attracted *professional* attentiveness,[116] measured through the rolling average of their *Education Week* coverage in the three years prior, and surveys that also were assigned a technical review panel were significantly more likely to receive ACES agenda space. Going from a survey or assessment without a technical review panel to one that has a technical review panel is associated with a 29 percent increase in the predicted probability of appearing on an ACES agenda. A one-standard-deviation increase in *Education Week* coverage (going from one article to five articles) is associated with an 11 percent increase in the predicted probability of ACES agenda attention.[117] Together, these results suggest ACES's agenda setting may have been amenable to forging links with NCES's professional community by highlighting technical tasks (for which the agency was receiving private advice) and professionally salient tasks. Reflecting on this period, Commissioner Elliott recalled:

> It was important that one of the people [who served on ACES] was a high official in the Census Bureau and one was in the Bureau of Labor and Statistics, and it was really important to me that those people would carry the message that NCES is really moving in the right direction and it really is part of the government statistics … I needed them.[118]

Given the tumult the agency experienced in the 1970s and 1980s, the Advisory Council offered the agency a way to connect with part of its professional community.

From a bureaucratic perspective, supporting interdependent task implementations is not the only reason for bureaucrats to consult with public advisers. Public committees can serve many purposes, and using public committees to connect with a professional community can be important for developing agency reputation and image. On the one hand, the Center's decision to use the ACES platform to discuss the surveys and assessments that also received technical review panel reviews could reflect an effort to invite public engagement

---

[116] The NCES models also include a lagged, three-year average measure of each task's *Education Week* coverage. This measure was obtained through systematic searches of *Education Week* using each survey or assessment name as the search term. *Education Week* articles are accessible at http://www.edweek.org.

[117] Predicted probabilities are calculated using the baseline case of a survey or assessment that does not have a technical review panel, is not mandated, is not new, occurs during divided government, and affects individuals, with all other variables held at their respective means. The 95 percent confidence interval around the change in the predicted probability for *Education Week* coverage ranges from −0.003 to 0.365. The 95 percent confidence interval around the change in predicted probability for the technical review panel measure ranges from 0.098 to 0.481 and it ranges from −0.174 to 0.012 for the measure of congressional attention.

[118] Interview with Emerson Elliott, conducted by Susan Moffitt on November 4, 2004.

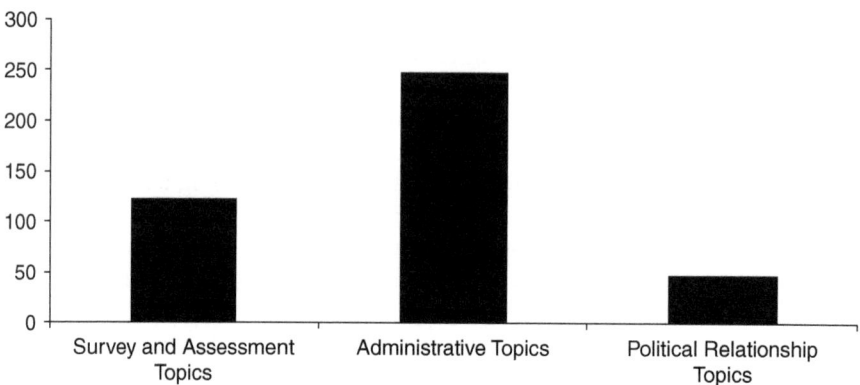

FIGURE 6.3. Count of Advisory Council on Education Statistics Agenda Topics by Type, 1985–2000.

for uncertain and interdependent tasks. However, recall that a long-standing critique of public advisory committees questions their contributions or usefulness. The Advisory Council's overlap with technical review panels may help explain some critics' perceptions that Council meetings were "show-and-tells" or "perfunctory" or "didn't do anything."[119]

Moreover, the ACES narrative cautions that fragility can appear when public engagement is not also grounded in task implementation. The preceding analysis considers agenda setting for assessment-specific topics. Figure 6.3 reveals the frequency of the Advisory Council's top twenty-one agenda items overall from 1985 to 2000, not only those restricted to specific assessments. Only eight of the agency's survey and assessment projects appeared frequently in the Council's deliberations, with the National Assessment appearing the most frequently.

The vast majority of the Council's agenda topics focused on general administration, such as Council administration, general methods topics, Center administration, Center reporting procedures, and the Center's budget. These general topics contrast with the specific implementation tasks that characterize FDA committees' agendas and participation.

The Advisory Council's agenda setting at times appeared consistent with helping NCES forge independence from the Department of Education and connecting the Center with parts of its professional community. But a systematic process for sustained and focused public engagement that liquefied knowledge largely failed to take root during the time period considered in this study. By the end of the Clinton administration and the beginning of the George W. Bush administration, Secretaries did not consistently fill open Council positions, the

---

[119] Eldridge, "The Status of Advisory Committees," pp. 154–162; Interview 81203, conducted by Susan Moffitt, August 12, 2003.

Council was unable to achieve quorum, and meetings did not take place for more than two years. Absent a systematic process linked to task implementation and dependent on shifting political winds, the Council was unable to survive and struggled to promote participatory bureaucracy during its tenure.[120]

LOOKING BEYOND AGENDA SETTING

To different degrees, both FDA committees and NAGB provide evidence of agenda setting consistent with participatory bureaucracy: public engagement focused on uncertain and interdependent task implementation. Though many political oversight measures developed for both cases fail to yield conclusive results, the FDA models display a positive association between divided government and agenda setting, consistent with participatory oversight. Topics mandated by Congress are significantly more likely to appear on NAGB agendas. Some aspects of participatory oversight and participatory bureaucracy can coexist.

Agenda setting – decisions and nondecisions – represents one pathway for public participation to develop policy and affect implementation by bringing publicity and openness to some policy tasks. Yet, who participates in those discussions? How public, open, and permeable are the discussions? How much "discussing" occurs, relative to "show-and-tell" presentations or "perfunctory" meetings? In addition to agenda setting, participatory bureaucracy also depends on bringing diverse expertise to bear on task implementations. Do FDA-style and National Assessment–style forms of public participation manage the democratic accountability side of the bureaucracy-democracy tension? Turning to analysis of who participates on public committees suggests when and how public committees may fulfill the "participatory" dimension of participatory bureaucracy.

[120] Other scholarship similarly suggests that focusing board work on specific "tangible" projects appears more amenable to committee contributions. See David S. Brown, *The Public Advisory Board in the Federal Government* (Syracuse University, Doctoral Dissertation, 1954), pp. 321–322.

7

Deliberate Participation

One of the great dangers in the unregulated use of advisory committees is that special interest groups may use their membership on such bodies to promote their private concerns.

House of Representatives Report 92–1017, April 25, 1972[1]

It's incumbent upon the members to listen carefully to the presentations from industry and to the Food and Drug Administration and neither act as advocates nor adversaries to the Agency or to the sponsors.

Statement by Chairman of the Pulmonary Allergy Drugs Advisory Committee, April 26, 1993

In 2010, American federal public committees offered upward of 70,000 people a seat at agency policymaking tables, at least in an advisory capacity.[2] Looking at the estimates of public participation on federal committees over

---

[1] U.S. Congress, House of Representatives, House Report 92–1017, *Federal Advisory Committee Standards Act*, 92nd Congress, 2nd Session, Committee on Government Operations, April 25 (Washington, DC: GPO, 1972), p. 6. An earlier House report called for advisory committees to offer "balanced and broader representation through appointment of members from varying social and economic constituencies," and continued: "Inclusion of environmentalists, consumers, geographic representatives, noninvolved persons and others would be helpful in providing a balance to a group." U.S. Congress, House or Representatives, House Report 91–1731, *The Role and Effectiveness of Federal Advisory Committees,* Committee on Government Operations, 91st Congress, 2nd Session, December 11 (Washington, DC: GPO 1970), p. 23.

[2] My estimated number of 73,723 advisory committee members in 2010 is based on data reported in the General Service Administration's advisory committee public data file for that year (see http://www.gsa.gov and http://facadatabase1997-2013.fido.gov/). For the time period from 1972 through 1998, estimates on committee membership are derived from the Annual Report of the President on Federal Advisory Committees. For the period from 1998 through 2010, estimates are based on data retrieved from the General Service Administration's public data file. These

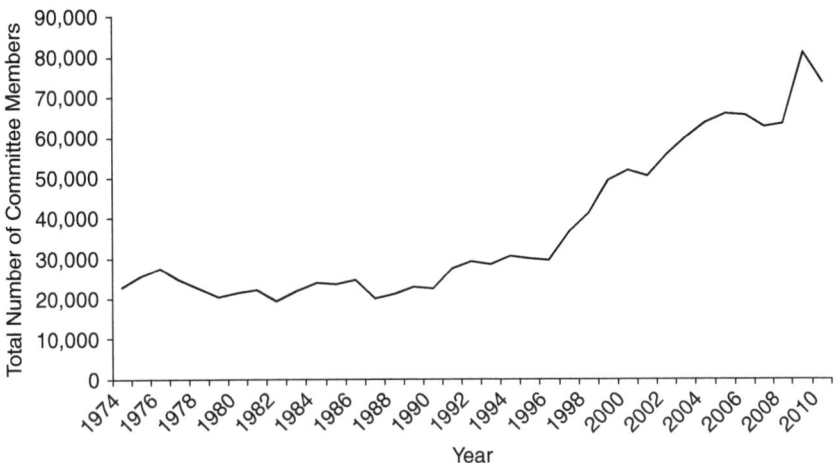

FIGURE 7.1. Count of Total Federal Advisory Committee Members across Agencies, 1974–2010.

time, depicted in Figure 7.1, represents a remarkable testament to public access to American bureaucracy.

Yet, how public are federal advisory committees in the sense of reflecting the various publics that policy affects? The vision of full group representation as a means of expressing and legitimizing democracy consistently fails to materialize in practice.[3] Participatory processes in government agencies, such as public committees, are vulnerable to similar limitations. Allegations abound that industry dominance on committees is not just an artifact of the past – such as the Business Advisory Council housed in the Department of Commerce in 1933 – but a persistent problem despite Federal Advisory Committee Act provisions. Estimates suggest approximately 38 percent of advisory committee members in 1985 hailed from private industry, for instance.[4] The danger of dominance is real.

estimates include all federal advisory committees, including grant committees; a rise in appointments to grants committees may help explain the steady rise in appointments over the past fifteen years. Some discrepancies appear across data sources. In 1998, the General Accounting Office reported 62,000 advisory committee members. U.S. General Accounting Office, *Federal Advisory Committee Act: Views of Committee Members and Agencies on Federal Advisory Committee Issues* (Washington, DC: GAO, 1998), p. 4. However, the "Twenty-Seventh Annual Report of the President on Federal Advisory Committees, Fiscal Year 1998" listed 41,259 members in 1998. See the Summary Table of Advisory Committee Data for Fiscal Year 1998, p. 12.

[3] E. E. Schattsneider, *The Semi-Sovereign People: A Realist's View of Democracy in America* (New York: Thompson Learning, 1960).

[4] White House, "14th Annual Report of the President on Federal Advisory Committees, Fiscal Year 1985," October 22, 1986.

When public administration scholar David S. Brown considered this question of representation with respect to federal advisory committees nearly half a century ago, he testified before Congress:

> Because of the complex nature of our society it is hardly possible to make the committee representative. Even though a number of my associates have condemned it because it is not and can never be truly representative, I see this as no real argument against it. A useful public purpose is served in my judgment by including within its membership sufficiently different points of view so that these at least will be heard.[5]

This pragmatic approach to public advisory committees raises related questions of how might "sufficiently different" points of view support bureaucratic administration, democratic accountability, or both?

From the perspective of bureaucratic administration, two features of public participation appear crucial for managing the complexity that Brown mentions in ways that are also consistent with bureaucratic reputation: diversity and expertise. Diversity can discourage dependence on or domination by a particular interest or perspective. Expertise provides a baseline of knowledge or ability that comes in many forms, depends on the policy task, and includes grassroots expertise. When task implementations present interdependence, uncertainty, or both, bureaucrats may find that they do not know enough, that implementers on whom they depend do not know enough, that no one knows enough, or that knowledge is insufficiently legitimate. As discussed in Chapter 2, building on that baseline of expertise, diverse perspectives and diverse cognitive heuristics render suboptimal policy decisions less likely. Again, from the vantage of bureaucratic administration, "suboptimal policy" means policy outcomes that are costly to reverse and/or damaging to agency reputation. Taking a cognitive approach differs from models of participation in bureaucratic policymaking that frame participation strictly as opportunities for communicating and advocating for particular *interests*. Managing complex problems requires different perspectives and heuristics, which may or may not align with traditional representations of interests and descriptive identity categories.

Though participatory bureaucracy allows for potentially autonomous bureaucratic action, elected officials may benefit from agency-initiated public engagement: participatory bureaucracy does not require a zero-sum trade-off where democracy loses whenever bureaucracy wins. Clearly, elected officials can benefit from bureaucratic competence that may accompany public participation. Elected officials, however, may seek a kind of participatory oversight that is inconsistent with bureaucratic reputation or that promotes responsiveness to elected officials, possibly at the expense of competent bureaucratic administration. Presidents, for instance, may depart from the conditions of participatory

[5] David S. Brown, U.S. Congress, Senate, *Advisory Committees*, Hearings on S.3067 before the Subcommittee on Intergovernmental Relations of the Committee on Government Operations, 91st Congress, 2nd Session, October 6 and 7, part 1 (Washington, DC: GPO, 1970), p. 33.

bureaucracy when they seek loyalty and ideological support among advisory committee appointees.[6] Public participation that works to support legislative oversight can differ from executive branch oversight by inviting both policy "winners" and "losers" to engage in participation: doing so may enhance legislators' abilities to oversee the bureaucracy,[7] but may frustrate administration. Yet, legislators, presidents, and bureaucrats alike may strive to "stack the deck" with privileged interests, enabling some groups to receive favored access to bureaucratic policymaking. Interest-dominated participation would yield participants who have systematic self-interested ties (such as financial ties) to a particular industry, group, or interest and/or who reflect a unified perspective, as described in models of cultural capture. These forms of participation teeter on the edge of the kind of group privilege that provokes cries of foul play among interests that feel excluded. Neither political responsiveness nor participation alone assures democratic accountability.

- *Participatory Bureaucracy:* Public participation is more likely to include diverse, task-specific experts and is less likely to abet privileged group dominance.
- *Participatory Oversight:* Legislatively initiated participation is more likely to: (1) privilege groups salient to the enacting legislative coalition; or (2) mirror the political environment by including winners and losers.
- *Participatory Oversight:* Presidentially initiated participation is more likely to include public participants who are loyal to the president and his policy positions than opponents.

Do institutional or organizational features abet or impede diversely expert participation consistent with participatory bureaucracy? Since the passage of FACA in 1972, some common procedures have governed the selection of official voting members to public committees. Vacancy announcements and the process for nominating candidates must be publicly reported in the *Federal Register*. Committee members who are considered "special government employees" for the purpose of serving on advisory committees cannot have conflicts of interest, or agencies must justify how their participation on the committee outweighs those conflicts.[8] Committee membership must reflect "balance"

---

[6] Bruce L. R. Smith, *The Advisers: Scientists in the Policy Process* (Washington, DC: Brookings Institution Press, 1992), pp. 42, 92–93. Smith discusses the role that presidential ideology plays in selecting advisory committee members.

[7] Steven J. Balla and John R. Wright, "Interest Groups, Advisory Committees, and Congressional Control of the Bureaucracy," *American Journal of Political Science*, 45 (2001): 799–812.

[8] These restrictions arise because of the application of the Ethics in Government Act to FACA. These provisions are limited to individuals who are designated "special government employees" and do not apply to committee members who are selected to represent specific groups or interests. For a discussion, see U.S. General Accounting Office, *Federal Advisory Committee Act: Views of Committee Members and Agencies on Federal Advisory Committee Issues* (Washington, DC: GAO, 1998); Steven P. Croley and William F. Funk, "The Federal Advisory Committee Act and Good Government," *Yale Journal on Regulation* 14(1997): 451–557.

TABLE 7.1. *Institutional and Organizational Attributes of Public Committees: Participation*

	FDA Drug Committees	National Assessment Governing Board
Institutional Origin	Authorized in statute	Mandated in statute
Policy Authority	Advisory	Policymaking
Appointments	Several designated positions, rest discretionary; variation in appointment authority	Explicit categories for each position; Secretary decision
Policy Type	Regulatory	Technical
Participatory Tasks	Discrete policy tasks	Discrete policy tasks

in terms of gender, race, and geography.[9] Typically, executive branch leadership – the president, presidential appointees, and senior agency staff – enjoy appointment authority, not Congress.[10] A General Accounting Office survey of government agencies and advisory committee members in 1998 revealed that the overwhelming majority of respondents – between 85 to 90 percent – perceived balance and representativeness on their committees.[11]

Even with the overarching institutional framework FACA provides, public committees can embody starkly different institutional arrangements. This chapter focuses on participation through NAGB and FDA drug review committees as examples of committees with pronounced organizational and institution differences, depicted in Table 7.1. Congress specified detailed National Assessment Governing Board membership categories in statute. While the FDA

---

[9] The Federal Advisory Committee Act required this of congressionally created advisory committees. The GSA expanded this requirement to all advisory committees. For a discussion, see Croley and Funk, "The Federal Advisory Committee Act and Good Government," p. 500.

[10] Robert Steinbrook, "Science, Politics and Federal Advisory Committees," *New England Journal of Medicine* 350 (2004): 1454–1460, p. 1457. Steinbrook notes that agency staffers are instrumental in collecting nominations for advisory committees and may be influential in the appointment process, but do not typically make appointments. Congressional participation in committee member selection can occur in the form of Senate confirmation of presidential appointments to committees, as in the case of the Public Advisory Board of the Economic Cooperation Administration in 1948. See David Brown, *Public Advisory Boards in the Federal Government* (Syracuse University, Doctoral dissertation, 1956), p. 105.

[11] Specifically, the survey found that "about 90 percent of the respondents generally or strongly agreed that committee membership was fairly balanced in terms of the points of view represented, and 85 percent generally or strongly agreed that their committees included a representative cross-section of those directly interested in and affected by the issues discussed by the committees." U.S. General Accounting Office, *Federal Advisory Committee Act: Views of Committee Members and Agencies on Federal Advisory Committee Issues* (Washington, DC: GAO, 1998), p. 7.

reserves a slot for a consumer/patient representative and a nonvoting industry representative, the FDA has considerable latitude in member appointments.

It is hard to imagine how an institutional arrangement could be any more supportive of diversity than the one established for NAGB. Yet, allegations of privilege have surfaced nonetheless. The diversity requirements contained in FACA alone, or through descriptive membership categories, are not necessarily able to ensure diversity or expertise in practice. Whereas NAGB seems designed for diversity, several aspects of FDA advisory committees appear amenable to industry dominance. Scholarship suggests highly technical tasks are more likely to diminish participation from "non-experts," even when they are invited to engage in policy discussions.[12] These sorts of tasks are also more conducive to industry capture, according to some accounts.[13] FDA advisory committees appear well suited, in both respects, to not only exclude but also enable industry dominance, as critics have periodically alleged.[14] Because appointment authority can reside with the Secretary for both agencies, FDA advisory committees and NAGB are also susceptible to membership selection to support executive branch policy positions.[15] The narrative and analysis of FDA committees and NAGB that follow, however, find evidence consistent with the diverse expertise necessary for participatory bureaucracy, even in unlikely committee circumstances.

PUBLIC PARTICIPATION FOR THE NATIONAL ASSESSMENT OF EDUCATIONAL PROGRESS

Controversy over members selected to NAGB emerged shortly after the Board moved from its position under the National Assessment's contractor to its more independent status. In a letter dated September 27, 1988, Chairman of the House Committee on Education and Labor Augustus Hawkins and his cosigners alleged that Secretary of Education William Bennett had "politicized" NAEP's public board – NAGB – by appointing members who did not

---

[12] William T. Gormley Jr., *The Politics of Public Utility Regulation* (Pittsburgh, PA: University of Pittsburgh Press, 1983).

[13] Nolan McCarty, "Complexity, Capacity and Capture," in *Preventing Regulatory Capture: Special Interest Influence and How to Limit It*, edited by Daniel Carpenter and David Moss (Cambridge: Cambridge University Press, 2013), pp. 99–123.

[14] Despite periodic complaints throughout the 1970s and 1980s, a GAO review of Department of Education and FDA conflict-of-interest procedures found that "not only were the procedures effective, but also they were followed with such consistency that we did not find a single instance where the appearance of a conflict of interest had not been identified and resolved in advance of an advisory committee meetings." Statement of Rosslyn Kleeman, Associate Director, General Accounting Office, prepared for the Subcommittee on Information Management and Regulatory Affairs, Committee on Governmental Affairs, U.S. Senate, June 21, 1984, p. 8.

[15] This chapter does not assess the Advisory Council on Education Statistics

meet "the high standards of expertise and balance intended by Congress."[16] Chairman Hawkins was clearly part of the coalition that codified the public board into law in 1988: the statute that authorized NAGB bore the chairman's name, the Augustus F. Hawkins–Robert T. Stafford Elementary and Secondary School Improvement Amendments of 1988. Yet the chairman's letter implied the outcome of the structure he sponsored did not support his preferences. House Democrats criticized Secretary Bennett for appointing members who supported the administration's view of "setting high performance standards and using comparisons of state test scores to spur reforms."[17] At the time, Secretary Bennett's appointments were understood as a potential assault on public education – part of a conservative effort to promote school privatization and a threat to faithful Democratic constituents.[18]

Allegations of politicization or imbalance are neither new nor unique to NAGB. Whereas most appointments to public committees garner little media attention, controversy over advisory committee appointments sporadically appears across committees and across government agencies. Charges that the president and his appointees removed advisory committee members who opposed administration views and appointed ideological and policy sympathizers erupted over Reagan administration's appointment decisions for the EPA's Science Advisory Board[19] and appeared during the George W. Bush administration for committees advising the Center for Disease Control, the National Center for Environmental Health, the Department of Health and Human Services Office for Human Research Protection, the Occupational Safety and Health Administration, and the National Institutes of Health. Public rebuke from the media and some women's organizations also arose after President George W. Bush appointed W. David Hager – an obstetrician and abortion opponent whose scholarship included work professing an evangelical Christian perspective on women's health – to the Food and Drug Administration's

---

[16] Reported by Richard Rothman, "Democrats Seek to Prevent 3 from Joining NAEP Panel," *Education Week*, October 12, 1988.

[17] Maris Vinovskis, *Overseeing the Nation's Report Card: The Creation and Evolution of the National Assessment Governing Board* (Washington, DC: National Assessment Governing Board, 1998), p. 22. Vinovskis notes that, despite the backlash over Bennett's appointments, the appointees who angered Chairman Hawkins were reappointed in 1992.

[18] John F. Jennings, "An Interview with John F. Jennings," in *The Nation's Report Card: Evolution and Perspectives*, edited by Lyle V. Jones and Ingram Olkin (Bloomington, IN: Phi Delta Kappa Press, 2004), pp. 279–280. It was the Senate that included state NAEP in its version of the 1988 legislation. The House focused its attention on amendments to Title I of the Elementary and Secondary Education Act. The former staff director for the Elementary and Secondary Education Subcommittee in the House of Representatives observed that he did not "think the members of Congress or the staff understood fully" the implications of the Senate amendments, which closely reflected the Reagan administration's Alexander-James panel's recommendations: Jennings "An Interview with John F. Jennings," pp. 279–281.

[19] Sheila Jasanoff, *The Fifth Branch: Science Advisors as Policy Makers* (Cambridge, MA: Harvard University Press, 1990), pp. 89–91. She notes that the controversy passed relatively quickly.

Reproductive Drugs advisory committee.[20] In this case, opponents claimed the appointee lacked appropriate expertise to serve. An even greater firestorm ignited after Vice President Dick Cheney refused to release the names of the individuals participating in his National Energy Policy Development Group and information about the group's consultations with oil companies, fueling charges of group dominance.[21]

To what extent, however, do allegations of imbalance map onto systematic privilege on Board appointments? NAGB contains a range of institutional features that appear amenable to separating the board from executive branch influence and patronage appointments, including detailed board membership categories. While many of NAGB's 1988 membership criteria were similar to those that defined 1978 membership, the 1988 legislation added new slots for a nonpublic school administrator, curriculum specialists, measurement and testing specialists, and principals. It also specified that individuals representing state elected officials (governors and legislators) should reflect different political parties. Moreover, Congress established the board outside the Department of Education's hierarchy, authorized the board to make binding policy decisions, and provided the board with its own staff and budget line item.[22] The National Assessment's governance arrangement from 1969 to 1988 included two primary institutional actors: the federal agency[23] and the National Assessment's grantee,[24] with the Assessment Policy Council operating under the auspices of the grantee. The 1988 legislation put the public board on more equal footing

---

[20] Controversy continued during the FDA's review of the over-the-counter contraceptive drug Plan B. Bureaucratic staffers in the FDA recommended approving Plan B for over-the-counter use without an age restriction. This recommendation was consistent with the public advice the FDA received from its public advisory committee, which voted 23–4 to approve Plan B for over-the-counter use. Hager was part of the minority voting against Plan B, and submitted a separate report to the FDA opposing the approval. The FDA decided not to approve Plan B for over-the-counter use, and Dr. Hager claimed he was persuasive in the FDA's decision. Marc Kaufman, "Memo May Have Swayed Plan B Ruling," *Washington Post*, May 12, 2005. The GAO investigated the FDA's review of Plan B for irregular procedures. Government Accountability Office, *Food and Drug Administration: Decision Process to Deny Initial Application for Over-the-Counter Marketing of Emergency Contraceptive Drug Plan B was Unusual* (Washington, DC: GAO, November 2005), pp. 15–16.

[21] For a summary, see Steinbrook, "Science, Politics and Federal Advisory Committees," pp. 1454–1460. The appointment of Governor Jeb Bush – President George W. Bush's brother – to NAGB in 2005, however, provoked little controversy or attention. Lynn Olson, "All in the Family: Another Bush helps shape federal policy on student testing," *Education Week*, February 16, 2005.

[22] P.L. 107–279. Having a separate budget line item can create a more direct link between the Board and Congress.

[23] Recall the federal agency for NAEP switched hands: The National Institute for Education assumed sponsorship responsibilities for NAEP in 1978. NAEP reverted back to NCES sponsorship in the early 1980s.

[24] Recall the NAEP grant/contract switched hands: the Education Commission of the States from 1969 to 1983, and the Educational Testing Service from 1983 to 1988.

with the agency and with the contractor, creating three principal institutional actors. If independence from the executive branch appears for any public committee, it should appear for the National Assessment's board.

Institutional provisions such as membership categories and budgetary independence represent only potential sources of independence. Countervailing institutional arrangements and the political environment may affect Board operations in practice. For instance, like most public committees, the departmental Secretary has appointment authority over NAGB, offering opportunities for executive branch influence. For another, the political environment in which the Board operates has witnessed sharply divided mobilized interests. Recall that some state and local opposition to national data collection and assessment efforts has been persistent and fierce since the federal government first got in the business in the nineteenth century.

Analysis of Governing Board Appointments, 1991, 1995, 1999

The analysis in this section assesses member selection to NAGB to test countervailing predictions of public participation. Do patterns of appointments reflect the diverse expertise that participatory bureaucracy requires, allegiance to executive branch policy preferences, opportunities for congressional oversight, or some combination of all of these? The Governing Board's membership criteria embody descriptive diversity. Substantive diversity, however, depends on the policy task. When diversity is consistent with participatory bureaucracy, it reflects diverse perspectives, not just diverse interests.

The context for assessing Board appointments in the 1990s included divisiveness over expanding the National Assessment to allow state comparisons. The National Assessment's 1988 foray into state-by-state comparisons mobilized distinct and opposing interests. Some states, localities, and their representative organizations supported state NAEP. Others strongly opposed it. These circumstances, plus divided government, plus a policy slated for implementation in a cabinet agency, suggest legislative conditions conducive to structuring public participation to mirror the political environment, to include both policy winners and losers in subsequent policy implementation, to make concessions to powerful interests, or even to design the policy to encourage failure. In other words, the political environment in the late 1980s and early 1990s suggest nearly ideal conditions for political oversight through a public board like NAGB.

Political oversight can occur directly or indirectly. When it works directly, legislators give privileged constituents unique access to agency policymaking. NAGB offers no evidence of direct oversight. *None* of the individuals nominated by a member of Congress was appointed to the Board in any of these three years. These descriptive statistics alone, however, are unable to speak systematically to whether appointments reflect public engagement for legislative oversight (with participants who represent privileged interests *or* participants who are more likely to "mirror" the political environment), public engagement for executive branch oversight (with public participants who are loyal to the president and his policy positions), and/or public engagement for participatory bureaucracy (with participants who are diversely expert), recognizing that legislators and presidents may benefit from diversely expert participants as well.

The logistic regression in Table 7.2 assesses the determinants of member selection to NAGB in 1991, 1995, and 1999 – the years for which data were available.[25] Consistent with other scholarship, the analysis is restricted to only the pool of individuals who were nominated to serve on NAGB, recognizing that the pool of nominees may reflect an underlying selection process. Considering the pool of people nominated to serve on NAGB in those three years,[26] the results in Table 7.2 offer a mixed portrait and suggest nuance instead of unequivocal claims of politicization or diverse expertise.

Most of the model's measures of potential political influence do not produce discernible effects on member selection and fail to achieve standard levels of statistical significance. For one, the results offer little support for claims that the Secretary, on behalf of the president, stacks the Board with party loyalists or uses the Board for patronage. Contributions to candidates in the president's political party before the individual's nomination fail to explain Board appointments: no "loyal" donors received Governing Board appointments during the time frame analyzed. More broadly, *campaign contributions* overall fail to yield a conclusive relationship with subsequent appointments.[27] Other political measures are similarly inconclusive, including nominees' and nominators' *appearances in Congressional hearings*.[28] Receiving a *nomination from*

---

[25] These are the only three years for which information on nominees was available to the author. Data for the pool of nominees come from board records publicly available in Chester E. Finn Jr.'s archived files at the Hoover Institution and from briefing materials reviewed at the NAGB's offices. Lists of nominees and their nominators were available for only 1991, 1995, and 1999. For other years, only the nominees recommended by the NAGB nominations committee were available. Acquiring data on committee nominations is difficult to achieve across government agencies, as Balla and Wright note in their article, "Interest Groups, Advisory Committees and Congressional Control of the Bureaucracy."

[26] The analysis assesses membership selection onto NAGB as a dichotomous choice. It considers the pool of nominees for slots on NAGB in 1991, 1995, and 1999, and it uses a logistic regression model to assess the factors associated with individuals' selection to the committee. The unit of analysis is the nominee.

[27] Data for this measure came from http://www.opensecrets.org/. Each nominee was used as a search term. Contributions were counted and averaged only for contributions made before the individual's nomination.

[28] Data for these measures were obtained by searching the *Lexis-Nexis Congressional* database (the database was subsequently acquired by Proquest): http://www.lexisnexis.com/academic/universe/congress/features.asp. Each nominee and nominator was used as a search term. One measure consists of the lagged, average number of appearances the nominee made before Congress (averaged across the 3 years before the nomination). A second measure consists of the lagged, average number of appearances the nominator or nominating group made before Congress (averaged across the three years before the nomination). These measures include only

TABLE 7.2. *Selection to NAGB, 1991, 1995, 1999, Logistic Regression*

Variable	Coefficient (SE)	Odds Ratio (SE)
Policy Position		
Publicly Opposed State NAEP Expansion (Opposed = 1)	−0.890 (1.357)	0.410 (0.557)
Nominator/Nominee Affiliated with 1988 NAEP Reform (Affiliated = 1)	**1.270 (0.568)**	**3.560 (2.024)**
Political, Group Prominence		
Nominated by Category Representative	−0.479 (0.575)	0.619 (0.356)
Nominee's Participation in Congressional Hearings	−0.599 (0.649)	0.549 (0.356)
Nominator's Participation in Congressional Hearings	−0.179 (0.218)	0.836 (0.182)
Log of Average Contributions Before Nomination	−0.050 (0.169)	0.951 (0.161)
Count of Different Nominations	.291 (0.199)	1.338 (0.266)
Policy Prominence		
Education Week References to Nominee, Rolling Ave 3 Years Prior	0.083+ (0.045)	1.086+ (0.048)
Descriptive Characteristics		
Nominee Race (White = 1)	−0.479 (0.605)	0.619 (0.375)
Nominee Gender (Male = 1)	0.646 (0.577)	1.908 (1.100)
Constant	**−2.827 (0.776)**	**0.059 (0.046)**
N = 249		

Boldface indicates significance at the $p<.05$ level; + indicates significance at the $p<.1$ level; all tests two-tailed.

a single-issue group, including teachers unions or the American Association of School Administrators, within the relevant membership category[29] and the *number of nominations* a nominee received also failed to produce a discernible association with membership selection. While *public opposition* to state NAEP

appearances prior to the individual's nomination. Moreover, these measures are not restricted to the period surrounding state NAEP's authorization in 1988. The NAEP and NAGB provisions were added to the 1988 legislation as Senate floor amendments: they did not "go through hearings or through the committee." See Jennings "An Interview with John F. Jennings," p. 278. Groups who signed the 1990 letter opposing state NAEP did testify at hearings in both the House and Senate relating to *other* parts of the 1988 Stafford-Hawkins amendments, such as Title I of the Elementary and Secondary Education Act. None of the nominees affiliated with state NAEP expansion participated in hearings related to any part of the 1988 amendments.

[29] Consistent with other scholarship such as Balla and Wright's article "Interest Groups, Advisory Committees, and Congressional Control of the Bureaucracy," the models include a measure of whether or not the individual was nominated by a representative of the category in which the nomination occurred: whether the Council of Chief State School Officers, for instance,

expansion appears in the negative direction, relative to a nominee who took no public position on the expansion, the results fail to achieve conventional levels of statistical significance.[30] Descriptive characteristics such as race and gender also fail to yield a systematic relationship with member selection.

The results point to two factors that appear systematically associated with membership selection: *affiliation with NAEP reform* in 1988 and *prominence in the education community*. Nominees whose nominators were affiliated with the Alexander-James panel and its recommendations for NAEP reform were significantly more likely to be selected to serve on the board compared with individuals who had no public affiliation with NAEP's reform.[31] Table 7.2 presents the results in terms of coefficients and odds ratios. Converting these results to predicted probabilities, individuals who were nominated by individuals with ties to the Alexander-James panel were about 16 percent more likely to receive a Board appointment than individuals who lacked such an affiliation.[32]

Participatory bureaucracy entails diversity built on a foundation of expertise. Traditional measures of expertise, such as advanced degrees or publications, fail to reflect the diversity of expertise of different categories of Governing Board members: teachers, measurement experts, elected officials, and public representatives. We would not expect most Governing Board members to have publication records or even advanced degrees, for instance. Prominence in the education community, however, offers a more reliable measure of expertise conducive to different backgrounds. Prominence in the field of education, measured through references in *Education Week*, helps explain Board appointments, but modestly so.[33] A one-standard-deviation increase in the average

nominated someone for the Chief State School Officer slot; whether the American Federation of Teachers nominated someone for the local school slot, and so forth.

[30] This is a dichotomous measure of public opposition to NAEP's expansion to State NAEP to test the claim that individuals who publicly oppose the administration's policy direction are less likely to receive slots on the board. Data for this measure come from two sources: an open and highly publicized letter released in 1990, with signers from more than seventy-five organized groups that opposed NAEP's expansion into state NAEP and a list of public opponents to national testing, collected by FairTest. FairTest provided this list to the author. Opponents in 1990 included the NAACP, the Urban League, the National Association of Secondary School Principals, the National Council for Social Studies, and some leadership from the American Federation of Teachers, among others.

[31] This measure is coded 1 if the *nominator* participated on the Alexander-James panel proposing state-by-state NAEP comparisons, if the *nominee* participated on the Alexander-James panel, or if the nominator or nominee made public statements, recorded in *Education Week*, supporting Alexander-James recommendations. The baseline group includes individuals who were affiliated neither with expansion proponents nor with its opponents.

[32] This predicted probability was calculated for the case of a white man who did not oppose NAEP expansion, who was not nominated by a single-issue group, with all other variables held at their respective means. The confidence interval around the change in the predicted probability was calculated by bootstrapping, and it ranges from 0.001 to 0.333.

[33] The model measures an individual's prominence in the general education community through a lagged, average count of the number of references to the individual in *Education Week*. Each nominee was used as a search term, and articles were retrieved from *Education Week's* online

number of references the individual received in *Education Week* in the three years before the individual was nominated (an increase from one reference to about six references) increases the predicted probability of receiving a board appointment by about 3 percent.[34] This measure achieves statistical significance at the 90 percent confidence level.

Though modest, the effects that prominence in the education community has on board appointments lend some support for the diverse expertise that participatory bureaucracy requires. The results are also conducive to aspects of executive branch and legislative oversight. Yet, instead of "politicization," the results suggest Board members shared a common trait: support for the National Assessment's general policy direction and a belief in the legitimacy of the federal assessment program, consistent with the findings of an historical review of the Governing Board conducted in 1998.[35] The inclusion of state NAEP supporters is consistent with program maintenance, a chief concern for bureaucratic administration. The results may also be understood as consistent with the president's and political appointees' pursuit of participation amenable to the President's policy agenda. Participatory bureaucracy, again, is not necessarily a zero-sum arrangement.

Board cohesiveness, however, does not mean unalloyed presidential, agency, or interest group dominance. The Board publicly criticized both President George H. W. Bush in 1991 and Vice President Al Gore in 1999 for prematurely reporting National Assessment results in violation of the assessment's reporting standards. The Governing Board also publicly took issue with aspects of President Clinton's Voluntary National Test proposals in 1999 and with the aspects of President George W. Bush's No Child Left Behind Act in 2003 that threatened to compromise test items' security. In each of these cases, the Board grounded its criticism in the policies' or actions' potential effects on the National Assessment's fundamental administration and its statistical integrity.

While Board support for the statistical integrity of the National Assessment is consistent with bureaucratic administration, it does not mean the federal agency, the National Center for Education Statistics, was able to steer the Board. The Center remained constrained in its efforts to structure NAEP and to advance some of the NAEP-related policies the Center preferred. Unlike FDA advisory committees, NAGB is not merely advisory but instead enjoys policymaking authority. This form of public engagement and participation appears on its face to be well situated to frustrate and possibly impair bureaucratic administration by curtailing the scope of agency authority. Yet the following illustration

---

archive of articles: http://www.edweek.org. The measure includes only *Education Week* references prior to the individual's nomination.

[34] As before, this predicted probability was calculated for the case of a white man who did not oppose NAEP expansion, who was not nominated by an Alexander-James affiliate, who was not nominated by a single issue group, with all other variables held at their respective means. The 95 percent confidence interval around this predicted probability ranges from 0.004 to 0.140.

[35] Vinovskis, *Overseeing the Nation's Report Card*, p. 22.

of the Governing Board's decision to prevent the National Assessment from sponsoring a survey of parents illustrates how participatory bureaucracy is *not* a matter of bureaucratic dominance, but instead weaves together bureaucratic initiative, diverse expertise, and multidirectional flows of information to support policy implementation for complex problems.

Case of Background Variables: Parent Survey

The debate that began in 1963 at the early meetings of assessment design over what background measures to include on the National Assessment persisted over several decades. As discussed in Chapter 6, an installment of this debate appeared again in 1994, when NCES staff proposed adding a parent survey to the National Assessment, justifying the survey as a potential contribution to making the assessment's results more meaningful to policy and practice. Center Commissioner Elliott argued:

> [P]eople don't just want a bunch of numbers from NAEP. They want to be able to say something about what is the relationship between achievement and different kinds of information about students. And one of the most important ones where NAEP is weakest is on socioeconomic background for students.[36]

For analysts, policymakers, practitioners, and the public to understand how schools, classrooms, and instruction could affect student achievement, the National Assessment would need a way to account for students' backgrounds, the Center argued.[37] Center staff argued that parent surveys – and surveys that were considerably longer than the one proposed for the National Assessment – were a staple of other prominent Center studies, including the National Education Longitudinal Study (NELS).[38] Parent surveys, in other words, were nothing new to other educational assessment efforts. Efforts to bypass parent surveys and to use proxy measures for socioeconomic status, the agency argued, were fraught with substantive and statistical limitations. Fourth graders unreliably answered questions about the number of books at home and parents' education levels. Comparing the proxies the National Assessment used to try to measure socioeconomic status with the direct measures that the NELS

---

[36] National Assessment Governing Board, "Transcript of National Assessment Governing Board Meeting," August 5, 1994.

[37] The federal agency presented the fundamental statistical issue: "There is no measure that is more strongly associated with student achievement than SES [socio-economic status] and if we are not able to parcel out SES from other information displaying the NAEP student achievement data, then we are not able ever to have satisfactory explanations of the NAEP data. It is so large an effect that it makes it difficult to sort out the effects of instructional variables. Things that are going on in the classroom which are regularly a part of our analyses are confounded because we are not able to sort out SES from those measures very well." National Assessment Governing Board, "Transcript of National Assessment Governing Board Meeting," August 6, 1994.

[38] National Assessment Governing Board, "Transcript of National Assessment Governing Board Meeting," August 5, 1994.

obtained through parent surveys helped demonstrate the problems with the proxy socioeconomic status measures. The technical argument for a parent survey also had a political dimension, as it did in 1974 when then-Commissioner Gilford pressed for more background measures. Center staff noted that "other parts of the Department … are very much interested in the SES issues beyond the NAEP issue," which included departmental interest in using NAEP to evaluate Title I of the Elementary and Secondary Education Act (the largest federal education program for elementary and secondary education) and to assess civil rights issues.[39]

While the Center focused on the contributions a parent survey might have for the Center's other products and for the department more broadly, NAGB focused on broader political dynamics and argued the parental survey could potentially damage the assessment's administration by compromising its political support. Governing Board opposition to the parental survey arose from a range of Board members, including principals, superintendents, university professors, industry representatives, and public representatives, along with Board staff. Parent survey opponents expressed concern that the surveys may be interpreted as violating privacy and may discourage the voluntary participation on which the National Assessment depended at the time.[40] Members noted the importance of collecting valid, reliable socioeconomic data but objected to the length of the proposed survey and to some of the questions.[41] As Governing Board staff summarized, the parent survey

> was well-intentioned. It would give us better socioeconomic data; there is no question about it. But it was long and could be considered by some intrusive.... how much money do you make? Where does your money come from? Who is your household partner? … in today's climate … somebody is going to say, 'Well, that is not the federal government's business, and are they keeping that data, and are they going to share it with the IRS? And is it going into this big computer?' … It may be well-intended, and it may be good, but could it derail us, and could it keep us from our primary mission?'[42]

---

[39] National Assessment Governing Board, "Transcript of National Assessment Governing Board Meeting," August 6, 1994.

[40] National Assessment Governing Board, "Transcript of National Assessment Governing Board Meeting," August 5, 1994. Recall that NAEP later became required, but not for another decade after these debates.

[41] A Board member argued, "You know I have deep concerns about this particular questionnaire but I also know that it is extremely important for us to be aware that if you can't factor out those powerful SES variables, you won't get out what we most important want to find out and that is what are the impact factors in the classroom and the teaching approaches and the curriculum variables and so on, and that is what we really want to get at. So SES is not an interesting by-line here, it is critical." National Assessment Governing Board, "Transcript of National Assessment Governing Board Meeting," August 6, 1994.

[42] National Assessment Governing Board, "Transcript of National Assessment Governing Board Meeting," August 5, 1994.

A Democratic governor on the board concurred, "It is a risk you don't need to run."[43] In the words of a Board member representing the public, "I mean, on the strictly statistical basis, sure, it may very well be the best way to go, but there may be reasons that we would choose, even in the light of that knowledge, not to go that way."[44] The Governing Board's cohesiveness on the issue also did not mean domination by a particular group or by experts: all but two of the Board members present actively participated in the deliberation. Only one of the two principals and a state board of education member did not go on record with a position.[45]

The government agency, NCES, proposed a field test to ascertain the potential scope of political problems a parent survey might provoke, to assess whether parents will "provide the personal information; will they allow their own sons and daughters to continue to participate in NAEP or will this somehow affect their view about whether their sons and daughters should participate in the National Assessment."[46] The Governing Board nonetheless passed a resolution that the "draft surveys" proposed by NCES "would not appropriately contribute to NAEP data collection and reporting, could threaten NAEP's future viability and therefore present a policy issue ... [and] should not be administered in the 1995 NAEP field trial nor included in the 1996 assessment."[47] The agency and the Governing Board then disagreed sharply over who had jurisdiction for deciding whether the parent survey should be administered: the federal agency or the board with its jurisdiction over policy.[48] Jurisdictional disputes such as this are precisely the sort that bureaucratic administration strives to avoid. The NCES commissioner publicly encouraged the committee to avoid engaging in a turf dispute,[49] and the subsequent subcommittee meeting between the public board and the agency was described as "very good" and "very open."[50]

---

[43] National Assessment Governing Board, "Transcript of National Assessment Governing Board Meeting," August 5, 1994.

[44] National Assessment Governing Board, "Transcript of National Assessment Governing Board Meeting," August 6, 1994.

[45] Seventeen of the nineteen members who were present for the August 6, 1994 Board meeting participated in full board deliberation, in writing the subcommittee resolution, or had their views mentioned as part of the board discussion.

[46] National Assessment Governing Board, "Transcript of National Assessment Governing Board Meeting," August 6, 1994.

[47] National Assessment Governing Board, "Transcript of National Assessment Governing Board Meeting," August 6, 1994.

[48] National Assessment Governing Board, "Transcript of National Assessment Governing Board Meeting," August 6, 1994. Individual background items required clearance from OMB. NAGB had authority over cognitive items.

[49] Commissioner Elliott argued against turning the disagreement into a turf fight: "[W]hat is in whose jurisdiction, it is really not very constructive and it is not helpful for the public, and I really hope that we don't have to do that sort of thing." National Assessment Governing Board, "Transcript of National Assessment Governing Board Meeting," August 6, 1994.

[50] National Assessment Governing Board, "Transcript of National Assessment Governing Board Meeting," November 1, 1994.

Yet, beneath the surface issue of turf resided a more fundamental challenge for the National Assessment's administration: the assessment's ultimate reliance on parent and student implementers outside the federal agency or assessment contractor, a prominent expression of NAEP's interdependent implementation. Leadership from the National Assessment's contractor, charged with administering the NAEP, asked the Board for advice on how to handle or communicate this interdependence:

> [O]ne of the things that we have to do is get schools – which is principals and superintendents – to agree to participate. It is a burden on them; it is time and it is effort.... And ... people ... are making it difficult for those superintendents and principals to give over time, because there is fear that their students are participating and giving information to the federal government ... I just met with 600 principals and superintendents, and this is a major concern of a large majority of them.[51]

The contractor went on to discuss wanting to be proactive and "searching for a spokesperson or spokespersons who could say that NAEP is okay; it is doing things that are good and nonintrusive and important for all segments of our society."[52] He asked the Governing Board how to "approach this." The Democratic governor on the Board offered, "I would be willing to help try to get governors universally to say, 'This is a very important tool.' But their endorsement may not be as important as finding a way to explain it to parents ... I would be willing to help on that problem of communication."[53] Recall that supporting multidirectional flows of information is one part of participatory bureaucracy. In this case, board members took an active role in facilitating that information flow.

In participatory bureaucracy, supporting bureaucratic administration differs from supporting bureaucrats' policy preferences. In the case of the parent survey, the government agency clearly preferred to develop and administer a new instrument – a preferences that collided with the Board's. The Board's participation, however, was key to supporting a fundamental tenant of NAEP's administration: sustaining state and local support for and participation in the National Assessment's administration.

* * *

Aspects of NAGB are not fully participatory in at least two ways. Participation on the Board, for one, is neither fully open nor fully free but instead reflects membership rights that may limit general citizen involvement. One portion of all Board meetings, for another, is closed to public attendance. Yet, NAGB

[51] National Assessment Governing Board, "Transcript of National Assessment Governing Board Meeting," August 5, 1994.

[52] National Assessment Governing Board, "Transcript of National Assessment Governing Board Meeting," August 5, 1994.

[53] National Assessment Governing Board, "Transcript of National Assessment Governing Board Meeting," August 5, 1994.

expresses diverse public engagement unified around common goals, notably expanding the National Assessment to offer state comparisons and protecting the assessment's operational integrity. The Board also challenges conventional sharp distinctions between "expert" and "public." At the grassroots level, teachers and administrators can appear to be experts who are part of the governing education bureaucracy, separate from citizens. At the federal level, however, school teachers and administrators represent relatively grassroots participation in national policymaking and may be described as "lay" instead of "expert." Rather than the full expression of active and latent interests, participatory bureaucracy depends on a more pragmatic standard: "sufficiently different points of view." In the development of diverse expertise that discourages domination, diverse need not mean full. To this end, NAGB included teachers, principals, superintendents, school board members, state chief school officers, state elected officials, measurement experts, industry representatives, and a few public members, which included lawyers, businessmen, and individuals prominent in education policy. Consistent with participatory bureaucracy, public engagement on the Governing Board was not dominated by any single group: teachers unions, local and state administrators, or either political party.

Aspects of NAGB are not bureaucratic in several traditional senses of bureaucracy. The Governing Board does not follow hierarchical lines of authority, nor does it defer to agency preferences. Yet, public participation through the Governing Board offered portals for participation to support ultimate bureaucratic administration and task implementation. Persuading state and local school officials, as well as parents and students, to participate in the assessment was a necessary condition for National Assessment implementation, from which the federal agency ultimately benefited. Instead of reflecting a case where negotiated compromise yields programs or agencies designed to fail, NAEP and NAGB offer illustrations of diverse expertise consistent with task implementation. The National Assessment works at the intersection of a group of agencies (NCES, the contractor, NAGB), is codified by Congress, and operates in a field fraught with controversy and a history of incompetence. The National Assessment nevertheless developed a reputation for being the "gold standard" assessment that embodies successful, complex policy implementation.

PARTICIPATION THROUGH FDA DRUG ADVISORY COMMITTEES

NAGB represents a case in which the public board's institutional design appears amenable to political oversight. Yet, it has indirectly buffered the assessment from political influence over the assessment. FDA drug committees, in contrast, have long faced allegations of abetting industry capture and/or cultural capture, in which the views of firms or a particular profession dominate the participatory process. In its 2007 assessment of the FDA's drug approval process, the Institute of Medicine argued,

FDA's credibility is its most crucial asset and recent concerns about the independence of advisory committee members ... along with broader concerns about scientific independence in the biomedical research establishment, have cast a shadow on the trustworthiness of the scientific advice received by the agency.[54]

Unlike NAGB meetings, FDA drug review meetings often attract considerable attendance and media attention: an average of 168 people attended each FDA advisory committee meeting in 2011.[55] And, unlike NAGB meetings, FDA drug review meetings often include audience comments during the open-mike portion of the meeting. Meetings convened in 2011 averaged four public speakers, often representatives from consumer protection groups such as Public Citizen, or disease sufferers speaking on behalf of the product under review.[56]

Open public comment periods can provide audience members with opportunities to bring perspectives to committee deliberations that might otherwise not be considered and provide provocative statements that make their way into subsequent media reports. "We have arrived in hell," AIDS research advocate Greg Gonsalves from the Treatment Action Group concluded at the open public comment portion of the Antiviral Drugs advisory committee considering the approval of ddC to use in combination with AZT. He offered his assessment of the evidence, "Let me be quite clear. I do not think ACTG study 155 meets the burden of proof for approval of ddC as part of a combination regimen with AZT. The intention-to-treat analysis of study 155 showed no difference in efficacy between the two treatment arms." He also advanced a normative policy conclusion:

> AIDS activists and government regulators have worked together with the best intentions over the years to speed access of drugs to individuals with life-threatening diseases.... What we have done, however, is to unleash drugs with well-documented toxicities onto the market without obtaining rigorous data on their clinical efficacy in order to provide the HIV positive and their care providers information they need to make rational treatment decisions.[57]

However, most of the active participation on FDA drug review committees arises from FDA staffers, the sponsoring firm, and committee members, with only occasional exchanges between committee members and individuals speaking during the open public comment portion of the meeting.

---

[54] Institute of Medicine, *The Future of Drug Safety: Promoting and Protecting the Health of the Public* (Washington, DC: National Academy Press, 2007), p. 9.

[55] The FDA does not keep records of who is sitting in meeting audiences. Audience members at the meetings I attended over the course of my research included reporters, Wall Street analysts, researchers in the pharmaceutical industry, organized interests, and disease sufferers.

[56] Committee chairmen may ask public speakers to disclose whether a firm has paid for them to attend.

[57] Comments of Gregg Gonsalves, Treatment Action Group, reported in "Food and Drug Administration Antiviral Drugs Advisory Committee transcript volume 1," September 20, 1993. Page numbers are not included on the transcript.

Concerns about ties between the FDA, its committee members, and the firms the FDA regulates are nothing new. A classic illustration comes from Dr. Julia Apter's 1974 Senate testimony, in which she alleged close ties between some of her advisory committee colleagues and the researchers whose drugs the committee reviewed. She testified,

> I was the only statistician in my advisory committee ... I would like to see more people who are scientists and not themselves involved in giving these drugs to patients. I would like to see more people who are not close personal friends of the people who are serving as investigators for the drug companies, to be on the advisory committees.[58]

In addition to ties between committee members and the researchers investigating the drugs the committee reviewed, Dr. Apter also perceived that she was the only statistician and that other committee members were connected to the drugs through their prescription practices. Dr. Apter argued that her status as an outsider allowed her to be "openly critical if I thought it was necessary."[59] Tapping industry knowledge has been part of the FDA advisory committee system since the 1950s, including the 1955 Citizens' Advisory Committee on the Food and Drug Administration, and has carried through to the 1997 Food and Drug Modernization Act requiring the FDA to include nonvoting industry representatives on new advisory committees.[60]

Single-interest dominance can foster perceptions of privilege, secrecy, and lack of general public accountability, whether or not such privilege actually occurs. When single-interest dominance occurs, it may discourage broad support as well as discourage an agency from considering potentially useful policy options, or, as Dr. Apter suggested, from receiving potentially helpful critiques. Over the past forty years, however, the FDA has developed elaborate procedures for screening committee members for inappropriate ties to industry through potential conflicts of interest. Before each committee meeting, committee members and invited guests must disclose any financial or "other" interests

---

[58] Testimony of Julia Apter, U.S. Congress, Senate, *Examination of the Pharmaceutical Industry* 73–74, Joint Hearings before the Subcommittee on Health of the Committee on Labor and Public Welfare and the Subcommittee on Administrative Practice and Procedure of the Committee on the Judiciary, 93rd Congress, 1st and 2nd Sessions, Part 7, August 15 (Washington, DC: Government Printing Office, 1974), p. 2885. The full quote reads, "I was the only statistician in my advisory committee. There were often other statisticians present during the time that we were reviewing drugs, but they were not voting members of the committee. I would have liked to have seen and still would like to see more statisticians. I would like to see more people who are scientists and not themselves involved in giving these drugs to patients. I would like to see more people who are not close personal friends of the people who are serving as investigators for the drug companies, to be on the advisory committees."

[59] Testimony of Julia Apter, *Examination of the Pharmaceutical Industry* 73–74, p. 2888. The full quote reads, "I have no personal contact with physicians who perform these investigations and that is largely because I am a woman and that, these contacts therefore could not prevent me from being openly critical if I thought it was necessary."

[60] Committees' consumer representatives have voting privileges.

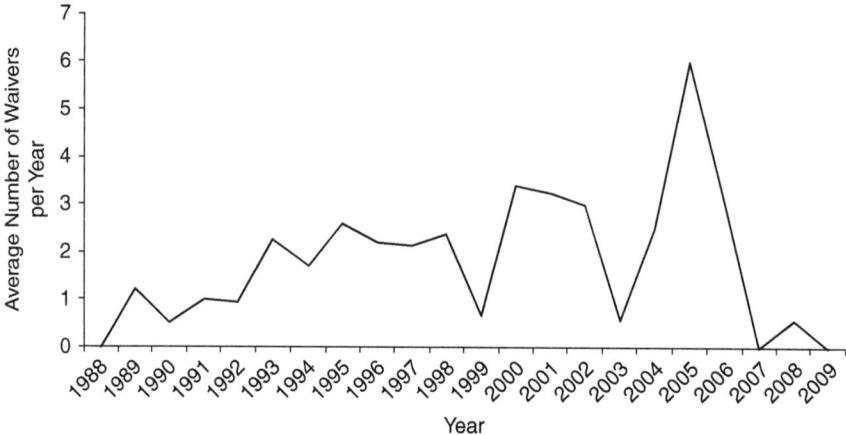

FIGURE 7.2. Average Number of Waivers per FDA Drug Advisory Committee Meeting, 1988–2009.

they have in the firm sponsoring the drug or in a competitor firm as well as research that may be impacted by the outcome of committee deliberation and decisions. When potential conflicts of interest arise, the agency has the option of granting the committee member a waiver to participate in the meeting none-theless. During the past twenty-five years, conflict-of-interest waivers have been a regular feature of many committee meetings. The agency granted at least one conflict of interest waiver at 137 of the 203 meetings for which records are available.[61] Yet, with the exception of waivers granted in 2005, Figure 7.2 suggests the average number of conflict-of-interest waivers has been relatively stable and relatively low over the past twenty years.

Diversity that builds on a foundation of expertise has the potential to sup-port interdependent task implementation in several ways. It can offer the agency diverse expertise that the agency would otherwise lack. Relatedly, it can expose problems outside the agency, notably with firms and their drug applications. It can also convey important information to implementers outside the agency. Who participates on and through FDA drug advisory committees? Do patterns of engagement support legislative oversight, executive branch oversight, and/or participatory bureaucracy?

Analysis of FDA Advisory Committee Participation

Examining committee meetings that reviewed New Molecular Entities from 1989 to 2009 produces usable information on 909 committee members involved in those reviews.[62] The sample is restricted to individuals who were

---

[61] My counts are restricted to meetings discussing NMEs. The estimates in Figure 7.2 are based on my review of transcripts obtained from 1988 to 2009, counting the number of individuals reported at the beginning of the meeting as receiving a waiver.

[62] Analysis is limited to NMEs and advisory committee meetings considering NMEs before the FDA issues its approval decision. Not all transcripts from NMEs reviewed between 1989 and

TABLE 7.3. *Descriptive Counts of FDA Advisory Committee Members, NME Meetings, 1989–2009*

	Men	Women	PharmD or SciD	MD	PhD	Other Degrees	RN
TOTAL	633	276	24	695	143	10	37

given voting rights at the meeting either on a continuing (ongoing) basis as a formal committee member or on a temporary basis as a committee guest. The sample was also restricted to meetings discussing the approval of a New Molecular Entity.[63] Individuals included in the sample participated in an average of three meetings discussing New Molecular Entities, with a range of one to nineteen meetings.

Descriptively, the portrait presented in Table 7.3 suggests FDA drug review committees in this time period consisted primarily of male MDs: 633 of the 909 committee members were men; 695 of the 909 committee members were MDs. Committees ranged from 0 percent to 70 percent female, with an average of 30 percent. At an average committee meeting, 78 percent of committee members held MDs. That figure ranged from 40 percent to 100 percent. Only about a quarter of the committee members ever received a conflict-of-interest waiver that allowed them to participate in a committee meeting despite a financial tie they might have had with either the firm sponsoring a drug or a competitor firm.

On the surface, these sorts of descriptive statistics appear to lend some support to Dr. Apter's 1974 lament about the scarcity of women and PhD statisticians on public committees. The prominence of medical doctors on FDA advisory committees appears consistent both with agency efforts to tap top technical expertise in the field and with concerns of cultural capture: a shared understanding of the world that yields regulatory decisions that benefit industry or dominant interests. Descriptive statistics alone, however, fall short of demonstrating capture or even the conditions for capture. And despite the preponderance of descriptive homogeneity, dissent appeared in more than 40 percent of the advisory committee meetings for which voting data was available from 1989 to 2009.

Does participation on FDA committees systematically privilege industry sympathizers? In other words, even if the choice to send a drug to committee does not exhibit firm privilege as Chapter 6 suggests, do aspects of committee operations and deliberation privilege industry overall and established firms in particular? Results presented in the following sections offer a fine-grained look

2009 yielded usable data. I was able to obtain complete data for all independent variables for 866 of the 909 individuals.

[63] The sample does not include general discussions on matters such as appropriate endpoints to use for studies of pain nor does it include meetings for drugs already approved.

at three important parts of committee participation: voting in the minority, testifying on behalf of industry, and serving as a committee chairperson.

Explaining Dissent

Unanimity alone is insufficient as evidence of cultural or industry capture; unanimity may arise either because of compelling features of the approval decision or because of a cohesive group view. While unanimous decisions may (or may not) include diverse perspectives that ultimately achieve consensus, split votes embody some measure of dissent and diverse perspective. The following models examine the determinants of individuals' minority voting decisions[64] at each meeting they attended, over time. Of the full sample of 909 individuals, voting information was available for 831 meeting participants.[65] The unit of analysis is the individual voting member by meeting,[66] and data were analyzed using logistic regression.[67] The models assess the impact of drug-specific characteristics, committee characteristics, and individual characteristics on voting decisions.

Drug-specific factors may bear on individuals' voting decisions, as uncertainty over drugs' effects may encourage greater dissent on public committees. In the models that follow, one measure of uncertainty comes from a drug's *priority status*, discussed in Chapter 6.[68] A second measure of relative uncertainty comes from a measure of *FDA experience with the firm sponsoring the drug*. Drugs sponsored by firms that have more experience with the FDA and with FDA advisors may induce less uncertainty about the potential quality of the product, and thus less dissent.[69] For each drug that was the topic of an advisory committee meeting, the models include a count of the number of drugs the sponsoring firm previously submitted to the FDA. Dissent over drug products might also arise from variation in *group demand for new therapies*: greater group demand for therapies may encourage members to vote as a bloc. To illustrate how group demand may influence committee members, consider the words of one former advisory committee member who observed: "[W]hen you hear the patients saying … 'If in doubt, approve, because there's nothing there

---

[64] The dependent variable is measured dichotomously, with 1 representing a minority vote. Abstentions are excluded from the analysis, coded as neither majority nor minority positions.

[65] Some meeting transcripts provided only overall vote outcomes (such as 7-3 in support of drug approval) but did not provide records of how individual members vote. Specific voting information was available for 831 participants.

[66] This dataset is linked to a primary sample consisting of NMEs approved between 1986 and 2009 discussed in Chapter 6. Individual participation data is available for NMEs reviewed between 1989 and 2009. Data on committee voting patterns were retrieved from transcripts of NME meetings obtained from a FOIA request.

[67] Supplemental models used random effects models for panel data for robustness checks.

[68] A drug's priority status is a dichotomous measure, coded 1 if the drug was a priority review. As mentioned in Chapter 6, information on drug priority status can be obtained from drugs@fda.gov.

[69] Daniel P. Carpenter, "Protection without Capture: Product Approval by a Politically Responsive, Learning Regulator," *American Political Science Review* 98 (2004): 613–631.

for us' … you hear the desperation … I understand that pain and I understand the risks. So I tended to go in that direction."[70] Like the agenda setting model in Chapter 6, this model includes the log of the number of drugs previously approved to treat the disease represented in each drug's primary indication, with a higher count representing lower drug demand, consistent with prevailing scholarship.[71]

The model also includes a count of *public comments* during the meeting: the number of individuals from the general audience who addressed the committee before committee deliberation and votes.[72] Public comments can entail desperate pleas from patients along with sharp rebuke for the FDA, as the examples presented earlier in the book illustrate. Committee members have also noted that the absence of public comments can send a signal too, akin to a dog that did not bark. Public comments are not unequivocally supportive of drug reviews, even when coming from patient advocates. The public comment portion of FDA advisory committee meetings typically includes comments from some disease sufferers recruited by firms to testify on behalf of the drug product under review, as well as comments from a representative of consumer interests. More public comments reflect potential opportunities for the committee to hear perspectives beyond a few patients recruited by firms to testify on behalf of the firm and its drug. The models also control for the committee type (i.e., Cardio-Renal, Antiviral, Anti-Infective, etc.) to consider significant but potentially unobservable committee differences.

In addition to the context of committee deliberation, the models consider several individual-level measures, including whether or not the committee member received a conflict-of-interest *waiver* to participate in the meeting.[73] To assess the committee member's technical expertise and prominence in the medical community, the models include the log of the number of each committee member's *publications* before the meeting in question.[74] The models also include indicator variables for the committee member's *gender* and whether the

[70] Interview 82603, conducted by Susan Moffitt on August 26, 2003.

[71] Carpenter, "Groups, the Media, Agency Waiting Costs and FDA Drug Approval," pp. 490–505. Supplemental models also included an index of the drugs' primary indications to consider significant but potentially unobservable differences between diseases the drugs are indicated to treat.

[72] Information on the number of public comments was obtained from each meeting transcript, available either at http://www.fda.gov/AdvisoryCommittees/ or obtained by the author through a FOIA request.

[73] Conflict of interest waiver information was derived from each meeting transcript. At the beginning of each advisory committee meeting, the FDA reports individuals who received waivers to participate.

[74] Publications were counted through systematic searches of the individual through the PubMed search engine (http://www.ncbi.nlm.nih.gov/pubmed) and through CVs posted on the web, using the committee participant's name as the search term. All available publications were included in the count.

individual holds a *PhD*.[75] These measures are designed to assess the extent to which the charges Dr. Apter levied in 1974 (and that other commentators have echoed since) are valid – that gender, professional training, and financial ties to the firm with the product under review bear systematically on dissent. Recall Dr. Apter claimed that her status as an "outsider" – as a woman, a biostatistician, and someone without financial ties to regulated industry – enabled her to be, in her words, "openly critical if I thought it was necessary."[76] Additional indicators reflect whether or not the individual served as the *consumer or patient representative* at the meeting, or served as a *voting guest* at the meeting. The final measure controls for the individual's number of *previous minority votes*.

The results in Table 7.4 suggest several drug, committee, and individual characteristics associated with committee dissent, but the substantive effects are modest. Consistent with leading scholarship on "protection without capture," firms with which the FDA has experience are significantly less likely to experience committee dissent.[77] The magnitude of the effect, however, is quite small. Converting the coefficients from Table 7.4 to changes in predicted probabilities, a one standard deviation increase in firm experience lowers the predicted probability of a minority vote by only one percent.[78] The effects of receiving a waiver on casting dissenting votes are inconclusive.[79] None of the other measures of disease- or drug-specific attributes obtains conventional levels of statistical significance.

The extent of public comments at committee meetings is associated with an increased likelihood of a minority vote, holding drug priority status and demand for the drug constant. The substantive effects, however, are quite small. A one-standard-deviation increase in the number of public comments (an increase from three to seven comments) is associated with only a 1 percent increase in the predicted probability of an individual casting a minority vote.[80]

Among the individual-level characteristics, only status as a voting guest appears associated with dissent. A committee guest is associated with a

---

[75] Degree information was obtained through online searches, using the individual's name as the search term.

[76] Testimony of Julia Apter, *Examination of the Pharmaceutical Industry 73–74*, p. 2888.

[77] Carpenter, "Protection without Capture," pp. 613–631.

[78] Predicted probabilities for this section are calculated for the case of a priority review, for an individual who did not receive a waiver to participate, does not hold a PhD, is not female, is not a consumer/patient representative, is not a committee guest, with all other variables held at their respective means. The 95 percent confidence interval around the change in the predicted probability for firm experience ranges from –0.018 to –0.006.

[79] See Genevieve Pham-Kanter for important variation on waivers. Genevieve Pham-Kanter, "Financial Conflicts of Interest in FDA Advisory Committees," paper presented at the 2013 Annual Meeting of the Law and Society Association, June 2013, Boston, MA.

[80] These predicted probabilities are calculated for the same case as described in footnote 78. The 95 percent confidence interval around the change in the predicted probability ranges from 0.001 to 0.014.

TABLE 7.4. *Minority Votes on FDA Drug Advisory Committees,*
1989–2009, Logistic Regression

	Minority Votes Coefficient (SE)	Minority Votes Odds Ratio (SE)
Drug Characteristics		
Firm: # Previous Submissions	**−0.036 (0.010)**	**0.964 (0.010)**
Priority Review (Priority = 1)	−0.222 (0.220)	0.801 (0.175)
Drug Demand (log order entry)	0.063 (0.092)	1.065 (0.098)
Committee Characteristics		
# Public Comments	**0.049 (0.017)**	**1.050 (0.018)**
Committee Type	−0.011 (0.019)	0.989 (0.019)
Individual Characteristics		
Individual Waiver (Waiver = 1)	0.070 (0.242)	1.072 (0.260)
Publications (log, before meeting)	0.071 (0.094)	1.074 (0.101)
Female (Female = 1)	−0.151 (0.211)	0.860 (0.182)
Consumer/Patient Rep (Rep = 1)	0.409 (0.446)	1.505 (0.671)
Voting Guest (Guest = 1)	**0.572 (0.231)**	**1.771 (0.409)**
PhD (PhD = 1)	0.178 (0.215)	1.194 (0.257)
# Previous Minority Votes	**0.904 (0.129)**	**2.469 (0.318)**
Constant	**−3.172 (0.513)**	**0.042 (0.022)**
Votes	2,337	
Individuals	831	

Boldface indicates significance at the p<.05 level; all tests two-tailed.

2.6 percent increase in the predicted probability of casting a minority vote compared with a committee member.[81] This suggests that the FDA invites guest "experts" who bring dissenting views to committee deliberations. Expertise, recall, is task specific; and the FDA appears to be systematically inviting guests who offer points of view that differ from standing committee members.

None of the other descriptive measures – degrees, gender, or consumer representative status – appears systematically related to voting patterns. Special membership categories have a long history on federal advisory committees, and they have appeared in recent calls for promoting greater diversity. Yet, the results listed in Table 7.4 find little evidence that such categories produce diverse or dissenting points of view expressed through votes. This appears consistent with the General Accounting Office's 2004 argument that demographic diversity criteria "alone do not provide a robust understanding of the points of view and potential biases the members may bring to the committee vis-à-vis

[81] These predicted probabilities are calculated for the same case as described in footnote 78. The 95 percent confidence interval around the change in the predicted probability ranges from 0.003 to 0.052.

the specific matters the committees will address." The report notes that demographic membership criteria "may achieve demographic diversity, but they cannot ensure an appropriate balance of viewpoints relative to the matters being considered by the committees."[82] However, procedures that provide committee guests with voting privileges and encourage open public comment, the results here suggest, may offer additional opportunities to invite diverse views to drug review deliberations. These results are correlational. Yet, they imply that including participants who are not regular committee members, such as guests and public commentators, is associated with greater dissent and brings some degree of diverse perspectives to public committees.

A Revolving Door?

Advisors to pharmaceutical industries encourage firms to recruit former advisory committee members to testify on the firm's behalf at advisory committee meetings,[83] suggesting public advisory committees may offer a form of revolving door. Individuals moving from government to industry, or from industry to government, reflect one form of potential cultural capture. In the sample used for this study, the revolving door between advisory committees and firms appears rarely. Only twenty-eight of the individuals in this study's sample, representing less than 3 percent of the sample, appeared before an advisory committee on behalf of a firm after previously serving as a committee member. Only nineteen individuals served as voting participants on FDA committees discussing NMEs after previously appearing on behalf of firms. Table 7.5 presents factors associated with the revolving door, when it occurs.[84]

Notably, firms appear more likely to recruit advisory committee members with more substantial publication records and who have more experience on FDA committees. Table 7.5 presents the results in terms of coefficients and odds ratios. Converting the results to predicted probabilities illustrates some small substantive effects associated with these results.[85] A one-standard-deviation increase in the log of publications an individual has before her first meeting appearance is associated with a 3 percent increase in the predicted probability of testifying for firms after serving as a committee member, and about a 1.6 percent increase in the predicted probability of serving as a committee

---

[82] U.S. General Accounting Office, *Federal Advisory Committees: Additional Guidance Could Help Agencies Better Ensure Independence and Balance* (Washington, DC: GAO, 2004), p. 40.

[83] On recruiting experts, see Wayne L. Pines and Mary Ann N. Cotton, "Preparing for an FDA Advisory Committee Meeting," *Drug Information Journal* 31(1997): 35–41.

[84] The data available for this study are not able to assess other ways industry may tap former advisory committee members, such as hiring former members to consult with firms to prepare for an advisory committee meeting, but not appear at the meeting on the firm's behalf.

[85] These predicted probabilities were calculated using the case of someone who was male, who did not hold a PhD, with the rest of the variables held at their respective means. The 95 percent confidence intervals around the predicted probabilities were constructed with bootstrapped standard errors. For the committee to firm model, the 95 percent confidence interval around

TABLE 7.5. *Changing Status from Committee Member to Firm Representative,*
FDA Drug Advisory Committees, Logistic Regression, 1989–2009

	Firm then Committee Coefficient (SE)	Firm then Committee Odds Ratio (SE)	Committee then Firm Coefficient (SE)	Committee then Firm Odds Ratio (SE)
Committee Characteristics				
Committee Type	–0.026 (0.045)	0.974 (0.044)	–0.078 (0.052)	0.925 (0.049)
Individual Characteristics				
PhD (PhD = 1)	–0.271 (0.759)	0.763 (0.579)	0.330 (0.641)	1.390 (0.891)
Publications (log, before meeting)	**0.430 (0.195)**	**1.538 (0.299)**	**0.847 (0.274)**	**2.332 (0.640)**
Female (Female = 1)	–1.544 (1.026)	0.214 (0.219)	–1.631 (1.189)	0.196 (0.233)
Total # NME Meetings Chaired			0.017 (0.156)	1.017 (0.158)
Voting Guest (Guest = 1)			**–1.443 (0.607)**	**0.236 (0.143)**
Total # Waivers			0.104 (0.099)	1.110 (0.109)
Total # Minority Votes			**–0.875 (0.324)**	**0.417 (0.135)**
# Years of Service on Committee			**0.392 (0.053)**	**1.479 (0.079)**
Constant	**–5.177 (0.931)**	**0.006 (0.005)**	**–7.460 (1.404)**	**0.001 (0.001)**
Individuals	867		867	

Boldface indicates significance at the p<.05 level; all tests two-tailed.

member after testifying on behalf of firms. A one-standard-deviation increase
in the number of years of advisory committee service (moving from three to six
years of service) is associated with a 3.5 percent increase in the predicted probability of testifying for firms. Casting minority votes is negatively associated

the change predicted probability associated with the change from member to guest ranges from
–0.023 to –0.001; with a one standard deviation change in the log of publications ranges from
0.010 to 0.060; with a one standard deviation change in the number of minority votes ranges
from –0.014 to –0.001; with a one standard deviation change in the number of years of service
ranges from 0.01 to 0.07. For the firm to committee model, the 95 percent confidence interval around the change in the predicted probability associated with a one standard deviation
increase in publications ranges from 0.003 to 0.035.

with subsequently testifying on behalf of firms, but modestly so: a one-standard-deviation increase in minority votes is associated with a 1 percent reduction in the predicted probability of testifying for firms.

Even though the revolving door may be rare, the results reveal the challenge that appears when firms and the FDA attempt to attract the same talent pool: individuals with prominent publication records. Yet, the results also suggest that firms are significantly less likely to recruit former advisory committee members who express minority or dissenting views, though the substantive effect of this result is quite modest. Not only might dissent buffer against cultural capture while on committees, but it might discourage the subsequent revolving door after service on a committee ends.

Privilege through Chairmanship?

Some committee observers contend that committee chairpersons can influence committee deliberation by: determining when firms can introduce previously unannounced speakers or materials, interacting or not with individuals participating in the open public comment period, and setting the tone of deliberation.[86] The results in Table 7.6 suggest that individuals with more extensive publication histories help explain FDA chairperson selection decisions.[87] A one-standard-deviation increase in the log of publications is associated with a 7.6 percent increase in the predicted probability of being selected to chair a meeting.[88] While the measure of publication histories speaks to potential expertise on FDA committees, diversity appears limited in several respects. Individuals who were committee guests as opposed to standing committee members were less likely to be appointed as chair for a committee meeting: the predicted probability of chairmanship declines by 8 percent.[89] Holding a PhD instead of an MD is also negatively associated with chairing an FDA meeting: the predicted probability declines by 8 percent here as well.[90] Measures of

---

[86] On the importance of committee chairs on committee member engagement and contributions, see David S. Brown, *The Public Advisory Board in the Federal Government* (Syracuse University, Doctoral Dissertation, 1954), pp. 65, 192, 415. House Report 91-1731 also noted the importance of committee chairs. See House Report 91-1731, *The Role and Effectiveness of Federal Advisory Committees*, House Committee on Government Operations, December 11, 1970, (Washington, DC: GPO, 1970), p. 17.

[87] Unclear from these results is whether the publication measure reflects independent expertise or individual dependence on firms sponsoring medical research.

[88] The publication measure includes work the individual published before her first meeting date. Predicted probabilities are calculated for the case of a male member who did not receive a waiver to participate in the meeting, who is not a consumer or patient representative or a voting guest, who does not have a PhD, who is serving on the Cardiovascular and Renal Drugs Advisory Committee, with all other variables held at their respective means. The 95 percent confidence interval ranges from 0.051 to 0.105.

[89] This is based on the same case conditions as described in footnote 88. The 95 percent confidence interval ranges from −0.102 to −0.059.

[90] This is based on the same case conditions as described in footnote 88. The 95 percent confidence interval ranges from −0.105 to −0.066.

TABLE 7.6. *Determinants of FDA Drug Committee Chairperson Selection, 1989–2009, Logistic Regression*

	Selecting Chairpersons Coefficient (SE)	Selecting Chairpersons Odds Ratio (SE)
Committee Characteristics		
Committee Type	0.023 (0.025)	1.023 (0.026)
Individual Characteristics		
Individual Waiver (Waiver = 1)	0.040 (0.211)	1.041 (0.219)
Publications (log, before meeting)	**0.533 (0.154)**	**1.704 (0.263)**
Female (Female = 1)	−0.128 (0.355)	0.880 (0.313)
Consumer/Patient Rep (Rep = 1)	−0.470 (0.982)	0.625 (0.613)
Voting Guest (Guest = 1)	**−2.119 (0.536)**	**0.120 (0.064)**
PhD (PhD = 1)	**−2.591 (0.766)**	**0.075 (0.057)**
# Previous Minority Votes	−0.237 (0.243)	0.789 (0.192)
Constant	**−4.352 (0.743)**	0.013 (0.010)
Observations	2,577	
Individuals	866	

Boldface indicates significance at the $p<.05$ level; all tests two-tailed.

gender and status as a consumer or patient representative fail to achieve standard levels of statistical significance, as does receiving a waiver to participate in the meeting. Nor does the model provide conclusive evidence that taking a minority position at a previous committee meeting yields "punishment" in terms of reduced opportunities to serve as chair.

IMPLICATIONS FOR PARTICIPATORY BUREAUCRACY: CONTRIBUTIONS AND VULNERABILITIES

This chapter set out to assess whether FDA drug committees and NAGB incorporate different perspectives on public committees consistent with participatory bureaucracy, recognizing that this approach is one among many ways to assess the diversity and expertise conveyed in public participation.[91] The FDA drug committees represent a case in which conditions seem ripe to find industry influence. Instead, drug review committees bore no systematic evidence of a revolving door between committees and industry; and the impact of conflict

[91] For scholarship that relies on surveys of agency staff and participants, see Robert S. Friedman, "Representation in Regulatory Decision-Making: Scientific, Industrial and Consumer Inputs to the FDA," *Public Administration Review* 38 (1978): 205–214. For scholarship that assesses the quality of deliberation, see Michael K. Gusmano, "FDA Decisions and Public Deliberation: Challenges and Opportunities," *Public Administration Review* 73 (2014): S115–S126.

of interest measures is inconclusive across models.[92] Yet, as the Institute of Medicine observed, even the appearance of an improper relationship can mar the agency's reputation; and the FDA began to restrict the percentage of committee members on public committees who may receive waivers. In 2010, this cap was 13 percent of members; and the agency reports that it granted waivers to less than 5 percent of committee members during that year.[93] Ultimately, however, advisory committee members' financial ties to pharmaceutical companies reflect a broader challenge facing the medical community.[94] Limits on the number of members who may receive waivers to participate in FDA meetings in which they may have a financial stake touch only lightly on the intricate ties among industry funding, physician education, and medical research. Moreover, new constraints on the number of waivers the FDA allows can heighten the challenge of attracting individuals with sufficient expertise but who are not tied to industry, given that industry and the agency both have incentives to recruit the same pool of talent.

As Michael Gusmano aptly observed, "Few are satisfied with range of public participants offering guidance and expertise to the FDA."[95] From the perspective of bureaucratic administration, however, the FDA results do not reveal patterns of domination incompatible with participatory bureaucracy. The finding that invited guests are more likely to offer dissenting views appears consistent with incorporating different perspectives on a task-specific basis and with some strategies for discouraging "group think." In their classic analysis of the government's troubled response to the threat of swine flu in 1976 and 1977, recall Neustadt and Fineberg's recommendation to convene public panels consisting of "a reservoir of talent, selected for practical knowledge not representation" and who "come from places where health interventions actually are carried out ... to bring a feel for the intricacies of implementation," to discourage group-think.[96] The FDA results on temporary members appear consistent with this general approach, though plenty of room remains to link FDA committees

---

[92] Lurie and colleagues found that members with conflicts of interest were more likely to vote for a drug's approval, but that removing individuals with conflicts of interests from committees would not change the ultimate outcome of committee votes. Peter Lurie et al., "Financial Conflicts of Interest Disclosure and Voting Patterns at Food and Drug Administration Advisory Committee Meetings," *Journal of the American Medical Association* 295 (2006): 1921–1928.

[93] Margaret A. Hamburg, "Commissioner's Letter to FDA Staff on Disclosure of Financial Conflicts of Interest," April 21, 2010. http://www.fda.gov/AdvisoryCommittees/AboutAdvisoryCommittees/ucm209001.htm (accessed October 18, 2011).

[94] Bernard Lo and Marilyn J. Field, *Conflict of Interest in Medical Research, Education and Practice* (Washington, DC: Institute of Medicine, 2009). For more on this argument, see Susan Moffitt, "The Policy Impact of Public Advice: The Effects of Advisory Committee Transparency on Product Safety," in *Regulatory Breakdown: The Crisis of Confidence in U.S. Regulation*, edited by Cary Coglianese (Philadelphia: University of Pennsylvania Press), pp. 180–199.

[95] Gusmano, " FDA Decisions and Public Deliberation," p. S121.

[96] Richard E. Neustadt and Harvey V. Fineberg, *The Swine Flu Affair: Decision-Making on a Slippery Disease* (Washington, DC: The National Academies Press, 1978), p. 94, p.89.

more closely with "places where health interventions are actually carried out," to use Neustadt and Fineberg's terms.

FDA drug committee meetings can also give witness to public learning, rather than perfunctory participation. Reviews of transcripts from the Cardiovascular and Renal Drugs committee from 1986 to 2002, for instance, reveal vigorous – and sometimes sizzling – exchanges between committee members, the sponsoring firm, and the agency. Unlike other drug review committees, the Cardiovascular and Renal Drugs committee during this time period frequently did not include a formal agency presentation as part of the typical advisory committee meeting. Instead, agency staff leadership would put both committee members and the firm on the spot through rigorous questions. "Ray, what else do you want to extract from us? We are a little bit at a loss to be other than sufficiently nebulous on this idea," the chairman of the Cardiovascular and Renal Drugs committee asked FDA division director, Dr. Raymond Lipicky, after hours of exchange about the drug Manoplex. Dr. Lipicky replied, "That sounds fine. I do not think you can push it any farther than you did."[97] Without a formal agency presentation, there may be fewer opportunities for committee meetings to become show-and-tell exercises, an accusation that faced the Advisory Council on Education Statistics. With the agency actively questioning the committee and the company sponsoring the drug, there may also be fewer opportunities for the committee to become the agency's adversary.[98] Both are consistent with bureaucratic administration, and there is room for the FDA to use this approach more frequently than it has in the past.

NAGB represents a case where conditions appear prime for representative participation. It is difficult to imagine institutional arrangements that could be descriptively more representative. Still, diversity did not necessarily manifest in terms of including both policy supporters and opponents on the Board, since few opponents to NAEP expansion appear to have been appointed to the board during this time period. Participatory bureaucracy, however, invites us to consider what "sufficiently different points of view" means from the perspective of bureaucratic administration and task implementation. Building diverse perspectives around some general common playing field, such as expanding NAEP, may have been one way to prevent participation from disintegrating into "a babble of conflict and controversy," as opponents of diversity warned.[99] Diverse perspectives appeared among NAEP appointees, but they did so with

---

[97] See "Food and Drug Administration, Cardiovascular and Renal Drugs Advisory Committee Transcript, 65th Meeting, Volume 1, October 24, 1991," discussing Manoplax (Flosequinan).

[98] For more discussion on implications of adversarial advisory arrangements, see Jasanoff, *The Fifth Branch*, Chapter 7, pp. 123–151.

[99] Chair of the Industrial Pollution Control Council, U.S. Congress, Senate, *Advisory Committees*, Hearings before the Subcommittee on Intergovernmental Relations of the Committee on Government Operations, 92nd Congress, 1st Session, part 2 (Washington, DC: GPO, 1971), p. 405.

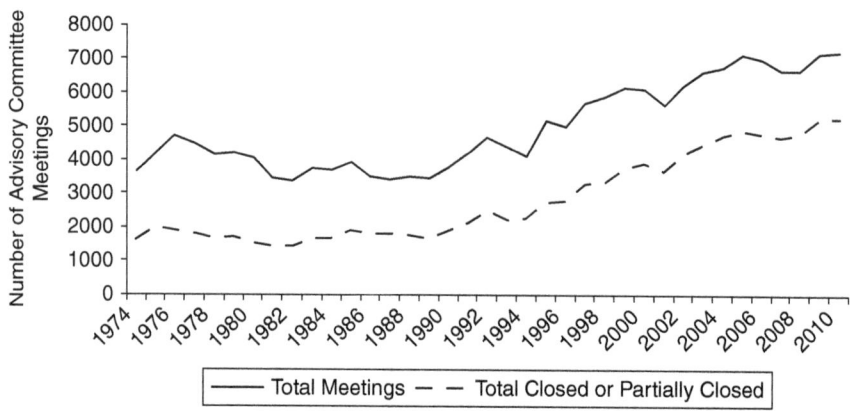

FIGURE 7.3. Count of Advisory Committee Meetings and Closed/Partially Closed Meetings, 1974–2010.

a common focus on how to expand NAEP while protecting its statistical integrity: one version of participatory bureaucracy in practice.

While drug advisory committees and NAGB reveal the potential of participatory bureaucracy, they also bear witness to its fragility. When bureaucracy is participatory, the scope of participation and information are fluid. When participatory bureaucracy works, it can put information into lots of active and latent participants' hands. Given the evolving and iterative nature of interdependent task implementations, participatory bureaucracy can get information "out there" for ongoing iterations of policy implementations even if all interested parties were not at the table for the original decision. For bureaucracy to be participatory, however, information and participation actually have to be fluid, knowledge has to actually get "out there," and doors need to be open. NAGB and FDA committees raise different challenges on this score.

NAGB closes a portion of every meeting, consistent with government procedures. There is nothing improper about this kind of closure, and agendas for the closed portion of the meeting (budget issues, member appointments, NAEP results that are not yet released) are publicly available. But closed meetings present a dilemma. Closing public meetings may enable the frank and open discussions needed to manage problems with uncertain and interdependent implementations. Conflict that spills into open public settings can challenge the development of bureaucratic expertise and administration.[100] Closed doors can be key to policy reform.[101] Neither public participation in agency policymaking

[100] Brian Balogh, *Chain Reaction: Expert Debate and Public Participation in American Commercial Nuclear Power, 1945–1975* (New York: Cambridge University Press, 1991).

[101] On the issue of closed doors supporting the development of general interest reform, see Eric Patashnik, *Reforms at Risk: What Happens After Major Policy Changes Are Enacted* (Princeton, NJ: Princeton University Press, 2008), p. 21.

nor transparency is an unalloyed good. Yet, closing meetings inherently limits the scope of the potential information flow to other implementers and to potential sources of democratic accountability. Closed meetings are in no way unique to the Governing Board. Figure 7.3 suggests that more than half of all public meetings convened have some portion of them that is closed.[102]

While FDA drug review committee meetings are rarely closed, they can limit participation in other ways. Committee meetings faithfully reserve time for open public comments, but the time to comment is typically quite limited; and conversation between committee members and public commentators rarely ensues. While FDA meetings are typically well attended and receive attention in the popular press, there are many degrees of separation between these meetings and doctor-patient office conversations. Information is getting "out there," but it is unclear if it ever reaches grassroots practice or if grassroots practice is even listening. Ultimately, does public participation through public committees help uncertain and interdependent task implementations in the way participatory bureaucracy predicts? We turn to the impact of public advice next.

[102] These estimates are derived from the Annual Report of the President on Federal Advisory Committees from 1972 through 1998. For the period from 1998 through 2010, these estimates come from data pooled from the General Service Administration's public data file. As noted earlier, some discrepancies appear between the GSS and Annual Report data sources. Estimates include all federal advisory committees, including grant committees. The inclusion of the grant review committees may account for the apparent rise in meeting closure.

8

The Impact of Public Advice

Outsiders holding advisory positions within bureaucracy have been at the center
of some of the most celebrated policy disputes that have arisen within the national
government since World War II.

Francis Rourke[1]

Energy's decision to undertake the Human Genome Project was based in part
on the 1987 recommendation of the department's Health and Environmental
Research Advisory Committee.

General Accounting Office, 2004[2]

Committee reports constitute a common descriptive measure of public committees' contributions, and federal public committees produce scores of reports
and recommendations, as Figure 8.1 suggests. When it works, however, participatory bureaucracy offers more than dense government reports filed in agency
archives or university libraries.[3] It liquefies knowledge and makes policy public
by bringing permeability to bureaucratic administration, which supports task
implementation. Has public participation for pharmaceutical regulation and
educational assessments been able to liquefy knowledge, promote competent
implementation, or both?

---

[1] Francis E. Rourke, *Bureaucracy, Politics and Public Policy* (Boston, MA: Little, Brown & Co,
1969), p. 100.

[2] The quote continues, "As a result, Energy, working with NIH, successfully coordinated the multi-
billion-dollar research effort that succeeded in identifying all of the genes on every chromosome
in the human body and determining their biochemical nature – leading the way to numerous
advances in medical science." U.S. General Accounting Office, *Federal Advisory Committees:
Additional Guidance Could Help Agencies Better Ensure Independence and Balance* (Washington,
DC: GAO, 2004), p. 14.

[3] Recall that congressional advisory committee reformers in the 1950s and 1970s called for a
more centralized and easily accessible way of retrieving and distributing committee reports and
recommendations.

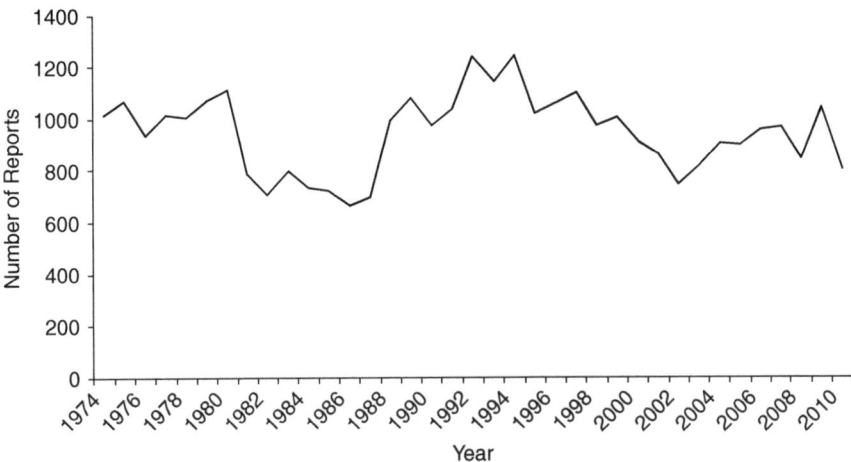

FIGURE 8.1. Total Number of Reports Produced by Federal Advisory Committees across Government Agencies, 1974–2010.

The Food and Drug Administration, like other agencies, justifies its consultations with public advisers in terms of expertise and reputation: "The primary role of an advisory committee is to provide independent advice that will contribute to the quality of the agency's regulatory decision-making and lend credibility to the product review process."[4] Public participation, from a bureaucratic perspective, can assist uncertain and interdependent task implementations. Results from FDA drug committees suggest they meet both the quality and legitimacy expectations of participatory bureaucracy. Drugs submitted to the FDA for review between 1989 and 2000 that went to an advisory committee for review before approval were significantly less likely to encounter post-marketing problems – subsequent boxed warnings and withdrawals from the market – than drugs that did not receive an advisory committee review, all else being equal. Moreover, results also suggest that, in this time period, drugs that received advisory committee reviews were less likely to be part of subsequent General Accounting Office reviews. These findings are an astonishing testament to the promise of participatory bureaucracy, given that Chapter 6 reveals that the FDA sends its most challenging drugs to committees for review, given allegations that firms corrupt the advisory process, and given periodic charges that committee reviews are perfunctory. When participatory bureaucracy works, evidence suggests it can make uncertain and interdependent implemen-

---

[4] Food and Drug Administration, "Advisory Committees: Critical to the FDA Review Process," in *From Test Tube to Patient: A Special Report from FDA Consumer Magazine.* Online at http://www.fda.gov/Drugs/ResourcesForYou/Consumers/ucm143538.htm (accessed January 20, 2014).

tations better, supporting bureaucratic administration and possibly democratic accountability as well.[5]

Assessing the impact of public participation for educational assessments requires a different analytic approach. Unlike drug regulation that offers reasonably clear indicators of policy quality or "bad" policy (serious side effects that warrant the drug's removal from the market), "quality" for educational statistics and assessments is more ambiguous. Assessment revisions, for instance, are not necessarily markers of a "bad" policy. To the contrary, they could signal vital evolution and learning. Mistakes sometimes occur, such as scoring problems in the late 1980s for the NAEP reading assessment, stemming from a contractor error. But these have been rare to the point of rendering them analytically suspect as a dependent variable, and low-stakes enough to render them substantively suspect as a marker of quality. However, public participation does not have to bear on life and death, as it does in the FDA, to matter to bureaucratic administration, democratic accountability, and policy outcomes. Educational assessments are well positioned to assess the contributions of public participation to the flow of knowledge. Does public participation help liquefy knowledge? The results that follow suggest that NAGB's design and its ancillary subcommittees and contracts offered a durable venue for policymaking: a stunning accomplishment when compared with the culture wars that engulfed the National History Standards Panel and dissolved the national standards setting process. They also suggest that public participation through the Governing Board helps get knowledge out of conference rooms and into the public domain, at least into the popular press.

On balance, the results that follow suggest how participation, as it has unfolded for drug regulation and educational assessments, can support bureaucratic administration while affording room for accountability: this is not necessarily a zero-sum game. Moreover, participation that is zero-sum – participation that flogs government agencies publicly, usurps bureaucratic authority, or abets privileged interest domination – appears relatively infrequently in the cases examined here. The conclusion will discuss the cases' generalizability in further detail.

---

[5] I have reported elsewhere that drugs receiving advisory committee reviews are *more* likely to be associated with subsequent safety alerts, all else being equal. I have also found that drugs receiving advisory committee reviews are *less* likely to be associated with subsequent safety alerts when few or none of the committee members have received conflict-of-interest waivers. Susan L. Moffitt, "The Policy Impact of Public Advice: The Effects of Advisory Committee Transparency on Product Safety," in *Regulatory Breakdown: The Crisis of Confidence in U.S. Regulation,* edited by Cary Coglianese (Philadelphia: University of Pennsylvania Press, 2012), pp. 180–199. These safety alert findings are not inconsistent with the findings reported later in this chapter. As I have argued elsewhere, unlike withdrawals, which are a clear sign of failure, safety alerts may be interpreted as another way of liquefying knowledge, and advisory committee reviews may be the first step in that liquefaction. Susan L. Moffitt, "Promoting Agency Reputation through Public Advice: Advisory Committee Use in the FDA," *Journal of Politics* 72 (2009): 880–893.

THE IMPACT OF DRUG ADVISORY COMMITTEE ADVICE

Recall that the results from Chapter 6 suggest the FDA consults with its advisors for tasks with uncertain and interdependent implementations. These tasks face high risks of implementation failure due to interdependence, where failure may arise at least in part from implementers who work outside the government agency's hierarchy, and where knowledge is emergent at best. In the case of the FDA, this interdependence includes firms, doctors and patients. The FDA has regulatory jurisdiction that bears on practice, despite the agency's frequent claim that it does not regulate the practice of medicine. The agency structures the availability of pharmaceutical therapies for sale in the United States, constraining and enhancing the choices doctors and patients enjoy as they approach treating and curing disease. The agency's charge, however – to ensure that the drugs that reach the market are safe and effective – extends well beyond the FDA's hierarchical regulatory authority. Drug safety and drug efficacy are partly matters of a drug's inherent characteristics. They are also fundamentally matters of physician and patient practice: safety and efficacy depend on how the therapies are used, in whom, for how long, and with what combinations of other therapies. The infamous drug Thalidomide, for instance, can help treat complications arising from leprosy as long as it stays far away from developing fetuses. Once a drug receives FDA's approval, the agency's hierarchical authority over practice dissipates dramatically.[6] FDA staff and leaders nevertheless have a stake in how implementation unfolds after agency approval decisions: the FDA can find itself facing criticism when other implementers fail to use approved drugs in safe and effective ways.

Recall that in the context of task uncertainty and interdependence, public participation has the potential to support implementation by helping agencies gather knowledge from outsiders (when outsiders have better information than insiders), distribute knowledge to outsiders (when insiders have better information than outsiders), develop new knowledge (when nobody has sufficient or appropriate knowledge), and legitimize knowledge (when knowledge does not speak for itself). All four can be crucial to policy implementation for tasks that appear in Quadrants C and D from Figure 1.1, and public advice has the potential to support all four in interconnected ways. Revisiting the case of the drug Lotronex, introduced in Chapter 6, illustrates how public participation enables these four interrelated flows of knowledge and may "contribute to the

---

[6] See Quirk for a discussion of how the ex ante focus of FDA regulatory work – regulating whether a drug is safe and effective enough to reach the market rather than regulating how the drug is used on the market – creates inefficiencies. In the context of weak post-marketing authority, the FDA faces difficult choices about "a drug that is useful for a narrowly defined patient population but that if approved (or allowed to remain on the market) would be prescribed excessively and would result in widespread harm." Paul Quirk, "Food and Drug Administration" in *The Politics of Regulation*, edited by James Q. Wilson (New York: Basic Books, 1980) p. 205.

quality of the agency's regulatory decision-making and lend credibility to the product review process" as the FDA claims.

The Case of Lotronex

The Gastrointesinal Drug Products Division reviewed Lotronex (alosetron) for the treatment of irritable bowel syndrome (IBS) in 1999. FDA reviewers had some doubts about Lotronex's efficacy in broad patient populations: Lotronex appeared only moderately effective and only in one form of IBS. Lotronex's safety, moreover, ranked high among the reviewers' concerns as the agency weighed whether or not to approve the drug. Troubling evidence of deadly ischemic colitis – artery blockage in the large and small intestines – appeared in clinical trials. Through a public meeting of the Gastrointestinal Drugs Advisory Committee in 1999, before the drug was approved, the FDA presented the dilemma that patients and doctors would face if Lotronex were to reach the market. The FDA's Lotronex safety reviewer asked the committee:

> How can a patient with IBS and her doctor weigh the chances of a good proba-
> bility of a modest benefit against a small probability of a serious adverse effect?
> That's a dilemma and that's the problem we're putting to you.[7]

Before bringing Lotronex to the Gastrointestinal Drugs Advisory Committee, FDA reviewers and Glaxo, the drug's sponsor, had engaged in internal debates over whether Lotronex could be linked with ischemic colitis and how the firm should communicate potential risk to health care professionals and patients. The committee meeting offered the FDA a venue for bringing those previously private debates into the public domain.

Yet, the advisory committee meeting offered the firm an opportunity to challenge FDA concerns about Lotronex risks, and to do so publicly. Glaxo appeared at the 1999 advisory committee meeting with a previously unannounced academic expert who came with analysis that neither the FDA nor the committee had been able to review ahead of time. She presented the committee with a pathology report casting doubt on the links between patients' cases of ischemic colitis and Lotronex. The pathology report suggested the cases of ischemic colitis may have been attributable to bacteria. While her testimony could not prove that the cases of ischemic colitis stemmed from something other than Lotronex, her testimony added uncertainty to the debate, blurring possible links between the drug and the deadly side effect.[8] The public forum enabled the agency to gather new knowledge, although it may not have been knowledge the agency wanted to receive. The public meeting also highlighted

---

[7] Comments of Dr. John Senior, "Food and Drug Administration, Gastrointestinal Drugs Advisory Committee Transcript, November 16, 1999," discussing the drug Lotronex. Page numbers do not appear on this transcript.

[8] A guest consultant who had been an investigator on Lotronex, who received other financial support from Glaxo, and who served on the committee in a nonvoting role that day noted, "I

the need to create new knowledge to figure out what was producing ischemic colitis.

While the links with ischemic colitis appeared unclear, patient desperation for a therapy to treat a disease that had no other treatment on the market was plain.[9] Two speakers addressed the committee during the open public comments portion of the first Lotronex meeting: a spokeswoman who represented the International Foundation for Functional Gastrointestinal Disorders and the Digestive Disease National Coalition and an IBS sufferer. Both described in graphic detail life with IBS, underscoring the need for new therapies. The committee recommended Lotronex for approval, and the FDA approved Lotronex with labeling that was consistent with the FDA Safety Reviewer's initial and internal recommendation.[10]

The FDA convened a second advisory committee meeting after Lotronex had been approved and after more cases of ischemic colitis appeared once the drug was used in practice. At the second public meeting, the FDA took the pathology of ischemic colitis off the table: Glaxo was not invited to challenge or discuss whether Lotronex caused ischemic colitis.[11] The meeting focused, instead, on how to expand communication with patients and doctors about the narrow population that should receive Lotronex and about the risks that accompany Lotronex use. The director of the FDA's Office of Drug Evaluation III, which oversees the Gastrointestinal Drug Products Division, argued that, for some drugs, communicating risk through labeling is an insufficient risk management strategy to implement drug safety. She asserted: "[L]abeling is important and it is the basis for all claims for advertising and truthful statements about the product, but maybe it is not enough for some drugs."[12] The FDA asked for the committee's advice on a range of risk-communication and risk-management strategies, including boxed warnings, medication guides, and restrictions on the types of physicians who could prescribe Lotronex.

Glaxo publicly attacked the FDA in spite of the meeting's limited agenda. Even when an agency sets the agenda and helps select participants, participation that is consistent with participatory bureaucracy is not perfunctory. Nor is participation risk free for the agency that calls the meeting. Glaxo alleged,

---

used to know what ischemic colitis is; I'm not sure I understand it now." See "Food and Drug Administration, Gastrointestinal Drugs Advisory Committee Transcript, November 16, 1999."

[9] Interview 82603, conducted by Susan Moffitt on August 26, 2003.

[10] See the Gastro-Intestinal Drug Product Team Leader's November 1999 memo to the Director of the Office of Drug Evaluation III for an expanded explanation, available in the drug review package. The drug's review package is available through the FDA at http://www.accessdata.fda.gov/drugsatfda_docs/nda/2000/21107a_Lotronex.cfm

[11] In their comments to the advisory committee, Glaxo representatives noted several times that the FDA had instructed them to restrict their committee presentation to risk management and not discuss adverse events' pathology reports.

[12] Comments of Dr. Florence Houn, "Food and Drug Administration, Gastrointestinal Drugs Advisory Committee Transcript, NDA 21-107, Lotronex, June 27, 2000," p. 9.

in front of an audience that contained IBS sufferers and reporters, that FDA efforts to regulate Lotronex more tightly revealed that the FDA did not take IBS patients' suffering seriously. It claimed that the FDA was holding Lotronex to a higher standard than it held other drugs – such as Non-Steroidal-Anti-Inflammatory-Drugs (NSAIDs) – that treat nonfatal conditions such as pain. In particular, it portrayed the FDA's proposals that the Lotronex label carry a boxed warning specifying its risks, that Lotronex patients receive a detailed medication guide, and that patients sign an informed consent form as inconsistent with other FDA decisions.[13]

Advisory committee members, however, publicly pressed Glaxo to articulate how a boxed warning could harm physician education.[14] Ensuing discussion revealed that it would not. The issue underlying Glaxo's opposition, the committee deliberation suggested, centered on the marketing restrictions that accompany boxed warnings. A boxed warning, for instance, would prohibit Glaxo from producing Lotronex pens and note pads for doctors' offices, because any advertisement would have to carry the boxed warning as well.[15] The advisory committee's deliberations implied Glaxo's opposition had much to do with the firm's bottom line.

Four IBS sufferers presented public testimony at the second Lotronex advisory committee meeting, revealing both the promise and limits of "public" participation. The chair of the advisory committee engaged with public speakers in several ways. For one, the committee chair specifically asked the public speakers to reveal any relationship they had with Glaxo. Consultants to firms preparing for advisory committees encourage firms to mobilize disease sufferers to attend and present testimony at the meetings to help "set the right tone."[16] Subsequent disclosures revealed that Glaxo had either paid for or encouraged three of the four public speakers to attend. For another, before hearing their statements, the committee chair admonished the public speakers to keep their comments to Lotronex's risk management strategy and not provide the committee with general, emotional descriptions of IBS.[17] The public speakers disregarded the committee request and offered their prepared testimonies on life with the disease. For yet another, the chair went on to ask the IBS sufferers how they had received information about Lotronex. Two of the speakers admitted

---

[13] The firm also pointed to Sildenafil for erectile dysfunction as another example of FDA inconsistency. See "Food and Drug Administration, Gastrointestinal Drugs Advisory Committee Transcript, NDA 21-107, Lotronex, June 27, 2000," p. 74.

[14] See "Food and Drug Administration, Gastrointestinal Drugs Advisory Committee Transcript, NDA 21-107, Lotronex, June 27, 2000," pp. 91–92, 209.

[15] See "Food and Drug Administration, Gastrointestinal Drugs Advisory Committee Transcript, NDA 21-107, Lotronex, June 27, 2000," p. 127.

[16] Pines, Wayne L. and Mary Ann N. Cotton, "Preparing for an FDA Advisory Committee Meeting," *Drug Information Journal* 31 (1997): 35–41. See p. 40.

[17] See "Food and Drug Administration, Gastrointestinal Drugs Advisory Committee Transcript, NDA 21-107, Lotronex, June 27, 2000," p. 164.

that neither their doctors nor their pharmacists had provided them with any information on Lotronex's risks. Committee members suggested this revelation, this new information that IBS sufferers were not receiving information on Lotronex's risks, supported agency claims for additional regulation and expanded physician and patient education.

In the fall of 2000, not long after the second Lotronex advisory committee meeting, the FDA received reports of deaths associated with complications from Lotronex use. In November 2000, Glaxo removed Lotronex from the market. Within two months of doing so, both the firm and the FDA received thousands of letters from IBS sufferers, asking for patient access to the drug. The FDA felt the heat from both sides – to help make the drug available to disease suffers who had no other treatment options and to keep off the market the drug that appeared prone to unsafe use. Glaxo and the FDA subsequently began negotiations over reintroducing Lotronex to the market.[18]

The FDA convened a third public meeting to discuss Lotronex, and the Office director began the meeting addressing allegations of implementation failure and the FDA's role in implementation. She used the forum to distribute information about what the FDA had done, had not done, could do, and could not do. She began by putting the burden of Lotronex's lack of availability to consumers on Glaxo. The very beginning of the implementation process – producing drugs – is up to firms. Even when drugs are not approved for public marketing, firms can make them available as Investigational New Drugs (IND). She noted:

> Contrary to public belief ... We don't stockpile drugs, we don't manufacture drugs, we don't conduct drug research trials, we don't run drug access programs. We just don't have the drugs. We can't force a pharmaceutical company to manufacture or market or conduct research or provide drug access programs.[19]

She went on to address allegations that the FDA, because of close relationships with firms in general and Glaxo in particular, had agreed to bring Lotronex back to the market, regardless of the safety risks it posed:

> FDA has been criticized that we have secretly come to an agreement with GSK [GlaxoSmithKline] on the return of Lotronex. This is false. There is no done deal ... New labeling has not been approved and we need your input on several aspects of this and other issues.[20]

---

[18] Glaxo declined to make the drug available on an IND basis through a drug access program. IND means that drugs are available as "investigational new drugs." They are not marketed, making them a costly option for firms. See "Food and Drug Administration, Gastrointestinal Drugs Advisory Committee and Risk Management Subcommittee of the Advisory Committee for Pharmaceutical Science, Transcript, April 23, 2002," p. 15.

[19] Comments of Florence Houn, "Food and Drug Administration, Gastrointestinal Drugs Advisory Committee and Risk Management Subcommittee of the Advisory Committee for Pharmaceutical Science, Transcript, April 23, 2002," p. 17.

[20] Houn, "Food and Drug Administration, Transcript, April 23, 2002," p. 17.

She went on to address allegations that the FDA was treating Lotronex differently than other drugs that treat nonlethal diseases but have been linked with death. Viagra is a notable example. Her statement highlights the complexity of drug safety in practice:

> FDA has been criticized that we don't take IBS seriously. Well, we take all disease and suffering seriously, IBS is no exception.... There is no uniform absolute way to manage drug risks for different diseases, different drugs, different adverse events, and with different risk tolerances by different people.[21]

From this last point, the FDA went on to discuss an expanded risk management strategy for Lotronex, building on the points from the second Lotronex meeting about better communication and stiffer regulation.

From a bureaucratic perspective, this kind of publicity opened the agency to public criticism: disease sufferers accused the FDA of not taking their suffering seriously and of denying them access to a "miracle" drug.[22] It also, however, provided the FDA an opportunity to apportion responsibility and make Glaxo's role more visible. To the audience of disease sufferers and the media, the FDA made plain that the firm could have provided Lotronex to IBS patients through a drug access program after the drug's recall. The firm chose not to, for profit reasons, deliberations implied. To the audience of consumer advocates and representatives of Lotronex-associated injuries, the FDA exposed what it considered flimsiness in the proposed Glaxo risk management plan. To the audience of pharmaceutical representatives, the FDA revealed what it did and did not consider acceptable about Glaxo's approach to risk management, providing other firms with information on how the FDA might expect them to approach risk management for their drug products. By making the Lotronex review visible, the FDA also brought visibility to Glaxo's part in implementation challenges.[23]

Three FDA public advisory committee meetings did not prevent Lotronex from experiencing implementation problems. Yet, this series of public meetings

---

[21] Houn, "Food and Drug Administration, Transcript, April 23, 2002," p. 18.

[22] "Food and Drug Administration, Gastrointestinal Drugs Advisory Committee and Risk Management Subcommittee of the Advisory Committee for Pharmaceutical Science, Transcript, April 23, 2002," p. 182. The committee chair in 2002 did not require public speakers to identify their relationship with Glaxo. Moreover, he extended the amount of time allotted for public comment to allow all fifteen registered public speakers time to testify. Unlike the previous Lotronex meetings public speakers represented both sides of the Lotronex debate. Some disease sufferers ardently argued for Lotronex's return to the market. A broad-based consumer advocate along with representatives of patients injured by and/or suing Glaxo argued against its return or for a severely restricted return. A representative of the American Society of Health System Pharmacists argued against devising a distribution plan that would impose restrictions on pharmacists.

[23] Some committee members received waivers to participate in the meetings. At the first Lotronex advisory committee meeting, convened before the drug was approved, two committee members received waivers to participate. One committee member was excluded from participating.

for a task in which the agency had insufficient information and high implementation interdependence provided opportunities to gather more information, begin the process of distributing information about Lotronex, and highlight firms', doctors', and patients' responsibilities for safe and effective drug implementations. Moreover, in spite of Lotronex's implementation problems, the agency successfully avoided the ultimate manifestation of policy failure and damage to the agency's reputation: a congressional oversight hearing or GAO investigation.

The Policy and Political Impact of FDA Drug Advisory Committee Reviews

Advisory committees can serve both internal and external audiences, depending on the task's implementation conditions and the terms of participation. Committees can facilitate the flow of expert information into an agency, assisting the agency's policymaking process and ultimate regulatory decision. Committees also facilitate the flow of information out of an agency, sending signals and providing expertise that may support ultimate drug implementation. Public advisory committees can provide the first opportunity for the agency to communicate publicly with various audiences about a drug's risk. Recall the words of the staffer who noted that FDA committees provide a way to release firm information that would otherwise be kept secret because of protections for proprietary information. The former staffer continued,

> [The FDA Advisory Committee System] provides a forum for discussing data and for getting different views. They could do that in private, as well … but … it enables them to disclose data publicly and to release those data, and I think that's an enormous public health benefit.[24]

From this viewpoint, the benefit from FDA advisory committees derives from their potential to distribute information in addition to shaping internal agency decision making about drug approval decisions, with the potential to yield a "public health benefit." The agency could obtain the information it acquires from advisory committee members privately. When it chooses to acquire and discuss information publicly, it provides agencies with a venue for making other implementers' secrets – such as firms' secrets – more visible: an attractive alternative for an agency worried about potential subsequent implementation

---

Moreover, a nonvoting invited guest at the meeting also had financial ties to Glaxo and served as an investigator for Lotronex. Two different committee members received waivers for the conflicts of interest at the second Lotronex meeting. Five committee members received waivers at the third meeting.

[24] Interview 112204 conducted by Susan Moffitt on November 22, 2004. He continued, "to this day, a lot of the data supporting the safety and efficacy of drugs is released only because of the advisory committee process … otherwise there isn't any mechanism … the advisory committees were the only place where any data was exposed publicly." Reference to this quote has appeared elsewhere in my published research. See Moffitt, "Promoting Agency Reputation through Public Advice," p. 889.

failure and damage to its reputation stemming from other implementers' actions. Do these consultations lend enough "credibility" to the review process to keep the agency off the congressional hot seat?

During the course of an advisory committee review for the drug Videx, an advisory committee member commented that in the event of a subsequent congressional hearing, "I hope they will be thankful that you made the right decision. It is a very difficult decision…. The company, the FDA and everybody here I think has done the very best that they can with the data they have available."[25] In the context of complex task implementation, doing "the very best" that is possible with the available data is what an agency hopes for; there are no guarantees that implementations will go well, but the participatory process can legitimize the knowledge the agency gathered and used. Though the FDA consulted with its public advisors before it approved Lotronex, the drug nevertheless experienced a fraught implementation. Did the preapproval review, and others like it, help keep the agency off the congressional hot seat? In other words, do public committee reviews appear associated with a "public health benefit" and sustained support for the agency?

The models that follow examine the overall relationship between advisory committee consultation and drug safety using two key measures of a drug's post-marketing safety: a measure of whether an approved drug later received a new, post-market boxed warning on its label for a significant new adverse drug reaction, and whether the drug was removed from the market.[26] It examines the political impact of public advice through subsequent GAO reports on FDA drug decisions. Elsewhere I have reported that drugs receiving advisory committee reviews are less likely to experience subsequent Congressional drug-oversight hearings, but more likely to experience subsequent safety alerts.

The following treatment effects model considers public advisory committees as the "treatment": whether or not each drug in the sample of NME's submitted for review between 1985 and 2000 experienced an advisory committee meeting.[27] This treatment model is identified through a yearly count of drug submissions to the Food and Drug Administration and through division staff levels.[28] The density of drug submissions to a particular reviewing division (i.e.

---

[25] Comments of Dr. Raymond L. Woosley. "Food and Drug Administration, Antiviral Drugs Advisory Meeting Transcript. Volume II, July 19, 1991," p. 174.

[26] Karen E. Lasser et al., "Timing of New Black Box Warnings and Withdrawals for Prescription Medications," *Journal of the American Medical Association* 287 (2002): 2215–2220.

[27] The model was restricted to the 1985–2000 time frame to use division-level measures that were not available to the author after 2000. Data on drug withdrawals and boxed warnings were generously provided by Daniel P. Carpenter.

[28] Measures of division staffing levels were available to the author for drugs approved between 1985 and 2000. These data were gathered through systematic reviews of FDA phone directories published between 1981 and 2000. Data were gathered by the author under the supervision of Daniel P. Carpenter in 2001.

Anti-infective, Oncology, etc.) and division staff levels should be related to each drug's likelihood of receiving an advisory committee review, but should be exogenous to the outcome measures.[29]

Consistent with the advisory committee agenda-setting models in Chapter 6, each model contains a measure of the drug's *priority* status, whether or not the drug treats a *lethal* disease, drug *pharmacological complexity*, *demand* for the drug, *elite* disease attention, *public media* disease attention, *congressional* disease attention, *divided* government, and a count of the number of drugs previously submitted by *the sponsoring firm* for both of the model's equations.

The results in Table 8.1 suggest that, when controlling for underlying drug risks, drugs receiving an advisory committee review are significantly less likely to experience boxed warnings on their labels and are significantly less likely to be withdrawn from the market. Even though public advisory committees review the riskiest drugs, the agency is also less likely to find itself on the congressional hot seat when it publicly consults its advisors. These results are a testament to the potential contributions of participatory bureaucracy when it focuses on uncertain and interdependent task implementations and enables diverse engagement, yielding more expert policy outcomes and less blame. Though congressional hearings have at times castigated the FDA over its advisory committee practices, the results presented here suggest advisory committee consultation may contribute to less political scrutiny for specific drug review decisions.

Public participation in the FDA is fundamentally a bureaucratic enterprise, with bureaucrats determining or playing an active role in committee operations including agenda setting, membership, staff support, and resources. NAGB, again, sits at the opposite end of the spectrum and removes participatory choices from bureaucratic control. What is the impact on bureaucratic administration for participation that resides beyond the agency's reach?

STABILITY AND PUBLICITY: THE IMPACT OF PARTICIPATION FOR THE NATIONAL ASSESSMENT

Unlike the FDA, the quality of educational assessments lacks the equivalent of a boxed warning or a withdrawal. The analysis that follows thus looks qualitatively at the impact of the National Assessment's participatory processes on assessment stability, assessment rigor, and getting information out into the public domain.

---

[29] The logic underlying this identification strategy suggests greater density of submissions should be negatively associated with advisory committee reviews (crowded agendas) and higher staffing levels would be positively associated with advisory committee reviews (sufficient capacity to host meetings).

TABLE 8.1. *Treatment Effects Models, Advisory Committee Reviews and Subsequent Implementation, Approved NMEs from 1986 to 2000*[30]

Variable	GAO Review Coefficient (SE)	Safety Withdrawal Coefficient (SE)	New Boxed Warning Coefficient (SE)
Implementation Uncertainty and Interdependence			
Drug Priority Classification (Priority = 1)	0.321 (0.101)	0.071 (0.034)	0.139 (0.043)
Drug for Lethal Disease (Lethal = 1)	0.049 (0.098)	0.017 (0.028)	0.015 (0.040)
Drug Pharmacological Complexity	0.160 (0.068)	0.039 (0.020)+	0.064 (0.028)
Political Oversight			
Firm Experience	0.007 (0.004)+	0.002 (0.001)	0.001 (0.002)
Demand for Therapy, Natural Log	0.016 (0.042)	−0.003 (0.012)	0.003 (0.017)
Elite Disease Attention	−0.006 (0.013)	0.003 (0.004)	0.001 (0.005)
Public Disease Attention	0.001 (0.000)	0.000 (0.000)	0.000 (0.000)
Congressional Disease Attention	−0.033 (0.066)	−0.026 (0.018)	0.063 (0.027)
Divided Government	0.101 (0.143)	0.033 (0.039)	0.038 (0.058)
Advisory Committee Review (Review = 1)	−0.903 (0.113)	−0.187 (0.066)	−0.332 (0.063)
Constant	−0.907 (0.480)+	−0.244 (0.139)+	−0.353 (0.197)+
Advisory Committee Selection			
Identification			
NME Density	−0.022 (0.007)	−0.023 (0.009)	−0.018 (0.008)
Division Staff	0.008 (0.005)+	0.008 (0.006)	0.009 (0.005)+
Implementation			
Drug Priority Classification (Priority = 1)	0.776 (0.145)	0.870 (0.149)	0.864 (0.148)
Drug for Lethal Disease (Lethal = 1)	0.249 (0.149)+	0.303 (0.154)	0.289 (0.153)+
Pharmacological Complexity	0.350 (0.108)	0.388 (0.118)	0.409 (0.113)
Political Oversight			
Firm Experience	−0.001 (0.006)	−0.001 (0.006)	−0.003 (0.006)
Demand for Therapy, Natural Log	−0.019 (0.064)	−0.009 (0.067)	−0.049 (0.066)

[30] Only drugs submitted for review between 1985 and 2000 were included in this sample. However, the approval date extended well beyond the 2000 submission cutoff.

Variable	GAO Review Coefficient (SE)	Safety Withdrawal Coefficient (SE)	New Boxed Warning Coefficient (SE)
Elite Disease Attention	−0.010 (0.020)	−0.019 (0.020)	−0.016 (0.020)
Public Disease Attention	0.001 (0.001)	0.001 (0.001)	0.001 (0.001)+
Congressional Disease Attention	0.127 (0.124)	0.190 (0.136)	0.201 (0.123)+
Divided Government	0.205 (0.223)	0.189 (0.232)	0.210 (0.228)
Constant	−3.042 (0.815)	−3.324 (0.890)	−3.641 (0.848)
	N = 391	N = 391	N = 389

Boldface indicates significance at the $p<.05$ level; + indicates significance at the $p<.1$ level; all tests two-tailed.

Policy Stability through Diverse Expertise

Public participation for the National Assessment comes via multiple venues. One venue is NAGB. Another, while it was in operation, was ACES. Throughout the Assessment's history, temporary panels have been convened to support various aspects of the National Assessment's development and implementation, including a "consensus" process for developing frameworks for subject areas and for determining cut points for performance levels, authorized through the Hawkins-Stafford amendments of 1988.

The consensus process for developing frameworks was contracted out to the Council of Chief State School Officers who appointed steering committees and planning committees for subject areas.[31] The planning committees consisted of subject area researchers, curriculum specialists, administrators, teachers, and teacher educators who proposed what the design and content of the National Assessment should include. In the words of an official who guided the consensus process, the planning committee was designed to "be able to balance different points of view about the subject."[32] The steering committees consisted of representatives from major interests including school administrators, the business community, school boards, policy makers, and members of the public. In addition to formal committee members, political and technical constituencies including states, teachers, and parent groups reviewed the frameworks. Both the steering and planning committees offered room for debate: controversy

[31] Specifically, the contract recipient proposed steering and planning committee members, but NAGB had final approval over membership. Before NAGB came into existence, the first framework committee for Math was supported by NCES (in 1986, 1987, and 1988). Ramsay Selden from the Council of Chief State School Officers directed the consensus effort, and William Cody provided key staff support.

[32] Interview 81803 conducted by Susan Moffitt on August 18, 2003.

could emerge in any subject area, such as the appropriateness of phonics in reading, the extent of Eurocentrism in history, or the place of evolution in science.[33] Yet, the framework-building process associated with the National Assessment managed the controversies without degenerating into "a babble of conflict and controversy," to use the phrase coined by a skeptic of advisory committee diversity before FACA passed.[34] In a review of articles published in *Education Week* between 1986 and 2010, congressional documents and GAO reports, little public opposition emerged to the frameworks that National Assessment committees developed.[35]

Content frameworks for NAEP stand in marked contrast to the experiences of several national standards-setting processes conducted during the same time period, including ones sponsored by the National Council on Education Standards and Testing (NCEST), the National Goals Panel, and other standards-setting efforts such as the National History Standards. Each of these efforts was more ambitious in scope: to specify the content that students should learn in various subject areas for the nation as a whole. Each was to have been voluntary at the time – standards that schools or districts may adopt – unlike the high-stakes assessments that trigger corrective action in the post–No Child Left Behind era. Yet, each dissolved amid profound normative disagreements that participants were unable to resolve about appropriate subject matter. The participatory process that ultimately led to the spectacular disintegration of the National History Standards, for instance, consisted of nationally renowned and ideologically opposed historians and public figures. The National Assessment's consensus processes, in contrast, were much lower-key affairs, both in terms of the notoriety of their participants and the scrutiny the process engendered. In the words of an architect of the National Assessment consensus process,

> The national history standards caused such a firestorm of controversy that at exactly the same time we were developing the history framework for NAEP … we attracted no fire or controversy … at the same time the draft of national standards were provoking such controversy … we … just sort of existed out of the limelight.[36]

---

[33] Interview 81803 conducted by Susan Moffitt on August 18, 2003.

[34] Recall this phrase arose in congressional testimony over FACA: it was not directed at the National Assessment. See the comments of the Chair of the Industrial Pollution Control Council, U.S. Congress, Senate, *Advisory Committees*, Hearings before the Subcommittee on Intergovernmental Relations of the Committee on Government Operations, 92nd Congress, 1st Session, part 2 (Washington, DC: GPO, 1971), p. 405. Observers recalled that NAGB moved away from the term "consensus" in 2003 partly out of concern that it implied a process that promoted the status quo or appealed to the lowest common denominator or was noncontroversial. Interview 81803 conducted by Susan Moffitt on August 18, 2003.

[35] Considerable controversy did emerge, however, over the cutpoints the Governing Board established. U.S. General Accounting Office, *Educational Achievement Standards: NAGB's Approach Yields Misleading Interpretations* (Washington, DC: GAO, 1993).

[36] Interview 81803 conducted by Susan Moffitt on August 18, 2003.

Leadership of the National Assessment framework process also noted that the Governing Board accepted the frameworks the consensus process produced and did not, for its part, degenerate into a babble of conflict and controversy either. Leadership understood the stability of the frameworks partly in terms of the participants:

> [T]he key thing is you have got to put together a set of personalities that will enable you to resolve the tough issues, because almost in every area there are differences of opinion, in science, history, geography. And for the planning committee the thing can't degenerate into a shouting match with no impasse.[37]

The common ground discussed in Chapter 7 – general support for the national assessment process – can offer a way to synthesize diverse perspectives in ways that support task implementation. When No Child Left Behind raised the National Assessment's visibility – making it mandatory for states – the assessment attracted some of the polarizing debate that has plagued other standard setting efforts. The opening narrative in Chapter 1 picks up one aspect of this debate: releasing test items. Yet, the National Assessment and its public Governing Board have remained remarkably stable and productive in the face of political firestorms surrounding them.

Rigor of the National Assessment: Buffering the Assessment from Political Winds

Including groups with vested interests in a policy is sometimes associated with watering down government action, such as being lenient on firms in the drug review process, for instance. Unlike the FDA participatory process, which discourages members with industry ties from participating in policy decisions, individuals are selected to NAGB and the framework committees because of their different affiliations, as occurs frequently on public committees across the federal government.[38] Has this resulted in a more lenient National Assessment? On balance, the evidence suggests the answer is decidedly "no." Even though the Chief State School Officers held the contract for the framework consensus process, and even though the National Assessment's early history highlights initial state and local opposition to the assessment, NAEP's frameworks and achievement levels[39] are notably more ambitious than the ones most states adopt. When No Child Left Behind made participation in the National Assessment mandatory, concerns arose over whether this would apply pressure

---

[37] Interview 81803 conducted by Susan Moffitt on August 18, 2003.

[38] Individuals who are designated as representatives do not face the conflict-of-interest standards that individuals appointed as special government employees experience. For estimates on the percent of committee members designated as representatives or special government employees, see U.S. Government Accountability Office, *FDA Advisory Committees: Process for Recruiting Members and Evaluating Potential Conflicts of Interest.* (Washington, DC: GAO, 2008), p. 13.

[39] Setting achievement levels is a different process than the framework setting process.

on the National Assessment to alter its frameworks and achievement levels. Instead, NAEP's frameworks and cut-points since No Child Left Behind have remained robust.

NAGB's process for reporting results also reflects a form of bureaucratization by constructing a barrier between the assessment and some kinds of direct political influence. The Governing Board's chairman and the Commissioner for Education Statistics release National Assessment results and offer careful interpretation before political officials – including the president and vice president – discuss the results. Deviations from the standard reporting process – when President George H. W. Bush discussed results prematurely or when Vice President Gore interpreted results before the Commissioner of Education – have generated swift rebuke and have been the exception rather than common practice.

Once results are released, however, National Assessment information can take on a life of its own, akin to drugs reaching the market. Once approved by the FDA, physicians may prescribe and patients may use therapies that deviate from the formal label, even though the participatory and technical processes yield carefully constructed information. Political leaders also point to the National Assessment and its results to validate their policy directions – to claim that students' improved math scores are attributable to the governor's policies or to claim that weak student scores affirm the governor's call for policy change. While political interests can upend the careful analysis that emerges from the participatory processes, the publicity that accompanies public participation can render the knowledge it produces more widely accessible.

Getting Information into the Public Domain

NAGB differs from FDA advisory committees in a range of ways, including committee design, authority, and participation. Like FDA committees, however, public participation through NAGB creates opportunities for information to flow in multiple directions in ways that might not exist otherwise. Participation goes beyond formal membership: open meetings can render policymaking venues accessible to audiences and participants who are not formal members. Governing Board meetings are open to anyone able to attend.[40] Congressional staffers, for instance, attended approximately one-quarter of Governing Board meetings between 1989 and 2002. Nearly three-quarters of Governing Board meetings received media coverage during that same time period.[41]

---

[40] Three of the four yearly board meetings occur in Washington, DC, rendering them accessible to DC-based organized interests, congressional staffers, and the media.

[41] The estimate of Congressional staffer attendance is based on lists of audience members recorded in meeting minutes. This may underreport staff member attendance if the staff member did not sign the meeting attendance list. Media coverage estimates are based on reviews of *Education Week* and *Washington Post* articles using National Assessment Governing Board or NAGB as search terms.

Overall media attentiveness to the National Assessment increased following the 1988 amendments. Does Board attentiveness to issues contribute to general media coverage of those items? The models that follow use the same dataset of 120 potential assessment agenda items followed over approximately twelve years that were discussed in Chapter 6 and used in the agenda-setting models. The dependent variable measures actual media attention to those potential agenda items, which were reported in *The Washington Post* to capture coverage in the mainstream media. The primary explanatory variable is a measure of *NAGB attention* to that agenda topic during one of its public board meetings. Controls include lagged Governing Board attention, lagged media attention, and *Congressional* and *Presidential* attention to the topic.

Across model specifications, the analysis presented in Table 8.2 suggests the Governing Board platform is associated with publicity for the topics it covers even when the article does not reference the Board. Additional models incorporate measures for presidential attention, which strongly predict media attention. The measure of congressional attention fails to achieve standard levels of statistical significance.

In a separate analysis, *Education Week* media coverage suggests that, as expected, media coverage of the National Assessment attends to controversy and conflict. Roughly half (153 out of 301 articles) of the *Education Week* articles covering the National Assessment and its Governing Board between April 20, 1988 and March 31, 2010 raised some matter of conflict. Very few of the articles – only eight – reported dissent within the National Assessment Governing Board.[42] Only fifteen reported conflict with the executive branch. The articles were more likely to present conflict within the broader community or among interests and report on how the Board managed the conflict.[43]

Implications for Bureaucratic Administration

Unlike the FDA, contributions to bureaucratic administration emanating from the National Assessment's participatory processes are more indirect. One contribution manifests through the Governing Board's efforts, working together with the agency, to fend off attempts to insert the assessment more directly into controversial policies. Both the Clinton administration and the George W. Bush administration sought to include the National Assessment in their broader accountability efforts. The Governing Board successfully separated the National Assessment from Clinton's Voluntary National Tests and from being

[42] Moreover, *none* of the 300 *Education Week* articles covering the NAEP in this time period reported conflict between NAGB board members over the creation and use of state NAEP.
[43] Media attention, however, is largely limited to topics raised during the open public portions of Governing Board meetings. Topics discussed during the closed portion of Board meetings – budgetary considerations and reviewing nominees for Board membership – received little media attention.

TABLE 8.2. *Media Attention to National Assessment Tasks, 1989–2000 Prais-Winston Regression, Panel Corrected Standard Errors*

Number of Washington Post Articles	Model 1 Coefficient (SE)	Model 2 Coefficient (SE)
Public Committee Agenda		
Topic Appeared on NAGB Agenda, Year	0.158 (0.050)	0.152 (0.050)
Political Oversight: Congress		
Congressional Committee Attention to Topic, Year	0.221+ (0.130)	0.238 (0.228)
Political Oversight: General Volatility, Divided Government		
Divided Government (1 = Divided)	0.156+ (0.093)	0.162 (0.079)
Political Oversight: Presidential Attention		
Presidential Attention to Topic, Year	—	0.754 (0.144)
Control: Lagged Washington Post Coverage		
Lagged Moving Average of Previous Washington Post Coverage	0.493 (0.212)	0.714 (0.252)
Control: Previous Board Attention		
Lagged Task Frequency, Previous Year	−0.002 (0.022)	−0.030 (0.022)
Constant	−0.077 (0.084)	−0.123+ (0.070)
Number of observations	1734	1053
Number of groups	183	117
R-squared	.113	.250

Boldface indicates significance at the $p<.05$ level; + indicates significance at the $p<.1$ level; all tests two-tailed.

a required vehicle for confirming the robustness of state assessments under the No Child Left Behind Act. In the words of one former board member, the Governing Board and its staff worked to "dampen expectations" of political leaders to keep the National Assessment separate from controversial presidential policies.[44] On the one hand, the National Assessment's political attractiveness is a testament to its legitimacy: Presidents tried to attach their new policies to this established, well-respected program. The National Assessment's success at fending off these entanglements is testament to its bureaucratization:[45] its success at building and protecting a stable, expert assessment program.

A second contribution manifests through the legitimacy the assessment confers on NCES, the government agency. The NCES remains at arm's length from the National Assessment and its public participatory processes, including its Governing Board. NAGB staff, moreover, enjoys responsibilities that may have

[44] Interview 82103 conducted by Susan Moffitt on August 21, 2003.
[45] Interview 82103 conducted by Susan Moffitt on August 21, 2003.

otherwise expanded the Center's role in the National Assessment. Responsibility for determining noncognitive items included on the assessment and for the framework development processes are two examples. In these ways, the National Assessment's participatory governing design may have limited the government agency's bureaucratic growth around the National Assessment. Yet, the Center oversees the National Assessment's budget,[46] the National Assessment remains the crown jewel in the Center's portfolio, and it remains a significant budget item. Assessment stability and political support mean significant National Assessment funding and support for the agency. The stature of the assessment has had spillover effects for the agency in terms of positive media coverage and congressional attention with respect to the National Assessment over the past twenty years.[47]

***

Public committees are known for their reports – such as the reports from the Citizens' Advisory Committee on the Food and Drug Administration or the Federal Advisory Committee on Emergency Aid in Education, both of which called for expanded resources and staff for the respective agencies, and both of which validated the positions their agency sponsors held. For more than sixty years, public committees have been scrutinized for their "usefulness" amid doubts that they tell the agency anything the agency did not already know. Educational assessments and the drug approval process, however, provide models of public engagement that intertwine meaningful participation with bureaucratic administration and go well beyond a formal report: both NAGB and FDA drug committees provide examples of making policy public. The National Assessment model offers the public board explicit policymaking authority. The FDA model intertwines participation into the agency's ongoing policymaking process for core agency tasks of drug approval, labeling and monitoring. The knowledge that public participation produces can extend well beyond the agency's boundaries. For both drug approval and educational assessments, the product of participation is not a one-time report but a systematic process of bringing three different meanings of public to bear on agency policymaking: public in the sense of government sponsored; public in the sense of visible; and public in the sense of participation from nongovernmental individuals.

Participation through public advisory committees offers bureaucrats a way to gather knowledge, develop knowledge, use knowledge, and put knowledge

---

[46] Budgetary discussions typically occurred during closed portions of NAGB meetings, when NCES officials would discuss the budgetary conditions, costs of various proposed projects, and options for proceeding, such as waiting several years for a subject matter assessment, or considering trade-offs to conduct which assessment when, or considering the cost of various sample sizes. One former committee member recalled that NAGB members would "basically rubber stamp" budgetary proposals from NCES. Interview 82103, conducted by Susan Moffitt, August 21, 2003.

[47] Recall, however, that NAEP's initial efforts to develop cut-points to report assessment results by achievement levels generated congressional attention and criticism.

into other implementers' hands deliberately. Building other implementers' knowledge benefits bureaucrats who depend on others for successful implementations. It benefits bureaucrats who want other implementers to shoulder responsibility in the event of failure. It benefits bureaucrats who want their knowledge to shape the course of policy development or implementation. Yet, it simultaneously benefits elected officials who seek to oversee the same external implementers on whom the agency depends. Participatory bureaucracy differs from the view that bureaucrats inevitably seek secrecy or that public participation necessarily comes at bureaucrats' and bureaucracy's expense. Instead, multiple political actors stand to benefit from participatory bureaucracy, when it works well.

APPENDIX FOR CHAPTER 8

The treatment-effects model assesses the effect of binary treatment z_j (advisory committee review) on variable y_j (drug safety) conditional on independent variables x_j and $w_{j:}$

$$y_j = x_j\beta + \delta z_j + \varepsilon_j,$$

where z^* is a linear function of exogenous covariates w_j and random component u_j,

$$z^*_j = w_j\gamma + u_j,$$

and

$$z_j = 1, \text{ if } z^*_j > 0$$

$$z_j = 0, \text{ otherwise.}$$

The w_j instrument is identified through measures of the density of workload and division staff levels.

9

Participatory Bureaucracy in American Democracy

> Access to competent advisors and good advice through sound management
> practice should create a wiser President, more confident and effective top executive
> branch officials, a Congress more knowledgeable in performing its legislative
> functions, and a citizenry more alert to the problems of the time.
>
> Committee on Government Operations, House Report 91–1731,
> *The Role and Effectiveness of Federal Advisory Committees*,
> December 11, 1970

This book set out to analyze participation from the perspective of bureaucratic task implementation. I did so to consider the implications of public participation for the enduring puzzle of how to reconcile bureaucratic capacity with democratic accountability. Engaging the public in policymaking with the aim of producing "better" outcomes may not be surprising from the perspective of democratic theory, but it fundamentally challenges traditional conceptions of public bureaucracy. Whereas democratic accountability is associated with openness, bureaucratic capacity is traditionally associated with closure. Another form of this dichotomy focuses on power: closure means power for the bureaucrats, whereas openness and participation cede power to someone else. More of one yields less of the other, and thus a trade-off ensures, conventional bureaucratic theory suggests.

But if public participation is an alternative to bureaucracy or a fundamental threat to bureaucratic power, why do bureaucrats open their doors to participation? When considering federal-level public committees over the past 100 years, evidence suggests that bureaucrats do a lot of door opening: considerable public participation has resulted from government agency initiative, not necessarily because Congress or the president require it or induce it. Bureaucrats – before and after the passage of the Federal Advisory Committee Act – have gone to great lengths to make public participation happen. Critics of public participation in agency policymaking point to bureaucratic door opening as merely a way to manipulate the public or to obtain a rubber stamp for preferred policies. The FDA case, however, stands boldly against the manipulation–rubber stamp critique: public participation through FDA drug review committees is associated with higher-quality policy outcomes manifested through safer drug post-marketing experiences and less frequent investigations of agency impropriety. In the right conditions, public participation yields not just better policy outcomes but better bureaucracy. Public participation is not necessarily bureaucracy's opposite but instead can be its complement.

What accounts for the differences between participation that impacts policy and bureaucratic administration and participation that does not? Evidence from drug review committees and from educational assessment boards and councils suggests focusing participation on uncertain and/or interdependent task implementation helps account for part of the difference. The drug review committees and the National Assessment Governing Board engage public participation for these kinds of tasks: tasks with evolving, interdependent implementations that exceed the scope of the agency's hierarchical reach. Analysis suggests that the Advisory Council on Education Statistics was less likely to do so. These cases were selected to reflect important, systematic institutional differences. ACES and NAGB were codified in statute, whereas drug committees were created at the FDA's discretion. ACES and FDA committees have only advisory authority and fall fully under FACA, whereas NAGB has policymaking authority and adheres to only some FACA provisions. NAGB and ACES work in the policy domain of educational assessments, whereas the FDA committees focus on pharmaceutical regulation. NAGB provides cases where members were selected as representatives of particular groups, whereas FDA drug committee members are appointed as special government employees subject to conflict-of-interest provisions. Across these institutional and organizational arrangements, task-specific implementation uncertainty and interdependence remain important explanations for public participation.

What do bureaucrats get out of public participation? I have taken care to avoid inferring intent from outcomes. Bureaucrats may pursue public participation for multiple reasons. Evidence suggests, however, that public participation for these kinds of tasks can be consistent with expertise and diverse engagement, the key building blocks of bureaucratic autonomy and reputation. If the agency faced only an information asymmetry, with outsiders holding better information than insiders (the police do not know where the drug dealers hang out, but community members know; so ask them), better information could be acquired privately, through personal communication. Agencies on the uninformed side of an information asymmetry do so, by obtaining knowledge from specific individuals or writing technical review panels into their contracts, and thus avoid triggering FACA sunshine requirements.[1] If the issue were just

---

[1] On this point, see Steven P. Croley and William F. Funk, "The Federal Advisory Committee Act and Good Government," *Yale Journal on Regulation* 14 (1997): 451–557, p. 513.

agency learning, we would have little reason to expect bureaucrats to open their doors in the post-FACA period. In other words, uncertainty offers an account for why bureaucrats may seek to learn *from* the public, but it fails to explain bureaucratic learning *in* public.

Tasks in Quadrants C and D from Figure 1.1, however, may not only be uncertain (we need more information) or difficult (we need a specialized kind of knowledge). They are fundamentally interdependent. That interdependence yields ever-evolving implementations: policy is made as practice unfolds. Drug safety ultimately depends on how frequently grandma takes her pain pills and whether she exceeds the recommended dose. Educational assessments depend on students showing up, on administrators letting special needs students take the test, and on the person scoring handwritten essays. Interdependent task implementations intertwine reputations – my success as a regulator depends on your prescribing practices as a physician – and creates incentives for bureaucrats to attend not only to their own learning (not only gathering knowledge) but also to getting information out the door to other parts of the implementation chain (watch out: Lotronex appears associated with ischemic colitis), creating new knowledge where none existed either inside or outside the agency (help us figure out how to determine if Lotronex is causing ischemic colitis: what markers should we look for?), and legitimating the knowledge that is used ("the agency and the firm have done the best that they could with the knowledge that they have" or "I do not think you can push it any farther than you did"). In the context of public participation for interdependent tasks, it is not just the federal bureaucrats who are learning in public.

To put this in slightly more formal terms, public participation for more interdependent tasks offers bureaucrats greater potential value than public participation offers for tasks with more independent implementations. Public participation, when constructed to yield diverse expertise, can support distributing knowledge, creating knowledge, legitimating knowledge, in addition to potentially gathering knowledge, which the agency is less likely to need when implementing independent tasks. Put another way, public participation is potentially more costly for tasks agencies perform independently and over which agencies enjoy unique information: recall Quadrant A from Figure 1.1. Turf and information are fundamental markers of bureaucratic power. The more independent and uniquely informed an agency is for a policy task, the greater the risks public participation poses to agency unique expertise. While public participation for such tasks – performing routine military aircraft maintenance, issuing drivers licenses, or even reviewing supplemental drug applications – may serve other purposes such as democratic oversight, it is less amenable to supporting bureaucratic administration. The lower relative cost of public participation for interdependent tasks also contributes to its relative value: by definition, bureaucrats cannot monopolize information for these kinds of tasks; and scholars including Herbert Simon and James Q. Wilson remind us of the higher costs of secrecy and exclusion for interdependent tasks.

While bureaucrats may cede some power to public participants in the course of implementing interdependent tasks, these are not the tasks where we would expect bureaucrats to enjoy monopoly power over information.

Two conditions of participatory bureaucracy provide the potential to assist democratic accountability and discourage manipulative knowledge distribution. One arises when the participatory process is indeterminate: when there is room for unanticipated testimony, for spontaneously proposed votes, for exchange between participants in their various forms – members, agency staffers, the rest of us in the room – and for knowledge to flow beyond the committee room, in multiple directions. My data are not amenable to reporting the prevalence of indeterminacy across the sprawling system of American federal advisory committees. I can report, however, my own surprise at the expressions of surprise I encountered lurking in the shadows of public meetings: audience members' whispers of shock over a committee vote, a sudden outburst of tears *from a bureaucrat*, a "last minute" addition to an agenda or a vote, or questions from committee members that make bureaucrats visibly squirm and stammer.

A second arises from fluid or permeable participation, one that is not habitually dominated by one or more interests. Having diverse experts is potentially beneficial to both bureaucrats and elected officials. For bureaucrats, it prevents their dependence on a single interest, which is an important building block for bureaucratic autonomy; and diverse expertise can support problem solving for complex tasks. Diverse participants can also offer elected officials more potential cues for monitoring bureaucrats. Participatory bureaucracy imposes some limits on the extent of diversity, which distinguish it in significant ways from full and free citizen participation. To prevent committees from disintegrating into a "babble of conflict and controversy," public committees for both drug reviews and for educational assessments sought diverse perspectives centered on the implementation of a particular task. In other words, participants brought diverse perspectives to bear on what the National Assessment's history framework should contain, not whether the National Assessment should have a history framework or if the National Assessment should occur at all. FDA committee participants brought diverse perspectives on whether a drug should be approved, how it should be labeled, and whether the sponsoring firm should conduct additional studies, not on whether the FDA should stop reviewing drugs before they reached the market. Diversity around how to implement rather than whether implementation is appropriate constitutes a limiting feature of participatory bureaucracy. Yet, it helps us understand participation from a bureaucratic perspective and suggests ways, albeit constrained ones, for public participation to support both bureaucratic administration and some aspects of democratic accountability.

The underlying democratic mechanism in participatory bureaucracy, in other words, depends on the extent to which knowledge is liquefied, to use Dewey's metaphor. Some theories of community organizing and participatory democracy discount information as token or ancillary to true decision-making power.

However, from a bureaucratic perspective, knowledge is power. Weber's foundational idea bears repeating: "bureaucratic administration means fundamentally the exercise of control on the basis of knowledge."[2] While information sharing may seem insignificant or insufficient from a grassroots perspective, it is monumental from a bureaucratic perspective.

Departure from "Backward-Mapping" Implementation and Participatory Democracy

Like "backward-mapping" implementation theories and participatory democracy, participatory bureaucracy recognizes that grassroots actors may be better informed than federal level bureaucrats are and that grassroots actors are vital to the implementation of interdependent tasks.[3] Unlike backward-mapping and participatory democracy, however, participatory bureaucracy does not assume the superiority of grassroots knowledge: it depends on the policy tasks. For some tasks, the lack of grassroots knowledge is a fundamental problem that public participation can help address: since IBS sufferers are not getting information on the dangerous side effects that Lotronex poses, what can we do to help potential Lotronex users become better informed and learn that the drug works well for one kind of IBS but not for another kind? For interdependent policy tasks, moreover, no one may have better information – neither federal officials nor the grassroots. Recall the AIDS activist who vividly argued before the Antiviral Drugs Advisory Committee,

> We have arrived in hell ... What we have done ... is to unleash drugs with well-documented toxicities onto the market without obtaining rigorous data on their clinical efficacy in order to provide the HIV positive and their care providers information they need to make rational treatment decisions.[4]

Nobody knows if these drugs are effective, he argued. In this case, grassroots empowerment – letting terminally ill patients choose how much risk to assume – was not, without vital information to make informed choices, really empowerment. For some tasks, the public or elected officials may need to learn as much as the federal bureaucrats know, or more. Participatory bureaucracy does not assume that local discretion and local knowledge will yield better policy outcomes or implementation: it depends on the existence and distribution of knowledge, relative to the policy task.

---

[2] Max Weber, *The Theory of Social and Economic Organizations* (London: Free Press of Glencoe, Collier-MacMillian Ltd., 1947), p. 339.

[3] On implementation, see: Richard Elmore, "Backward Mapping: Implementation Research and Policy Decisions," *Political Science Quarterly* 94 (1979–1980): 601–616; Jeffrey Pressman and Aaron Wildavsky, *Implementation: How Great Expectations in Washington are Dashed in Oakland* (Berkeley: University of California Press, 1984).

[4] Comments of Gregg Gonsalves, Treatment Action Group. "Food and Drug Administration, Antiviral Drugs Advisory Committee, transcript volume 1, September 20, 1993." Page number does not appear on transcript.

Departure from Full and Free Expression

My account of participatory bureaucracy differs from the diversity expectations advanced in some democratic theories. In different ways, pluralism and deliberative democracy ultimately hinge on the opportunity for the full expression of interests at the policymaking table, though that diversity manifests in different forms. In pluralism, it manifests through groups. David Truman's *Governmental Process* points to federal advisory committees as one venue for expressing group interests. He argued, "Basically the creation of advisory committees marks a recognition ... that individuals and groups likely to be affected should be consulted before governmental action is taken."[5] And his critique of advisory committees echoes the mid-century allegations that appeared in 1957 congressional testimony of committees cultivating industry privilege and agency spokespersons. Deliberative democracy calls for individuals, not just their group representatives, to engage in the full and free expression of values and reasons to reach legitimate decisions. Participatory bureaucracy is neither full nor free. As NAGB illustrates, even with detailed descriptive categories, all interests – namely the interests that opposed the existence of the assessment – were not necessarily at the table and were not necessarily expressed. If a detailed institutional design like the Governing Board's is unable to represent fully the array of interests, it is difficult to imagine how an alternative institutional design can.

While it does not meet the standards of full expression of all interests, participatory bureaucracy creates the potential for future engagement in a way that closed bureaucratic processes fundamentally cannot.[6] When we start from the perspective of the bureaucracy, the counterfactual is Weberian bureaucracy as opposed to starting from a democratic ideal. When policymaking is public – when doors are open, when transcripts are kept, when the media reports on the process, and when tens or hundreds or thousands of people are involved in interdependent tasks that continue to change and evolve – I may not have a chair at the table this time, but at least there is a way for me to find out what is going on, where to show up next time, what happened in the past, and who else might be there. The democratic mechanism works through its potential: laying the groundwork for an inattentive public to become engaged, should it choose to or is roused to engage. This again highlights the importance of interdependent tasks – tasks that intertwine implementers and that evolve.[7]

---

[5] David B. Truman, *The Governmental Process: Political Interests and Public Opinion* (New York: Alfred A. Knopf, 1962), p. 458.

[6] Participatory bureaucracy is consistent with the pragmatist view of building capacity to manage future as well as current problems. See Christopher Ansell, *Pragmatist Democracy: Evolutionary Learning as Public Philosophy* (New York: Oxford University Press, 2011), p. 97.

[7] For interdependent, iterative tasks, round one may be an opening salvo. Path dependence matters, but drug labels are revised and history frameworks are rewritten.

Participatory bureaucracy is ill equipped to resolve the tension between bureaucracy and democracy for tasks that are fully performed within the bureaucratic hierarchy. Here, participation comes at the expense of bureaucratic information and jurisdiction, unless it is the kind of agency promotion campaign that Truman and others highlight. Participatory *oversight* is more likely to ensue when bureaucrats have full information and jurisdiction for their tasks, producing the bureaucracy-democracy trade-off. This trade-off for these kinds of tasks persists. Yet, much of American bureaucratic policymaking falls outside our metaphorical Quadrant A from Figure 1.1. The fragmentation in American bureaucracy that has been portrayed as a weakness in the American state can instead provide portals of opportunity to manage the bureaucracy-democracy tension.

Dimly lit Holiday Inn ballrooms in suburban Maryland, packed with rows of suited Wall Street analysts, reporters, and industry competitors facing a Last Supper-type table of medical advisors who ask questions, answer questions, but rarely talk to each other or to the audience, bear little resemblance to a vibrant New England town meeting that Dewey might have imagined.[8] But consider the Weberian alternative, where there is no opportunity for AIDS activists to grab the open mike, because neither the activists nor the microphone nor the media are in the same room as the policymakers. In a fully closed bureaucracy, hundreds of "lay" participants would not have been invited to review National Assessment test items in the 1960s, and 70,000 people would not have been systematically part of policymaking across federal agencies in 2010. David Brown's 1970 assessment of public committees bears repeating: "A useful public purpose is served ... by including within its membership sufficiently different points of view so that these at least will be heard."[9]

ENDURING CHALLENGES FOR PARTICIPATORY BUREAUCRACY

What Is Not Seen?

As Figure 7.3 in Chapter 7 reports, many public meetings remain fully or partially closed to public audiences and transcripts, even when accounting for closed peer review grant committees. Participatory bureaucracy suggests that when agencies face an information asymmetry – when outsiders have better information than insiders do – closed or private meetings can help agencies gather knowledge. Agencies could receive advice from some members of the public, but not in public. Closed meetings, however, limit the potential

[8] During the early part of this study, FDA advisory committee meetings were typically held in hotels rather than in FDA headquarters.

[9] Statement of David S. Brown, U.S. Congress, Senate, *Advisory Committees: Hearings on S.3067 before the Subcommittee on Intergovernmental Relations of the Committee on Government Operations*, 91st Congress, 2nd Session October 6 and 7, part 1 (Washington, DC: GPO, 1970), p. 33.

democratic accountability mechanism in participatory bureaucracy and the ability to liquefy knowledge through audience members, media accounts, transcripts and the potential for future action or revision. Future assessments of the full advisory committee system should consider the effects of *both* open and closed meetings, their implications for democratic accountability, and their implications for task implementation.

What Is Not Said?

My analysis has looked at decisions and nondecisions – topics that are on public agendas and topics that are not. My analysis also has looked at whether dissent is more or less likely depending on different task conditions. My reviews of drug committee transcripts revealed very few instances of agency disagreement brought before the public committee; the agency typically presented questions or issues, but did not present them as internal disagreements. Were some internal disagreements but not others brought before committees? Future analysis mapping drug applications and public committees could examine this more fully. Democracy *within organizations* may have implications for democratic governance more broadly.[10] Moreover, the analysis presented here cannot assess what debate looks like with and without an audience or a transcriptionist.

Recall that FDA Commissioner Alexander Schmidt warned of market speculation that could arise by introducing greater transparency into the FDA drug review process. While public participation can induce firms to provide important information they may otherwise not provide, concerns about whether public venues shut down debate linger. Moreover, when an FDA drug advisory committee publicly reacts negatively to a drug, does it have reverberating effects for drug research and development, possibly leading firms to abandon drugs? Scholars are beginning to probe this question.[11] Moreover, recall the case of Propulsid, in which Janssen removed the drug from the market before an advisory committee could meet. A common agency justification for opposing congressional advisory committee openness proposals in 1957 and 1971 claimed the danger more openness would pose to vigorous debate. One agency leader went so far as to say that openness would discourage the public's ability to engage with its government. Future research should assess both sources of

---

[10] Martha Feldman, Ann M. Khademian, and Kathy Quick, "Ways of Knowing, Inclusive Management, and Promoting Democratic Engagement: Introduction to the Special Issue," *International Public Management Journal* 12 (2009): 123–136; Martha Feldman and Ann M. Khademian, "The Role of the Public Manager in Inclusion: Creating Communities of Participation," *Governance* 20 (2007): 305–324.

[11] Jessica Blankshain, Daniel P. Carpenter, and Susan L. Moffitt, "R&D Abandonment in Regulatory Equilibrium: Evidence from Asset Price Shocks Induced by FDA Decisions." Unpublished paper. Harvard University.

silence: silence because of exclusion and silence because the microphone is on and the cameras are rolling.[12]

What Else Matters to Implementation?

Public engagement alone will not solve all of the problems facing the FDA's drug review process, or the rollout of the Affordable Care Act, or the development and implementation of the Common Core state standards in education. Big structural problems remain for interdependent task implementations. I have deliberately offered examples, such as Vioxx and Lotronex, to illustrate that policies can encounter implementation problems even when they are the focus of public reviews. Public participation is not a panacea.

The systematic analysis, however, demonstrates the contributions that public participation can make for discrete tasks: a particular drug review, a particular assessment framework. Structural challenges facing the Common Core, for instance, include the design of teacher education in the United States, the unequal distribution of financial resources to support public education, and residential segregation, to name just a few. These are not discrete tasks that public meetings consisting of a dozen diverse experts convened four times per year in Washington, DC can fully address. Moreover, actually liquefying knowledge – getting it out to the public – and making use of liquefied knowledge can require additional institutional supports beyond the participatory forum and ongoing opportunities to receive information. Attending meetings is costly. Meeting agendas are designed to help address particular policy tasks, not provide general information citizens can easily use. Liquefied knowledge does not necessarily attenuate inequalities, but can instead exacerbate them.

What about Other Venues for Participation?

I selected the agencies and public committees for this study on the basis of systematic variation and overlap in institutional variables: mandated/agency-created, advisory/policymaking, representative membership/special government employee membership, and so on. I also selected agencies that were originally part of the Department of Health, Education and Welfare to allow for some comparability across the cases and because HEW represented the agency in mid-twentieth-century United States with more public committees than any other agency. Recall that HEW – and the FDA in particular – received a dismal committee openness

---

[12] On whether public committees may discourage firms from providing full information, see Cary Coglianese, Richard Zeckhauser, and Edward Parson, "Seeking Truth for Power: Informational Strategy and Regulatory Policymaking," *Minnesota Law Review* 89 (2004): 277–341. On other potential "chilling" effects of Federal Advisory Committee Act requirements on public participation, see Rebecca J. Long and Thomas C. Bierle, "The Federal Advisory Committee Act and Public Participation in Environmental Policy," Discussion Paper 99-17 (Washington, DC: Resources for the Future, 1999).

score in the early 1970s. This selection strategy and looking closely at micro-level agency agenda and participation decisions have enabled me to isolate and demonstrate the importance of task implementation conditions across institutional designs and demonstrate the policy impact of public advice. This selection strategy enables me to generalize not only across HEW/HHS/ED committees but also across two types of committees (technical and policy).

The vast and varied system of American advisory committees that the House Committee on Operations struggled to understand in the mid-1950s remains vast and varied today. I have supplemented my original analysis of public committees for drug reviews and educational assessments with select descriptive summaries of the broader advisory committee system. Some parts of the vast public committee system remain outside the theoretical and empirical scope of this work. For one, presidential commissions warrant separate analysis.[13] Throughout the post-FACA period, roughly fifty presidential advisory committees have been in operation, on average, each year. We would expect such committees to adhere closely to presidential incentives and to promote the president's policy positions, rather than follow the logic of participatory bureaucracy. For another, with its attention on the federal government, this book does not focus principally on what is typically referred to as mass citizen participation or on the effects of public participation on mass citizen pharmaceutical consumption or public school performance. Moreover, state and local advisory committees can generate little visibility, which challenges their compatibility with participatory bureaucracy's tenets of multidirectional information exchanges. Further outside the scope of this work are conditions when policy implementation depends on secrecy, as it can in areas of national defense and law enforcement.[14] Public participation certainly can help soldiers, spies, and law enforcement know where to look. However, the value of that information plummets when the targets know where and when they are being watched and who is watching them.

What about Congress?

This book has emphasized the importance of executive branch action in the development and use of public committees. Bureaucrats' pursuit of participation invites nuance to prominent theories of delegation. While Congress and executive branch agencies alike may benefit from diverse expertise and participatory bureaucracy, zero-sum conditions remain where participation may give

---

[13] Presidential commissions, for instance, may be better suited than agency committees as vehicles for political patronage. On this point, see Thomas E. Cronin and Norman C. Thomas, "Federal Advisory Processes: Advice and Discontent," *Science* 171 (1971): 771–779. See p. 773. On presidential commissions, see Amy Zegart, "Blue Ribbons, Black Boxes: Toward a Better Understanding of Presidential Commissions," *Presidential Studies Quarterly* 34 (2004): 366–393.

[14] Recall some committees are exempt from FACA provisions, including committees that advise the Central Intelligence Agency and the Federal Reserve. Advisory committees created at the state and local level are also exempt. See Croley and Funk, p. 490.

Congress an upper hand for oversight. While federal advisory committees have historically been instruments of the executive branch, FACA gave Congress new tools both to oversee the executive branch enterprise and to use it for congressional advantage. My analysis finds mixed evidence of direct congressional influence on agenda setting or participation. The issues and people that generate congressional attention were not systematically included in and on the public committees I have examined. NAGB presents a stunning example of how committee appointments even with congressionally mandated membership categories can nonetheless leave powerful members of Congress fuming. We would expect, however, that the transparency provided by public committees prevents public committees from straying too far from congressional wishes. The promise of transparency, however, depends on committee meetings' openness, and the extent of closed meetings could inhibit congressional benefits as well. Two other areas merit further exploration: appropriation riders[15] and appointment authority. Recall that one of the earliest manifestations of congressional involvement with federal-level public committees came in 1842 with a restriction on the use of funds for committees. While committee membership appointment authority typically resides in the executive branch's hands, some committees, such as the Advisory Committee on Student Financial Assistance, grant Congress authority over appointing some of its members. Future work should assess whether appropriation riders and Congressional appointment authority appear more likely for tasks over which bureaucrats enjoy information and jurisdiction: for tasks in Quadrant A and the classic political struggle they abet.

Participatory Bureaucracy through Other Administrative Procedures?

Recall that participatory bureaucracy is a systematic process of public engagement that brings diverse expertise to interdependent task implementations. The 1946 Administrative Procedure Act and 1966 Freedom of Information Act embody some aspects of participatory bureaucracy by offering opportunities for greater information flows, but both depart from core features of participatory bureaucracy. FOIA enables individuals and groups to submit requests to government agencies and to obtain access to previously unreleased information and documents.[16] Like participatory bureaucracy, FOIA offers the public opportunities to learn. But its information flow is only one way – from the government to the individual who requested the information – rather than multidirectional. The notice and comment provisions of the Administrative Procedure Act enable interested groups and individuals to see and comment on proposed agency rules before they become law.[17] These APA provisions allow

---

[15] Jason A. McDonald, "Limitation Riders and Congressional Influence Over Bureaucratic Policy Decisions," *The American Political Science Review* 104 (2010): 766–782.
[16] 5 USC 552, *The Freedom of Information Act*, 1966.
[17] 60 Stat. 237. *The Administrative Procedure Act (APA)*, P.L. 79–404, enacted June 11, 1946.

for limited flows of information: from the agency to the public, from the public back to the agency, and then, possibly, from the agency back to the public through a final rule. The opportunity to comment on rules is, in principle, open to anyone, although scholarship suggests that business interests participate more frequently than other interests do. Participatory bureaucracy in contrast allows for an information exchange between multiple participants, potentially creating new knowledge beyond the scope of a dyadic relationship. Whereas notice-and-comment provisions offer opportunities for the public to comment on policy design, participatory bureaucracy is amenable to both policy implementation and policy design.

Pragmatic Participatory Bureaucracy

Participatory bureaucracy offers a way to support capable implementation and democratic accountability for interdependent tasks that rely on implementers outside the agency's direct jurisdiction. It is less amenable to managing the bureaucracy-democracy tension for tasks implemented within a unified, closed hierarchy. The promise of participatory bureaucracy, the FDA and the Governing Board cases suggest, can yield a policy process that is public in the sense of government sponsored, public in the sense of visible, and public in the sense of resulting from engagement with individuals and groups outside the government's jurisdiction. It also makes policy public by equipping the governance space beyond the scope of the agency with potentially usable knowledge. Although the participatory process may be bureaucratic in terms of systematic, predictable, and expert, the products of that process can take on a life of their own, when and if the information reaches attentive publics.

From a Weberian view of bureaucracy, the puzzle of public advice appears to be "why do we see agencies actively pursuing public participation?" From the perspective of participatory bureaucracy and interdependent tasks, the puzzle becomes "why don't we see more public participation that looks like the FDA or NAGB?" From a bureaucratic perspective, incentives for closure and secrecy persist, especially for tasks that bear a closer resemblance to Weberian bureaucracy. Incentives to use public participation for purposes other than implementing complex tasks also persist. From a congressional perspective, committees can be oversight tools, enabling Congress to keep an eye on agency actions. From a presidential or executive branch appointee perspective, committees can offer ways to marshal support for the president's policies. At times, committees can serve multiple masters. Public participation in agency policy-making comes with well-known limitations. However, it is uniquely situated to manage the tension between bureaucracy and democracy, to expand the space of governance in a potentially non-zero sum fashion, and to make policy public.

Appendix

TABLE A.I. *FDA Drug Review Advisory Committees Descriptive Statistics*

	#Obs	Mean	SD	Min	Max
Drug Priority Classification (Priority=1)	474	0.457	0.499	0	1
Drug for Lethal Disease (Lethal=1)	474	0.580	0.494	0	1
Drug Pharmacological Complexity, Natural Log of Label Word Count	474	7.025	0.669	3.219	8.573
Number of Staff, Reviewing Division	391	51.746	12.660	18	93
Number of NMEs Reviewed During Submission Year	474	26.949	8.098	14	45
Drug Demand: Order of Drug Entry to the Market, Natural Log	474	1.778	1.251	0	4.382
Elite Disease Attention: Average *NEJM* Attention, Rolling Average, 3 Years Prior	474	3.549	5.203	0	21.333
Public Disease Attention: Average *Washington Post* Attention, Rolling Average, 3 Years Prior	474	71.530	130.513	0	899.667
Firm Experience: Number of Previous Firm NME Submissions	474	10.901	11.516	1	48
Average Congressional Committee Disease Attention, Rolling Average, 3 Years Prior	474	0.314	0.799	0	7.333

(*cont.*)

TABLE A.I. *(cont.)*

	#Obs	Mean	SD	Min	Max
Divided Government (Divided = 1)	474	0.741	0.438	0	1
Boxed Warning Added Post-Marketing (Warning = 1)	472	0.104	0.305	0	1
Count of GAO Reports on Drug/FDA	474	0.184	0.668	0	6
Safety Based Withdrawal (Withdrawal=1)	474	0.042	0.201	0	1
Pre-approval Advisory Committee Review (Review = 1)	474	0.418	0.494	0	1
Individual Vote in Minority (Minority = 1)	2670	0.054	0.225	0	1
Natural Log of Publications	2590	3.739	1.325	0	6.735
Female (Female = 1)	2670	0.291	0.454	0	1
PhD (PhD = 1)	2648	0.143	0.350	0	1
Serve as Committee Chair (Chair = 1)	2669	0.084	0.277	0	1
Serve as Patient/Consumer Rep (Rep = 1)	2669	0.075	0.263	0	1
Waiver for Meeting (Waiver = 1)	2669	0.196	0.397	0	1
Number of Public Speakers	2521	2.564	4.442	0	33

TABLE A.2. *National Assessment Governing Board Agenda and Impact Descriptive Statistics*

Variable	#Obs	Mean	SD	Min	Max
NAEP Task (1 = Task Appeared on Agenda during Year)	1747	0.360	0.480	0	1
Number of NAEP Task Appearances on Agenda during Year	1747	0.823	1.298	0	7
First Time or Special Project Task (1 = Novel)	1747	0.316	0.465	0	1
NAEP Mandated Tasks (1 = NAEP Mandate)	1747	0.234	0.423	0	1
Technical Tasks: Moving Average of Process Publications	1416	0.138	0.349	0	2.667
Statutorily Mandated NAGB Task (1 = Mandate)	1747	0.278	0.448	0	1
Congressional Committee Attention, Lagged Moving Average 3 Years Prior	1734	0.023	0.109	0	1.333
Congressional Committee Attention, Year	1734	0.032	0.207	0	3
Presidential Attention, Year	1062	0.015	0.156	0	3
Education Week Attention, Lagged Moving Average, 3 Years Prior	1747	1.310	2.153	0	19.333
Education Week, Year	1747	1.424	2.742	0	30
Divided Government (1 = Divided)	1747	0.833	0.373	0	1
NCES Staff/Budget Ratio	1747	2.345	0.874	1.44	4.28
Lagged Task Frequency on Agenda in Previous Year	1747	0.767	1.261	0	7
Count of Previous Agenda Appearances	1747	5.720	8.167	0	50
Washington Post Attention, Lagged Moving Average, 3 Years Prior	1746	0.183	0.451	0	4.333
Washington Post Attention, Year	1746	0.208	0.702	0	9

TABLE A.3. *National Assessment Governing Board Member Selection Descriptive Statistics*

	# Obs	Mean	SD	Min.	Max
Chosen to Serve on NAGB (Selected = 1)	249	0.084	0.278	0	1
Opposed State NAEP (Opposed = 1)	249	0.096	0.296	0	1
Nominator/Nominee Affiliated with 1988 NAEP Reform (Affiliated = 1)	249	0.161	0.368	0	1
Nominated by Category Representative	249	0.353	0.479	0	1
Education Week References to Individual	249	1.467	4.185	0	27.667
Nominee's Participation in Congressional Hearings, Before Nomination	249	0.147	0.499	0	3.667
Nominator's Participation in Congressional Hearings, Before Nomination	249	0.893	1.434	0	6.667
Nominee's Average Campaign Contributions, Before Nomination	249	317.229	1650.842	0	17000
Log of Average Contributions Before Nomination	249	0.527	1.865	0	8.889
Count of Different Nominations	249	1.269	0.935	1	12
Nominee Race (White = 1)	249	0.835	0.372	0	1
Nominee Gender (Male = 1)	249	0.635	0.483	0	1

TABLE A.4. *Advisory Council on Education Statistics Descriptive Statistics*

Variable	#Obs	Mean	SD	Min	Max
NCES Task ACES Agenda Appearance	263	0.354	0.479	0	1
Survey Scope Number of Assessment Respondents	263	28456.940	112992.700	1	1440000
Natural Log of Assessment of Respondents	263	8.132	2.336	0	14.180
Task Novelty: First Time or Expedited Data Collection (1 = Novel)	263	0.494	0.501	0	1
Technical Review Panel in Contract (1 = Technical Panel)	263	0.468	0.500	0	1
Agency Resources: NCES Staff/Budget Ratio	263	3.302	1.941	1.44	7.35
Profession: Lagged Moving Average *Education Week* Attention, 3 Years Prior	263	1.392	3.560	0	19.667
Congressionally Mandated Survey/ Assessment (1 = Mandated)	263	0.540	0.499	0	1
Congress: Lagged Moving Average Congressional Committee Attention, 3 Years Prior	263	0.128	0.369	0	2
Divided Government (1 = Divided)	263	0.871	0.336	0	1
Survey Impact on Individuals (1 = Individual)	262	0.584	0.494	0	1
Survey Impact on State or Local Govts (1 = Govt)	262	0.458	0.499	0	1
Survey Impact on For-Profits Firms (1 = For-Profit)	262	0.279	0.449	0	1

(cont.)

TABLE A.4. *(cont.)*

Variable	#Obs	Mean	SD	Min	Max
Survey Impact on Non-Profits Firms (1 = Non-Profit)	262	0.450	0.498	0	1
Number of *Washington Post* Task References, Year	263	1.262	4.167	0	29
Control: Lagged Moving Average, *Washington Post* Attention, 3 Years Prior	263	1.037	3.312	0	19.667
Control: Lagged Task Frequency on Agenda in Previous Year	263	4.540	6.191	0	29
NAEP or NAEP Related Task (NAEP = 1)	263	0.080	0.272	0	1

Bibliography

Alexander, Lamar and H. Thomas James. 1987. *The Nation's Report Card: Improving the Assessment of Student Achievement*. Washington, DC: National Academy of Education.

Allen, Nancy L., John R. Donoghue, and Terry L. Schoeps. 2001. *The NAEP 1998 Technical Report*. Washington, DC: National Center for Education Statistics.

Ansell, Christopher K. 2011. *Pragmatist Democracy: Evolutionary Learning as Public Philosophy*. New York: Oxford University Press.

Bachrach, Peter and Morton S. Baratz. 1962. Two Faces of Power. *American Political Science Review* 56 (4): 947–951.

Balla, Steven J. 1998. Administrative Procedures and Political Control of the Bureaucracy. *American Political Science Review* 92 (3): 663–673.

Balla, Steven J. and John R. Wright. 2000. Can Advisory Committees Facilitate Congressional Oversight of the Bureaucracy? In *Congress on Display, Congress at Work*, William T. Bianco (ed.). Ann Arbor: University of Michigan Press, pp. 167–187.

  2001. Interest Groups, Advisory Committees, and Congressional Control of the Bureaucracy. *American Journal of Political Science* 45 (4): 799–812.

Balogh, Brian. 1991. *Chain Reaction: Expert Debate and Public Participation in American Commercial Nuclear Power, 1945–1975*. New York: Cambridge University Press.

Baram, Michael, Ellen Flannery, Patricia Davis, and Gary Marchant. 2000. Symposium: Regulatory and Liability Considerations. *Boston University Journal of Science and Technology Law* 6: 86.

Baumgartner, Frank R. and Bryan D. Jones. 1993. *Agendas and Instability in American Politics*. Chicago: University of Chicago Press.

Bawn, Kathleen. 1995. Political Control versus Expertise: Congressional Choices about Administrative Procedures. *American Political Science Review* 89 (1): 62–73.

Bertelli, Anthony and Laurence E. Lynn, Jr. 2006. *Madison's Managers: Public Administration and the Constitution*. Baltimore, MD: Johns Hopkins University Press.

Blankshain, Jessica, Daniel P. Carpenter, and Susan L. Moffitt. "R&D Abandonment in Regulatory Equilibrium: Evidence from Asset Price Shocks Induced by FDA Decisions." Unpublished paper. Harvard University, Cambridge, MA.

Bohman, James. 1996. *Public Deliberation: Pluralism, Complexity and Democracy.* Cambridge, MA: MIT Press.

Bok, Sissela. 1983. *Secrets: On the Ethics of Concealment and Revelation.* New York: Random House, Inc.

Bombardier, Claire, Loren Laine, Alise Reicin, Deborah Shapiro, Ruben Burgos-Vargas, et al. 2000. Comparison of Upper Gastrointestinal Toxicity of Rofecoxib and Naproxen in Patients with Rheumatoid Arthritis. *New England Journal of Medicine* 343: 1520–1528.

Bourque, Mary Lyn. 2004. A History of the National Assessment Governing Board. In *The Nation's Report Card: Evolution and Perspectives*, Lyle V. Jones and Ingram Olkin (eds.). Bloomington, IN: Phi Delta Kappa Educational Foundation, pp. 201–231.

Bowles, Chester. 1945. OPA Volunteers: Big Democracy in Action. *Public Administration Review* 4 (5): 350–359.

Brehm, John and Scott Gates. 1997. *Working, Shirking and Sabotage: Bureaucratic Response to a Democratic Public.* Ann Arbor: University of Michigan Press.

Brown, David S. 1954. *The Public Advisory Board in the Federal Government.* Doctoral Dissertation, Syracuse University. Ann Arbor, MI: ProQuest/UMI.

Brown, Mark B. 2008. Fairly Balanced: The Politics of Representation on Government Advisory Committees. *Political Research Quarterly* 61 (4): 547–560.

Brudney, Jeffrey and Robert England. 1983. Toward a definition of the co-production concept. *Public Administration Review* 43 (1): 59–65.

Cannan, R. Keith. 1968. Status of the Drug Efficacy Study of the National Academy of Sciences-National Research Council. *Food, Drug and Cosmetic Law Journal* (January): 32–35.

Cardozo, Michael. 1981. The Federal Advisory Committee Act in Operation. *Administrative Law Review* 33 (1): 1–62.

Carpenter, Daniel P. 2001. *The Forging of Bureaucratic Autonomy: Reputations, Networks, and Policy Innovation in Executive Branch Agencies, 1862–1928.* Princeton, NJ: Princeton University Press.

2002. Groups, the Media, Agency Waiting Costs and FDA Drug Approval. *American Journal of Political Science* 46 (3): 490–505.

2004. Protection without Capture: Product Approval by a Politically Responsive, Learning Regulator. *American Political Science Review* 98 (4):613–631.

2010. *Reputation and Power: Organizational Image and Pharmaceutical Regulation at the FDA.* Princeton, NJ: Princeton University Press.

Carpenter, Daniel P., Jacqueline Chattopadhyay, Susan Moffitt, and Clayton Nall. 2012. The Complications of Controlling Agency Time Discretion: FDA Review Deadlines and Postmarket Safety. *American Journal of Political Science* 56 (1): 98–114.

Carpenter, Daniel P. and George A. Krause. 2012. Reputation and Public Administration. *Public Administration Review* 72 (1): 26–32.

Carr, Peggy. 2004. Preface. In *The Nation's Report Card: Evolution and Perspectives*, Lyle V. Jones and Ingram Olkin (eds). Bloomington, IN: Phi Delta Kappa Educational Foundation, pp. vii–xi.

Clemens, Elisabeth S. 2006. Lineages of the Rube Goldberg State: Building and Blurring Public Programs, 1990–1940. In *Rethinking Political Institutions: The Art of the State*, Ian Shapiro, Stephen Skowronek, and Daniel Galvin (eds.). New York: New York University Press, pp. 187–215.

Coglianese, Cary. 1997. Assessing Consensus: The Promise and Performance of Negotiated Rulemaking. *Duke Law Journal* 46 (6): 1255–1349.

Coglianese, Cary, Richard Zeckhauser, and Edward Parson. 2004. Seeking Truth for Power: Informational Strategy and Regulatory Policymaking. *Minnesota Law Review* 89: 277–341.

Cohen, David K. 1982. Policy and Organization: The Impact of State and Federal Educational Policy on School Governance. *Harvard Educational Review* 52(4): 474–499.

Cohen, David K. and James P. Spillane. 1992. Policy and Practice: The Relations Between Governance and Instruction. *Review of Research in Education* 18: 3–49.

Cohen, David K. and Susan L. Moffitt. 2009. *The Ordeal of Equality: Did Federal Regulation Fix the Schools?* Cambridge, MA: Harvard University Press.

Croley, Steven P. and William F. Funk. 1997. The Federal Advisory Committee Act and Good Government. *Yale Journal on Regulation* 14: 451–557.

Cronbach, Lee J. 2004. An Interview with Lee Cronbach. In *The Nation's Report Card: Evolution and Perspectives*, Lyle V. Jones and Ingram Olkin (eds.). Bloomington, IN: Phi Delta Kappa Educational Foundation, pp. 139–153.

Cronin, Thomas E. and Norman C. Thomas. 1971. Federal Advisory Processes: Advice and Discontent. *Science* 26 (February): 771–779.

Crout, J. Richard. 1974. In Praise of the Lowly Package Insert. *Food, Drug, Cosmetic Law Journal* 29: 139–145.

Crozier, Michel. 1964. *The Bureaucratic Phenomenon*. Chicago: University of Chicago Press.

Cyert, Richard M. and James G. March. 1963. *A Behavioral Theory of the Firm*. Englewood Cliffs, NJ: Prentice Hall.

Dahl, Robert. 1961. *Who Governs? Democracy and Power in an American City*. New Haven, CT: Yale University Press.

Derthick, Martha. 1979. *Policymaking for Social Security*. Washington, DC: Brookings Institution Press.

Dewey, John. 1927. *The Public and Its Problems*. Athens, OH: Swallow Press.
   1956. *The School and Society and the Child and the Curriculum*. Chicago: University of Chicago Press.

Dow, Peter B. 1991. *Schoolhouse Politics: Lessons from the Sputnik Era*. Cambridge, MA: Harvard University Press.

Downs, Anthony. 1967. *Inside Bureaucracy*. Boston: Little, Brown.

Eldridge, Marie D. 1990. The Status of Advisory Committees to the Federal Statistical Agencies. *The American Statistician* 44 (2): 154–162.

Elliott, Emerson, and Gary Phillips. 2004. A View from the NCES. In *The Nation's Report Card: Evolution and Perspectives*, Lyle V. Jones and Ingram Olkin (eds.). Bloomington, IN: Phi Delta Kappa Educational Foundation, pp. 233–249.

Elmore, Richard. 1979–1980. Backward Mapping: Implementation Research and Policy Decisions. *Political Science Quarterly* 94 (4): 601–616.

Epstein, David and Sharyn O'Halloran. 1999. *Delegating Powers: A Transaction Cost Politics Approach to Policy Making under Separate Powers*. New York: Cambridge University Press.

Epstein, Steven. 1996. *Impure Science: AIDS, Activism, and the Politics of Knowledge.* Berkeley: University of California Press.

Esterling, Kevin. 2004. *The Political Economy of Expertise.* Ann Arbor: University of Michigan Press.

Farley, Dixie. 1988. Getting Outside Advice for the Close Calls. *New Drug Development in the United States.* FDA Consumer Special Report.

Feldman, Martha and Anne M. Khademian. 2007. The Role of the Public Manager in Inclusion: Creating Communities of Participation. *Governance* 20 (2): 305–324.

Feldman, Martha, Anne Khademian, and Kathy Quick. 2009. Ways of Knowing, Inclusive Management, and Promoting Democratic Engagement: Introduction to the Special Issue. *International Public Management Journal* 12 (2): 123–136.

Fiorina, Morris P. 1989. *Congress: Keystone of the Washington Establishment.* New Haven, CT: Yale University Press.

Friedman, Robert S. 1978. Representation in Regulatory Decision-Making: Scientific, Industrial and Consumer Inputs to the FDA. *Public Administration Review* 38 (3): 205–214.

Fung, Archon and Erik Olin Wright. 2001. Deepening Democracy: Innovations in Empowered Participatory Governance. *Politics and Society* 29 (1): 5–41.

Fung, Archon. 2004. *Empowered Participation: Reinventing Urban Democracy.* Princeton, NJ: Princeton University Press.

2006. Varieties of Participation in Complex Governance. *Public Administration Review* 66: 66–75.

Gailmard, Sean and John W. Patty. 2012. *Learning While Governing: Expertise and Accountability in the Executive Branch.* Chicago: University of Chicago Press.

Galley, Michelle. 2001. Governing Board Considers Scrapping Long-Term NAEP. *Education Week* 21 (13): 22.

Garfield, Harry. 1924. Recent Political Developments: Progress or Change? *American Political Science Review* 18 (1): 1–17.

Gilford, Dorothy. 2004. NAEP and the US Office of Education, 1971–1974. In *The Nation's Report Card: Evolution and Perspectives,* Lyle V. Jones and Ingram Olkin (eds). Bloomington, IN: Phi Delta Kappa Educational Foundation, pp. 165–183.

Gill, Norman N. 1940. Permanent Advisory Committees in the Federal Government. *Journal of Politics* 2 (4): 411–435.

Golden, Marissa Martino. 2000. *What Motivates Bureaucrats? Politics and Administration During the Reagan Years.* New York: Columbia University Press.

Gormley Jr., William T. 1983. *The Politics of Public Utility Regulation.* Pittsburgh, PA: University of Pittsburgh Press.

Gormley Jr., William T. and Steven J. Balla. 2007. *Bureaucracy and Democracy: Accountability and Performance.* Washington, DC: CQ Press.

Grant, W. Vance. 1993. Statistics in the US Department of Education: Highlights from the past 120 years. In *120 Years of American Education: A Statistical Portrait.* Thomas D. Snyder (ed.). Washington, DC: National Center for Education Statistics, pp. 1–5.

Greenbaum, William, Michael S. Garet, and Ellen R. Solomon. 1977. *Measuring Educational Progress: A Study of the National Assessment.* New York: McGraw-Hill Book Company.

Gusmano, Michael K. 2014. FDA Decisions and Public Deliberation: Challenges and Opportunities. *Public Administration Review* 73 (51): S115–S126.

Harris, Gardiner and Eric Koli. 2005. "Lucrative Drug, Danger Signal and the FDA." *New York Times*, June 10.

Hazlett, J. A. 1974. *A History of the National Assessment of Educational Progress, 1963–1974*. Doctoral Dissertation, University of Kansas. Ann Arbor, MI: ProQuest/ UMI.

Heclo, Hugh. 1978. Issue Networks and the Executive Establishment. In *The New American Political System*, Anthony King (ed.). Washington, DC: American Enterprise Institute, pp. 87–124.

Heimann, C. F. Larry. 1997. *Acceptable Risks: Politics, Policy and Risky Technologies*. Ann Arbor: University of Michigan Press.

Hilgartner, Stephen. 2000. *Science on Stage: Expert Advice as Public Drama*. Stanford, CA: Stanford University Press.

Huber, John and Charles R. Shipan. 2002. *Deliberate Discretion: The Institutional Foundations of Bureaucratic Autonomy*. New York: Cambridge University Press.

Huber, John and Nolan McCarty. 2004. Bureaucratic Capacity, Delegation, and Political Reform. *American Political Science Review* 98 (3): 481–494.

Hutt, Peter Barton. 1983. Investigations and reports respecting FDA regulation of new drugs (Part 1). *Clinical Pharmacology and Therapeutics* 33 (5): 539–540.

Institute of Education Sciences. 2007. *Mapping 2005 State Proficiency Standards onto the NAEP Scales*. Washington, DC: Institute of Education Sciences.

Institute of Medicine. 2007. *The Future of Drug Safety: Promoting and Protecting the Health of the Public*. Washington, DC: National Academy Press.

Jasanoff, Sheila. 1990. *The Fifth Branch: Science Advisors as Policy Makers*. Cambridge, MA: Harvard University Press.

Jeffrey, Julie Roy. 1978. *Education for Children of the Poor: A Study of the Origins and Implementation of the Elementary and Secondary Education Act of 1965*. Columbus: Ohio State University Press.

Jennings, John F. 1991. Chapter 1: A View from Congress. *Educational Evaluation and Policy Analysis* 13 (4): 335–338.

Jones, Lyle V. and Ingram Olkin (eds). 2004. *The Nation's Report Card: Evolution and Perspectives*. Bloomington, IN: Phi Delta Kappa Educational Foundation.

Kaitin, Kenneth I. Ann Melville, and Betsy Morris. 1989. FDA Advisory Committees and the New Drug Approval Process. *Journal of Clinical Pharmacology* 29: 886–890.

Kanthak, Kristin and George A. Krause. 2012. *The Diversity Paradox: Political Parties, Legislatures and the Organizational Foundations of Representation in America*. New York: Oxford University Press.

Karty, Kevin D. 2002. Closure and Capture in Federal Advisory Committees. *Business and Politics* 4(2): 213–238.

Kaufman, Herbert. 1981. *The Administrative Behavior of Federal Bureau Chiefs*. Washington, DC: The Brookings Institution.

Keiser, Lael R., Vicky M. Wilkins, Kenneth J. Meier, and Catherine A. Holland. 2002. Lipstick and Logarithms: Gender, Institutional Context and Representative Bureaucracy. *American Political Science Review* 96 (3): 553–564.

Keppel, Francis. 1966. *The Necessary Revolution in American Education*. New York: Harper & Row, Publishers.

Kerwin, Cornelius. 2003. *Rulemaking: How Government Agencies Write Law and Make Public Policy*. Washington, DC: CQ Press.

Kingdon, John W. 1984. *Agendas, Alternatives and Public Policies*. Boston: Little, Brown and Company.

Kluempke, Gerald. 1976. *A Descriptive Analysis of the Attitudes, Make-Up, Function, and Utilization of Advisory Councils of the U.S. Department of Education.* Doctoral Dissertation, George Washington University. Ann Arbor, MI: ProQuest/UMI.

Knippenberg, Daan van and Michaéla C. Schippers. 2007. Work Group Diversity. *Annual Review of Psychology* 58: 515–541.

Krause, George A. 2003. Coping with Uncertainty: Analyzing Risk Propensities of SEC Budgetary Decisions, 1949–1997. *American Political Science Review* (97) 1: 171–188.

Krause, George A. and J. Kevin Corder. 2007. Explaining Bureaucratic Optimism: Theory and Evidence from U.S. Executive Agency Macroeconomic Forecasts. *American Political Science Review* 101 (1): 129–142.

Kursh, Harry. 1965. *The United States Office of Education.* Philadelphia: Chilton Company.

Kwak, James. 2013. Cultural Capture and the Financial Crisis. In *Preventing Regulatory Capture: Special Interest Influence and How to Limit It,* Daniel Carpenter and David Moss (eds.). Cambridge: Cambridge University Press, pp. 71–98.

Langbein, Laura. 2002. Responsive Bureaus, Equity and Regulatory Negotiation. *Journal of Public Policy Analysis and Management* 21 (3): 446–465.

Lasser, Karen E., Paul D. Allen, Steffie J. Woolhandler, David U. Himmelstein, Sidney M. Wolfe, et al. 2002. Timing of New Black Box Warnings and Withdrawals for Prescription Medications. *Journal of the American Medical Association* 287: 2215–20.

Laugesen, Miriam J. 2013. Policy Complexity and Professional Capture in Federal Rulemaking. Paper presented at the Annual Meeting of the American Political Science Association, August 31–September 2, Chicago, IL.

Laugesen, Miriam. J., Roy Wada, and Eric M. Chen. 2012. In Setting Doctors' Medicare Fees, CMS Almost Always Accepts the Relative Value Update Panel's Advice on Work Values. *Health Affairs* 31 (5): 965–972.

Lavertu, Stéphane, Daniel E. Walters, and David L. Weimer. 2012. Scientific Expertise and the Balance of Interests: MEDCAC and Medicare Coverage Decisions. *Journal of Public Administration Research and Theory* 22 (1): 55–81.

Lavertu, Stéphane and David L. Weimer. 2011. Federal Advisory Committees, Policy Expertise, and the Approval of Drugs and Medical Devices at the FDA. *Journal of Public Administration Research and Theory* 21 (2): 211–237.

Lehmann, Irvin J. 2004. The Genesis of NAEP. In *The Nation's Report Card: Evolution and Perspectives,* Lyle V. Jones and Ingram Olkin (eds.). Bloomington, IN: Phi Delta Kappa Educational Foundation, pp. 25–92.

Leiserson, Avery. 1942. *Administrative Regulation: A Study in Representation of Interests.* Chicago: University of Chicago Press.

Levine, Daniel B. 1986. *Creating a Center for Education Statistics: A Time for Action.* Washington, DC: National Academy Press.

Lewis, David E. 2003. *Presidents and the Politics of Agency Design: Political Insulation in the United States Government Bureaucracy, 1947–1997.* Stanford, CA: Stanford University Press.

  2008. *The Politics of Presidential Appointments: Political Control and Bureaucratic Performance.* Princeton, NJ: Princeton University Press.

Lindblom, Charles. 1977. *Politics and Markets.* New York: Basic Books, Inc.

Lindblom, Charles and David K. Cohen. 1979. *Usable Knowledge: Social Science and Social Problem Solving.* New Haven, CT: Yale University Press.

Linn, Robert L. 2004. The Influence of External Evaluations. In *The Nation's Report Card: Evolution and Perspectives*, Lyle V. Jones and Ingram Olkin (eds.). Bloomington, IN: Phi Delta Kappa Educational Foundation, pp. 291–308.

Lipsky, Michael. 1980. *Street-Level Bureaucracy: Dilemmas of the Individual in Public Services*. New York: Russell Sage Foundation.

Lo, Bernard and Marilyn J. Field. 2009. *Conflict of Interest in Medical Research, Education and Practice*. Washington, DC: Institute of Medicine.

Lurie, Peter et al. 2006. Financial Conflicts of Interest Disclosure and Voting Patterns at Food and Drug Administration Advisory Committee Meetings. *Journal of the American Medical Association* 295 (16): 1921–1928.

Mansbridge, Jane J. 1983. *Beyond Adversary Democracy*. Chicago: University of Chicago Press.

1992. A Deliberative Theory of Interest Representation. In *The Politics of Interests: Interest Groups Transformed*, Mark P. Petracca (ed.). Boulder, CO: Westview Press, pp. 32–57.

Maor, Moshe. 2010. Organizational Reputation and Jurisdictional Claims: The Case of the US Food and Drug Administration. *Governance* 23 (1): 133–159.

Maor, Moshe, Sharon Gilad, and Pazit Ben-Nun Bloom. 2013. Organizational Reputation, Regulatory Talk, and Strategic Silence. *Journal of Public Administration Research and Theory* 23 (3): 581–608.

March, James G. 1999. *The Pursuit of Organizational Intelligence*. Malden, MA: Blackwell.

Martin, Wayne. 2004. NAEP from Three Different Perspectives. In *The Nation's Report Card: Evolution and Perspectives*, Lyle V. Jones and Ingram Olkin (eds.). Bloomington, IN: Phi Delta Kappa Educational Foundation.

McCarty, Nolan. 2013. Complexity, Capacity and Capture. In *Preventing Regulatory Capture: Special Interest Influence and How to Limit It*, Daniel Carpenter and David Moss (eds.). Cambridge: Cambridge University Press, pp. 99–123.

McCubbins, Matthew and Thomas Schwartz. 1984. Congressional Oversight Overlooked: Police Patrols vs. Fire Alarms. *American Journal of Political Science* 28 (1): 165–179.

McCubbins, Matthew, Roger Noll, and Barry Weingast. 1987. Administrative Procedures as Instruments of Control. *Journal of Law, Economics and Organization* 3 (2): 243–277.

1989. Structure and Process, Policy and Politics: Administrative Arrangements and the Political Control of Agencies. *Virginia Law Review* 75: 431–482.

McDonald, Jason A. 2010. Limitation Riders and Congressional Influence over Bureaucratic Policy Decisions. *American Political Science Review* 104 (4): 766–782.

McDonnell, Lorraine. 2004. *Politics, Persuasion and Educational Testing*. Cambridge, MA: Harvard University Press.

McNollGast. 1999. The Political Origins of the Administrative Procedures Act. *Journal of Law, Economics and Organizations* 15(1):180–217.

Meier, Kenneth J. 1993. *Politics and the Bureaucracy: Policymaking in the Fourth Branch of Government*, 3rd ed. Belmont, CA: Wadsworth Publishing Company.

Meier, Kenneth J. and John Bohte. 2007. *Politics and the Bureaucracy: Policymaking in the Fourth Branch of Government*, 5th ed. Belmont, CA: Thomson Wadsworth.

Meier, Kenneth J., Eric Gonzalez Juenke, Robert D. Wrinkle, and J. L. Polinard. 2005. Structural Choices and Representational Biases: The Post-Election Color of Representation. *American Journal of Political Science* 49 (4): 758–768.

Meier, Kenneth J. and Laurence J. O'Toole. 2006. *Bureaucracy in a Democratic State: A Governance Perspective*. Baltimore, MD: Johns Hopkins University Press.

Messick, Samuel, Albert Beaton, and Frederic Lord. 1983. *National Assessment of Educational Progress Reconsidered: A New Design for a New Era*. Princeton, NJ: Educational Testing Service.

Moe, Terry M. 1987. Interests, Institutions and Positive Theory: The Politics of the NLRB. *Studies in American Political Development* 2: 236–299.

1990. The Politics of Structural Choice: Toward a Theory of Public Bureaucracy. In *Organization Theory: From Chester Barnard to the Present and Beyond*, Oliver E. Williamson (ed.). New York: Oxford University Press, pp. 116–153.

2005. Power and Political Institutions. *Perspectives on Politics* 3(2): 215–223.

Moffitt, Susan L. 2010. Promoting Agency Reputation through Public Advice: Advisory Committee Use in the FDA. *Journal of Politics* 72 (3): 880–893.

2012. The Policy Impact of Public Advice: The Effects of Advisory Committee Transparency on Product Safety. In *Regulatory Breakdown: The Crisis of Confidence in U.S. Regulation*, Cary Coglianese (ed.). Philadelphia: University of Pennsylvania Press, pp. 180–199.

Monsees, Carl Henry. 1943. Industry Advisory Committees in the War Agencies. *Public Administration Review* 3 (3): 254–262.

Monsees, Carl H. 1944. *Industry-Government Cooperation: A Study of the Participation of Advisory Committees in Public Administration*. Washington, DC: Public Affairs Press.

Morgan, Kimberly and Andrea Campbell. 2011. *The Delegated Welfare State: Medicare, Markets, and the Governance of Social Policy*. New York: Oxford University Press.

Morrato, Elaine H. and S. Ling. 2012. The FDA Drug Safety and Risk Management Advisory Committee: A Case Study Evaluation of Meeting Frequency, Content and Outcomes Before and After FDAAA. *Medical Care* 50 (11): 970–986.

Morrisett, Lloyd. 2004. An Interview with Lloyd Morrisett. In *The Nation's Report Card: Evolution and Perspectives*, Lyle V. Jones and Ingram Olkin (eds.). Bloomington, IN: Phi Delta Kappa Educational Foundation, pp.122–132.

Mosher, Frederic A. 2004. An Age of Innocence. In *The Nation's Report Card: Evolution and Perspectives*, Lyle V. Jones and Ingram Olkin (eds.). Bloomington, IN: Phi Delta Kappa Educational Foundation, pp. 93–111.

Moynihan, Daniel Patrick. 1998. *Secrecy: The American Experience*. New Haven, CT: Yale University Press.

Mukherjee, Debabrata, Steven E. Nissen, and Eric J. Topol. 2001. Risk of Cardiovascular Events Associated with Selective COX-2 Inhibitors. *Journal of the American Medical Association* 286 (8): 954–959.

Mullis, Ina V. S., John A. Dossey, Eugene H. Owen, and Gary W. Phillips. 1993. *NAEP 1992 Mathematics Report Card for the Nation and the States: Data from the National and Trial State Assessments*. Washington, DC: National Center for Education Statistics.

Munger, Frank J. and Richard F. Fenno. 1962. *National Politics and Federal Aid to Education*. Syracuse, NY: Syracuse University Press.

Nathan, Richard P. 1983. *The Administrative Presidency*. New York: MacMillan Publishing Company.

National Center for Education Statistics. 1999. *Directory of NAEP Publications*. Washington, DC: U.S. Department of Education.

Neustadt, Richard E. and Harvey V. Fineberg. 1978. *The Swine Flu Affair: Decision-Making on a Slippery Disease*. Washington, DC: The National Academies Press.

Newman, William H. 1946. Government-Industry Cooperation that Works. *Public Administration Review* 6 (3): 240–248.

Nissen, Steven E. 2006. ADHD Drugs and Cardiovascular Risk. *New England Journal of Medicine* 354: 1445–1448.

Olson, Lynn. 2002a. Board Acts to Bring NAEP in Line with ESEA. *Education Week* 21 (38): 22–24.

2002b. Want to Confirm State Test Scores? It's Complex, But NAEP Can Do It. *Education Week* 21 (26): 1, 10–11.

2005. All in the Family: Another Bush Helps Shape Federal Policy on Student Testing. *Education Week* 24 (23): 32.

Osborne, David and Ted Gaebler. 1992. *Reinventing Government: How the Entrepreneurial Spirit is Transforming the Public Sector*. Reading, MA: Addison-Wesley.

Osborne, Sean P. 2010. Delivering Public Services: Time for a New Theory? *Public Management Review* 12 (1): 1–10.

Page, Scott E. 2007. *The Difference: How the Power of Diversity Creates Better Groups, Firms, Schools and Societies*. Princeton, NJ: Princeton University Press.

2008. Uncertainty, Difficulty and Complexity. *Journal of Theoretical Politics* 20 (2): 115–149.

Patashnik, Eric. 2008. *Reforms at Risk: What Happens after Major Policy Changes Are Enacted*. Princeton, NJ: Princeton University Press, 2008.

Pateman, Carol. 1970. *Participation and Democratic Theory*. Cambridge: Cambridge University Press.

Pellegrino, James W., Lee R. Jones, and Karen J. Mitchell (eds.). 1999. *Grading the Nation's Report Card: Evaluating NAEP and Transforming the Assessment of Educational Progress*. Washington, DC: National Academy Press.

Petracca, Mark P. 1986. Federal Advisory Committees, Interest Groups and the Administrative State. *Congress & The Presidency* 13(1):83–114.

Pfeffer, Jeffrey and Gerald R. Salancik. 2003. *The External Control of Organizations*. New York: Harper and Row.

Pham-Kanter, Genevieve. 2013. Financial Conflicts of Interest in FDA Advisory Committees. Paper Presented at the 2013 Annual Meeting of the Law and Society Association, June, Boston, MA.

Pines, Wayne L. and Mary Ann N. Cotton. 1997. Preparing for an FDA Advisory Committee Meeting. *Drug Information Journal* 31: 35–41.

Pressman, Jeffrey and Aaron Wildavsky. 1984. *Implementation: How Great Expectations in Washington are Dashed in Oakland*. Berkeley: University of California Press.

Price, Don K. 1962. *Government and Science: Their Dynamic Relation in American Democracy*. New York: Oxford University Press.

Quirk, Paul J. 1980. Food and Drug Administration. In *The Politics of Regulation*, James Q. Wilson (ed.). New York: Basic Books, pp. 191–235.

Redford, Emmette S. 1969. *Democracy in the Administrative State*. New York: Oxford University Press.

Rettig, Richard, Laurence E. Earley, and Richard A. Merrill (eds.). 1992. *Food and Drug Administration Advisory Committees*. Washington, DC: National Academy Press.

Roberts, Alasdair. 2006. *Blacked Out: Government Secrecy in the Information Age*. New York: Cambridge University Press.

Roberts, Patrick S. 2006. FEMA and the Prospects for Reputation-Based Autonomy. *Studies in American Political Development* 20 (1): 57–87.

Rothman, Robert. 1988. Democrats Seek to Prevent 3 from Joining NAEP Panel. *Education Week*, October 12.

Rothman, Robert. 1990. 75 Groups Sound Warning over Expansion of Assessment. *Education Week*, June 20.

Rourke, Francis E. 1961. *Secrecy and Publicity: Dilemmas of Democracy*. Baltimore, MD: Johns Hopkins University Press.

Rourke, Francis E. (ed.). 1965. *Bureaucratic Power in National Politics*. Boston: Little, Brown & Co.

Rourke, Francis E. 1976. *Bureaucracy, Politics and Public Policy*, 2nd ed. Boston: Little, Brown & Co.

Ryan, Ann Marie. 2007. Keeping Every Catholic Child in a Catholic School During the Great Depression, 1933–1939. *Catholic Education* 11 (2): 157–175.

Salamon, Lester M. 2002. *The Tools of Government: A Guide to the New Governance*. New York: Oxford University Press.

Schattschneider, E. E. 1960. *The Semi-Sovereign People: A Realist's View of Democracy in America*. New York: Thompson Learning.

Schneider, Anne and Helen Ingram. 1990. Behavioral Assumptions of Policy Tools. *Journal of Politics* 52 (2): 510–529.

Schuck, Peter H. and Steven Kochevar. 2014. Reg Neg Redux: The Career of a Procedural Reform. *Theoretical Inquiries in Law*; Yale Law School, Public Law Working Paper No. 308; Yale Law & Economics Research Paper No. 478.

Scott, W. Richard. 1992. *Organizations: Rational, Natural, and Open Systems*, 3rd ed. Englewood Cliffs, NJ: Prentice Hall.

Selden, Ramsay. 2004. Making NAEP State-By-State. In *The Nation's Report Card: Evolution and Perspectives*, Lyle V. Jones and Ingram Olkin (eds.). Bloomington, IN: Phi Delta Kappa Educational Foundation, pp. 195–199.

Sellers, Jeffrey M. 2011. State-Society Relations. In *The Sage Handbook of Governance*, Mark Bevir (ed.). London: Sage, pp. 124–141.

Selznik, Philip. 1949. *TVA and the Grass Roots: A Study in the Sociology of Formal Organizations*: Berkeley: University of California Press.

Simon, Herbert A. 1965. *The Shape of Automation for Men and Management*. New York: Harper & Row.

Simon, Herbert A., Donald W. Smithburg, and Victor A. Thompson. 1950. *Public Administration*. New York: Alfred A. Knopf.

Skowronek, Stephen. 1982. *Building a New American State: The Expansion of National Administrative Capacities, 1877–1920*. Cambridge: Cambridge University Press.

Smith, Bruce L. R. 1992. *The Advisers: Scientists in the Policy Process*. Washington, DC: Brookings Institution Press.

Steffes, Tracy. 2012. *School, Society and the State: A New Education to Govern Modern America, 1890–1940*. Chicago: University of Chicago Press.

Steinbrook, Robert. 2004. Science, Politics and Federal Advisory Committees. *New England Journal of Medicine* 350: 1454–1460.

Stone, Deborah. 2002. *The Policy Paradox*. New York: W. W. Norton & Company.

Thomas, John Clayton. 2012. *Citizen, Customer, Partner: Engaging the Public in Public Management*. New York: M.E. Sharpe.

Thompson, James D. 1967. *Organizations in Action: Social Science Bases of Administrative Theory*. New York: McGraw–Hill.

Truman, David B. 1962. *The Governmental Process: Political Interests and Public Opinion*. New York: Alfred A. Knopf.

Urfalino, Philippe. 2005. *Le Grand Méchant Loup Pharmaceutique*. Paris: Les éditions Textuel.

Forthcoming. Secret-Public Voting in FDA Advisory Committees. In *Private Public Debate and Voting*, Jon Elster (ed.). New York: Cambridge University Press.

U.S. Congress, House of Representatives. 1955. *Interim report of the Antitrust Subcommittee of the House Judiciary Committee on the Business Advisory Council*, 84th Congress, 1st session. Washington, DC: Government Printing Office.

1956. Committee Print, *Replies from Executive Departments and Federal Agencies to Inquiry Regarding Use of Advisory Committees, January 1, 1953–January 1, 1956, Part 3: Department of Health, Education and Welfare, June 5, 1956*. Washington, DC: Government Printing Office.

1957. House Report 85–576, *Amending the Administrative Expenses Act of 1946, and for Other Purposes*, 85th Congress, 1st session, June 17, 1957. Washington, DC: Government Printing Office.

1970. House Report No. 91–1731, *The Role and Effectiveness of Federal Advisory Committees*, Committee on Government Operations, 43rd Report, 91st Congress, 2nd Session, December 11, 1970. Washington, DC: Government Printing Office.

1971. *Advisory Committees*, Hearings before the Subcommittee of the Committee on Government Operations on HR. 4383, 92nd Congress, 1st Session, November 4, 1971. Washington, DC: Government Printing Office.

1972. House Report No. 92–1017, *Federal Advisory Committee Standards Act*, Committee on Government Operations, 92nd Congress, 2nd Session, April 25, 1972. Washington, DC: Government Printing Office.

1972. *US Government Information Policies and Practices – Public Access to Information from Executive Branch Advisory Groups*, Hearings before the Subcommittee of the Committee on Government Operations, 92nd Congress, 2nd Session, June 6, 8, and 19, 1972, part 9. Washington, DC: Government Printing Office.

1974. *Use of Advisory Committees by the Food and Drug Administration*, Hearings before the Committee of Government Operations, 93rd Congress, 2nd Session, March 6, 7, 8, 12, 13; April 30; May 21, 1974. Washington, DC: Government Printing Office.

1975. *Use of Advisory Committees by the Food and Drug Administration Part 2*, Hearings before the Committee of Government Operations, 94th Congress, 1st Session, April 23, May 9 and 12, 1975. Washington, DC: Government Printing Office.

1976. House Report No 94–787, *Use of Advisory Committees by the Food and Drug Administration*, Committee on Government Operations, 94th Congress, 2nd Session, January 26, 1976. Washington, DC: Government Printing Office.

U.S. Congress, Senate. 1970. *Advisory Committees*, Hearings on S.3067 before the Subcommittee on Intergovernmental Relations of the Committee on Government Operations, 91st Congress, 2nd Session, October 6 and 7, 1970, part 1. Washington, DC: Government Printing Office.

1970. *Advisory Committees*, Hearings on S.3067 before the Subcommittee on Intergovernmental Relations of the Committee on Government Operations, 91st Congress, 2nd Session, October 8 and 9, 1970, part 2. Washington, DC: Government Printing Office.

1970. *Advisory Committees*, Hearings on S.3067 before the Subcommittee on Intergovernmental Relations of the Committee on Government Operations, 91st Congress, 2nd Session, December 8, 10, 17, 1970, part 3. Washington, DC: Government Printing Office.

1971. *Advisory Committees*, Hearings on S.1637 before the Subcommittee on Intergovernmental Relations of the Committee on Government Operations, S.1964, and S.2064, 92nd Congress, 1st Session, June 10 and 11, 1971 part 1. Washington, DC: Government Printing Office.

1971. *Advisory Committees*, Hearings on S.1637 before the Subcommittee on Intergovernmental Relations of the Committee on Government Operations S.1964, and S.2064, 92nd Congress, 1st Session, June 15, 17, 22 and July 13, 27, 28, 1971, part 2. Washington, DC: Government Printing Office.

1971. *Advisory Committees,* Hearings before the Subcommittee on Intergovernmental Relations of the Committee on Government Operations on S.1637, S.1964, and S.2064, 92nd Congress, 1st Session, October 6, 7, 8, and 11, 1971, part 3. Washington, DC: Government Printing Office.

1972. Senate Report No. 92–1098, *Federal Advisory Committee Act,* Committee on Government Operations, 92nd Congress, 2nd Session, September 7, 1972. Washington, DC: Government Printing Office.

1974. *Advisory Committees,* Oversight Hearings before the Subcommittee on Budgeting, Management and Expenditures of the Committee on Government Operations on P.L. 92–463, 93rd Congress, 1st and 2nd Sessions, November 29, December 13, 1973; February 5, 1974. Washington, DC: Government Printing Office.

1974. *Examination of the Pharmaceutical Industry 73–74,* Joint Hearings before the Subcommittee on Health of the Committee on Labor and Public Welfare and the Subcommittee on Administrative Practice and Procedure of the Committee on the Judiciary, 93rd Congress, 1st and 2nd Sessions, Part 7, August 15–16, 1974. Washington, DC: Government Printing Office.

2004. *FDA, Merck, and Vioxx: Putting Patient Safety First?* Hearings before the Senate Committee on Finance, part 1, 108th Congress, 2nd Session, November 18, 2004. Washington, DC: Government Printing Office.

U.S. Congressional Research Service. 2008. *Advisory Committees: A Primer, A Report by Wendy Ginsburg.* Washington, DC: U.S. Congressional Research Service.

2010. *Advisory Committees: A Primer, A Report by Wendy Ginsburg.* Washington, DC: U.S. Congressional Research Service.

U.S. Department of Health and Human Services Office of the Inspector General. 2002. *FDA Review Process for New Drug Applications*. Washington, DC: Department of Health and Human Services.

U.S. Department of Labor. 1953. *Womanpower Committees During World War II, Women's Bureau Bulletin 244*. Washington, D.C.: U.S. Department of Labor.

U.S. General Accounting Office. 1976. *The National Assessment of Educational Progress: Its Results Need to be Made More Useful*. Washington, DC: GAO.

1977. *Better Evaluations Needed to Weed Out Useless Federal Advisory Committees*. Washington, DC: GAO.

1986. *The Condition of Information on Education*. Washington, DC: GAO.

1988. *Federal Advisory Committee Act: Report to the Chairman, Committee on Government Affairs, U.S. Senate*. Washington, DC: GAO.

1993. *Educational Achievement Standards: NAGB's Approach Yields Misleading Interpretations*. Washington, DC: GAO.

1997. *Federal Advisory Committee Act: Overview of Advisory Committees Since 1993, Statement of L. Nye Stevens*. Washington, DC: GAO.

1998a. *Federal Advisory Committee Act: Views of Committee Members and Agencies on Federal Advisory Committee Issues*. Washington, DC: GAO.

1998b. *Federal Advisory Committee Act: General Services Administration Oversight of Advisory Committees*. Washington, DC: GAO.

1998c. *Federal Advisory Act: Advisory Committee Process Appears to be Working, but Some Concerns Exist, Statement by L. Nye Stevens*. Washington, DC: GAO.

2001. *EPA's Science Advisory Board Panels: Improved Policies and Procedures Needed to Ensure Independence and Balance*. Washington, DC: GAO.

2004. *Federal Advisory Committees: Additional Guidance Could Help Agencies Better Ensure Independence and Balance*. Washington, DC: GAO.

U.S. General Services Administration. 2007. *The Federal Advisory Committee Act: An Overview*. Washington, DC: GSA.

U.S. Government Accountability Office. 2006. *Drug Safety: Improvement Needed in FDA's Postmarket Decision-Making and Oversight Process*. Washington, DC: GAO.

2008a. *Federal Advisory Committee Act: Issues Related to the Independence and Balance of Advisory Committees*, Statement from *Robin M. Nazarro* Washington, DC: GAO.

2008b. *FDA Advisory Committees: Process for Recruiting Members and Evaluating Potential Conflicts of Interest*. Washington, DC: GAO.

U.S. Office of Education, U.S. Department of Health, Education and Welfare. 1958. *Biennial Survey of Education in the United States: Statistical Summary of Education 1953–54*. Washington, D.C.: Government Printing Office.

Van Meter, Donald S. and Carl E. Van Horn. 1975. The Policy Implementation Process: A Conceptual Framework. *Administration & Society* 6 (4): 445–488.

Viadero, Debra. 1994. House Subcommittee Approves Proposal to Abolish NAEP Board. *Education Week*, February 9.

Vinovskis, Maris. 1998. *Overseeing the Nation's Report Card: The Creation and Evolution of the National Assessment Governing Board*. Washington, DC: National Assessment Governing Board.

Wagner, Wendy. 2013. The Participation-Centered Model Meets Administrative Practice. *Wisconsin Law Review* 2013 (2): 671–692.

Walker, Jack L. 1977. Setting the Agenda in the U.S. Senate: A Theory of Problem Selection. *British Journal of Political Science* 7 (4): 423–445.

Warren, Kenneth F., 2004. *Administrative Law in the Political System*, 4th ed. Boulder, CO: Westview Press.

Weaver, R. Kent. 1986. The Politics of Blame Avoidance. *Journal of Public Policy* 6 (4): 371–398.

Weber, Edward P. and Anne Khademian. 2008. Wicked Problems, Knowledge Challenges, and Collaborative Capacity Builders in Network Settings. *Public Administration Review* 68 (2): 334–349.

Weber, Max. 1946. Bureaucracy. In *Max Weber: Essays in Sociology*, Hans Heinrich Gerth (ed.) and C. Wright Mills (trans.). New York: Oxford University Press, pp. 146–244.

  1947. *The Theory of Social and Economic Organizations*. London: Free Press of Glencoe, Collier-MacMillian Ltd.

  1965. Essays on Bureaucracy. In *Bureaucratic Power in National Politics*, Francis E Rourke (ed.). Boston: Little, Brown and Company, pp. 3–14.

Weick, Karl. 1976. Educational Organizations as Loosely Coupled Systems. *Administrative Science Quarterly* 21: 1–19.

Weiss, Janet A. 2002. Public Information. In *The Tools of Government: A Guide to the New Governance*, Lester M. Salamon (ed.). New York: Oxford University Press, pp. 217–254.

Weiss, Janet A. and Judith Gruber. 1984. Using Knowledge for Control in Fragmented Policy Arenas. *Journal of Policy Analysis and Management* 3 (2): 225–247.

Weiss, Janet A. and Mary Tschirhart. 1994. Public Information Campaigns as Policy Instruments. *Journal of Policy Analysis and Management* 13 (1): 82–119.

White, Eileen. 1981. Reagan Weighing Much Deeper Education Cuts and Faster Dismantling of Federal Department. *Education Week*, September 28.

  1983. Better Proposal Said to Win Assessment Project for ETS. *Education Week*, March 2.

Whyte, Warren E. 1970. Effectiveness of the NAS-NRC Drug Effectiveness Study. *Food, Drug, Cosmetic Law Journal* (February): 91–100.

Wilensky, Harold. 1969. *Organizational Intelligence*. New York: Basic Books.

Wilson, James Q. 1989. *Bureaucracy: What Government Agencies Do and Why They Do It*. New York: Basic Books.

Wolanin, Thomas. 1975. *Presidential Advisory Commissions*. Madison: University of Wisconsin Press.

Womer, Frank. 1968. *What Is National Assessment?* Denver, CO: Education Commission of the States.

Yackee, Jason Webb and Susan Webb Yackee. 2006. A Bias Toward Business? Assessing Interest Group Influence on the Bureaucracy. *Journal of Politics* 68 (1): 128–139.

Yackee, Susan Webb. Forthcoming. Lifecycle of Medical Product Rules Issued by the Food and Drug Administration. *Journal of Health Politics, Policy and Law*.

Zegart, Amy B. 2004. Blue Ribbons, Black Boxes: Toward a Better Understanding of Presidential Commissions. *Presidential Studies Quarterly* 34 (2): 366–393.

Statutes, Public Laws, and Federal Regulations

An Act to Establish a Department of Education, March 2, 1867, 14 Stat. 434.
Pure Food and Drug Act of 1906, P.L. 59–384, 34 Stat. 768.
Food, Drug and Cosmetic Act of 1938, P.L. 75–717, 52 Stat. 1040.
The Administrative Procedure Act, enacted June 11, 1946, P.L. 79–404, 60 Stat. 237.
Harris Kefauver Act, Drug Amendments of 1962, P.L. 87–781, 76 Stat. 780.
The Freedom of Information Act of 1966, P.L. 89-487, 80 Stat. 250.
Federal Advisory Committee Act of 1972, P.L. 92–463, 86 Stat. 770.
An Act to Extend and Amend the Elementary and Secondary Education Act of 1965, P.L. 93–380, 88 Stat. 556–558.
Education Amendment of 1978, P.L.95–561, 92 Stat. 2353.
Augustus F. Hawkins-Robert T. Stafford Elementary and Secondary School Improvement Amendments of 1988, P.L. 100–297, 102 Stat. 347.
Improving America's Schools Act, October 20, 1994, P.L. 103–382, 108 Stat. 4041.
Food and Drug Modernization Act of 1997, P.L. 105–115, 111 Stat. 2296.
Food and Drug Administration Amendments of 2007, P.L. 110–85, 121 Stat. 823.
21 CFR 14.80, revised as of April 1, 2013.

Published Interviews and Oral Histories

Cronbach, Lee 2004. An Interview with Lee Cronbach. In *The Nation's Report Card: Evolution and Perspectives*, Lyle V. Jones and Ingram Olkin (eds.). Bloomington, IN: Phi Delta Kappa Educational Foundation, pp. 139–153.

Crout, J. Richard. Oral History, History of the Food and Drug Administration, Interview, November 12, 1997.

Finn, Chester E. Jr. 2004. An Interview with Chester E. Finn, Jr. In *The Nation's Report Card: Evolution and Perspectives*, Lyle V. Jones and Ingram Olkin (eds.). Bloomington, IN: Phi Delta Kappa Educational Foundation, pp. 251–265.

Gardner, John. 2004. An Interview with John Gardner. In *The Nation's Report Card: Evolution and Perspectives*, Lyle V. Jones and Ingram Olkin (eds.). Bloomington, IN: Phi Delta Kappa Educational Foundation, pp. 113–122.

Jennings, John F. 2004. An Interview with John F. Jennings. In *The Nation's Report Card: Evolution and Perspectives*, Lyle V. Jones and Ingram Olkin (eds.). Bloomington, IN: Phi Delta Kappa Press, pp. 278–289.

Morrisett, Lloyd. 2004. An Interview with Lloyd Morrisett. In *The Nation's Report Card: Evolution and Perspectives*, Lyle V. Jones and Ingram Olkin (eds.). Bloomington, IN: Phi Delta Kappa Educational Foundation, pp. 122–132

Smith, Marshall S. 2004. An Interview with Marshall S. Smith. What NAEP Really Could Do. In *The Nation's Report Card: Evolution and Perspectives*, Lyle V. Jones and Ingram Olkin (eds.). Bloomington, IN: Phi Delta Kappa Educational Foundation, pp. 266–277.

Index

For EU product safety concerns, contact us at Calle de José Abascal, 56–1°, 28003 Madrid, Spain or eugpsr@cambridge.org.

www.ingramcontent.com/pod-product-compliance
Ingram Content Group UK Ltd.
Pitfield, Milton Keynes, MK11 3LW, UK
UKHW020453240426
470322UK00016B/335